Aristotle on the Human Good

Richard Kraut

PRINCETON UNIVERSITY PRESS

PRINCETON, NEW JERSEY

Published by Princeton University Press, 41 William Street,
Princeton, New Jersey 08540
In the United Kingdom: Princeton University Press, Oxford

Library of Congress Cataloging-in-Publication Data

Kraut, Richard, 1944–
Aristotle on the human good / Richard Kraut.
p.   cm.   Bibliography: p.   Includes index.
ISBN 0–691–07349–X
ISBN 0–691–02071–X (pbk.)
1. Aristotle. Nicomachean ethics. 2. Aristotle—Ethics.
3. Good and evil—History. 4. Happiness—History. I. Title.
B430.K73 1990   171′.3—dc20   89–32443

First Princeton Paperback printing, 1991

This book has been composed in Linotron Bembo

Princeton University Press paperbacks are printed on acid-free paper,
and meet the guidelines for permanence and durability of the
Committee on Production Guidelines for Book Longevity of the
Council on Library Resources

Printed in the United States of America by Princeton University Press
Princeton, New Jersey

9 8 7 6 5 4 3 2

For Anthea, Naomi, and Jonah

Contents

Acknowledgments

I am grateful to many generous people who offered encouragement and criticism when I was struggling with the initial stages of my work: Elizabeth Asmis, Norman Dahl, Cynthia Freeland, Christine Korsgaard, Joan Kung, Jon Moline, Terry Penner, Ian Mueller, John Rist, Jennifer Whiting, and Charles Young. Many others, too numerous to mention, raised important questions in discussion. At the final stage of this project, I received excellent criticism from Daniel Devereux and another referee, who read the manuscript for Princeton University Press. Frank Hunt, my copyeditor, helped in many other ways. I have tried to respond to many of the objections I received over several years, but no doubt I have not learned as much from others as I should have. Whatever the defects of this book, I am indebted to those who have tried to make it better.

I would like to add a note of tribute to my friend and fellow worker Joan Kung, who died of cancer in 1987. She not only sustained me with encouragement and detailed comments while I was engaged in this project, but throughout the time I knew her inspired me by her unique combination of generosity, integrity, ebullience, modesty, and wholehearted dedication to philosophy, its history, and the intellectual life. I was fortunate to have been her friend, and she is sorely missed.

I also wish to thank the University of Illinois at Chicago, and its philosophy department, for the support they have given this project over several years. During the 1983–84 academic year, I was a Fellow of its Humanities Institute, and was able to begin the research that resulted in this book. Further work was undertaken during a sabbatical leave granted me during the fall and winter of the 1986–87 academic year. Relief from teaching responsibilities during the spring of 1988 helped me during the final stages of writing. In addition, during this period, I had the good fortune to receive a fellowship from the National Endowment for the Humanities. Without the abundant support of these institutions, my work would have been long delayed.

Abbreviations

Ath. Pol.	*Constitution of Athens*
De An.	*De Anima*
De Gen. An.	*Generation of Animals*
De Juv.	*On Youth, Old Age, Life and Death, and Respiration*
De Part. An.	*Parts of Animals*
EE	*Eudemian Ethics*
Met.	*Metaphysics*
Meteor.	*Meteorologica*
MM	*Magna Moralia*
NE	*Nicomachean Ethics*
Pol.	*Politics*
Post. An.	*Posterior Analytics*

Aristotle on the Human Good

1. Consistency, Hierarchy, Inclusivism

In the opening pages of the *Nicomachean Ethics*, Aristotle asks: what is the good for a human being? And he then gives a sketch of an answer—a sketch that becomes increasingly detailed, as he proceeds within and beyond Book I. We are told, at an early point (I.4), that the human good consists in *eudaimonia* (conventionally translated "happiness"),[1] and although Aristotle reports that this answer is widely accepted, it does not take him very far, as he realizes (1095a16–22). For different people have different conceptions of what happiness is. And so, in order to determine what the human good consists in, we must decide which of the many competing conceptions of happiness is correct: does it consist in pleasure, or wealth, or honor, or health, or virtue, or in some combination of these and other goods? My aim in this book is to understand the answer Aristotle gives to this question.[2]

[1] This rendering has its drawbacks: "Happiness" is sometimes used simply as the name of a feeling, and it is often thought that if one feels happy, then one is happy. By contrast, for Aristotle, *eudaimonia* is the name of the highest good at which one can aim, and a person is *eudaimon* by having that good; accordingly, if one's conception of that highest good is mistaken, one can think oneself *eudaimon* even though one is not. Nonetheless, we do sometimes ask "What is happiness?" in a way that makes the question similar to Aristotle's question "What is *eudaimonia*?" We are not asking for a description or analysis of a feeling, but are raising a question about what kind of life would be good to live. Aristotle points out (I.4 1095a19–20), that *eudaimonia* is often equated with living well (*eu zēn*) and doing well (*eu prattein*). Note, however, that although he thinks other animals besides human beings can live well (*De An.* III.12 434b22–5, *De Part. An.* II.10 656a3–8, *EE* I.7 1217a29), only human beings and gods can be called *eudaimon* (*NE* I.9 1099b32–3, X.8 1178b24–8). His meaning at *NE* I.4 1095a19–20 must be that *human beings* who live well or do well are called *eudaimon*. For the sake of variety, I shall sometimes use "well-being," "living well," "a good life," or "flourishing" instead of "happiness," despite the important differences among them. "Flourishing" is defended as a translation, and "happiness" criticized, in Cooper, *RHGA*, pp. 89–90 n. 1. See too Ackrill, "Aristotle on *Eudaimonia*," p. 24. I discuss this issue more fully in "Two Conceptions of Happiness." (See the Bibliography for full information on works cited.)

[2] My aim is simply to understand Aristotle's conception of happiness in the *NE*. His treatment of this topic in the *Eudemian Ethics*, and in other works, deserves a separate study, and I shall make use of these additional sources only to the extent that they shed light on particular passages in the *NE*. My opinion is that Aristotle does not change his mind about how we should lead our lives; his practical works differ in emphasis and verbal formulation, but he does not move from one conception of happiness to another. I will do little to defend this interpretation here, but for further discussion, see 5.9. I hold the orthodox view that

One difficulty in interpreting his conception of happiness stems from the fact that he returns to this topic near the end of the *NE*, and gives an account whose relation to earlier material is unclear. He says in X.7–8 that happiness—or, as he sometimes puts it, perfect (*teleia*)[3] happiness—consists in an intellectual activity called "contemplation" (*theōria*).[4] According to one way of interpreting these chapters, they say that happiness consists in *just* this one activity.[5] But if that is the correct way of reading X.7–8, then there seems, at least on the surface, to be a conflict with what Aristotle had claimed earlier, in Book I. For that book is generally taken to hold that happiness consists in a number of different goods: one of them may be contemplation, but there are others besides.[6] Of course, if Aristotle says in one place that happiness consists in contemplation alone, and says elsewhere that it consists in other goods as well, then he has contradicted himself.[7] One of my main concerns will be to argue that the

---

the *NE* is later than the *EE*, but nothing in my argument depends on this. For a challenge to this orthodoxy, see Kenny, *The Aristotelian Ethics*.

[3] See X.7 1177a17, 1177b24, X.8 1178b7. The term *teleia* and its cognates can also be translated "complete" or "final." Which term best conveys Aristotle's meaning is sometimes an important interpretive issue. In particular, what he means by *teleia* happiness in X.7–8 is one of the issues that make the interpretation of these chapters difficult. I take up this problem in Chapter 1; see 1.9, 1.10, 1.13, and 1.16. (References to sections of this study will be abbreviated thus: 1.9 = Chapter 1, Section 9. References to Aristotle's works will mix roman and arabic numerals: X.7 = Book X, chapter 7.)

[4] The conventional rendering of *theōria*—"contemplation"—can be seriously misleading, as can the alternative—"study"—suggested by Irwin's translation. I will say more about what *theōria* is, and why these translations are inexact, in 1.19.

[5] See, for example, Nussbaum, *The Fragility of Goodness*, pp. 375–6. She takes X.7 1177b1–4 to be saying that only contemplation has intrinsic value. Since Aristotle holds that goods not desired for themselves cannot be identified with happiness (I.5 1096a5–9), 1177b1–4 seems to commit him to the view that only one good—contemplation—can be correctly equated with happiness. A similar reading can be found in Cooper, *RHGA*, pp. 155–180: he takes Aristotle to be saying (X.7 1178a2–4) that human beings are to be identified solely with their theoretical reason, and that all goods besides contemplation are therefore "alien" (p. 163). This interpretation is revised in his "Contemplation and Happiness: A Reconsideration."

[6] To my knowledge, the fullest defense of this interpretation is found in Ackrill, "Aristotle on *Eudaimonia*." A competing interpretation, found in Hardie, "The Final Good in Aristotle's *Ethics*," holds that Aristotle wavers in Book I, sometimes identifying happiness with one good, sometimes with many.

[7] Doubts about the consistency of X.7–8 with preceding material, or affirmations of its inconsistency, are quite common. See, for example, Ackrill, "Aristotle on *Eudaimonia*"; Adkins, "*Theōria* versus *Praxis* in the *Nicomachean Ethics* and the *Republic*"; Allan, *The Philosophy of Aristotle*, p. 139; Cooper, *RHGA*, pp. 156–164; Hardie, "The Final Good in Aristotle's *Ethics*"; Jaeger, *Aristotle*, pp. 439–440; Moline, "Contemplation and the Human Good"; Monan, *Moral Knowledge and Its Methodology in Aristotle*, p. 114; Nagel, "Aristotle on *Eudaimonia*," p. 7; Nussbaum, *The Fragility of Goodness*, pp. 373–7; Ross, *Aristotle*, pp. 233–4; White, "Goodness and Human Aims in Aristotle's Ethics," pp. 242–3; and Wilkes, "The Good Man and the Good for Man in Aristotle's Ethics," pp. 341, 351–2. Recent at-

NE does not contain this internal conflict. I shall try to show that the treatment of happiness in Books I and X forms an integrated unit, neither part of which can be fully understood in isolation from the other.

On my reading, Aristotle holds that there are two good ways of answering the question "What is happiness?" According to the best of these two answers, happiness consists in just one good: this is the virtuous exercise of the theoretical part of reason, that is, the activity called *theōria*. Every other good (including the ethical virtues) is desirable for the sake of this one activity. According to the second-best answer, happiness consists in virtuous practical activity:[8] it is the exercise of such virtues as magnanimity, courage, justice, temperance, practical wisdom, and so on. Just as every good in the best life is desirable for the sake of contemplation, so every good in the second-best life is desirable for the sake of activity in accordance with the practical virtues. Aristotle presents, in other words, two models of how one should lead one's life: one should be either a philosopher (that is, someone who devotes himself above all to exercising the virtues of theoretical reason) or a statesman[9] (that is, someone who devotes himself above all to the fullest exercise of moral virtue). If one chooses the first option and circumstances are favorable, then one attains perfect happiness; if one chooses the second, one will at best be happy in a secondary way. Unphilosophical and apolitical careers cannot be held up as models of how to live one's life, but are acceptable to the degree that they approximate these two paradigms.

An important ingredient of this interpretation is that every good of human life is to be located somewhere within a hierarchy that has a single end at its pinnacle. The lowest row of this hierarchy contains ends (such as wealth) that are not good in themselves, but are desirable only on condition that they lead to further goods. Above this row, Aristotle places

---

tempts to defend the consistency of X.7–8 with preceding material can be found in Cooper, "Contemplation and Happiness: A Reconsideration"; Devereux, "Aristotle on the Essence of Happiness"; Eriksen, *Bios Theoretikos*, pp. 135–6, 148, 151–3; Gauthier and Jolif, *L'Éthique à Nicomaque*, vol. 2, pp. 891–6; Keyt, "Intellectualism in Aristotle"; Rorty, "The Place of Contemplation in Aristotle's *Nicomachean Ethics*"; Urmson, *Aristotle's Ethics*, pp. 14–15 (but contrast pp. 123–5); and Whiting, "Human Nature and Intellectualism in Aristotle."

[8] Here I use "practical" as Aristotle sometimes does (X.7 1177b3, 6), to draw a contrast with theoretical activity or virtue. The practical virtues include all of those (such as temperance, justice, and courage) that Aristotle calls "ethical" and some of those (such as practical wisdom) that he calls "intellectual." For this contrast, see I.13 1103a4–10. I will use the term "moral virtue" interchangeably with "practical virtue," and "moral activity" interchangeably with "activity in accordance with practical virtue." I will sometimes use "excellent" and "excellence" instead of "virtuous" and "virtue."

[9] I will use the terms "statesman" and "politician" as translations of Aristotle's term *politikos*. The Greek term can refer broadly to anyone who plays a leading part in civic affairs, or more restrictively to those who exercise outstanding ability in this sphere. Obviously, someone leading the second-best life falls into the latter category.

goods (such as honor) that are desirable in themselves, though they are not to be identified with happiness. Still higher are those intrinsically desirable ends (virtuous activities) that are properly identified with happiness. Each good on a lower row is choiceworthy for the sake of some good on a higher row. From the fact that one good is desirable for the sake of a second, Aristotle infers that the second is more desirable than the first (I.1 1094a14–16), and as a result the single good at the top of the scale will be the best good within its hierarchy (I.2 1094a18–22).

The political life can be represented in the following way:

B

M   N

X   Y   Z

B: ethical activity
M, N: other goods that are desirable in themselves
X, Y, Z: goods that are conditionally desirable

And the philosophical life can be represented by adding another good, A, representing contemplation, above B, at the top of the hierarchy:

A

B

M   N

X   Y   Z

Notice that, according to this interpretation, the philosophical life is the life of a good person, that is, someone who has and exercises the ethical virtues.[10] Although one must decide whether to become a theoretician or a political leader, there are certain paramount goods one will need whichever alternative one adopts, and these are the virtues of justice, courage, practical wisdom, and so on. Since these are the most important ends that the two lives have in common, they receive most of Aristotle's attention. The *NE* is a political work, and therefore it focuses primarily on the qualities that every citizen should have. For all the importance of theoretical activity—every other good should be desired for its sake—it is in a sense an optional ideal: one can live well without being a philosopher.

Nonetheless, it should not be thought that Aristotle's defense of the philosophical life in X.7–8 is a mere addendum, which readers may ignore without impairing their understanding of what precedes it. On the contrary, if we misread this late segment of the *NE*, and fail to see how it

[10] Contrast Cooper, *RHGA*, pp. 163–5: the person leading the best life has an attitude incompatible with moral virtue.

coheres with the account of happiness given in Book I, then we will distort much that falls between the opening and closing portions of Aristotle's work. In particular, we will fail to see why Aristotle thinks that the *ethical* virtues are so valuable. As I will try to show, his defense of the philosophical life is of a piece with his defense of the practical virtues: he intellectualizes such excellences as courage, generosity, and justice, and regards them as approximations of the theoretical virtues. For the ultimate aim of human life, and the proper function of human beings, is to use reason well, and this goal can be reached in either of two ways: ideally, by leading a philosophical life and making contemplation one's highest aim; but if that option cannot be taken, then we do best by fully developing the practical virtues and exercising them on a grand scale, in the political arena. If one fails to see the common core that unites these two lives—the idea that happiness, our ultimate aim, consists *solely* in excellent reasoning activity—then one will have missed a central feature of Aristotle's conception of the good.

To defend my interpretation against alternatives, I will have to confront a passage in which he seems to be saying that happiness consists not simply in contemplation or ethically virtuous activity, but in a much broader group of intrinsic goods—so broad, in fact, as to include all the intrinsic goods there are. The passage in question reads as follows:

> The self-sufficient we posit as that which when taken by itself makes life choiceworthy and in need of nothing. Such we think happiness to be. Furthermore, it is the most choiceworthy of all, without being counted in addition—being counted in addition, it is obviously more choiceworthy [when taken] with the least of goods. For what is added on is an increase of goods, and of goods the greater is always more choiceworthy. (I.7 1097b14–20)[11]

These obscure lines are widely taken to mean that human happiness needs nothing because it already contains as components all of the intrinsic goods there are, or all that can be fit into a single life.[12] It is the most

[11] Translations are my own. But I have consulted those of Ross, Ostwald, and Irwin, and frequently conform to the choice of terms made by one or more of them. I use Bywater's Greek text.

[12] See, for example, Burnet, *The Ethics of Aristotle*, ad loc.; Gauthier and Jolif, *L'Éthique à Nicomaque*, ad loc.; Ackrill, "Aristotle on *Eudaimonia*," pp. 21–2. They take Aristotle to be saying that happiness consists in all intrinsic goods; I add such phrases as "all that can be fit into a single life" or "all compossible intrinsic goods" to cover the possibility that some intrinsic goods might have to be omitted from happiness because no life can contain them all. But I do not think that this refinement on their interpretation is necessarily an improvement. The important question is whether Aristotle thinks that happiness consists not only in virtuous activities, but also in such intrinsic goods as honor, pleasure, and friends. If he does have this expansive conception of happiness, then it does not matter, for my purposes, whether he thinks it consists in *all* intrinsic goods or only in all *compossible* intrinsic goods.

choiceworthy good in a special way: it is not most desirable in the way in which some noncomposite good like contemplation is more desirable when it is compared, one by one, with every other noncomposite good (justice, friendship, honor, and so on). Rather, happiness is the most choiceworthy good because of its all-inclusive structure: all compossible intrinsic goods are included within it, so that there is no way to make it more desirable by adding something else to it.

I will argue that this interpretation (sometimes called "inclusivism")[13] is fundamentally misguided, and is based on a misreading of the above passage and several others.[14] My thesis is not simply that inclusivism runs into trouble because of what Aristotle says about contemplation in Book X. Rather, I claim that it also gives a poor account of Book I. For the fundamental thesis of Book I, as I understand it, is that happiness consists in a long stretch of perfect virtuous activity of the rational soul.[15] That one good can be analyzed into several subdivisions, since Aristotle distinguishes several kinds of perfect virtues of the rational soul. But happiness is not a composite of all compossible intrinsic goods: for example, it does not include physical pleasures, or honor, or friends. Though inclusivism is widely accepted, I shall argue that it impedes our understanding of both Book I and Book X, and prevents us from grasping the central role of virtuous activity in Aristotle's theory. He thinks that, in order to lead our lives well, we need more than a list of intrinsic goods: we must determine which of them is most worthwhile, and how much each should be pursued. His way of imposing this kind of order on the diversity of human

[13] The term "inclusive end" and the contrasting term "dominant end" were introduced into discussions of Aristotle by Hardie, "The Final Good in Aristotle's *Ethics*." Of course, these phrases can be used in different and conflicting ways. Note, for example, that there is a sense in which my interpretation takes Aristotle to have an inclusive-end conception of happiness: if inclusivism is the view that, according to Aristotle, happiness consists in two or more goods (thus Ackrill, "Aristotle on *Eudaimonia*," p. 17), then in a way I am putting forward a version of inclusivism. For on my view happiness does not consist only in contemplation: there is also a secondary form of happiness, which consists in moral activity. However, if inclusivism is the view that happiness consists in *all* intrinsic goods (or all compossible intrinsic goods), then I do not take Aristotle to be an inclusivist. Note too that there is an important difference between (a) "Human happiness consists in all the intrinsic goods" and (b) "A happy life for a human being contains all the intrinsic goods." I reject (a), but accept something close to (b). See 5.13. A happy life for a human being contains friends, physical pleasures, honors, health, and so on. These subordinate goods promote human happiness, but on my interpretation they are not what happiness consists in.

[14] The interpretation of I.7 1097b14–20 that is now widely accepted has been challenged by Kenny, *The Aristotelian Ethics*, pp. 204–205. Cf. his paper "Happiness," p. 51. He is backed by Clark, *Aristotle's Man*, pp. 153–5. But I believe that their alternative reading is less well supported than the current orthodoxy. See 5.2.

[15] See I.9 1100a4, I.10 1101a14–15, I.13 1102a5–6. Of course, it is not at all clear what Aristotle means by activity of the soul in accordance with perfect virtue. For what is "perfect" (*teleia*) virtue? (An alternative translation would be "complete virtue.") I take up this issue in 4.16–17.

goals is to arrange our ends in a hierarchy, and to place virtuous activity (whether practical or theoretical) at the top. Happiness is the end for the sake of which all others are desired; it consists solely in virtuous activity, and is not a composite of all intrinsic goods.

Since happiness consists in virtuous activity alone, no increase or decrease in the degree to which we possess other kinds of goods by itself constitutes an increase or decrease in happiness. And since *perfect* happiness consists in contemplation alone, there is no upper bound on the value of this activity. There is no such thing as a life that has more philosophical activity than is desirable; the more such activity one engages in, the better off one is.[16] Furthermore, I take Aristotle to be saying that moral activity has this kind of priority over goods that are subordinate to it: when we compare two nonphilosophical lives and see that one has a higher degree of ethical activity than the other, then we can immediately infer that the more ethical life is happier. Even if the less moral life has a larger number of other goods (for example, more physical pleasures), that fact should not affect our comparison. For happiness does not consist in any of these lower goods: just as perfect happiness consists in contemplation alone, so the secondary form of happiness consists in ethical activity alone.

2. EGOISM

Another important feature of my interpretation is that I do not take Aristotle to be an egoist.[17] That is, I do not take him to be assuming,

[16] As we shall see in Chapter 1, however, a proviso must be added, because Aristotle believes that if there is too little contemplative activity in a life, then that activity does not make the life happy. If a person engages in only a slight amount of philosophical activity, and then adds only a slight bit more, that addition does not advance him from a happy life to an even happier life. Increases in theoretical activity increase happiness only when the initial amount is above a certain threshold. When two lives are above that threshold, then whichever has more philosophical activity is the happier life. Lives that differ in length present a different problem: Suppose A and B lead philosophical lives for thirty years, and during this time A engages in a bit less philosophical activity than B; then B dies, and A changes careers, so that for twenty more years he leads a life filled with excellent practical activity but devoid of philosophical thought. B's life is slightly better than A's for thirty years, but Aristotle can say that A's whole life is better than B's whole life. Just as a tiny amount of contemplation is not enough to make a life happy, so a tiny difference in the amount of contemplation contained by two unequal periods may not be enough to make the shorter period happier. See too Chapter 5, note 23.

[17] Some form of egoism—either as a doctrine about how one should act or as a theory about how human beings necessarily act—is commonly ascribed to Aristotle, either as his main tendency or as his consistent conviction. See, for example, Allan, *The Philosophy of Aristotle*, p. 140; Field, *Moral Theory*, pp. 110–111; Hardie, "The Final Good in Aristotle's Ethics," pp. 317–320; Irwin, *Plato's Moral Theory*, p. 255; Prichard, "The Meaning of *Agathon* in the *Ethics* of Aristotle," p. 40; Ross, *Aristotle*, p. 230; Sidgwick, *The Methods of Ethics*, pp. 91–2. A dissenting voice can be found in Annas, "Plato and Aristotle on Friendship and Altruism," pp. 539–544. However, the term "egoism" is not used by all of those who ascribe

implicitly or explicitly, that each human being must or should do whatever promotes the greatest amount of good for himself. On my reading,
he believes that although the best one can do for oneself is to lead a philosophical life, there may be circumstances in which one should lead a
political life instead. Consider the following example: The king of a small
Greek city sends his son to Athens in order to study political theory with
Aristotle. The son shall some day inherit his father's position, and his
training in Athens is undertaken in the expectation that he will rule more
wisely after attending Aristotle's political lectures, and after studying the
constitutions of other cities. When the son hears Aristotle's defense of the
contemplative ideal, he decides that the life for which he has been
groomed is not as desirable as the one he would have were he to stay in
Athens and discuss philosophy for the rest of his days. If he returns to his
city, he will have so much political work to do that no time will be left to
undertake the study of theoretical subjects. But he thinks that he owes it
to his father and his native city to lead the political life for which he has
been prepared since early childhood. He would be better off were he to
become a philosopher, but others with whom he has special ties would
be worse off. And so he returns to his city, and leads a good—but not the
best—life.

In saying that Aristotle is not an egoist, I am claiming that nothing in
his writings requires him to disapprove of the son's decision. When he
argues, in *NE* X.7–8, that the philosopher's life is better than the statesman's, he is addressing those who are free to choose either kind of life.
They are not constrained by special circumstances, and so they quite
properly will choose the life that is best for them. Each asks, "How will
I be happiest?" and Aristotle tries to show why each will be happiest by
leading the philosophical life. But this allows him to say that in certain
circumstances one should act for the sake of someone else's happiness,
even if this means that in doing so one has less happiness for oneself. He
gives no formula for determining what one should do when such conflicts
occur, that is, when the act that optimizes one's own well-being would
prevent others from fully achieving their good. In fact, he denies that
there can be such a formula.

Consider another example: An old man is ill, and his son, a philosopher, is trying to decide what to do about it. If the son devotes himself to
restoring his father's health, he knows that he will have to give up a certain amount of philosophical activity, and this loss cannot be recovered;

---

to Aristotle a form of that doctrine, and more importantly, there may be no one moral or
psychological doctrine that all ascribe to him. There are a number of different views that
can be called egoistic, and so it is possible that my denial that Aristotle is an egoist is consistent with some of what these authors say. The kind of egoism that I claim cannot be found
in his works will be more fully described in 2.1.

he does not think that if he gives up some time for theorizing now, he will as a result eventually have more time for this activity. Furthermore, his father is not a philosopher, and never will be; contemplation is not one of his activities. And so, if the son gives up some amount of theoretical activity, he cannot justify his choice by saying that although he will have less, others will have more, and the total amount of contemplation going on in the world will increase.

On my interpretation, Aristotle is not committed to saying that the son must refuse to help his father. Although he thinks that perfect happiness consists entirely in contemplation, he is not claiming that this is a good that one must maximize. How then should the son make his decision? Again, Aristotle would say that there is no formula. Presumably, he would agree that such factors as these should be taken into consideration: How serious is the father's illness? How much good can the son do? How much does the father want the son's care? How much time would it require? Are there others who would be willing and better able to help? Has he been a good father and is he a good man? Is the amount of care that would be needed beyond what is normally expected of children? If these questions are answered in a certain way, then Aristotle would say that the son must help his father, despite the fact that as a result his life is less desirable than it would otherwise have been. In this case, it is not just the father who has suffered a misfortune; the son suffers a loss too, since he must give up the best activity, to some extent. Of course this is not a major sacrifice, since he still leads a philosophical life; although he is not as happy as he might have been, he is still leading the best kind of life. In fact, on my interpretation, the son could still live well even if he entirely gave up philosophy, for a secondary form of happiness is available to those who do not exercise the theoretical virtues.

3. AN OVERVIEW

I shall proceed in the following way:

In Chapter 1, I argue that X.7–8 contains a striking thesis about the value of contemplation: the more such activity a life contains, the better a life it is. This is not the weak claim that it would always be desirable to increase theoretical activity provided that this brings no loss in other goods. Rather, Aristotle's thesis is that it would always be desirable to change the mixture of goods in one's life so that contemplation increases, even if the level of other goods decreases. The best way to improve a life is to add a greater amount of philosophical activity to it. In this sense, there is no limit to the value of theoretical activity; more is always better than less.

But, as I try to show in Chapter 2, this striking thesis does not commit

Aristotle to the view that, whatever one's circumstances, one should maximize the amount of time one spends contemplating. For he nowhere assumes or claims that human beings should be devoted to their own *maximal* good. He believes that what is best for one person can sometimes conflict with what is best for another, and he does not think that in these circumstances each should always give priority to his own optimal well-being. Some just accommodation must be reached, in order to resolve such conflicts, and this requires attention to the proper relationship between the conflicting parties. My treatment of these issues shall draw on several doctrines put forward in Aristotle's political writings: the rotation of rule among equals, the justification of slavery, and the occasional need for ostracism. I will also draw heavily on his discussion of friendship, in Books VIII and IX of the *NE*; for although Aristotle endorses self-love in these books, we should not take him to mean that one's own happiness is to be maximized, come what may for others. My principal claim in this chapter is that egoism—the view that each act should maximize one's own good—is too great a simplification of proper human relationships to fit Aristotle's thought.

In Chapter 3, I argue that when Aristotle defends the philosophical ideal, in X.7–8, he does not abandon the psychological or normative assumptions he has been making throughout the *NE*. He continues to believe that many different types of human ends (besides contemplation) are desirable in themselves, and he assumes that the philosopher will need them all, to some degree, in order to lead a life that is regularly devoted to theoretical activity over a long period of time. He takes it for granted that all human beings need friends in order to live well, and that philosophers will be best equipped to achieve their ultimate end over the course of a lifetime if they carry out their activities with others who have both the practical and the theoretical virtues. So contemplation is not an *alternative* to the other goods (ethical virtue, friendship, pleasure) that are taken so seriously throughout the *NE*; rather, it is a way of organizing those subordinate ends into a coherent system: the best amount of lower goods to have, from one's own point of view, is the amount that most fully contributes to one's ultimate end. Of every other good besides contemplation, there can be too much or too little for one's own good. By aiming at this ultimate end, we have a target which helps us determine how much is too much, and how little too little. Similarly, if we do not lead a philosophical life, but a political life instead, then ethical activity provides us with a guideline for answering quantitative questions about subordinate goods: the best amount of honor, the right number of friends, the appropriate amount of time spent on relaxation, is determined by looking to the effects differing quantities will have on ethical activity.

In Chapter 4, I turn to Aristotle's main discussion of happiness, in Book I, and argue that he equates it with just one type of good: virtuous activity. One of the principal topics we will examine is his conception of the "for-the-sake-of" relation: what is it for one thing to be desired or desirable for the sake of another? My claim is that there is only one such relation recognized in Aristotle's text, and that it involves both normative and causal elements: when B (for example, a bridle) is for the sake of A (for example, riding horses), then B causally promotes A, and A provides a standard that regulates the production of B. In Book I, Aristotle is looking for an end for the sake of which every other end is pursued—and this "for the sake of" is to be understood in normative-causal terms. Happiness is the good that is *causally promoted* by every other end, and that provides a *standard* for the regulation of every other end. According to an alternative interpretation, which I shall reject, there is a second for-the-sake-of relation in Book I: B is for the sake of A when A is a whole of which B is a part. Inclusivism requires such a relationship, for it takes every good (including ethically virtuous activity and contemplation) to be desirable for the sake of the all-inclusive composite that Aristotle allegedly identifies with happiness. I shall try to show that the for-the-sake-of relation never takes this form in Aristotle.

Once this issue has been settled, we will be able to understand the distinction he makes between perfect and most perfect virtues: just as he thinks that such ends as wealth, honor, pleasure, and virtue can be arranged in a hierarchy, some of these ends being for the sake of others, so he thinks that the virtues themselves can be arranged hierarchically. Some virtues of the rational soul are not perfect, because they are desirable only on condition that they lead to other virtues; others are perfect but not most perfect because, although they are choiceworthy in themselves, they are also desirable for the sake of some further virtue. And in X.7–8, we learn that the most perfect virtue is the one that enables us to engage in our highest activity, contemplation.

Chapter 5 then turns to the passage that has misled so many into thinking that Aristotle has an inclusivist conception of happiness: these are the lines, cited above in Section 1, in which he holds that happiness is self-sufficient (it "makes life choiceworthy and in need of nothing") and that it is "most choiceworthy of all, without being counted in addition" (1097b14–20). Partly because this passage contains the premise "of goods the greater is always more choiceworthy," many readers have inferred that happiness is inclusive of as many goods as a life can contain. I shall try to show how this inference can be blocked, and how the passage can be made consistent with Aristotle's frequent claim that happiness is to be identified with virtuous activity and with no other type of good. One of the advantages of my reading is that it allows us to see how his observation in I.7 that happiness is self-sufficient is compatible with the thesis of X.7 that contemplation is the most self-sufficient good (1177a27–8). That thesis is nonsense if the self-sufficiency of a good consists in its containing all others. Once we reject this way of interpreting self-sufficiency, we can see how a single noncomposite good, like contemplation, can be most self-sufficient.

Finally, in Chapter 6, I turn to the "function argument" of I.7, and show how it helps prepare the way for Aristotle's defense of both the political and the philosophical lives. I will try to explain why Aristotle thinks that one kind of good life is devoted to the ultimate end of exercising, as fully as possible, such virtues as justice, generosity, temperance, and practical wisdom. To have these virtues, one must structure one's ends so that everything else in one's life is done for the sake of reasoning well, and for no further end. And so the political life resembles the life of the philosopher: each is devoted ultimately to excellence in reasoning, and in each case subordinate goods (pleasure, honor, and so on) are pursued with moderation, since too few or too many would undermine one's highest end.

When we read Aristotle in this way, we see that his famous doctrine of the mean is connected with his conception of happiness, and is therefore more controversial and substantive than has been realized. His thesis is far more interesting than the claim that we must do neither more nor less than we should; as he himself says, the doctrine of the mean is too general, unless it is tied to a definite target which helps us fix the boundary between extremes (VI.1 1138b18–34). That target is constituted by the intellectual virtues discussed in Book VI: we should educate our emotions and our desires for subordinate goods in such a way that we will be best able to exercise practical or theoretical reason. In other words, we should live in order to reason well; and to reason well is to exercise the virtues of the thinking part of the soul. All of our desires, and all of our external resources, should be regulated in such a way that they contribute fully to this ideal, as it is expressed either in the philosophical life or, failing that, in the political life.

CHAPTER ONE

Two Lives

1.1. The Philosophical Life and the Political Life

The main burden of *NE* X.7–8 is to argue that "the life in accordance with understanding" (*nous*), as Aristotle calls it, is the happiest kind of life a human being can lead (1178a6–8). But precisely what kind of life is it? Which goods will it contain, and how are they to be organized? These are among the principal questions I will try to answer in this study. Before I present and defend my interpretation, however, I would like to begin with some elementary observations.

Aristotle defends this life by giving a number of arguments designed to show that contemplation is the best activity available to human beings; and he also points to certain ways in which the virtue of *sophia* (theoretical wisdom) is superior to such practical excellences as justice, courage, and temperance. So, "the life in accordance with understanding" is obviously one that contains a certain amount of contemplative activity; and the person who engages in this activity thereby activates the virtue of theoretical wisdom. That virtue, we are told in VI.7 (1141a17–20), is a composite of understanding and knowledge (*epistēmē*): to have theoretical wisdom is to be able (by means of *nous*) to grasp the first principles of certain theoretical disciplines, and to be able (by means of *epistēmē*) to derive conclusions from those principles in an appropriate way.[1] To exercise any of these intellectual virtues is to bring to mind—to contemplate[2]—the eternal and

[1] See VI.3 on *epistēmē*, VI.6 on *nous*, and VI.7 on *sophia*. We are told at 1139b19–24 that the objects of scientific knowledge must be necessary and eternal. Aristotle's conception of such knowledge is most fully presented in *Post An.* I.2–9; and see *Post An.* II.19 on the division of labor between *epistēmē* and *nous*. Note that at *NE* VI.7 1141a20 Aristotle says that wisdom requires scientific knowledge "of things held most in honor" (so too 1141b3). I take him to mean that someone has theoretical wisdom *simpliciter* (and is not merely *sophos* in some respect) only when he has understood the divine first causes of the universe. See *Met.* I.2 (especially 983a5–11) on the objects of the highest form of wisdom. Note too the implied distinction at *NE* VI.8 1142a17–18 between expertise in mathematical or natural science, on the one hand, and theoretical wisdom on the other. The important point is that the ideal life is not one in which just any theoretical object (such as plane figures or winged animals) is contemplated; ideally, one should contemplate the first cause of the universe. I return to this point in 1.19.

[2] Aristotle uses *theōria* to cover a wide range of cases, and it does not always designate the activity in which one exercises theoretical wisdom. One can be said to be engaged in *theōria* whenever one closely observes or studies something—whatever that something is. For ex-

necessary truths of a theoretical discipline that one has mastered. And so a "life in accordance with understanding" could just as well be called "a contemplative life." And since *philosophia* is another name Aristotle gives to the activity of contemplation (1177a25), we can also say that the person who leads the best kind of life is a philosopher.[3]

But after Aristotle argues that the life in accordance with understanding is happiest, he adds: "secondarily, the [life] in accordance with the other virtue" (1178a9).[4] There is, in other words, another life besides the philosophical life and another happiness (a21–2); it is a life in accordance with practical rather than theoretical virtue, and its happiness is in some way secondary. Though it is uncontroversial that in X.7–8 Aristotle discusses these two lives—one in accordance with understanding, the other in accordance with practical virtue—it is not at all clear what the relation between them is. Is he saying that one should lead the philosophical life

---

ample, every craft studies (*theōrein*) the process by which contingent objects come into being (VI.4 1140a11–12); the person of practical wisdom studies his own good (VI.7 1141a25); and we can study the actions of our neighbors better than our own (IX.9 1169b33). But the *theōria* Aristotle is talking about in X.7–8 is not the study of just any objects or truths. It is the activation of theoretical wisdom, and this state of mind does not take human happiness as an object of study—a point Aristotle emphasizes in VI.12 (1143b18–20). When he uses *theōria* in this narrow way, he contrasts it with practical activity and practical thought; see, for example, I.5 1095b18–19, VI.2 1139a27–8, X.7 1177b2–3, X.9 1180b20–21. Whether *theōria* is used narrowly or broadly, it is always a condition in which one is actually directing one's attention to something (see, for example, VII.3 1146b34–5, X.4 1175a1); it is an activity and not merely a capacity or disposition. It is important to bear in mind that to activate the virtue of theoretical wisdom—to contemplate—is not to be seeking knowledge, but to be bringing to mind the knowledge one already has. (Aristotle claims that the thoughts of the knower are more pleasant than those of the seeker: X.7 1177a26–7.) Someone who first undertakes an investigation is engaged in *theōria* in the broad (see, for example, X.9 1181b18, 20) but not the narrow sense.

[3] Aristotle uses *philosophia* and its cognates to name both (a) the search for wisdom undertaken by those who do not yet have it (*Met.* I.2 982b12–21) and (b) the activity engaged in by the wise when they bring to mind the truths they know (*Met.* II.1 993b19–20). Since X.7 is a defense of the activity that actualizes our best virtue (1177a12–17), *philosophia* at 1177a25 presumably refers to (b) rather than (a). I therefore take 1177a25–7 to be saying that philosophy is reasonably thought to be our best activity, since those who know (that is, those who contemplate the truth) engage in a more pleasant pursuit than those who are still seeking the truth. (If *philosophia* at 1177a25 meant "seeking wisdom," then Aristotle's argument at 1177a25–7 would be that since the pleasures of philosophy are so great, those of knowing must be even greater.)

[4] It is not clear what word should be used to fill out Aristotle's sentence. Is he saying at 1178a9 "secondarily, the life in accordance with the other virtue is happiest"? Or is he saying "secondarily, the life in accordance with the other virtue is happy"? Fortunately, nothing of importance turns on this indeterminacy. He is saying either that the practical life is second-happiest or that it is happy in a secondary way, and these are equivalent ways of making the same point: the philosophical life is best, the other life second-best. Irwin supplies "happiest" at 1178a9, Ross and Ostwald "happy."

rather than the other one?[5] Or are we to combine the two lives and lead them both?[6] That is a question to which we will soon return.

We should also note that at times, when Aristotle argues that exercising theoretical virtue has certain advantages over exercising practical virtue, he makes his point by drawing a contrast between the philosopher and the politician. For example, at 1178a23–b5, he claims that the politician (the *politikos*: 1178a26–7) will need more external goods than will the person who contemplates. And he also points out that political activity is not as leisurely as contemplation (1177b4–24). This contrast between the philosopher and the politician is not a different contrast from the one he has been drawing between the life in accordance with understanding and the life in accordance with practical virtue. Just as the philosopher is the person who leads the life in accordance with understanding, so the politician is the person who leads the life in accordance with the other virtues. Of course, it may be that, properly interpreted, X.7–8 is urging us to lead a life that is both philosophical and political: Aristotle may be saying that although some kind of primacy should be given to philosophical activity, the best life will be that of someone who is both a philosopher and a statesman. That is a possibility I am still leaving open.

I now want to put forward a suggestion that goes beyond the uncontroversial points I have been making: I believe that there is a certain connection between the project Aristotle is undertaking in X.7–8 and a question he discusses in I.5. Before I say what that connection is, let me briefly describe the contents of that earlier chapter: There are, Aristotle says (1095b14–19), three main answers to the question "What is happiness?" and each corresponds to a different way of life. The first kind of life is one preferred by the many: they think that happiness consists in physical pleasure. After briefly criticizing this conception of the good (b19–22), he turns to a second kind of life—the political life—and tries to associate it with a way of answering the question "What is happiness?" At first, he takes those who lead a political life to be saying that happiness consists in honor. But then, after criticizing this conception of happiness (b22–30), he considers another conception that might be attributed to those who lead a political life: perhaps the end of this life is virtue (b30–31). Again, Aristotle argues against this way of saying what happiness is (1095b31–1096a4). He then postpones discussion of the third main kind of life—the contemplative life—and instead criticizes the view that happiness consists

[5] Thus Hardie, *Aristotle's Ethical Theory*, p. 422; Ross, *Aristotle*, p. 233; Cooper, *RHGA*, p. 160.

[6] Thus Gauthier and Jolif, *L'Éthique à Nicomaque*, vol. 2, p. 862; Stewart, *Notes on the Nicomachean Ethics of Aristotle*, vol. 1 (pp. 59–62), vol. 2 (pp. 443–5); Keyt, "Intellectualism in Aristotle," pp. 372–4, 377.

in wealth (a4–7). The chapter concludes with the observation that none of the rival conceptions of happiness considered thus far has been successful (a7–10).

Does Aristotle think that he has in I.5 given good reasons for not leading a political life? Is he saying here that the only acceptable conception of happiness must be the one put forward by those who favor the contemplative life? I suggest that we answer these questions in the negative. We should not take Aristotle to be saying in I.5 that he has completed his discussion of the political life. For as we have seen, he continues his discussion of that life in X.7–8, where he argues that the life of a philosopher is happier than that of a politician. Furthermore, in X.7–8 he does not base his comparison between the philosophical and the political lives on the assumption that the statesman's end is either honor or virtue—the two conceptions of happiness that have been rejected in in I.5. Rather, the starting point of X.7 is that happiness consists not in virtue itself but in activity in accordance with virtue (1177a12).

I suggest, therefore, that we read I.5 in the following way: It is not claiming that a person leading a political life must say either that happiness is honor or that it is virtue. If Aristotle were doing that, then, having rejected both answers, he would be in a position to say that we should not lead a political life. Instead, I.5 is saying that *if* honor or virtue is taken to be the end of the political life, then that kind of life is based on an unacceptable answer to the question "What is happiness?" Furthermore, I suggest that in X.7–8 Aristotle is assuming that the political life can be associated with a better answer to that question than either "honor" or "virtue." The best answer it can give to that question is "activity in accordance with such practical virtues as courage, justice, and temperance and so on." The contemplative life, by contrast, rests on the thesis that happiness consists in activity in accordance with theoretical wisdom. If we connect I.5 with X.7–8 in this way, then we should say that the treatment of the political life in I.5 is merely introductory: Aristotle is not rejecting the political life there, but is instead trying out and rejecting two conceptions of happiness that can, with some reason, be associated with that life. The *proper* way to associate that kind of life with a conception of happiness is to take its end to be activity in accordance with moral virtue. So, when we finish I.5, we do not yet know how politicians should best defend their way of life by basing it on a certain conception of happiness. The comparison between the political and the philosophical lives is barely touched upon in that early chapter, but rather than leave it unfinished, Aristotle returns to it in X.7–8. In fact, when we consider that X.6 argues against identifying happiness with pleasant amusements (1176b9–1177a11), then we can say that X.6–8 returns to the theme of I.5: the three most favored kinds of life are those dedicated to pleasure, politics, and philosophy.[7]

What I have said so far is compatible with the possibility that in X.7–8 Aristotle is urging his readers to lead a life that is both philosophical and political. He might believe that the best answer to the question "What is happiness?" is not one that would be given by a single-minded philosopher ("theoretical activity"), or one that would be given by a single-minded statesman ("practical activity"), but rather one that combines both answers: happiness is activity in accordance with theoretical and practical virtue. In that case, he would be saying that we should not be merely philosophers or merely politicians, but should instead lead the life of someone who is both a theoretician and a statesman. That is an interpretation I shall soon consider. My proposal, at this point, is simply that we make a certain connection between I.5 and X.7–8. The later chapters return to a question that has been raised but not answered in the earlier chapter: should we lead a political or a philosophical life? Perhaps Aristotle's answer is that we do not need to choose, since we should ideally combine both careers.

The interpretation I have given so far is open to two challenges. First, I have used portions of Book I to help explain what Aristotle is doing in Book X: noticing that in X.7–8 he takes the life in accordance with ethical virtue to be the life of a politician, I claimed that he is investigating the difference between the kinds of lives that were first mentioned in I.5. But it may be objected that I am not justified in making any such connection between Aristotle's two treatments of happiness in the *NE*. For, as I noted in the Introduction, some have argued that there is a deep conflict between these two portions of the *NE*, and if they are correct, then in studying X.7–8 we must be prepared to set aside everything Aristotle says in earlier parts of his work. Second, it can be argued that in Book I, and throughout the bulk of the *NE*, Aristotle takes the advocate of the political life to give an all-inclusive answer to the question "What is happiness?" That is, human happiness consists in all compossible intrinsic goods, and since this is the end that politics tries to bring about, the advocate of the political life will answer the question "What is happiness?" by equating it with all such goods. By contrast, on the reading I have proposed, Aristotle takes the advocate of the political life to be saying that the one good with which happiness should be identified is activity in accordance with the practical virtues.

---

[7] The idea that the three most prominent lives of I.5 correspond to the three lives of X.6–8 is not new. See, for example, Gauthier and Jolif, *L'Éthique à Nicomaque*, on 1177a6–9; Keyt, "Intellectualism in Aristotle," p. 375.

Neither objection can be answered at the moment. First, I cannot show yet that the *NE* is a unified work; that conclusion can emerge only when all of my arguments have been presented, and the reader is in a position to judge how good a case I have made. What I can say now in my defense is that good methodology requires us to start with the assumption that the *NE* is internally consistent, and to abandon this assumption only when we have good reason to do so. We should try to see how far we can explain what Aristotle says in one place by appealing to what he says elsewhere, and we should give up this attempt only when our project fails. And so I will continue to range back and forth between Books I and X, on the assumption that they present different aspects of a single coherent theory. I assume that no one objects *in principle* to this method, though many may be skeptical about the project's chances of success.

As for the second objection, I must again ask the reader to wait patiently for arguments that will be given later. In order to develop my interpretation, I must postpone discussion of those passages that seem to undermine it. I will argue later that Aristotle never commits himself to an all-inclusive conception of happiness. If I am right about this, and if X.7–8 can eventually be shown to form a unity with what precedes it, then we should develop and explore the suggestions I have been making about the relation between I.5 and X.7–8: The comparison between political and philosophical lives, initiated in I.5, is not abandoned, but is finally addressed in the later part of Aristotle's work. X.7–8 confirms the point, made in I.5, that each of the different lives is associated with a different conception of happiness: the philosopher says it is theoretical activity, the statesman that it is practical activity. Aristotle implies in I.5 that the differences between political and philosophical careers must be considered if we are to lead our lives as best we can. And it is only in X.7–8 that those differences are brought to light, and we are told which of those two lives is better.

1.2. CHOOSING ETHICAL ACTIVITY

Proceeding on the assumption that X.6–8 returns to the project, initiated in I.5, of comparing lives, and that X.7–8 focuses on the philosophical and the political lives, let us now ask what these two lives consist in. Precisely what is involved in leading a philosophical life, and in leading a political life? How do they differ, and in what ways are they similar? (Bear in mind that, however much or little they differ, it is possible that they are, ideally, to be combined.)

It is uncontroversial that there will be some similarities. For Aristotle is willing to assume (1178a25–6) that theoretical virtue and ethical virtue need the necessary goods (such as health and food: see 1178b34–5) to the same degree. So it is not the case that leading a philosophical life requires having goods A, B, C, . . . , whereas leading a political life requires M, N, O, . . . , there being no overlap between the two classes. But can we be more precise than this? Can we say more about which goods they have in common, and which goods (if any) are peculiar to each life?

I will soon say what I think the differences are between these two lives, and I will argue that, ideally, they are *not* to be combined; on my interpretation, Aristotle thinks that we do best to choose a philosophical *rather than* a political life. But for now I would like to remind the reader of a feature of my interpretation that was emphasized in the Introduction. One of the major claims of this book is that the two lives have a great deal in common, beyond the necessary goods: in particular, I hold that both the philosopher and the statesman have the ethical virtues of justice, courage, temperance, and so on. One part of this claim is of course uncontroversial, for everyone agrees that the statesman has these traits of character. As we saw in the previous section, X.7–8 assumes that the life in accordance with ethical virtue is the life of a *politikos*. But the other part of my claim can be called into question. What reason do we have for thinking that, in Aristotle's opinion, the person leading the philosophical life will have the ethical virtues? In fact, why should we not take Aristotle to be saying that this is precisely where the two lives will differ: the politician has ethical but not theoretical virtue, whereas the philosopher has theoretical but not ethical virtue?

My reply is that there is some textual basis within X.7–8 for rejecting this suggestion. For Aristotle reminds his readers in X.8 that the philosopher is a human being (1178b5, 33); and, he adds: "Insofar as he is a human being and lives together with a larger group, he chooses to do the things that are in accordance with virtue. Therefore, he will need such things [external goods] in order to live a human life (*anthrōpeuesthai*)" (b5–7). We will return to this passage in Chapter 3, but for now we need only observe that Aristotle thinks of the philosopher as someone who has this much in common with the statesman: both of them choose to act in accordance with the ethical virtues. For it is clear from the context that this is the kind of virtue he has in mind in the above passage.

It can be argued, however, that although Aristotle's philosophers choose to do ethically virtuous acts, they see nothing intrinsically desirable in such behavior. On this interpretation, the best life consists in maximizing the amount of theoretical activity one engages in, on the grounds that this is the only intrinsically worthwhile good. Philosophers will, on certain occasions, perform just acts—not because they have the virtue of justice, but because in those circumstances just action will be the most effective means to their selfish and intellectual ends.[8] If this interpretation is correct, then the statesman and the philosopher do have more in common than their possession of the necessary external goods; statesmen will always act in accordance with the ethical virtues, and philosophers will at least sometimes do the same. But the difference (indeed, incompatibility) between the two lives would be far more striking than their similarities. Philosophers would not have the ethical virtues; instead, they would hold themselves ready to do whatever is contrary to virtue in order to increase their opportunities for contemplating. By contrast, politicians, being good people, would never do anything contrary to virtue (I.10 1100b34–5); they choose ethical activity for its own sake (II.4 1105a32).

But this way of contrasting the philosopher and the politician could be plausible only to those who have already become convinced that the treatment of happiness in Book X is inconsistent with earlier parts of the *NE*. For on this reading, X.7–8 ranks the life of someone indifferent to the virtues of character above the life of someone dedicated to expressing those virtues. And so these chapters would be committed to the view that we are better off if we do not have such virtues as justice and courage. But this doctrine must be inconsistent with the bulk of the *NE*. For Aristotle makes it quite clear in earlier parts of this work that he is not merely describing certain qualities—called ethical "virtues"—that some people have and others lack. He does not adopt the attitude of an anthropologist who studies certain ideals without committing himself to their worth. Rather, he studies the ethical virtues because he thinks they are goods we want to possess, and he expects his audience to agree. As he says in II.2: "The present inquiry is not for the sake of contemplation,[9] as others are. For we examine virtue not in order to know what it is, but in order to become good, since otherwise there would be no benefit in it . . ." (1103b26–9). But there would have been no benefit in examining the ethical virtues for those in Aristotle's audience who eventually decide to lead the immoral life he allegedly advocates in X.7–8.

Since I am taking the unity of the *NE* as my working hypothesis, I will set aside this way of contrasting the philosopher and the statesman. Instead, I will assume that the philosopher, like the statesman, is a good person, and has benefited from undertaking a study of ethical virtue. Nothing in X.7–8 should be read as undermining what precedes these

---

[8] This is how Cooper reads this passage. See *RHGA*, pp. 160–68, especially 164. In "Contemplation and Happiness: A Reconsideration," he abandons this reading.

[9] Aristotle's point is that we do not study politics merely in order to contemplate its truths. Of course, in the narrow sense of *theōria* (see note 2 above), the only truths contemplated are the ones known by virtue of theoretical wisdom, and these do not include political truths. In this passage, Aristotle is using *theōria* more broadly, to include any object of study whatsoever.

chapters if we can avoid doing so, and so when Aristotle says that philosophers choose to act ethically (1178b6), we should take this to express his assumption that they have the ethical virtues. If we ask, "Why do Aristotle's philosophers choose to act ethically?" we have no reason, at this stage of our study, to reply: "as a mere means." Rather, we should say that since they are human beings and not gods, they live with others, and a good life for those who are in these circumstances requires the possession and exercise of the ethical virtues.

Of course, we cannot rest content with this answer, however true it may be. For we want to know *why* Aristotle thinks that someone leading the philosophical life will choose to possess and exercise the ethical virtues. More important, we want to know why he thinks *anyone*—philosopher or not—should have the virtues of character. I will tackle the first of these questions in Chapter 3, and the second in Chapter 6. For now, I simply proceed on the assumption that, for whatever reason, leading the philosophical life involves activities that express the ethical virtues.

1.3. THE PHILOSOPHICAL-POLITICAL LIFE

I now want to consider the possibility that in X.7–8 Aristotle is not urging his readers to lead a philosophical life *rather than* a political life, but is instead saying that we should lead a life in accordance with both understanding and practical virtue. In other words, according to this interpretation, X.7–8 tells us to be philosophers and statesmen, just as Plato's *Republic* tells the highest class of citizens to be both philosophers and rulers. At certain times, Aristotle believes, we should take up leading positions in the polis, and deliberate with others about which laws should be adopted and which decrees issued;[10] but at other times, we should withdraw from the political arena, and study philosophy instead.

Of course, this interpretation cannot deny that much of X.7–8 is devoted to drawing a contrast between the life in accordance with understanding and the life in accordance with ethical virtue. But it warns us not to be misled by this contrast. Aristotle's intention, it holds, is to show that one aspect of the philosophical-political life is superior to the other:

[10] I take Aristotle to be assuming that a *politikos* is not merely a citizen of a certain community, but also someone who regularly takes an active part in such typically political activities as legislating, adjudicating, and deliberating on behalf of the whole community. See VI.8 1141b24–33. And of course he does not merely engage in these activities, but does them well; he has undertaken the further political studies Aristotle recommends in X.9 (see especially 1180b7–28, 1181b3–12), and rules in light of the conception of virtue put forward in the *NE*. So, leading the political life is not merely a matter of having and exercising such virtues as justice and temperance. It involves studying and exercising the science that rules over all other practical disciplines (I.2 1094b2–3) and that issues laws governing them (b4–6).

when a person contemplates, he is at his happiest; when he engages in politics, he is involved in a second-best activity. So read, X.7–8 is merely saying that higher priority should be given to the philosophical aspect of our lives than to their political aspect. The happy life is analyzed into two parts—one's life as a philosopher and one's life as a politician—and the first of these components is the one that is happiest.

How might one arrive at this interpretation? The reasoning that under-lies it could be put as follows: Suppose Aristotle were saying that we should lead the life in accordance with understanding *rather than* the life in accordance with practical virtue. In that case, he would be rejecting the ethical virtues: he would be saying that we should develop the theoretical virtues *rather than* such moral excellences as justice and courage. But that is a highly unpalatable reading, for Aristotle indicates throughout the bulk of the *NE* that we ought to possess and exercise these virtues of character. Accordingly, if we want to read the *NE* as a unity, we should take the life in accordance with understanding and the life in accordance with practical virtue as two aspects of the one life that Aristotle is urging us to lead. And since one aspect of this life is philosophical and the other political, he is in effect telling his readers to be both philosophers and politicians.[11]

But this argument rests on a mistake. It moves from:

(a) The happiest life is a life in accordance with understanding; it is not a life in accordance with practical virtue.

to:

(b) The happiest life is that of someone who has understanding but not practical virtue.

[11] I take this to be the gist of the argument that lies behind the interpretation of Stewart, Gauthier and Jolif, and Keyt. See note 6 above. Their position, as I here represent it, need not rest on any thesis about how the term *bios* ("life," "way of life") is used. That is, it does not commit them to the claim that in Greek usage a single person can be said to lead two different *bioi* at the same time. Aristotle, on their reading, argues that one should lead a life in which one is both a philosopher and a politician; this need not be expressed by saying that one is to lead two lives. For the claim that a single person cannot be said to have simul-taneously several *bioi*, see Cooper, *RHGA*, pp. 159–160. Keyt, "Intellectualism in Aris-totle," p. 373, cites texts that he takes to undermine Cooper's position, and Cooper replies in "Contemplation and Happiness: A Reconsideration," pp. 213–215 n. 14. I think that Pla-to's *Laws* 734d–e casts some doubt on Cooper's claim, but does not decisively refute it. The important point is that the interpretation defended by Keyt and the others can be defeated on independent grounds. If X.7–8 advocates a combined life, it must be a life that alternates between philosophical and political activity. And there is strong evidence that Aristotle does not take such a dual career to be the best available to human beings.

And it holds that since (b) should be rejected, so should (a). But the move from (a) to (b) rests on a dubious way of construing "the life in accordance with understanding." It assumes that if a life is in accordance with X rather than Y, then it is a life that has X but no Y. But there is no reason to take "life in accordance with X" in this way: a life that is in accordance with X can have lots of goods besides X. We have seen that, according to Aristotle, the philosopher must be equipped with necessary goods, and will choose to act ethically. But this does not mean that his life is one that is *in accordance with* food, shelter, health, ethical virtue, and so on. The philosophical life is one that gives a certain kind of primacy to theoretical reason and to contemplation, and that is why Aristotle calls it a life in accordance with understanding. (We shall soon discuss what kind of primacy that is.) It is not a life in accordance with practical virtue, because those virtues do not have primacy in it. But we should not infer that these practical excellences play no role whatsoever in the philosophical life. (That role will be discussed in Chapter 3.) And so we should not assume that Aristotle's consistency can be preserved only if we take him to be urging his readers to lead a life that is both in accordance with understanding and in accordance with ethical virtue. A life can contain ethical activity without giving primacy to that activity—that is, without being a life in accordance with ethical virtue.

According to the interpretation I shall defend, this talk of primacy can be made more precise. A good has primacy in a life, and that life is in accordance with that good, when it is the ultimate end of that life; and the ultimate end of a life is one that has three features: (a) all other ends in that life are desired for its sake; (b) it is desired for itself; and (c) it is not desired for the sake of any other good in that life. On my reading, contemplation is the ultimate end of the philosophical life, and activity in accordance with ethical virtue is the ultimate end of the political life. The philosopher will engage in ethical activity, but will do so for the sake of contemplation;[12] therefore, his life is "in accordance with understanding" and not in accordance with practical virtue. By contrast, the political life is one that omits contemplation: the politician always acts for the sake of moral activity, and since contemplation is not desirable for the sake of any further good, it plays no role in the second-best life.

But before I try to defend this interpretation, I would like to say more about the alternative under consideration in this section. I have rejected one argument that might be used to reach the conclusion that the two

[12] Valuing ethical activity because it promotes contemplation is of course compatible with valuing ethical activity for its own sake. The philosopher who fully understands what happiness is will not only see that ethical activity is desirable in itself, but also realize that such activity constitutes a secondary form of happiness. For further discussion, see 3.8.

lives discussed in X.7–8 are to be combined. But can we give reasons for rejecting that conclusion? Can we say why Aristotle should not be taken to be claiming that the ideal life for a human being is one that is a mixed philosophical-political life, that is, one in which we alternate between theoretical activities and such typically political activities as making laws, adjudicating conflicts, debating policy, and so on?

To begin with, there is a powerful argument from silence: It was commonly assumed by Aristotle's contemporaries that politics and philosophy are two alternatives between which one must choose. Those with sufficient leisure had to decide whether to become philosophers or political leaders.[13] And although someone advising a young man faced with this choice could advocate a dual career—as Plato does in the *Republic*—there is absolutely no evidence in *NE* X.7–8 or in any of his other writings that Aristotle did so. In these chapters, he argues that the philosophical life is superior to the political life, and says nothing at all to suggest that one should not choose one rather than the other, but should instead combine them. In the absence of any such suggestion, his audience would have naturally taken him to mean that ideally one should be a philosopher rather than a political leader. Imagine present-day students asking their teacher whether they should enter the academic world or pursue a political career. Suppose the teacher replies by enumerating all the advantages of an intellectual life. Would the students infer that they were being told to pursue both of their options?

This argument from silence is reinforced by positive evidence drawn from X.7–8. One of the points Aristotle makes, when he tries to show the superiority of contemplation to the politician's activities, is that the philosopher needs fewer external supplies than does the politician (1177a27–b1, 1178a25–b6). The greater the undertakings of the statesman, the more he will need in the way of external goods (1178b1–3); by contrast, these sorts of goods are not needed for contemplative activity, and might even be called hindrances (b3–5). These remarks of Aristotle's will receive fuller attention in Chapter 3, but for now we can say that they

---

[13] See *Pol.* I.7 1255b35–7: those who have sufficient resources appoint someone to oversee their slaves, and devote their time to either philosophy or politics. In *Pol.* VII.2, Aristotle considers which of these two alternatives is more choiceworthy, and says nothing to suggest that they should be combined. The decision about which life to lead is momentous (1324a25–35), but instead of declaring himself in favor of one or the other, Aristotle finds fault with arguments that have been given on both sides (1324a35–1325a5). *NE* I.4–5 also assumes that the political and philosophical lives are competing alternatives: people lead different lives because they have different conceptions of happiness (1095a20–22, b14–16); and those who lead political or philosophical lives are parties to this dispute. These passages clearly indicate that political and philosophical careers were generally regarded as alternatives between which one must choose.

suggest that a choice must be made between the philosophical and the political lives. For if one level of external goods best suits a philosopher, and a higher level best suits the statesman, then one had better decide which kind of career one will pursue, and make appropriate adjustments in the other goods by means of which one supports such a life. It would be silly to take Aristotle to be suggesting that we should strike a mean between the level of goods best for philosophy and that best for political action. There is no textual support for such a reading, and one can easily see why such a middling approach would be doubly defective: the level of supplies would be too low for one sort of life and too high for the other.

We will see, later in this chapter, that Aristotle puts forward a definite view about how much theoretical activity it is good for a human being to engage in. His formula, as I understand it, is that the more one contemplates, the better one's life; there is no such thing as a human being who has studied philosophy too much for his own good. Now, if I am right about this, it will provide decisive evidence against the view that the best life for a human being must be one that combines the activities of a philosopher and a political leader. For obviously the political activities involved in holding office and participating in legislative or judicial decisions take a great deal of time, and so they leave one with less time for developing one's understanding of the theoretical disciplines and contemplating their truths. If, as I shall argue, Aristotle holds that human beings become happier the more they contemplate, then he cannot also believe that the best life we can lead is one in which we willingly give up time we could spend on theoretical pursuits in order to engage in political activity. In normal circumstances, philosophers who are not burdened with the responsibilities of Plato's philosopher-king will have more time for theoretical studies, and, since more contemplation is always better than less, they will have better lives.

I conclude that the most plausible way to read X.7–8 is to take Aristotle to be considering two models of how to lead one's life. The two lives— one in accordance with understanding, the other in accordance with practical virtue—are the main options between which Aristotle's leisured male audience had to choose. And the obvious way to read him is to take him to be saying that the first option is better than the second. For though both will be happy lives (if each is equipped with resources at its own appropriate level), the life of the philosopher is happier than that of the politician. That is what Aristotle means when he says (1178a6–8) that the life in accordance with understanding is happiest, and then adds, "secondarily, the [life] in accordance with the other virtue" (a9–10).

1.4. THE PRIMACY OF CONTEMPLATION

Having agreed that the philosophical and political lives are not to be combined, but are instead alternatives between which we must choose, let us return to the question of how those lives differ. One possible reading would be this: according to Aristotle, the only important difference between these two lives is that the first contains some theoretical activity whereas the second has none. The best life is that of a person who, upon occasion, exercises the virtue of theoretical wisdom; but where this activity is ranked, in one's scale of values, is immaterial, so long as one engages in it to some extent.

To see more fully what this reading involves, consider two different philosophers: the first contemplates for six hours every day, and prefers this activity to all others; the second contemplates for only one hour every other day, because there are many other activities that he enjoys more and takes to be better goods than contemplation. According to this interpretation, Aristotle thinks that both are leading a life in accordance with understanding, and both have the happiest kind of life there is for a human being. Neither philosophical life is better than the other, and the choice between them is a matter of indifference. Both kinds of life are better than the second-best life, which is that of a statesman who has no theoretical wisdom and who never contemplates.

I know of no one who has proposed such a reading of X.7–8, but that does not mean that it is wrong. If it is a bad reading, we should be able to say why. And in fact it is quite easy to do so: Aristotle believes that contemplation is the best kind of activity and the highest single good. Therefore, he could not believe that there is nothing to choose between a life that ranks this activity first and a life that gives it a lower priority. He must think that the person who ranks other goods above contemplation is making a mistake about how best to lead his life; such a person does not have a perfect understanding of what his goal in life should be, and such a life cannot be the happiest there is for human beings.

The evidence that, according to X.7–8, contemplation is the best single good is abundant: It is the activity of the best virtue (1177a12–13), and so it is the best activity (a19–20). And Aristotle tries to substantiate this ranking: the objects studied by the philosopher are the best that can be grasped (a20–21); contemplation is the activity we can engage in most continuously (a21); it gives us our greatest pleasures (a23–5); it is more self-sufficient than ethical activity (a27–8); a human being is most of all to be identified with theoretical reason (1178a7); and this part of the human soul is the one that is most akin to the gods (1179a26–7).

Clearly, Aristotle would not bother making these claims if he thought that where one ranks contemplation among goods is a matter of no practical importance. In some way or other, our lives should give expression to the fact that contemplation is superior to every other good. But precisely how is this to be done? If one agrees with Aristotle that theoretical activity is the highest good available to us, then what follows about the way one decides to act? What plans or methods of decision making are ruled out or required by such a ranking? Surely, in order to lead the best life, it is not sufficient that one merely *believes* that contemplation is our best activity: such a belief must in some way affect the way one makes choices. And it is not sufficient if one merely engages in this activity at some point or other in one's life: that is not giving it enough prominence. What then must one do, in order to give expression to one's belief that contemplation is the best single activity?

One way of answering this question would be as follows: Before you act, always check to see how much contemplation each of the alternatives will bring you over the long run, and choose the act that brings you no less of this good than any of the others. For example, if your father is ill, and helping him would bring you less contemplation over the long run than not helping him, then you must refuse to help—regardless of the consequences for him or for anyone else. Suppose helping him would bring you one day less of contemplation than you might otherwise have; then, even if he should die as a result of your neglect, you must not go to his aid.

Such a reading assumes that Aristotle is an egoist, at least in X.7–8. That is, it takes him to be saying that one should always choose the action that is best for oneself, regardless of the consequences for others. But, as I will argue in Chapter 2, there is no evidence that Aristotle adopts such a view in X.7–8 or anywhere else. For now, we should notice that if we take Aristotle to be saying that the extent of one's own theoretical activity should be maximized, then we must admit that X.7–8 is inconsistent with what precedes it. For these late chapters would be advising us to perform acts that ethically virtuous people, as Aristotle conceives them, would never do. He thinks that we should recognize the great debt we owe our parents, and that we should support them when they are old;[14] and surely giving up a few hours or days of our time in order to save their lives would be the least we could do for them. But such minimal support would be prohibited by X.7–8 if these chapters are urging us to do everything we can to maximize our own opportunities for contemplation. Since we are looking for a way of reading the *NE* that will preserve its consistency, we should set aside this egoistic way of expressing the prior-

[14] See VIII.11 1161a15–17, VIII.12 1162a4–7, IX.1 1164b3–6, IX.2 1164b33–1165a2, IX.2 1165a21–4.

ity of contemplation. It should be seriously entertained as a reading of X.7–8 only if the project of discovering a unified *NE* proves hopeless.[15]

Another way of giving expression to the priority of contemplation would be this: those leading the best life should assign a number to each good in that life, and the highest number should be assigned to contemplation. This assignment is not to be made in an arbitrary way; rather, it should reflect the objective importance of various goods. Giving the highest number to contemplation reflects the fact that it is the best single good. The second-best good (activity in accordance with ethical virtue) should receive a lower number—but not just any lower number will do: it must reflect the real difference in value between ethical and theoretical activity. And then each of the other goods must receive some number, so that the whole assignment reflects the real differences in value between them. After these weights are correctly assigned, one should schedule one's activities in a way that reflects their relative worth. For example, if contemplation receives a number twice as large as the number assigned to physical pleasures, then one must arrange one's time so that over the long run one devotes twice as much time to the first good as to the second.

The problem with this suggestion is that there is no hint in any work of Aristotle's about how such a project is to be carried out. He nowhere says that contemplation is related to some other good as one number is to a second; nor does he assign numbers to any other pairs of goods in an effort to represent how much more desirable one is than the other. He often claims that the study of the human good lacks the precision available in theoretical subjects,[16] and he could not say this if he thought that

---

[15] It might be claimed that there is a passage in X.7 that requires us to maximize theoretical activity, come what may for others: "We should not—as we are advised—think human thoughts, since we are human, and mortal thoughts, since we are mortal, but should engage in immortal activity (*athanatizein*) so far as possible, and should do all things with a view to living in accordance with what is best in us" (1177b31–4). This could be taken to mean that, regardless of the consequences for others, we should contemplate as much as we can: *athanatizein* is what the gods do, and we are to engage in this divine activity as much as we can. But once we recognize the nonegoistic character of Aristotle's thought, and see how X.7–8 can be harmonized with the rest of the *NE*, it will not be plausible to read these lines as an expression of intellectual egoism. Given the context, Aristotle's claim in this passage is that, to be as happy as possible, one should engage in as much theoretical activity as possible. But he recognizes that one's maximal happiness can conflict with that of others, and does not insist that in all such cases one must give priority to oneself. It is implausible to think that X.7–8 suggests that in deciding what kind of life to lead one should disregard the consequences such a decision will have for others. These chapters are concerned "merely" with the problem of what the best kind of human life is. They leave aside the difficult question of how one should act when leading such a life is not what is best for others. Nothing in the context suggests that Aristotle is here concerned with that interpersonal issue.

[16] See I.3 1094b12–28, I.7 1098a26–b8, II.2 1103b34–1104a10, IV.5 1126b2–9, IX.2 1164b27–30.

assigning numbers to goods were a feasible project. In fact, a passage in *Politics* III.12 explicitly says that goods cannot be related in this way.[17] Although some goods are more desirable than others, we cannot say how much better they are. And therefore we cannot assign a number to contemplation in a way that would accurately represent its degree of superiority to all other goods.

1.5. UPPER AND LOWER BOUNDS

Someone who tries to have three hours of physical enjoyment for every hour of contemplation, because he prefers the former to the latter, is not being guided by Aristotle's conception of the ideal life. So, we can say that we have a rough idea of what the lower bound on contemplation is, in the happiest life. If one ranks physical pleasure or any other good above contemplation, then one is not trying to lead the best life, as Aristotle conceives it. This does not give us a lower bound on how many hours per day we should ideally spend on contemplation. But it does allow us to say, in a great many cases, that someone is spending too little time on philosophical activity: someone who spends no time on it, or ranks other activities ahead of it, is not leading the best life.

What we would like to know is whether we can plausibly attribute to Aristotle any view about whether contemplation has an upper bound. And if it does have one, where does it lie? We have seen that, on his view, one can contemplate too *little* for one's own good. And we have a workable standard that will decide in a great many cases when a life fails to be best because it falls below this standard. Our question now is whether one can contemplate too *much* for one's own good. More precisely, we want to know whether a human life can fail to be happiest because the person leading it assigns too much weight to contemplation and overestimates its intrinsic worth. And if it is possible for human beings to think too highly of contemplation, does Aristotle give us a workable standard for determining when a person is open to this criticism?

---

[17] Aristotle argues there that merit should be the basis of distribution both in politics and in the crafts; the most outstanding flute-player, for example, should have the best flute, even if he is ill-born or ugly. An alternative to this principle is then considered: an inferior musician should get the best flute if his superiority in looks (for example) outweighs his inferiority in ability. Aristotle replies that such extrinsic factors as birth and appearance should play no role in these decisions, and then adds that, in any case, we cannot take account of them unless "every good is commensurable (*sumblēton*) with every other" (1283a3–4). In other words, those who want to take other goods besides musical ability into account must tell us how valuable these additional goods are in comparison with such skill. If A is a better musician than B, but B is better-looking, and we are to weigh these two considerations against each other, then we must say how much better one good is than the other. But this cannot be done.

It is important not to confuse these questions with others. One might ask, for example, whether, according to Aristotle, one should sometimes give up a certain amount of contemplation in order to foster the well-being of someone else. Since I take Aristotle's moral thought to be non-egoistic, I think the answer is yes: to recall the examples used in the Introduction, a son may sometimes have to help his ailing father, when this means a net loss of time for contemplation; and sometimes one's debt to one's parents and community may require one to renounce a philosophical life. Now, if a person should in certain circumstances give up some philosophical activity for the sake of others, then there are cases in which one can contemplate too much. But these are not cases in which one contemplates too much *for one's own good*. Nor are they examples of someone overestimating the worth of contemplation. The person who philosophizes when he should be helping others might not be making a mistake about the value of contemplation; rather, his mistake may consist in his insufficient concern for the good of others.

Our question is not "Can there be cases in which someone decides to contemplate now, and as a result has less time, over the long run, to contemplate?" The answer to this question, presumably, is yes. Suppose some malicious person has accused me of a crime I did not commit, and the penalty for those convicted is death; if I spend the next month devoting my full attention to preparing a defense, I am assured of acquittal. Obviously, in this situation, if I were to spend all available time, during the next month, engaged in theoretical activity, I would be contemplating too much, during that period of time, for my own good. But this is not a case in which a person overestimates the intrinsic value of contemplation, in comparison with the intrinsic worth of other goods. Rather, it is a case in which someone decides to have more contemplation now even though this will mean less contemplation in the future. If I decide to ignore my future, I could be criticized for engaging in too much contemplation, during a limited period of time. But our question is not whether it is possible to contemplate too much during one period of time, because of the consequences for a later period. It is whether Aristotle would in certain cases look at the whole of a person's life and say: "This was not the best kind of life, because it had too much contemplation. In having so much contemplation, this person had too few other goods, and did not achieve the right kind of balance. He overestimated the degree to which contemplation is a better good than any others."

On my interpretation, Aristotle does not think this is a legitimate way of criticizing someone's life. There is, in this sense, no upper bound on the amount of contemplation that is desirable. Of course, this allows him to say that, during certain periods of time, one may be contemplating too much for one's own good. For example, Aristotle himself observes that contemplation is sometimes harmful to one's health (VII.12 1153a20). This is an empirical claim, and he is presumably thinking of such phenomena as overwork, neglect of good nutrition, failure to exercise, and so on. These facts about health, and other ineliminable features of the human situation, put an upper bound on how much one should contemplate over various stretches of time. They are constraints that the person who aims at the best life should not ignore, as Aristotle emphasizes in X.8 when he says that, being human, we need the external goods in order to contemplate (1178b33–5). But on my interpretation, health does not set an upper bound on the extent to which contemplation is desirable. In designing one's life so that it will be as valuable as possible, one should strive to have as much contemplation as possible. Such a plan will occasionally involve having less contemplation in the short run; for overwork will ruin one's health, and as a result one will in the long run have less time for philosophical activity. And the same holds true for all other goods, including ethical virtue: none of them sets an upper bound on the extent to which contemplation is desirable.

I have been suggesting that, according to Aristotle, there is no such thing as too much philosophical activity, over the course of a lifetime, for one's own good. But suppose I am wrong about this. Suppose Aristotle thinks that contemplation can be overrated, and that a human life can lack balance because it contains an excess of philosophy. In that case, we can reasonably ask how we are to determine when we have stepped over this boundary. On this reading, X.7–8 would be telling us not to contemplate too much, because at a certain point an increase in contemplation diminishes one's own happiness; but these chapters would not say anything about where that point lies. For all that Aristotle's fellow philosophers are told, they might be spending too much time engaged in theoretical activity. Then again, perhaps some have not yet reached that point, and should be devoting more of their time to this activity. Or perhaps, without realizing it, some are giving just the right amount of emphasis to contemplation. Aristotle would have given no way of determining in which direction he and his audience should ideally move. I find it hard to believe that he would give his readers no guidance on this issue, and we will soon (1.8ff.) see textual evidence that he *does* provide the help we can legitimately request: in X.8, he claims that ideally we should engage in as much philosophical activity as possible.[18]

---

[18] Three points of clarification are needed here: (a) I am not claiming that Aristotle must assign numerical weights to various goods if he wants to help his readers recognize when a life contains too much philosophical activity for one's own good. In 1.6, I discuss other ways in which he might have provided a guideline for making this judgment. (b) I am not ruling out the possibility that, according to Aristotle, no verbal formula can help us decide how much philosophy is too much. He might think that we simply need to develop the

It might be objected, however, that if I take Aristotle to be saying that philosophy's value is unlimited, then I should go one step further and take him to be urging his readers to maximize the amount of theoretical activity they engage in. For why would he propose that more contemplation is always better than less, if he did not want his readers to act on this thesis? And how else is one to act on it, if one does not maximize one's own philosophical activity? But to this last question there is an easy answer: The egoist is not the only one who needs to know what is in the best interests of a human being. If more contemplation is always better than less, then that fact should guide us in our deliberations, whether we are acting in our own interests or in the interests of others. For when we are in a position to benefit others, we will know that the best way to help them is to increase their opportunities for philosophical activities. And when it is appropriate for us to think of ourselves, we will know that we should turn to intellectual activity. The formula "more contemplation is better than less" will not help us resolve conflicts between one person's good and another's, but it will tell us where each person's good lies, and so it will play a vital role in decision making, whether one is an egoist or not.

So we cannot tell, just by looking at someone's actions, whether he accepts the conception of happiness that Aristotle puts forward in X.7–8. What we must know is how he makes decisions—how he justifies his actions. If he leads a political life because he thinks this is the best available to human beings, then of course Aristotle would find fault with his conception of the good. But one might accept Aristotle's conception and lead a political life nonetheless. Similarly, one might spend five hours a day on theoretical matters, and then devote three to ethical activities, because one thinks that this is the best mixture for human beings; that is, one might think that a six-to-two ratio would be a balance too heavily weighted, for one's own good, in favor of philosophy. Again, Aristotle, as I understand him, would criticize this conception of happiness. Though his defense of

---

ability to "see" that some lives are defective because they are overly theoretical. I take up this possibility in 1.7. (c) I am not arguing that since it would be nice to know how much theorizing is too much, Aristotle must have something helpful to say about this. Rather, my claim that he does have something helpful to say is backed by textual evidence, to be provided in 1.8ff. At this point, I am simply calling attention to the gap that would exist in his conception of happiness if he believed that we can undermine our well-being through excessive philosophizing but said nothing about where this point or zone of excess lies. My argument that Aristotle tells us how much philosophy would be best will be strengthened if I can show that he provides similar guidance regarding all the other goods. (It would be odd if philosophy were the only good for which he provided no quantitative directions.) This strengthening of my argument begins in Chapter 3, where I suggest that Aristotle tells us how much to pursue such goods as friends and amusements. I return to this theme in Chapter 6 when I discuss the doctrine of the mean.

the philosophical life does not determine how much time to devote to philosophy, it puts a definite constraint on how we should ideally make decisions about scheduling our activities.

1.6. MINIMAL PRIORITY

I believe that there is strong textual warrant in X.7–8 for the interpretation I have just put forward. But before we turn to that evidence, I want to consider what the alternatives to my interpretation are. How else can we construe the primacy of contemplation, without making these chapters inconsistent with the rest of the *NE*? The assignment of weights has no textual warrant, as we saw earlier in 1.4. But is there some way of putting an upper bound on the value of contemplation without assigning weights?

The following possibility should be explored: The most desirable life for a human being is one in which we give more time to contemplation than to any other single activity, but it is also one that has no additional contemplation beyond that point. In other words, the best plan of life is to minimize the priority of contemplation: it should have as little priority as is compatible with its being the best good. We should contemplate only as much as is needed in order to reflect the fact that it is the most desirable good; and then, after that, we should attend to other goods.

There are two ways in which such an idea might be worked out. First, one might take Aristotle to believe that one should have as many diverse types of good as is compatible with giving priority to contemplation. He does say, "of goods the greater is always more choiceworthy" (I.7 1097b19–20), and that could be taken to mean that, other things being equal, it is better to have $n + 1$ types of good than n. In that case, he might think that someone who engages in contemplation a great deal has too little diversity in his life: he just goes on and on enjoying a single kind of pleasure, and this way of using his time has its price, since he could be using that time to experience pleasures he has never known. And so, according to this way of thinking, the best plan would be this: give contemplation its due, by spending more time on this good than on any other, but subject to that constraint, seek as much diversity as possible. If we find someone who has failed to experience certain pleasures, and could have done so without unduly slighting philosophical activity, then we can criticize him for having the wrong priorities.

This way of reading the *NE* seems unpromising. I know of nothing in X.7–8 that can be construed as an endorsement of the widest diversity compatible with contemplation's primacy. And as I shall argue in Chapter 5, the best reading of Aristotle's statement "of goods the greater is always more choiceworthy" will not treat this as a recommendation of increasing diversity. If I am right about this, then there simply is no evidence for the interpretation in question.

But there is a second way of working out the idea that the priority of contemplation should be kept to a minimum. One can say that only certain types of ends (such as contemplation, ethical virtue, physical pleasure, friends, and honor) are to be pursued: their number is limited, and one should seek no other types beyond these. But, on this interpretation, one should have the right balance between these goods, and in particular one should spend no more time on contemplation than is called for by the fact that it is the best single good. In other words, the difference between the amount of time (t) one spends on contemplation and the amount of time (less than t) one spends on the next-best activity should be as small as one can possibly make it. Those who do not strive for this goal can be criticized for overestimating the intrinsic worth of contemplation.

Again, I find no reason to attribute such a view to Aristotle. This way of achieving balance between contemplation and other goods would be justified only if the value of the second-best good approached the value of contemplation asymptotically. That is, they would have to be so close in value that any numerical attempt to represent the superiority of one to the other would overestimate it. There is no textual basis for such an interpretation.

If Aristotle is not urging his readers to give contemplation minimal priority over other goods, then he must believe that it has more weight than that. But how much more weight? The fact that no numbers can be assigned seems to prevent us from giving any other answer than the one I favor: one cannot overvalue contemplation (although one can at times pursue it more than one ought, either for one's own sake or for the sake of another). One cannot make its worth equal to that of any other: it must be higher. But it cannot be just barely higher. Nor can we use numbers to express its superiority. And so we are naturally led to the view that the more contemplation one has, the better one's life. I am not suggesting that Aristotle himself was forced to this position willy-nilly. On the contrary, I take it to be a thesis he finds naturally appealing. The *NE* gives us no way of telling how to find the limit of contemplation's worth, and a natural explanation for this omission suggests itself: Aristotle sees no reason why there should be such a limit.

1.7. INTUITIONISM

At this point, someone might protest that the question I am asking—how much contemplation would be too much?—is misconceived. For Aristotle warns us many times not to expect precision in ethics.[19] This point applies to contemplation no less than to any other good, and so it is not surprising that X.7–8 gives us no formula for deciding how many hours of philosophy is the right number. In deciding when to contemplate and when not to, we need a certain kind of perception or insight or judgment, and that ability is an important part of practical wisdom.[20] It cannot be expressed by means of a substantive rule; we can only say: "contemplate as much as a person of practical wisdom would."[21]

The surface plausibility of this objection depends on the fact that it runs together two issues that I have been trying to keep separate.

First, there is the question "How much of one's time should be devoted to contemplation?" To this there can be no single answer, for people find themselves in different circumstances, and the amount of contemplation one should strive for depends on those circumstances. To recall our familiar examples: The son who is being trained to inherit his father's kingdom should not spend any time on theoretical activities; his end should be the secondary happiness of a political life, and he should devote all of his time to the well-being of his community. Similarly, the son whose father is ill should, in certain circumstances, accept a loss of time for contemplation, in order to pay back what he owes his father.

Second, there is the question "How much contemplation is it good for a human being to have?" Here, I think that Aristotle would *not* reply that the correct answer depends on the circumstances. Rather, he would say that the more time one has for contemplation, the better off one is. It would have been better for each of the two sons if they had had more opportunities for philosophical activity: they make the right decisions when they give up this activity to a large or a small extent, but that is because they should, in their circumstances, act for the sake of others.

But the objector may persist as follows: "I recognize that these are different questions, but Aristotle gives the same response to both. If practical wisdom reaches the conclusion that the son should help his ailing father, and should give up some contemplation, then the son is better off with this mix of goods than he would be with any other mix. This amount of contemplation is the right amount and the best amount for

[19] For references, see note 16 above.

[20] Practical wisdom is concerned not only with universals but with particulars as well (VI.7 1141b14–21; cf. VI.11 1143b4–5), and since it requires a certain kind of perception (VI.8 1142a25–9), it is called an "eye of the soul" (VI.12 1144a29–30). In general, difficult issues in the practical realm must be decided by a kind of perception (II.9 1109b22–3).

[21] The person of practical wisdom determines where the mean lies (II.6 1107a1–2); the ethically virtuous person is the standard of what is really good and pleasant (III.4 1113a25–33, IX.4 1166a12–13, X.5 1176a15–19); and one cannot acquire the ethical virtues in the strict sense unless one has practical wisdom (VI.13 1144b16–17).

him. And if the other son leads a political life devoid of contemplation, because this is what practical wisdom requires, then this is the right amount and the best amount for him. But there is no such thing as the best amount of contemplation *simpliciter*. For there is no one right or best mixture of goods for all human beings. One simply judges each situation according to its merits, and the best life for you is the life in which each of these decisions is wisely made."

Put in this form, I believe the objection loses whatever plausibility it may first have had. For in effect the objector is now denying that the contemplative life is always better than the political life; those who are free to lead a life filled with philosophical activity may be no better off than those who have none, for each may be doing what is appropriate to his circumstances. This interpretation is undermined by the fact that X.7–8 compares two lives—the philosophical and the political—and that Aristotle unequivocally says (1179a31–2) that the first of them is happiest. This is incompatible with the proposition that the political life is just as happy. If the philosophical life is ideal and the political life second-best, then the son who returns to his kingdom is accepting a less happy life. And similarly, the son who gives up some contemplation to help his father does not have as good a life as he might have.[22]

There is a more general point to be made: we should not attribute to Aristotle the view that so long as one has and exercises practical wisdom,

---

[22] I do not think my interpretation is undermined by any of the passages cited in notes 20 and 21 above. For if my reading is correct, Aristotle can still say that we need "an eye of the soul" in order to discern how to act in particular cases. The philosopher will need the ethical virtues (for reasons to be discussed in Chapter 3), and his conception of happiness does not in itself tell him which act is fitting on particular occasions; and he will also have to make decisions about when to pursue his own optimal good and when to promote that of others. It would be silly to think that Aristotle's answer to the question "What is happiness?" is "Whatever the person of practical wisdom says it is." Aristotle is trying to give such a person a general guideline for making decisions; for practical wisdom requires knowledge not only of particulars, but of universals as well. The person of practical wisdom deliberates well about "living well in general" (VI.5 1140a25–8) and understands what the end of human life is (VI.9 1142b32–3), but his conception of the good must be the one put forward in the *NE*, since that is the correct conception. Once we figure out what kind of life is being advocated in X.7–8, we know what the person of practical wisdom would say, at a highly general level, about how to make decisions. Similarly, I do not think that my interpretation is put in doubt by the fact that, according to Aristotle, we should not pursue one and the same mean in all cases, but rather the mean relative to us (II.6 1106a26–b7). Aristotle's point is that, for example, there is no one right amount of anger to feel on all occasions: we must feel neither too much nor too little, but the amount that is appropriate at this time, towards this person, for this reason, and so on (1106b18–24). This claim about anger (and similar claims about other emotions and the actions to which they lead) is not incompatible with the view that the more we exercise theoretical wisdom the better our lives. The doctrine of the mean should not be equated with the view that too much of anything (including virtue) is bad for us; Aristotle himself warns against this (1107a22–3).

always making the right decision in a way that reflects one's circumstances, one will be ideally happy. For disastrous circumstances beyond
one's control may constrain one's choices. Suppose one is sold as a slave
to a tyrant, and hard physical labor becomes one's daily lot. One will use
practical wisdom to do the best one can, given these severe limitations,
but happiness during this period of time is not a possibility (I.10 1100b28–
1101a8). It is therefore a mistake to think that, since the son who returns
to his community is (by hypothesis) making the right decision for the
right reasons, he must be leading an ideally happy life. Good practical
reasoning does not ensure that one will have a happy life, let alone an
ideally happy life.

1.8. THE ARGUMENT FROM DIVINITY: A FIRST LOOK

I would now like to discuss an argument Aristotle gives in X.8 on behalf
of the philosophical life, for I believe that it reveals his commitment to
the thesis that more contemplation is always better than less. It is an argument that appeals to the kind of life the gods have: of all living beings,
they are the ones who are happiest (1178b8–9). What does their happiness
consist in? Aristotle argues that, properly conceived, they do not engage
in ethical activity, and so the only kind of life that remains for them is
contemplative (b10–21). Then he draws the following conclusion:

> As a result, the activity of the god, outstanding in blessedness, would be con-
> templative. And among human activities the one that is most akin to this has
> the character of happiness (*eudaimonikōtatē*) most of all. A sign of this is that the
> other animals do not share in happiness, since they are completely deprived of
> such activity. For, among gods, the whole of life is blessed, and among human
> beings [life is blessed] to the extent that they have something resembling such
> activity. But none of the other animals is happy, since in no way do they share
> in contemplation. As far as contemplation extends, thus far happiness extends,
> and those who have more contemplation also have more happiness, not inci-
> dentally, but by virtue of the contemplation. For it is in itself worthy of honor.
> As a result, happiness would be a certain contemplation. (1178b21–32)

The first part of this text ranks the well-being of gods, humans, and
lower animals; and the last few lines suggest that the criterion by which
this interspecies ordering is made can also be used within a single species.
For Aristotle says that those who have more contemplation have more
happiness; and this is a perfectly general formula that can be used to compare the well-being of any two humans, and not merely the well-being of
a god, a human being, and a lower animal. And so, if one human being
devotes more time to this activity than does another, then the first has
more happiness than the second. If happiness is a certain contemplation

(1178b32), and if different living beings have varying amounts of happiness, or none at all, because of their differing proximity to the divine, then those human beings who most closely resemble gods will have the most happiness.

Is there any other plausible reading? It might be protested that in the passage just cited Aristotle does not explicitly use his formula (the more contemplation, the more happiness) to make comparisons among human beings. Does this indicate that he thinks the formula lacks validity for such intraspecies judgments? It is hard to see how he could justify restricting its use in this *ad hoc* way. If we are better off than lower animals precisely because and to the extent that we bear a greater resemblance to the gods, then it should follow that when one human being resembles the gods more than another, he should for that reason be happier. And we know that, according to Aristotle, philosophers lead happier lives than do statesmen because, being more akin to the divine, they are more dear to the gods, if the latter have any concern for human life (X.8 1179a22–32). Whether statesmen engage in no theoretical activity at all, or engage in this activity less than do philosophers, they in any case fail to be as happy as philosophers precisely because of their lower level of theoretical activity. So Aristotle clearly does make comparisons between human lives on the basis of their differing degrees of philosophical activity. Furthermore, we have already (1.4) rejected the idea that X.7–8 merely calls upon us to engage in contemplation to some extent, and that it is a matter of indifference whether one devotes more or less time to this activity. If that were all Aristotle meant, then he would not have wasted his time arguing for the superiority of contemplation to all other activities. He must be saying that how much we engage in this activity matters, and he nowhere suggests that there is an upper limit on its value.

Suppose we agree, then, that Aristotle does intend his formula (the more contemplation, the more happiness) to apply to comparisons among human beings. Still, it might be said, this does not mean that no other factors are relevant. According to this proposal, Aristotle means that so long as there are no other differences between A and B, aside from the fact that A contemplates more than B, then A is happier than B. But, if there are such differences, then they might compensate for the philosophical disparity between their lives.

This suggestion has a number of liabilities. First, it lacks textual support. Aristotle says, quite simply: "those who have more contemplation also have more happiness" (1178b29–30); there is no qualification to the effect that this formula applies only when all other things are equal.

Second, as we have seen (1.4), Aristotle denies that one can say how much the worth of one good exceeds that of another. Therefore there is no way to measure the worth of contemplation in comparison with other goods, and without such a measure, there is no basis for saying that the loss of a certain amount of philosophy would be compensated by an increase in other goods.

Third, if Aristotle were merely making the weak point that more contemplation is better than less, other things being equal, then he could not, by means of that principle alone, arrive at any conclusions about which kinds of living beings are best off. Gods contemplate more than human beings do, and if this were their only difference, then Aristotle could infer, by means of his all-things-being-equal principle, that divine life is happier than any human life. But human beings have many goods that the gods lack: might not these many differences compensate for the fact that we contemplate less than the gods do?[23] Aristotle would have to admit the possibility that, for the duration of adult human life, we are better off than the gods. He would have to say that, since we cannot assign numbers to goods in a way that reflects their relative value, we must be skeptics about whether philosophers surpass gods in well-being. But obviously Aristotle is no such skeptic: he ranks divine life above human life with utter confidence. And we can easily understand the basis of this confidence if we take him at his word: "those who have more contemplation also have more happiness." Human beings must, for all sorts of reasons, interrupt their contemplative activity, and this diminishes the amount of happiness they can have over the course of a lifetime. By contrast, "among gods, the whole of life is blessed" (1178b25–6). The extent to which they engage in contemplation exceeds the extent to which we can, and this fact by itself is sufficient to show that they are happier than we can be.

1.9. PERFECT HAPPINESS

We must now consider the possibility that the argument of the preceding section has gone awry, because of a feature of the text that we have not yet taken into account. When Aristotle introduces his "argument from divinity"—the argument that we should contemplate because the gods do—he says: "It would appear from what follows that perfect (*teleia*) happiness is a certain contemplative activity" (1178b7–8). What does he mean by the phrase "perfect happiness"? Are we supposed to read the rest of the passage in such a way that whenever "happiness" occurs, we should

[23] Aristotle thinks that the unmoved mover's contemplation is superior in quality to our own (*Met.* XII.7 1072b24–6), but this doctrine does not affect the point I am making. Divine contemplation is of greater duration and higher quality than human contemplation, but why cannot human superiority in all other respects (we have friends, enjoy physical pleasures, exercise practical virtues) outweigh the few points in favor of divine life? Aristotle needs a conception of happiness that answers this question.

take this as an abbreviation for "perfect happiness"? And if we do interpret the passage in that way, how will it change our understanding of
Aristotle's argument? In particular, will we no longer be able to use this
passage as evidence that the value of contemplation lacks an upper bound?

To begin with, we should notice that 1178b7–8 is not the only sentence
in X.7–8 that contains the expression "perfect happiness." It first occurs
near the beginning of X.7, when Aristotle claims that happiness is activity in accordance with the best virtue, that is, the virtue of the best part
of the rational soul (*nous*). Of this part he says, "Whether it itself is divine
or the most divine thing in us, its activity in accordance with its own
virtue would be perfect happiness" (1177a15–17). We come across the
phrase a second time after Aristotle has given a number of arguments for
the superiority of contemplation. He affirms, as his conclusion: "this
[contemplative activity] would be the perfect happiness of a human
being" (1177b24–5). The third and final occurrence of the phrase is in the
lines cited in the previous paragraph, which introduce the argument from
divinity (1178b7–8).

What does Aristotle mean by "perfect happiness"? He does not explain
this term, and it occurs nowhere else in the *NE*. But if (as I argued in 1.3)
X.7–8 compares two competing plans of life, both of which are happy
but one of which is happiest, then a certain interpretation of "perfect happiness" suggests itself. The two lives differ in that each assigns a certain
primacy to a different good, a primacy that consists in being an ultimate
end. So, on my reading, when Aristotle says that perfect happiness consists in contemplation, he means that it is the best candidate for the ultimate end.[24] Contemplation is desirable in itself, it is not desirable for the

---

[24] According to *Met.* V.16, to say that something is *teleion* can mean (a) that it has all of
its parts, (b) that it is unsurpassed in excellence, or (c) that it has reached its end (its *telos*).
"Complete" best fits (a), "perfect" (b), and either "perfect" or "final" (c). My position is
that according to Aristotle we can properly speak of the happiness of a philosopher and the
happiness of a politician, but that the first of these is superior to the second, because contemplation is a better candidate for the ultimate end than ethical activity. There are two ultimate
ends of two kinds of happy lives, but the first is unsurpassed in excellence as an end, and
the second is not. I do not think that senses (a) and (c) fit as well. As for (a): if *teleia* happiness
is happiness that has all its parts, and Aristotle equates this with contemplation, then he is
saying that to contemplate is to have every part of happiness. But when Aristotle speaks of
happiness as having parts, he clearly indicates that exercising theoretical virtue (or any other
single virtue) is only one of them. See, for example, *EE* II.1 1219a35–9, 1219b13, 1220a2–
4. (I will later return to the idea that happiness has parts; I do not take this to constitute
evidence against my noninclusivist interpretation.) As for (c): I am not sure what to make
of the idea that happiness has an end which it must reach in order to be *teleia*. Happiness *is*
the ultimate end, so what could it mean for it to have an end? Perhaps it could be said that
the happiness of the statesman is not *teleia* because the ethical activity he engages in, and the
happiness he has attained, has not reached its end: ethical activity is for the sake of contemplation, but in the life of the statesman it does not promote this end. In this case, the hap-

sake of anything else, and every other good is desirable for its sake. And, as the arguments of X.7–8 are intended to show, contemplation has other features that indicate how appropriate it is for human beings to assign it this central place in their lives, if this option is open to them. By contrast, the good that is nonperfect happiness, namely, virtuous practical activity, is the second-best choice for an ultimate end: although it has certain features we are looking for in an ultimate end (such as intrinsic goodness, pleasantness, and self-sufficiency), it has them to a lesser degree than contemplation; and one feature of an ultimate end (not being desirable for the sake of other goods) is missing.[25]

This way of reading "perfect happiness" requires further defense, but I will not undertake this task immediately. Instead, I will argue in the next section that even if we construe "perfect happiness" in a very different way, doing so will not provide a plausible alternative to my reading of the argument from divinity. Even when "perfect happiness" is construed in a way I do not accept, we must take Aristotle to be saying that the more we contemplate, the better our lives.

According to the interpretation of "perfect happiness" that I reject, the phrase is to be read as though Aristotle meant to say "perfect part of happiness." That is, when he says that perfect happiness consists in contemplation, he means only that it is the best single good there is. It is not happiness itself, but just the best part of it; for on this interpretation, the *NE* rejects the identification of human happiness with any one good. Instead, happiness in Book I is a composite of all compossible intrinsic goods; and what X.7–8 adds is that the perfect part of this composite, the single most valuable good, is contemplation.[26] And so, on this reading,

---

piness that is *teleia* would be the ultimate end (contemplation), and the happiness that is not *teleia* would be one that is subordinate to that. When (c) is interpreted in this way, it comes to the same thing as (b). On *teleia eudaimonia* and its connection with *Met.* V.16, see Keyt, "Intellectualism in Aristotle," pp. 377–8. He believes that Aristotle is using *teleia* in either sense (b) or sense (c), and tries to show how this allows for an "inclusivist" reading of X.7–8: though perfect happiness consists in contemplation, this activity is only the best of the many components included within happiness.

[25] More fully, my position is that ethical activity comes close to being the best choice for an ultimate end. It is desirable in itself, and when contemplation is left aside, we can say that all other goods are desirable for its sake, while it is not desirable for the sake of any other. In this way, it approximates the self-sufficiency of contemplation. (Self-sufficiency, as defined by Aristotle at I.7 1097b14–15, will be discussed in 5.11.) Furthermore, although both ethical virtue and theoretical virtue are excellent conditions of the rational soul that account for our superiority to other creatures, the latter virtue more fully explains our position in the hierarchy of *all* living beings.

[26] This is the interpretation endorsed by Keyt, "Intellectualism in Aristotle." He precedes his discussion of *teleia* happiness with the question, "[I]s [Aristotle] making the more modest assertion, as Stewart and Gauthier claim, that the best *element* of the best total life for a man is its theoretical activity?" (p. 377, his emphasis); and he answers in the affirmative. He

Books I and X are concerned with different questions: the first asks "What is happiness?" ("What is the best composite?"), while the last asks "What is *perfect* happiness?" ("What is best in that composite?").

As I will argue in Chapter 5, there is no textual support for the view that, according to Aristotle, happiness is a combination of many diverse intrinsic goods. If I am right about this, then of course it cannot be true that "perfect happiness" picks out the best good in the all-inclusive composite that Aristotle equates with happiness: there is no such composite. For now, let us simply remind ourselves that it is plausible to connect I.5 with X.7–8: in the earlier chapter, Aristotle wants to know what the end of the political life is, and he sees the political and contemplative lives, each with its own conception of happiness, as alternatives between which we must choose. In X.7–8, the two lives are finally compared: we should choose the philosophical life because its end (contemplation) is superior to the end of the political life (activity in accordance with practical virtue). The comparison between lives in X.7–8 is carried out in precisely the same manner as the comparison in Book I: different lives have different ultimate ends, and one life is better than another if its ultimate end is superior. And so, when Aristotle argues in X.7–8 that perfect happiness consists in contemplation, he is answering the question raised in Book I: "What is happiness?" To think that Books I and X are addressed to different questions is to ignore the fact that the opening book raises a major question—should we be philosophers or politicians?—that is answered only in the closing pages of the *NE*.

1.10. AN ALTERNATIVE READING

In the preceding section, I pointed out that the argument from divinity in X.8 is introduced by a sentence that uses the term "perfect happiness." Aristotle says, "It would appear from what follows that perfect happiness is a certain contemplative activity" (1178b7–8). The rest of the argument does not use that phrase; instead, Aristotle speaks simply of happiness, and concludes that, by virtue of this argument, "happiness would be a certain contemplation" (b32). But it is possible that he drops the term

---

refers to Stewart, *Notes on the Nicomachean Ethics of Aristotle*, vol. 1 (pp. 59–62), vol. 2 (pp. 443–5); and Gauthier and Jolif, *L'Éthique à Nicomaque*, vol. 2, p. 862. See too Cooper, "Contemplation and Happiness: A Reconsideration," pp. 205–206. According to Keyt, p. 368, if Aristotle went further than this "more modest assertion," then he would be a "strict intellectualist," that is, someone who believes that "practical activity has value only as a means to theoretical activity." See too Keyt's diagram, p. 371. But these are not the only two alternatives: Aristotle can believe that contemplation is the ultimate end (not just the best component of the ultimate end) without regarding ethical activity as a mere means to this end. He can say that moral activity is good in itself, and more significantly, that it comes close to fulfilling the conditions demanded of an ultimate end.

"perfect" merely for the sake of convenience, and that every time he uses *eudaimonia* and related expressions, we are supposed to supply *teleia*.[27] In that case, the claims of the argument from divinity must be more fully spelled out in the following way:

(a) The gods have more perfect happiness than human beings.
(b) Certain human beings have more perfect happiness than lower animals.
(c) The more contemplation a being has, the more perfect happiness that being has.

If this is what Aristotle means, then what implications does that have for my thesis that more contemplation is always better than less? Does the argument from divinity no longer provide support for my view that, according to X.7–8, human beings cannot have too much philosophical activity for their own good?

Certainly, if "perfect happiness" is taken in the way I suggested in the last section, there is no reason to abandon the thesis that the value of contemplation is unbounded. On my view, Aristotle identifies contemplation with "perfect happiness" because he thinks there is a different good—activity in accordance with moral virtue—that can also be identified with happiness. To record the fact that two kinds of life are happy, and to indicate that one is nonetheless happier, he makes a distinction between the best (that is, perfect) happiness and a life that is happy in a secondary way. On this reading, the best kind of life has contemplation as its sole ultimate end, and the more fully one can realize this end, that is, the more often one can engage in this activity, the better off one is. So, on this construal of "perfect happiness," there is no need to modify my way of interpreting Aristotle's statement that "those who have more contemplation also have more happiness" (1178b29–30). If we take this to mean that those who have more contemplation thereby have a higher degree of perfect happiness, it will still be true that the more contemplation a life has, the better a life it is.

But we have seen that there is another way of construing Aristotle's claim that contemplation is perfect happiness: he might mean that happiness is a complex good whose best (that is, perfect) component is contemplation. Although I will later argue against the inclusivism on which this reading is based, let us now reconsider Aristotle's ranking of gods, humans, and lower animals in the light of this alternative construal of perfect happiness. Happiness, let us now suppose, is a complex good (as Book I allegedly tells us), and one of its components, contemplation, is perfect happiness. The gods have more perfect happiness than human

[27] I take this to be Keyt's reading. See "Intellectualism in Aristotle," p. 382.

beings, because they contemplate more. Should we also say that, according to Aristotle, the gods have better lives than human beings, by virtue of the fact that they have more perfect happiness? Surely the answer is yes. He clearly believes, in X.7–8 and elsewhere, that there are divine beings whose lives are superior to our own.[28] And the only way he can explain this is by saying that the gods contemplate more than we do. From the fact that one kind of living being contemplates more than another, Aristotle immediately infers that the first has a better life than the second. Since this inference holds of any two living beings, it can be used to make comparisons among human beings: if one human life has more contemplation than another, then it is a better life. If they have the same amount, they are equally desirable.

So even if perfect happiness were just one component of happiness, it would be a component of an extraordinary kind, according to X.7–8: just by looking at this one component, and noticing differences between the degrees to which different human beings possess it, we can draw conclusions about which has a better life. The other alleged components of happiness could of course have an indirect bearing on well-being: variations in the degree to which one possesses the other goods would make a difference in happiness, to the extent that those variations promote larger or smaller amounts of philosophical activity. But such variations in subordinate goods could never by themselves outweigh differences in theoretical activity.

I therefore see no reason for thinking that in X.7–8 Aristotle leaves the value of contemplation undetermined. There is simply no reason to take him to be saying that there is a point beyond which we do ourselves no further good by spending more time on philosophy. He tells us that "those who have more contemplation also have more happiness" (1178b29–30), and even if we supply the term "perfect" before "happiness," he will be saying that there is no upper bound on the value of contemplation. Furthermore, as I have said before, if contemplation can be overrated, and a human life can lack balance because it contains an excess of philosophy, then Aristotle owes his readers an explanation of how we can know where this boundary should be placed. But there is no reason

[28] See *Met.* XII.7 1072b24–6. It is standard Aristotelian doctrine that all other living things strive to imitate the gods. "All things desire that [sc. to participate in the divine, so far as they can], and whatever they do in accordance with nature, they do for the sake of that" (*De An.* II.4 415b1–2). Because of the presence of this divine element in all living beings, they can be said to strive after the same kind of pleasure (*NE* VII.13 1153b31–2, X.2 1173a4–5). And of course if all living things imitate the gods, these divine beings must have the best kind of life; otherwise, they would be inappropriate objects of emulation. Aristotle appeals to the superiority of the unmoved mover in his account of celestial movement (*De Caelo* II.12, especially 292a22–b25); biological generation too is explained as an approximation to divine life (*De An.* II.4 415a26–b2, *De Gen. An.* II.1 731b24–732a1).

to accuse him of failure to answer the question "How much contemplation would do one the most good?" In the argument from divinity, his
answer is staring us in the face.

1.11. Individuating Lives

More needs to be said about Aristotle's argument from divinity, but for
the moment I would like to consider an objection to my way of describing the two competing lives of X.7–8. I take these chapters to be saying
that the best kind of life human beings could want for themselves is one
that has the greatest possible amount of philosophical activity. But I also
take Aristotle to be saying that there is a second-best kind of life: one in
which one tries to have as much excellent practical activity as possible.
This second choice is a happy life, even though it contains no theoretical
activity at all. Now, someone might object that this cannot be what Aristotle means, for if my reading were correct, there would be indefinitely
many different kinds of lives that are happy, not just two. The best kind
of life would be the one that has the largest number of contemplative
hours (or minutes or seconds—the unit is unimportant); the second-best
would be the one that falls just short of that number; the third-best would
have slightly less philosophical activity than the second; and so on, until
at some point one ranks nonphilosophical lives in terms of the amount of
time they devote to moral activity. Since X.7–8 says that there are exactly
two kinds of happy life, it might be thought that my reading must be
abandoned.

But I do not think that this objection has any merit. For although one
way to individuate kinds of lives would be to count philosophical or political hours and to say that when the numbers differ we have different
kinds of lives, that is not the only way, nor is it a particularly useful or
revealing method of individuation. Suppose you try to philosophize as
much as possible, when you consider only your own happiness, and I
have the same goal, but we succeed to slightly different degrees. If we say
that we have different kinds of lives because of their different degree of
success, then in all likelihood every human being will have a different
kind of life from every other. But then sorting individual lives into different categories will be uninteresting and useless: what is the point of
putting individuals into groups if each goes into a different group, and
we notice nothing but differences between lives and never similarities? It
is more revealing to point out that your life and mine have a great similarity as well as a small difference: they are of the same type, since each of
us pursues the same goal.

And of course this way of individuating lives seems to be one that Aristotle has in mind. In *NE* I.2 he says that we need to determine what the

target (*skopos*: 1094a24) of human life is, and in I.5 we are told that those who lead different lives answer this question differently. The hedonistic, political, and philosophical lives do not differ quantitatively, by having different degrees of success in their pursuit of the same goal; rather they differ because they aim at different targets. Since types of lives are individuated in Book I by distinguishing their targets, and since this seems to be a useful way of classifying our options, it is reasonable to assume that Aristotle is adopting the same method of individuation in Book X. His readers are trying to decide whether to be philosophers or statesmen (or perhaps whether a change in career would be justified). It is perfectly reasonable for Aristotle to look upon these as two different modes of life, and to point out at the same time that the more one achieves the goal of the best life, the better off one is. Insisting that more contemplation is better than less does not commit him to classifying lives according to degrees of contemplation rather than according to kinds of goals.

On my reading, Aristotle is claiming that the best target to aim at, when one seeks one's happiness, is not one that is itself a complex mixture of goods. The best any life can achieve is to have as much of one good, contemplation, as possible. The second-best kind of life similarly aims at one good, excellent ethical activity, and tries to achieve this as much as possible. But it is not part of my interpretation that, according to Aristotle, anyone who tries to mix these two goods, and proposes that as his target, is bound to lack happiness. In other words, I do not take Aristotle to be saying that we should in all circumstances choose one of these goods or the other as our target, and never some combination of them both.

Suppose, for example, that someone wants to combine the two careers of philosophy and politics. He has no precise formula about how this mixture is to be achieved; rather, he simply wants a high degree of both activities, and does not care about achieving any precise proportion between them. I take Aristotle to be saying that if one is trying to have the best life one can, then this mixture of goods is not the best target to aim at. If one succeeds in achieving this balance, one still will not have as good a life as someone who makes contemplation his sole ultimate end. The goal of having a mixture of philosophy and politics is intermediate between the best goal and the second-best; and for reasons we have just given, there is nothing absurd about saying that there are lives that fall between the best and the second-best. Aristotle can say that anyone who succeeds at this mixed life is happy—not as happy as those who contemplate more, but happier than those who do not contemplate at all. Although the philosophical and political lives are viewed as competing alternatives, he has a way of evaluating the decision and the success of those who think they will be best off if they try to combine them.

It may sometimes happen that by trying to pursue a mixed career, one fails in both areas. By spending a good deal of time in purely intellectual pursuits, one may falter as a politician: in complex political situations, one may not have as much time as one needs in order to determine what an ethically virtuous person should now do for the community; even if one knows what to do, one may fail to achieve one's ends, if one has not spent enough time cultivating political alliances. Or the problem may be reversed: through having spent so much time on politics, one may have too little time left to master the subjects by means of which one acquires theoretical wisdom.

It would be silly for Aristotle to deny these points. It is a matter of common sense that these conflicts can sometimes occur, and it would be dogmatic to insist otherwise. But on my reading, there is a further point about the philosophical-political life, and it is one that Aristotle commits himself to: one could do better for oneself if one's ultimate end were simply contemplation. Those who try to combine philosophy and politics may end up failing at one or the other or both, but the possibility of failure will vary with circumstances, and some extremely able and fortunate people may be able to combine the two careers. Even in these cases, however, Aristotle would claim that one can have a better life by trying to engage in philosophical activity as much as possible.

1.12. THE POLITICAL LIFE

One feature of my interpretation that I have not yet defended is the thesis that, according to the *NE*, one can lead a happy life even if one never engages in philosophical activity. Those who make ethical activity their ultimate end, and who have the resources to achieve this end over the course of a lifetime, lead good lives, even if they do not develop the virtues of theoretical reason. What textual basis is there for ascribing this thesis to the *NE*?

As we have seen, Aristotle says several times that *perfect* happiness consists in contemplation, and it is natural to take these statements to entail that if one does not engage in this activity, then one does not have perfect happiness. That leaves room for the possibility that one can be happy—though not perfectly happy—even if one does not philosophize. And it is plausible to assume that, precisely because Aristotle recognizes this possibility, he equates contemplation with *perfect* happiness rather than with happiness *simpliciter*. I will supplement this argument in Chapter 4, when I discuss his statement in Book I that happiness consists in activity in accordance with perfect virtue, as well as his claim that it consists in activity in accordance with the most perfect virtue.[29] I will try to show that these formulae refer to different virtues: a perfect but not most perfect virtue is one that is practical, whereas the most perfect virtue is theoretical. If I am right about this, then Book I contains two accounts of what happiness is: it is activity in accordance with practical virtue, and it is activity in accordance with theoretical virtue. This dual account corresponds with the fact that in X.7–8 two competing lives are considered, one of them happier than the other. So, what Aristotle should be taken to mean in Book I is that perfect happiness consists in one kind (the most perfect kind) of virtuous activity, and a secondary form of happiness consists in another (less perfect) kind of virtuous activity. In other words, one can be happy—though not perfectly so—if one has and exercises the practical virtues, but lacks the theoretical virtues.

It may be useful to supplement these considerations by considering some alternatives to my interpretation, and seeing that they are defective in various ways. To keep the number of options manageable, let us agree on these three points:

(a) In X.7–8, Aristotle considers two competing kinds of lives.
(b) One of them gives some kind of primacy to philosophical activity, the other to virtuous practical activity.
(c) The philosophical life is happiest, while the political life is happy to a secondary degree.

On my reading, each life has one ultimate end: contemplation in one case, moral activity in the other. But what kinds of lives might X.7–8 have in mind, if they are not the ones I propose?

One possibility would be this: The two lives are both devoted to a mixture of philosophy and politics, but they differ in that each places more emphasis on one or the other of these two kinds of activity. When one aims at one's own happiness, one's target should ideally be a mixed ultimate end, and the two ingredients in that mixture should be contemplation and practical activity, with more emphasis going to the former. Someone who succeeds in achieving that mixture is happiest. This life is philosophical, and it is a life in accordance with understanding, because theoretical activity is the main ingredient of its ultimate end. There is, however, a second-best life, in which one again aims at a mixed ultimate end, but in this case one puts more emphasis on politics than on philosophy. This second life is political, and is a life in accordance with ethical virtue, because such activity receives more emphasis than any other. So interpreted, Aristotle would be saying that in order to be happy, one must

[29] Perfect virtue: I.9 1100a4, I.10 1101a14, I.13 1102a6; most perfect virtue: I.7 1098a17–18.

be both a philosopher and a politician. Those who emphasize the former role are happier than those who emphasize the latter.

The problem with this interpretation is that it allows the two kinds of lives to be almost identical. One person puts more emphasis on philosophy and the other on politics, but each is a philosopher-statesman, and they may differ only in that one wants to spend a bit more time than the other does on philosophy. I have already argued (1.11) that it is not fruitful to classify lives into types if the distinction between them is based merely on the different amount of time each devotes to various activities. It does not seem any more interesting to distinguish lives merely on the grounds that one aims at slightly more and the other slightly less of a certain ingredient in a mixture that is otherwise the same. If there are really two competing lives in X.7–8, then they presumably differ markedly enough to make it worthwhile to count them as different lives.

Here is another possibility: The goal of the best life is a mixture of philosophical and political activity, with more emphasis going to the former than to the latter. The second-best life, by contrast, is one that has no philosophical activity at all. This interpretation does succeed in making the two lives quite different, but it coincides with my own reading in one crucial respect: it takes the second-best life to have a single ultimate end—activity in accordance with moral virtue—and it agrees that, according to X.7–8, a life devoid of philosophical activity can still be happy. It differs from my reading only in its description of the best life, and at the moment we are looking for a plausible alternative to my way of understanding the second-best life. (In any case, I have already given my reason for thinking that, according to X.7–8, the best life is not one that achieves some ideal balance between philosophy and politics, but is instead the one that has the greatest amount of philosophical activity.)

One remaining alternative should be considered: The best life is the one I have described; those who want to be ideally happy should not take time away from philosophy in order to pursue political careers. The second-best life is one that assigns some place to philosophical activity, but keeps that place as small as possible; all of one's remaining time should be devoted to political activity. According to this interpretation, the advocate of the philosophical life and the advocate of the political life agree that some time must be spent on contemplation if one is to be happy. But they disagree about how much time is best devoted to this activity: one party thinks that more is always better, and this is the side of the dispute that Aristotle takes; the other party thinks that contemplation should be kept to a minimum, though it should not diminish to zero.

Here we do have a significant difference between ideals, and the portrayal of the political life does differ from the one I have given; for on this last interpretation, Aristotle holds that no life can be happy unless it contains some philosophical activity. The trouble with this alternative to my reading is that it does not accord well with my thesis that the treatment of the conflict between philosophy and politics in X.7–8 is continuous with the preliminary discussion of that same subject in I.5. In the earlier chapter, Aristotle asks what the end of the political life is, and his assumption is that competing ways of life differ because they put forward different conceptions of the ultimate end. Nothing is said there or in X.7–8 to the effect that the ultimate end of the political life is a mixture of theorizing and something else. The end of politics will be something for the sake of which everything else in the political life is pursued, and so if contemplation is to have any place at all in the political life, it must be something sought for the sake of the unique end of politics. But we know from X.7 that contemplation cannot play this subordinate role: it produces no further good beyond itself, and is desired only because of its intrinsic value (1177b1–4).

Furthermore, in X.7 Aristotle declares his opposition to those who urge us to leave divine activity to the gods, and to concentrate solely on what is human (1177b31–3); by contrast, he never considers the thesis that we should engage in divine activity but should do so as little as possible. This suggests that when he argues in X.7–8 for the superiority of one way of life over another, the kind of life that he has in mind as the inferior one is the life we would lead if we followed the dictum that we should not try to make ourselves godlike. In any case, it is reasonable to assume that the political life is the one that gives to political activity the same kind of priority that the philosophical life gives to philosophy. If it can be shown that in the philosophical life every other good is desired for the sake of contemplation, then the political life will differ in that it proposes a different conception of the ultimate end. For these reasons, it is plausible to think that philosophy is absent from the political life.

One further point should be made about the political life, before we turn back to the argument from divinity: This is a life that people can decide to lead for very different sorts of reasons. Recall the son who has been specially prepared to take over from his father the rule of his kingdom. When he hears Aristotle's defense of the philosophical life, he is convinced by the arguments, but decides that nonetheless he should lead the second life, because this is what he owes his father and the other members of his community. His life does not have the highest kind of happiness, but he recognizes this fact.

A slightly different situation would be this: Someone may take himself to be incapable of developing the theoretical virtues, and of understanding the truths contemplated in the philosophical life. He too may decide to lead the political life, although he agrees with Aristotle that the philosophical life is best.

Both types should be distinguished from the person who leads the political life because he mistakenly thinks that this is the best kind of life for a human being. Such a person is presumably aware that some choose to lead philosophical lives instead, but he thinks they are making an inferior choice. On my interpretation, Aristotle is granting that this third type of person—like the first two—can lead a happy life. Of course, the fact that he leads a political life does not guarantee that he is happy. He might be leading such a life merely as a means of increasing his wealth, power, and honor; and in that case his conception of the end is so badly mistaken that he cannot be counted as someone whose life is a good one. But it is also possible for this person to want to lead a political life for good reasons: he thinks that happiness is activity in accordance with such practical virtues as justice, courage, and temperance. His conception of happiness, in other words, is to a large extent correct, for he makes virtuous activity of the rational soul his ultimate end, and he desires external and bodily goods for the sake of this one highest end. His one important mistake is his failure to realize that there is an activity of reason that has an even better claim to be the ultimate end of human life. But, on my interpretation, Aristotle does not demand of those who lead happy lives that they have a *perfect* understanding of human well-being. If they reason to the conclusion that happiness consists in exercising the practical virtues, and they therefore have a sound basis for choosing the political life, then they can achieve an imperfect form of happiness.

Why should we take Aristotle to be making this concession? Why not read him in such a way that only the first two kinds of individuals mentioned above (the encumbered son, the person with no talent for theory) can be happy in a secondary way? Once again, I am relying on a certain way of connecting I.5 and X.7–8. The political and philosophical lives are introduced as competitors, each resting on a different conception of the ultimate end. Since X.7–8 returns to this dispute, and grants that one who leads the inferior life can nonetheless live well, these chapters are granting that a secondary form of happiness can be achieved even when one's conception of the ultimate end is not all that it should be.[30]

---

[30] If this interpretation is right, then Aristotle would do best to recognize second-best versions of the practical virtues, just as he recognizes a second-best form of happiness. If someone fails to realize that the philosophical life is best, but nonetheless has good reasons for taking moral activity as his ultimate end, then he does not have perfect practical wisdom, but a second-best kind. He partially understands what the end of human life is. And for this reason, he has second-best versions of the ethical virtues. I see nothing in Aristotle's moral philosophy that would prevent him from adopting this view. (Note that this does not commit him to the view that only philosophers fully possess the ethical virtues. For one may recognize the superiority of the philosophical life without being able to lead it, for lack of opportunity or ability.)

1.13. PERFECT HAPPINESS AGAIN

We must now take a closer look at the argument from divinity, for there
is a way of reading it that conflicts with my thesis that a nonphilosophical
life can be happy. After Aristotle assumes that the gods are the happiest
living beings in the universe (1178b8–9), and argues that the only activity
in which they can engage is contemplation (b10–22), he goes on to compare their condition with that of humans and other animals:

> Among human activities the one that is most akin to this [divine contempla-
> tion] would have the character of happiness most of all (*eudaimonikōtatē*). A sign
> of this is that the other animals do not share in happiness, since they are com-
> pletely deprived of such activity. For, among gods, the whole of life is blessed,
> and among human beings [life is blessed] to the extent that they have something
> resembling such activity. But none of the other animals is happy, since in no
> way do they share in contemplation. As far as contemplation extends, thus far
> happiness extends, and those who have more contemplation also have more
> happiness, not incidentally, but by virtue of the contemplation. (1178b23–31)

These claims—the lower animals are not happy because they do not contemplate; to be happy, a living being must share in contemplation; happiness extends as far as contemplation does—suggest that in X.7–8 Aristotle is embracing a position far more restrictive than the one I have been
attributing to him. It looks as though he is saying that any creature—be
it human or not—that engages in no theoretical activity is lacking in happiness. Read in this way, Aristotle would be saying that no matter how
outstanding a person is in character, no matter how honored and meri-
torious he is as a statesman, no matter how unblemished his life is by
misfortune, and no matter how well supplied he is with external and bodily goods, he is not happy if he fails to contemplate. He would be in the
same category as lower animals, evildoers, and victims of severe misfortune: though they have different kinds and amounts of good, none of
them should be called *eudaimon*. Aristotle's description of Priam in I.10
(1101a6–8) would in this case be quite misleading: he should not say that
Priam was deprived of happiness because of his great misfortunes; rather,
since he was not a philosopher, he never had any happiness to begin with.

Is there a way to read our passage that avoids committing Aristotle to
this low estimate of outstanding and successful statesmen? One strategy
is to take up an idea that was mentioned earlier, in 1.9: whenever Aristotle
talks about happiness in the argument from divinity, we should take him
to be referring to *perfect* happiness. In 1.9–10, I argued neither in favor of
nor against that way of construing the passage: rather, I tried to show that
even if we do so construe it, Aristotle will still be saying that it is always
better to engage in more contemplation rather than less. But now it is

necessary to consider the merits of reading "perfect" into Aristotle's argument at various points. Doing so gives us one way of upholding the thesis that nonphilosophers can be happy in a secondary way.

The passage cited above is preceded by the statement "It would appear from what follows that perfect happiness is a certain contemplative activity" (1178b7–8). And although the phrase "perfect happiness" does not recur in the argument from divinity, it may be that Aristotle is dropping it merely for the sake of convenience. So let us see what his argument looks like if we introduce the word "perfect" at appropriate places. We must now take Aristotle to be saying that no other animals besides human beings are *perfectly* happy, since none of them shares in contemplation. That is, we will not take him to be saying *in this passage* that animals lack happiness altogether; he will only be saying here that they are completely deprived of *perfect* happiness. Similarly, he will merely be claiming that nonphilosophical statesmen lack perfect happiness. He will be leaving open the possibility that these two groups—politicians and lower animals—are happy in a secondary, imperfect way.

Elsewhere, of course, he makes a distinction between these groups: he says that we do not call the lower animals happy, and he thinks this is justified, since these creatures do not engage in ethical activity (I.9 1099b32–1100a1). So, it might seem that horses and oxen fail two independent tests for happiness: first, they do not contemplate, and thus they fail to attain perfect happiness; second, they do not engage in moral activity, and therefore they fail to attain the less perfect form of happiness. The first test uses the gods as exemplars of perfect happiness; but the second test is independent of any divine comparison, and instead uses ethical human beings as exemplars of happiness. It is this second test that outstanding politicians pass: though they are like animals in their failure to engage in activity akin to divine contemplation, they are themselves the models of happiness used by the second test.[31]

1.14. Gods, Philosophers, Statesmen

If we read "perfect" into the argument from divinity in the way just suggested, we can reach the result that happiness is available even to those who do not contemplate. But I want to reject this strategy, and achieve

---

[31] This way of reading the argument is suggested by Keyt, "Intellectualism in Aristotle," p. 382. He says that Aristotle's argument might at first seem inadequate: the lower animals need not be deprived of happiness merely because they do not contemplate, for they might achieve happiness through practical thinking. But on second glance, Keyt suggests, Aristotle can be rescued: he is only trying to explain why the lower animals lack perfect happiness, and their failure to contemplate is in this case a perfectly satisfactory explanation. As Keyt notes, the same puzzle is raised by Ackrill, *Aristotle's Ethics*, p. 265.

this result in a different way, for I believe that Aristotle's argument in X.8 is an attempt to show why animals and certain human beings simply fail to be happy; it is not merely an attempt to show why they fail to be perfectly happy. Let us look once again at this portion of our passage:

> And among human activities the one that is most akin to this would have the character of happiness most of all (*eudaimonikōtatē*). A sign of this is that the other animals do not share in happiness, since they are completely deprived of such activity. For, among gods, the whole of life is blessed, and among human beings [life is blessed] to the extent that they have something resembling such activity. But none of the other animals is happy, since in no way do they share in contemplation. (1178b22–8)

On the reading I favor, Aristotle is here making the following claims: (a) The gods are paradigms of happiness, since they have perfect happiness at all times. (b) All other living beings have a greater or a lesser degree of similarity to the gods, or no similarity at all (in the relevant respect). (c) This comparison yields a ranking of living beings in terms of happiness: the degree of well-being achieved by all other living things can be assessed by comparing their lives with divine life. (d) Judged in this fashion, human beings have different degrees of happiness, for some of their activities have more resemblance to divine activity than others; but in any case, no human being is happy for the entire duration of his lifetime, from beginning to end.[32] (e) The lives of other animals are not as good as our lives can be, and they are not happy, because "in no way do they share in contemplation."

So interpreted, Aristotle is not merely claiming here that other animals lack perfect happiness. He means precisely what he says: these creatures "do not share in happiness" *simpliciter*. It is not as though he had one test to determine whether they are *perfectly* happy, and an independent test— one that does not require some semblance of contemplative activity—to determine whether they are *happy*. The well-being of all creatures—human beings, other animals, or plants—can be assessed by seeing how closely they approximate the divine.

Why should we read our passage in this way? Because it is standard Aristotelian doctrine that living beings form a hierarchy, and that the best any creature can do is resemble the gods. The stars in the outermost sphere come closest to unchanging life, because of the simplicity of their

---

[32] The period of happiness for human beings begins only when they have emerged from their earlier years (I.9 1100a1–4, *EE* II.1 1219b5). And the fact that we cannot contemplate continuously (*NE* X.4 1175a3–5) means that even during our adult lives we cannot achieve as much happiness as a god can during that same period of time. (It should not be inferred, however, that if a philosopher is not at the moment engaged in theoretical activity, he is not happy. See 1.17.)

motion; the movement of the intermediate spheres is more complex, and so the divinities of this region attain a lesser good.[33] On earth, only the good of human beings is sufficiently similar to the divine good to deserve the same name, *eudaimonia*. But animals, or at least some of them, can be said to live well,[34] because they have such low-grade forms of knowledge as perception[35] and (in some cases) memory.[36] Plants are still further removed from the divine. Their only way of approximating eternal activity is through reproduction: though the individual plant has nothing like knowledge or reason, it does help perpetuate the species, and this is as close as it can get to the activity of the gods.[37] At the bottom of the scale are lifeless objects: since they lack a soul, whatever goodness they have derives from their serving human ends.[38]

So Aristotle does not have or need two different standards for determining how well off a species is. He does not take the measure of certain living things by comparing them with his god, and then evaluate other species by means of some different and independent test. Everything can be ordered by a single measure. The highest form of life is one of supreme, eternal, and uninterrupted intellectual activity. Humans are the only nondivine beings that can exhibit enough similarity to the gods' supreme activity to justify the claim that we, like they, can be happy. In fact, some human beings can achieve perfect happiness, since they engage in the very same activity as the gods; but they are of course not as happy as gods, since their contemplation is not eternal and uninterrupted. Other human lives approximate divine life to a lesser degree, and are happy in a secondary way—a point I will soon return to. Lower animals are not as well off as human beings, because they have only a low-grade form of knowledge. But they have better lives than plants, since the latter have no cognitive dimension at all. The similarity between gods and nonhuman lives is so remote that it is understandable that the term *eudaimon* should not be applied to the latter, even when they live well.[39]

[33] *De Caelo* II.12, especially 292a22–b25.

[34] *De Part An.* II.10 656a5–8, *De An.* III.12 434b24–6, *EE* I.7 1217a28–9.

[35] *De Gen An.* I.23 731a30–b5, *De Sensu* 1 437a1–3.

[36] *Met.* I.1 980a27–b25. Since animals that have memory are here said to be more intelligent (*phronimōtera*: b21) than others, it is clear that they occupy a higher position in the *scala naturae*.

[37] *De Gen An.* I.23 731a24–6, II.1 731b31–732a1; *De An.* II.4 415a23–b7.

[38] *De Gen An.* II.1 731b24–31.

[39] At times, as in X.8, Aristotle says that sub-human forms of life have no share in the divine; see too *EE* I.7 1217a26–9. At other times, he says they share in the divine, so far as they can: *De An.* II.4 415a29–b1. In *De Part An.* II.10 656a7–8, he says that either human beings alone share in the divine, or they do so most of all. I do not think there is any real inconsistency here. Strictly speaking, no other type of animal engages in reasoning; this is the basis of the function argument in *NE* I.7. And when reasoning is taken as the respect in

What then are we to make of Aristotle's remark in I.9 that the other animals cannot be happy because they do not engage in ethical activity (1099b32–1100a1)? We need not take this to mean that man is an independent measure of how well off other living beings are. That is, Aristotle is not saying that, quite apart from any comparison that can be made between god and lower animals, there is a further standard by which their well-being can be measured—namely, the standard provided by human beings. If he were saying that, then he would mean that no matter how utterly ungodlike a form of life is, it still might be happy, if it comes close enough to human life. And Aristotle rejects this thought, for he believes that the extent to which a creature lives well is the extent to which it approximates the divine. Because he believes this, he thinks that one way to see that lower animals have no *eudaimonia* is to notice how far removed they are from us with respect to one of the capacities that make us godlike. To be distant from human beings is to be even more distant from the single paradigm of happiness, namely, the activity of the unmoved mover. So I take Aristotle to be saying in I.9 that an animal's failure to engage in ethical activity is one good reason for denying that it is happy. What X.8 adds is that there is a deeper reason, a reason that explains why the I.9 test is appropriate: whether a living thing is happy, and how happy it is, does not depend *ultimately* on whether it engages in the same kinds of activities that human beings engage in. It depends on its similarity to the gods. Because there is a way in which the ethical activity of human beings is godlike, the failure of other animals to engage in such moral activity helps explain why they are not to be considered happy.

If we look at Aristotle in the way I am suggesting, then we must say that those who possess the practical virtues and act in accordance with them thereby share in (*metechein*: 1178b24; *koinōnei*: b28) the contemplative activity of the gods. This does not mean that practical activity is itself a form of theoretical thinking: Aristotle nowhere says that when a good person acts in an ethical way, the virtue of theoretical wisdom is brought into play. What it does mean is that there is a certain similarity (*homoiōma ti*: 1178b27) between excellent practical activity and contemplation, a similarity great enough to account for the fact that both are forms of happiness. In other words, one way of sharing in contemplative activity is to act in accordance with practical wisdom: there is enough kinship between the two forms of wisdom (theoretical and practical) to make exercising the latter the same kind of thing as exercising the former.

This kinship can be seen in several different ways. Aristotle thinks that

---

which comparisons are made, the lower animals are said to lack a kinship with the gods, and do not share in the divine. But they resemble the gods in other ways, and by this loose standard they share in the divine to some small extent.

the function of practical reason is in an important respect similar to that of its theoretical counterpart: it is to grasp a certain body of truths. And the intellectual virtues of a practically wise person are therefore similar to those of a philosopher: they are the qualities that put one into the best position to attain the truth.[40] Furthermore, the development of practical wisdom requires a methodology similar to the one used by the theoretician: starting from appearances, common opinions, and puzzles, those who achieve theoretical or practical wisdom work towards an understanding of first principles, and then base all of their reasoning on those first principles.[41] And as we shall see later, Aristotle believes that in order to lead a good human life, whether one is a philosopher or a politician, one must take one's ultimate end to be reasoning well; the theoretician and the statesman are akin in that each engages in excellent reasoning not for the sake of some different type of good (honor, power, physical pleasure), but simply because such reasoning is the best activity for a human being to undertake. When one makes theoretical reasoning one's ultimate end, one engages in godlike activity, because the gods also contemplate. But if one leads a political life, one is devoting oneself to a lesser form of reasoning, and one thereby more distantly approximates the condition of the gods. In addition, the statesman has this kind of similarity to the unmoved mover: because of their reasoning activity, each is a cause of order and goodness among those subject to their influence.[42]

This similarity between political and divine life is not the focus of Aristotle's "argument from divinity" in X.8. The point of that argument is to show why one should lead a philosophical rather than a political life: since the gods achieve the highest degree of happiness by contemplating,

[40] NE VI.2 1139b12–13. Practical reasoning must also be in accord with right desire (1139a29–31), and in this respect differs from theoretical reasoning. In Chapter 6, I take Aristotle to be saying (VI.1 1139a14–17) that either of these two tasks—using practical or theoretical reasoning well—provides a standard that gives more precision to the doctrine of the mean. Both the philosopher and the politician try to hit the mean, and they use similar standards to determine the boundary between too much and too little.

[41] See NE I.4 1095a30–b8: in all subjects, we begin with points familiar to us but not well understood, and seek other starting points, which will be explanatory of all else. In practical philosophy, the familiar starting points include the various things we take to be good—health, wealth, honor, virtue, and so on (EE I.8 1218a15–24); and the most fundamental starting point we seek to understand is happiness—the "starting point and cause" of the other goods (NE I.12 1102a3–4). For the methodological role of appearances (phainomena), common opinions (endoxa), and puzzles (aporiai), see NE VII.1 1145b2–7, Topics I.2 101a34–b4, Met. III.1 995a24–b4. Aristotle's method is discussed in Owen, "Tithenai ta Phainomena"; Barnes, "Aristotle and the Methods of Ethics"; and Irwin, "Aristotle's Methods of Ethics" and "Ways to First Principles: Aristotle's Methods of Discovery."

[42] The godlike status of the politician is pointed out at NE I.2 1094b10: he is the cause of good throughout the whole community. (I will discuss this passage more fully in 6.8.) The unmoved mover is said to be the ruler of the universe at Met. XII.10 1076a4.

the best kind of human life is the one that is devoted to that very activity. But even though Aristotle is not concerned, in this passage, to spell out the similarity between excellent practical reasoning and divine contemplation, he expresses himself in a way that allows that further point to be made. When he says, "among human activities, the one that is most akin to this would have the character of happiness most of all" (1178b23), he can be taken to mean that human contemplation is more akin to divine activity than is excellent practical reasoning. Theoretical reasoning is most akin, but practical reasoning is still akin to some extent. Similarly, when he goes on to say that humans have as much happiness as they have something resembling (*homoiōma ti*: b27) divine contemplation, we should take him to be thinking of the two highest forms of human reasoning. Those who live in accordance with excellent theoretical reasoning bear the strongest resemblance to the gods, and can attain perfect happiness; those who instead live in accordance with excellent practical reasoning are farther removed from the gods, but they still have enough of a similarity to be called happy to a secondary degree.

As my account of the *NE* proceeds, I will try to strengthen the case for reading Aristotle in this way. For I will eventually try to show that his function argument in I.7 should be read as the beginning of a defense of two kinds of life—one philosophical, the other political. That argument should be taken to mean that reasoning well is the ultimate end of any happy human life; and Aristotle goes on to say, in X.7–8, that of the two kinds of life that exhibit this structure, the theoretical is more choiceworthy than the political. It is by virtue of the kinship between the philosophical and the moral lives that Aristotle is able to provide a common foundation for both.

But quite apart from the question of how the function argument should be interpreted, we have excellent reason for taking Aristotle to be assuming that such a kinship exists. For it would be incredible if he held that politicians are the sole exception to his general rule that the well-being of all forms of life can be assessed by determining the extent to which they resemble the unmoved mover. If plants, lower animals, philosophers, and the souls of heavenly spheres strive to approximate the highest form of life, and can be called *eudaimon* when they take on some definite resemblance to the divine, then the same test must also be applied to those who lead a political life.[43] Since they are happy, they must resemble the un-

---

[43] According to Nussbaum, *The Fragility of Goodness*, p. 292, Aristotle is opposed to "a unified account of The Good Life for all beings in the universe, ranking them and ordering them in a non-species-relative way." We can only say what it is for a member of a species to do well; we cannot justify the claim that certain species are better off than others. She admits (p. 373) that "a number of passages scattered through the corpus" tell a different story, but thinks they are "plainly at odds with the numerous arguments in all the ethical works to the

moved mover in some respect, even though they do not contemplate. And surely what grounds this resemblance is the fact that the political life is organized around a reasoning activity; in such a life, the highest good is reasoning in accordance with practical virtue.

We can now return to the problem posed in the preceding section: does the argument from divinity commit Aristotle to the view that only those who contemplate can be happy? If other animals completely lack happiness because their activities are so dissimilar to that of the gods, then must Aristotle also say that nonphilosophical statesmen are in the same predicament? One way to avoid this result is to read "perfect happiness" wherever we find "happiness" in the argument from divinity: it is only saying that lower animals lack perfect happiness, and similarly, it is only saying that a political leader who never theorizes lacks perfect happiness. But we have seen that this strategy is unsatisfactory, since Aristotle typically uses a divine standard to assess the well-being of all creatures. He compares every species with the gods to determine how well off it is, and whether it can be called *eudaimon*; a divine test is not used merely to decide the narrow question of whether a species is perfectly happy. So I have proposed that we take a different tack when we interpret the argument from divinity: we should take Aristotle to be assuming that human beings can

---

effect that ethics and politics must confine themselves to the question, 'What is the good for a human being?' " (p. 374).

Where are these numerous arguments? She cites (p. 292) this evidence: (a) In *MM* I.1 (1182b1–5), Aristotle says that politics must not take the good without qualification to be its subject, but rather the good *for us*. It therefore does not study the good of the gods: that topic belongs to a different study. (b) The *NE* says, "The good is not single for all animals, but is different in the case of each" (VI.7 1141a31–2). (This is her translation; I would translate: "There will not be one wisdom concerning the good of all animals.") (c) "All three ethical works announce that their subject is the *human* good, or the good life for a human being" (p. 292, her emphasis).

But these texts allow Aristotle to hold that certain kinds of living things have better lives than others. (a) The *MM* passage simply says that the study of the good for gods belongs to a different investigation. This further inquiry could reach the conclusion that the well-being of humans and other creatures is an approximation of the divine good. (b) In the *NE* chapter cited (VI.7) Aristotle affirms the inferiority of our lives to those of the gods (1141a20–22, 1141a34–b2). Therefore, we should not take his remark at 1141a31–2 (there is no "one wisdom concerning the good of all animals") to be incompatible with interspecies comparisons of well-being; he makes such comparisons in this very chapter. From the fact that what is good for plants differs from what is good for animals, it does not follow that animals cannot attain a higher degree of well-being than plants. (c) Although the subject of the *NE* is the human good (I.2 1094b7, I.7 1098a16), the merits of the contemplative life are explicitly included within the scope of its inquiry (I.5 1095b19, 1096a4–5). In I.13, nutrition and growth are dismissed, since they are not specifically human (1102a32–b3), but theoretical wisdom is among the virtues to be examined (1103a5). (Aristotle later uses *anthrōpinon* ["human"] more narrowly; see Chapter 6, note 6.) The *NE*, unlike the *MM*, does not promise to ignore the way the gods live.

resemble the gods to a greater or lesser extent. Although statesmen are deprived of perfect happiness, because they do not engage in the same activity as gods, they can lead happy lives nonetheless, because their ultimate end is the godlike goal of reasoning well.

1.15. More on 1178b28–32

I have been arguing that in one portion of Aristotle's argument from divinity—the one in which he compares the lives of gods, humans, and animals (1178b22–8)—we should not insert the word "perfect" wherever Aristotle talks about happiness. He is saying here that animals lack happiness, and not merely that they lack perfect happiness. Now let us proceed to the lines that bring the argument from divinity to a close: "As far as contemplation extends, thus far happiness extends, and those who have more contemplation also have more happiness, not incidentally, but by virtue of the contemplation. For it is in itself worthy of honor. As a result, happiness would be a certain contemplation" (b28–32). These words could be taken to mean that happiness and contemplation have the same extent, and if that is what Aristotle is saying, then he is committed to the view that when contemplation is entirely absent from a person's life, that person is deprived of happiness. But, on my interpretation, he believes no such thing; on the contrary, he thinks that those who lead political lives can be happy even if they engage in no philosophical activity whatsoever. So we should ask: is there any way to read the words just cited that allows for the possibility of good lives devoid of philosophical thinking? And once again, it might be suggested that the solution to our problem consists in adding the word "perfect" to what Aristotle says. In that case, he means: as far as contemplation extends, thus far *perfect* happiness extends; those who have more contemplation have more *perfect* happiness.

But this is a strategy we have reason to reject, if the interpretation I have defended is correct. On my view, Aristotle holds that there is no such thing as a human life that contains too much contemplation for its own good. If I am right about this, then he does want to say that those who have more contemplation (whether they are divine or human) have more happiness. They do not merely have more *perfect* happiness; they also have more happiness *simpliciter*. And so we should resist any attempt to water down what he says in our present passage, by inserting "perfect" before happiness. He does not mean that those who contemplate more, though they have more perfect happiness, might nonetheless have less happiness *simpliciter* than those who contemplate less.

Furthermore, we can avoid committing him to the thesis that non-philosophical politicians lack happiness without reading "perfect" into these lines. All we need do is notice a distinction between these two statements:

(a) Those who have more contemplation also have more happiness.
(b) Those who have more happiness also have more contemplation.

The first statement is the one Aristotle makes; the second is not. The latter entails that if a politician is happier than a pig, then the politician contemplates more than the pig. But since contemplation (that is, the activation of theoretical wisdom) is an activity that only gods and a few philosophers engage in, it is not true that politicians contemplate more than pigs. If we were to attribute (b) to Aristotle, we would have to say that nonphilosophical statesmen are no happier than other animals.

By contrast, (a)—the statement Aristotle actually makes—can be read in a way that avoids such disparaging comparisons. It says that if one living being contemplates more than another, then the first is happier than the second. And what if neither of two living beings contemplates at all? One might think that (a) tells us how to answer this question: since neither contemplates more than the other, neither has more happiness than the other. But it is also possible to read (a) in a different way: it merely concerns beings who contemplate to some extent, and it says that in these cases the amount of happiness equals the amount of contemplation. On this reading, it is not addressed to the question of how to compare two living beings who do not contemplate at all. That kind of comparison would have to appeal to something other than contemplation. Instead of asking who contemplates more, we would have to look for some other activity that is sufficiently similar to divine activity, and determine which of the two has more of that activity.

Similarly, there are two ways of reading Aristotle's statement that "as far as contemplation extends, thus far happiness extends" (1178b28–9). This could simply be taken to mean that as one expands the amount of contemplative activity one engages in, the happiness of one's life increases. That, I think, is what Aristotle is saying. Read differently, he would be claiming that when someone's happiness increases, that increase must be constituted by an increase in contemplation. This interpretation would eliminate the possibility that one's happiness might grow by virtue of an increment in some other good.

The correct interpretation is the one that best fits the context, and so if my earlier arguments were correct, we should take Aristotle to be allowing for increases in happiness that are not constituted by increases in contemplation. For the earlier part of the passage (1178b23, 26–7) suggests that human activities vary in their degree of similarity to a god's contemplation, and as I shall argue in Chapter 6, the similarity between philosophical and moral activity underlies the function argument of I.7. If Aristotle does think that the statesman and the philosopher both approximate the condition of the gods, the latter being a closer approximation than the former, then he cannot be claiming, in the above passage, that when two lives are devoid of contemplative activity, they are equally removed from the divine. Rather, he should be taken to mean that among contemplators, those who contemplate more are happier; and among noncontemplators, those who have more of the next-best approximation to the divine are happier. If we read him in this way, then we can continue to attribute to him the view that those who lead a political life, devoid of contemplation, may be happy in a secondary way. And when he says that "those who have more contemplation also have more happiness" (b29–30), it will not be necessary to insert "perfect" before "happiness."

1.16. THE ARGUMENT FROM DIVINITY: A SECOND LOOK

How does the argument from divinity arrive at the conclusion that perfect happiness consists in contemplation (1178b7–8)? Why does Aristotle think that, to decide how we should lead our lives, we should look to the kind of life the gods have? It may seem as though he is pulling a rabbit out of a hat: he merely argues that the gods must be doing something, and since it is unreasonable to think that they engage in ethical activity, all that remains for them is contemplation (b10–22). But even if we agree that this is their sole occupation, and that their lives are happy, why should we take these claims to provide us with a reason to engage in contemplation, and to think that the more we do so the better off we are?

Aristotle would reply as follows: When we say that the gods are happy, and when we say that certain human beings are happy, we are using the term "happiness" in precisely the same way.[44] We are using a single measure to evaluate the lives of divine and human beings. Now, suppose we make the assumption that the gods are not only happy, but happier than human beings—an assumption entailed by Aristotle's claim at 1178b8–9 that the gods are the happiest beings there are. It follows that whatever it

[44] Aristotle's account of human happiness does in a way differ from his account of divine happiness. For us, the good is a certain virtuous activity carried out over the course of a sizable but finite period of time (I.7 1098a18, I.10 1101a16, X.7 1177b24–6; I discuss these passages in the next section). If we engage in virtuous activity during that period of time, that is the best we can attain. And in order to attain that good, we must be sufficiently equipped with other goods as well (I.10 1101a15). No such restrictions are required in the account of the good for divine beings, since they exist at all times and need no resources in order to contemplate eternally. But this difference between the highest good for humans and the good for gods is not a difference in ends: happiness for us and for them consists in virtuous activity of the rational soul. The best we can hope for is a limited amount of what they have eternally; and so, when we understand what happiness is, we see why we are attributing the same good to gods and to humans when we call each kind of being *eudaimon*.

is that they do to achieve their happiness, we can at best approximate that activity. And it also follows that the more closely we approximate their condition, the better off we are.[45]

Aristotle thinks that all of this is so obvious to his audience that he need not argue for it. He therefore concentrates on the proposition his audience may not already accept: that divine activity is contemplative. And once he reaches this conclusion, it suits his purposes perfectly, for the gods' contemplative activity is a condition that human beings can try to approximate in various ways. Obviously, the best we can do to approach their condition is to contemplate—though this activity will have to be interrupted for various reasons. But there is another way of measuring up to the standard of happiness set by the gods, for even if we do not engage in excellent *theoretical* reasoning, we can still make excellent *practical* reasoning our ultimate end. This will not be perfect happiness, because it is a different kind of activity from the one the gods engage in; but the statesman's life is nonetheless lived for the sake of excellent reasoning, and so it bears enough similarity to divine life to be considered happy. By contrast, the lives of animals are so far removed from divine activity that we can understand why they are not called happy: though they have some degree of well-being, to the extent that they exercise certain cognitive capacities, this semblance to divine life is so slight that they are rightly thought to lack happiness.

To justify the common view that the lives of animals, humans, and gods can be placed on an ascending scale of well-being, happiness must be some good that the animals lack, that human beings achieve to greater or lesser degrees, and that the gods have without end. Contemplation fits the bill perfectly: it is the only good that the gods can have, it is a good that lower animals cannot come close to having, and it is a good that two of the most favored kinds of human lives approximate in varying degrees. Therefore, perfect happiness is contemplation: the term "perfect" is used merely to set off the activity that completely meets Aristotle's specifications from the activity that is a second-best approximation to divine contemplation.

As I mentioned earlier (1.9), Aristotle's identification of perfect happi-

---

[45] Nussbaum, *The Fragility of Goodness*, p. 293, takes Aristotle to be saying: "The life of a divine being might be ever so admirable; but the study of this life, insofar as it lies beyond our capabilities, is not pertinent to the practical aims of ethics." I agree that, according to Aristotle, it is impossible for a human being to contemplate continuously and eternally. Furthermore, he does not think that we should attempt to do what is impossible. But on my reading he does not infer from this that we should not try to approximate the condition of the gods, by contemplating as much as we can. Nor would this be a reasonable inference. If unattainable ideals can be approximated, they may properly guide our conduct. For example, although musicians of average talent cannot play as well as prodigies, they may emulate such models, and approximate their excellence as much as they can.

ness with contemplation is sometimes taken to mean that, of all the components of happiness, contemplation is the one that is perfect, that is, best. But if my reading of the argument from divine activity is correct, this way of watering down X.7–8 must be rejected. Happiness is not treated in X.7–8 as a composite of various goods, of which the gods have just one. Such a view would force Aristotle to admit that the gods have a deficiency, since however valuable contemplation is, they lack the other components of happiness. And were he to admit this, he would have to ask such questions as these: Does the fact that the gods lack the other components of happiness make them less happy than human beings, since human beings can attain all of these goods to some extent? During the time that human beings are alive, are they happier than gods? Are humans inferior with respect to happiness only because they eventually die, while the gods go on enjoying their single good forever? Or are gods happier than human beings not just because of their greater longevity, but also because it is better to contemplate uninterruptedly and do nothing else than to contemplate at times and possess a variety of other goods?

This last question would be answerable only if there were a way of saying how much more valuable contemplation is than any other good: only then could Aristotle say whether having a great deal of this good and nothing else is better than having just some of this good and much else. Since he has no such way of measuring goods, he would have to leave our questions unanswered. That is, once he admits that a god's happiness is diminished by its lack of the other goods alleged to be components of happiness, he must become a skeptic as regards comparisons between gods and humans. And of course he rejects such skepticism.

It might be suggested that if he relativizes the concept of happiness, he can avoid the conclusion that the gods fall short of perfect happiness by lacking some of its components. According to this proposal, the happiness of gods and human beings would be measured by different standards: a one-good standard for gods, a multiple-good standard for human beings. But surely he must resist this proposal, if he wants to say that gods are happier than we are, for any such judgment presupposes a single basis of comparison. Suppose a god does as well as possible by divine standards, and a person does as well as possible by human standards. Aristotle could not say that the god is nonetheless happier, if he always construed *eudaimonia* as "happiness for a god" or "happiness for a human being" and never as "happiness" *simpliciter*.

Aristotle never suggests, in the *NE* or in any other work, that comparisons between the happiness of gods and the happiness of human beings cannot be made. He accepts the view of his contemporaries and predecessors that the gods are happier than we are, and he provides a place for this proposition within his metaphysics and his moral thought. To be as happy as we can, we must approximate the condition of the gods; for a single standard of well-being ranks all living creatures and places the gods at the top. Accordingly, if the gods merely contemplate, then the more we contemplate the happier we are. Any other way we have of being happy must be a second-best and imperfect way of leading our lives.

1.17. LENGTH OF TIME

We must now take notice of a proviso attached to the thesis that perfect happiness consists in contemplation. In X.7, after Aristotle argues for the superiority of contemplation to ethical activity, he concludes: "The perfect happiness of a human being would be this [contemplation], if it receives a perfect length of life; for among the things pertaining to happiness, none is imperfect" (1177b24–6). The phrase "perfect length of life" brings to mind the proviso that Aristotle had attached to his conclusion in I.7. There, after arguing that the human good consists in activity in accordance with virtue, he adds: "Furthermore [the human good] is in a perfect life.[46] For one swallow does not make a spring, nor does one day; so too, one day or a short time does not make one blessed and happy" (1098a18–20). It is clear that "a perfect life" in this passage means the same as "a perfect length of life" in X.7. Aristotle is insisting that happiness consists not merely in having a certain good, but in having that good over a considerable period of time.[47] I take him to be saying in X.7 that if one engages in theoretical activity for too short a time—for example, one day—then one's life fails to be happy, even though one has engaged in the activity that constitutes perfect happiness. For perfect happiness does not consist in just any amount of philosophical activity; rather, it consists in

[46] The usual translation (see, for example, Ross, Ostwald, Irwin) is "in a complete life." However, if we want to use a single translation of *teleios* throughout I.7 and X.7–8, and if my interpretation of these chapters is correct, then "perfect" is preferable to "complete." For the most *teleion* end (1097a30) and the most *teleia* virtue (1098a18) in I.7 are not the most complete end and the most complete virtue in the sense that these terms are sometimes given—the end that includes all ends and the virtue that includes all virtues. If, as I believe, "perfect end" and "perfect virtue" are the best translations to use in I.7, then "perfect happiness" would be most suitable for X.7–8; accordingly, "perfect" should be used in 1177b24–6 and, for the sake of consistency, at 1098a18. ("Most final end" and "most final virtue" would also be acceptable in I.7, but "final happiness" would be a poor choice for X.7.) In any case, whether we use "complete life" or "perfect life," it is clear that Aristotle's phrase refers to a period of time that is of sufficient length.

[47] It might be suggested that "in a perfect life" at 1098a18 alludes not only to duration but to the additional goods beyond virtuous activity that are needed in a happy life. But this suggestion is made doubtful by I.10 1101a14–16, where we are told that one needs not only perfect virtuous activity and external goods, *but also* a period of time that is perfect. This indicates that "in a perfect life" at 1098a18 refers solely to time, since it is later distinguished from the point that we need external equipment.

contemplation that endures over a period of time that is not brief. I also assume that this point applies to the secondary form of happiness as well. If, having just passed one's youth and having only recently commenced one's political career, one is struck down by a disease, then one's life is not happy, even though one may have attained, for a brief period of time, the good in which secondary happiness consists.[48]

Aristotle's general point is that when we look at a person's way of life and try to decide whether or not he should be considered happy, we should not look at the activities he is undertaking at this very moment, or on this very day, or over any other brief period of time. We must take a sizable period of time, and ask whether, in view of the person's activities during this period, his life is happy. Philosophers or politicians who have only recently attained their ultimate end (contemplation in one case, moral activity in the other) will not yet have securely passed this test. Should misfortune cut them down just when they have achieved their highest goals, their lives cannot be considered happy. For we do not merely want the good, however briefly; quite properly, we want the good for a sizable stretch of time.[49]

[48] Since contemplation is an activity (*energeia*) rather than a process (*kinēsis*) in the technical sense, it is not something that develops over time toward a stage of completion. See *Met.* IX.6 1048b18–36, *NE* X.4 1174a14–b9. Of course, acquiring the virtue of theoretical wisdom and searching for theoretical truths are processes. But contemplation is the activity of reflecting on truths that have already been discovered (X.7 1177a26–7); seeking theoretical truth is desirable for the sake of contemplating those truths, but the ultimate end is not something that is desirable for the sake of anything further. So, in saying that perfect happiness consists in contemplation if it receives a perfect length of life, Aristotle cannot mean that in order to be perfectly happy one must bring the project of contemplating the truth to a stage of completion: there is no such stage. Similarly, he should not be taken to mean that secondary happiness requires a certain duration merely because it takes that long to complete various moral projects (that is, acts of justice, courage, and so on). Rather, he is saying that happiness consists in engaging in such acts over a considerable period of time. His point is that there is a purely temporal dimension to happiness: it requires a certain period of time not because the activities in which it consists necessarily take up much time (one can contemplate for a short time), but simply because a happy life, or a happy period of one's life, cannot be a short one. There is an imperfection in having the good briefly. I am not sure that this is what Gauthier and Jolif have in mind in their note on 1098a18: "l'homme mûr doit encore pouvoir disposer d'un espace de temps assez long pour que cet exercice de la vertu puisse s'y déployer largement, s'y épanouir à son aise" (*L'Éthique à Nicomaque*, vol. 1, p. 60). My view is at odds with that of Irwin, who says, "since the projects of a virtuous friend or of a magnificent and magnanimous person take some time to realize, a complete time will not be a short time" ("Permanent Happiness: Aristotle and Solon," p. 105). The point he makes here about moral activity cannot be applied to contemplation.

[49] I do not take Aristotle to be making a point about the use of words when he says that happiness requires a considerable period of time. Greek usage allows one to say that a person was *eudaimon* just for a day; see, for example, Euripides, *Bacchae* 910–911. Rather, Aristotle is proposing that happiness be attributed to people only if they attain the good over a long period of time. To have the good briefly is to have it for too little time, and since a happy

How sizable a stretch? How long is a "perfect length of life"? Aristotle merely says, in the passage cited above from I.7, that it is not a day or any other short period of time. Presumably he would add that any attempt to say precisely how long it is would be arbitrary. Ideally, of course, one would undertake theoretical studies as soon as one is mentally prepared to do so, and one would regularly exercise theoretical wisdom, without any significant period of decline or lengthy interruption, for as many years as human beings can reasonably expect. But Aristotle need not insist that perfect happiness be ascribed to a person only when we consider that maximal stretch of time. He holds that happiness can be lost and then recovered (I.10 1101a9–13), and so he is committed to the view that if we take some period of a person's life that is less than the whole, and less than the maximum that is feasible for human beings, it can still be a long enough period of time during which to call someone happy.[50] So, if the person in question was engaged in theoretical activity during that long period of time, he then achieved perfect happiness, even if he later lost it and failed to have as much perfect happiness as a human being can hope for.

All of this Aristotle takes for granted when he says, "As far as contemplation extends, thus far happiness extends, and those who have more contemplation also have more happiness . . ." (X.8 1178b28–30). He does not mean that if someone contemplates to some extent, however small, he is to that extent happy. Rather, he is assuming that contemplation must extend over a sufficiently long period of time before a person can be considered happy. His point is that once this period of time is long enough, then increases in contemplation constitute increases in happiness. If we take a temporal unit of sufficient length, we can say that the more contemplation contained by that unit, the more happiness one has within that period of time; and the longer these units continue, the greater the extent of one's happy life.

Because Aristotle does not say what the minimal units of time are during which one can be called *eudaimon*, he must admit that there will be

---

life, or a happy period of life, must be free of imperfection, a person must possess the good for a sizable period of time if we are to call him happy. This argument can be called conceptual, in that it does not rely on a particular conception of what happiness consists in. But it is not a report on how words are used. If it is argued, against Aristotle, that however long we possess the good, we possess it too briefly, and that therefore the length of our lives is necessarily imperfect, he can respond that happiness (including perfect happiness) must be a humanly attainable goal (I.6 1096b31–4). It would also be unreasonable to demand that happiness be attributed only to those who have achieved the good for the maximum period of time possible for a human being. For we do not know what that period of time is; and when someone lives longer than any human being has hitherto, we are not tempted to infer that no one who lived earlier was happy or perfectly happy.

[50] Contrast *EE* 1219b5–8 and *MM* 1185a5.

cases in which it is unclear whether we should say that someone was or is happy. This question will in some cases admit of no determinate answer, even when we know all the facts about someone's activities. But this degree of indeterminacy is not a serious flaw in his theory, for there will be many other cases in which he can say with complete confidence that a person is leading a happy life, and other cases in which he can confidently deny this.

A further point should be noticed: It can happen that a life containing no contemplation is more desirable than a life that contains some small amount of this activity. Compare A, a philosopher who dies soon after he begins exercising theoretical wisdom, and B, an outstanding political leader who has exercised practical wisdom throughout his adult life and has suffered no major misfortunes. The first life has no happiness, perfect or imperfect, whereas the second has a long span of secondary happiness. The second must be happier than the first, since it is happy and the first is not. But this fact hardly undermines Aristotle's defense of the philosophical life. In deciding which of the two lives one should lead, one must be guided by one's knowledge of special circumstances, and not simply by general considerations that favor the philosophical life. If one foresees that a philosophical career would be cut short in its infancy, and that a political career offers brighter prospects, then one's choice becomes obvious, despite the superiority of contemplation.

Suppose, however, that one's alternatives (a lengthy political career versus a briefer philosophical career) are not quite so stark: one must now choose between ten years as a philosopher and thirty years as a statesman. If we assume that one can call a person happy over a period of ten years, then the two alternatives here are (a) a shorter amount of perfect happiness and (b) a longer period of secondary happiness. Were Aristotle to say that (b) is better than (a), then he would have to face further questions: what if it were a choice between ten philosophical years and twenty-nine political years? what if . . . ? If Aristotle begins by saying that (b) is better than (a), he will eventually want to give the opposite answer, as the questions proceed, but there will be no reason to reverse himself at one point rather than another. Perhaps he is well advised to say that (a) is better than (b), and that this holds true whenever one's philosophical career is sufficiently long to be called a happy period of one's life. His position would be that quality is more important than quantity, so long as the quality is not too short-lived. Just as a short period of great pleasure is more desirable than a longer period of inferior pleasure (IX.8 1169a22–5), so a period of perfect happiness is better than a longer term of secondary happiness.

In certain hypothetical situations Aristotle gives no clear advice about what kind of life to lead. He cannot say with any precision what the minimal temporal unit of happiness is, but in some cases this is what one would have to know in order to make the proper decision about which career to pursue. His position, as I have described it, is that in some cases quality should be sacrificed for quantity: when the amount of contemplation is too small, one should pursue a political career instead. But when the quantity is above a certain threshold, then one should lead a philosophical life, even if it is shorter than the political life. One can say that one day does not make for happiness, and that a period of ten years can be happy; but there will be a sizable gray area in which one will not be able to say which career should be chosen.

I do not think this is a serious problem for Aristotle, for in most cases his readers have no reason to suppose that a philosophical life will be especially short, or shorter than a political life. If anything, it was the political life that was fraught with danger, as Plato reminds us in the *Apology* (31d6–32a3). Barring special circumstances, the choice between the philosophical and the political lives should be made on the basis of the differing merits of philosophical and political activity. If one does not owe it to others to lead a political life, and if there is no reason to believe that a philosophical career would be cut short in its infancy, then one should make contemplation one's ultimate end. And although there is no formula for deciding when one should give up some amount of philosophical activity in order to benefit others, Aristotle does tell us precisely how we should spend our time when the time is right to spend it on ourselves: the more we contemplate, the better off we are.

1.18. A Second Indeterminacy

I now would like to suggest that Aristotle's conception of happiness is indeterminate in another way, closely related to the one just discussed. Suppose we look at someone's life over a long stretch of time, from early adulthood until old age, for example. At some time during that period, he acquires both practical and theoretical wisdom. But then, soon afterward, he develops a sleeping sickness and is largely inactive, with only a few hours of normal activity here and there. For brief periods he activates the virtues of his rational soul, but then he soon lapses back into a state of passivity.

This thought experiment is not too distant from one Aristotle himself proposes. In *NE* I.5, he considers the thesis that happiness consists in virtue, and rejects it for the following reason: "It seems possible to have virtue even when one is asleep or inactive throughout one's life, and in addition to these [cases, it seems possible to have virtue while] suffering evil and being unfortunate in the greatest of ways. No one would consider such a life happy, unless he were going all out to defend a thesis"

(1095b32–1096a2). The person in my example is not asleep or inactive throughout the whole of his life, but he is quite close to that condition. And the question I would like to ask about him is this: Should Aristotle say that his life is happy?

I think the answer is clearly no. The individual I am thinking of engages in no more virtuous activity over the course of a lifetime than does someone who acts virtuously for the better part of a day or two and then dies. As we have seen, Aristotle thinks that this activity must go on for more than a day or a short amount of time before it constitutes happiness. For this reason alone, he ought to say that when that same amount of virtuous activity is divided into small segments and distributed here and there over the course of a whole life, the individual is still not happy. It is hard to see how the person whose virtuous activity is scattered over the course of a lifelong sleeping sickness is better off than someone who dies after just a few full days of virtuous activity. Furthermore, Aristotle explicitly says that if one is asleep or inactive throughout one's life, one cannot be considered happy. It should not matter whether this inactivity is total and uninterrupted or whether it is nearly so.

Surely Aristotle's point is that there must be a good deal of virtuous activity over a long stretch of time if that activity is to constitute happiness. But it is impossible to say how much of that activity there must be during that period of time. This is a second form of indeterminacy, though it is similar to the one we observed in the previous section. There, we realized that when we ask whether or not someone is happy, we must look at his life over a long stretch of time—how long, we cannot say. Now, the point is that even after one picks out a period of time that is clearly long enough, there is a further indeterminacy, in that the person must, during that time, engage in virtuous activity with some regularity and frequency—how much, we again cannot say.

Important though it is to recognize this second gray area, we should remember that it does not undermine Aristotle's conception of happiness. It simply means that there may be cases in which it is arbitrary to say or deny that someone is happy, even though we know all the relevant facts about his life, and even though he has lived for a long period of time. In spite of this indeterminacy, it is possible to recognize clear cases when they occur, and we know exactly what to strive for when we want to do ourselves the most good. Some people spend as much time on philosophy as ideal circumstances allow, and these are Aristotle's clearest cases of happy lives; similarly, some people are fully devoted to and occupied with politics, and they count as exemplars of a secondary form of happiness. The greater the distance between a life and these two ideals, the less happiness (perfect or secondary) it has, and eventually it becomes too remote from either ideal to be called happy at all. It does not matter that there is no precise cutoff point; what matters is that we know what to strive for. By contrast, suppose Aristotle were saying that a life can be unhappy because it contains too much contemplation, but did not tell us how this excess can be recognized. In the absence of this information, we would not know how to lead the most important part of our lives: we would not know whether the amount of time we are spending on philosophy is too much, too little, or just enough.

1.19. MORE ON CONTEMPLATION

We have been discussing the connection Aristotle makes between happiness and contemplation, but more should be said now about what contemplation actually is. I noted in 1.1 that to contemplate is to bring to mind the truths of some theoretical discipline. It is not the activity of searching for the truth within some field, but rather a process of reflection on a system of truths already discovered. This activity, as Aristotle points out in X.7, may be carried on by a person who is at the moment not in the presence of others (1177a32–3), but he nowhere suggests that it requires isolation. We should not be misled by the connotations of our term "contemplation" into thinking that Aristotle's *theōria* is necessarily a pensive and meditative withdrawal from interaction with others. Rather, *theōria* is an activity that goes on whenever one brings certain truths to mind: it occurs not only when one silently reflects, but also when one lectures or writes about a certain subject, when one reads a book, when one listens to a book being read, or when one hears someone presenting a lecture. The teacher who is preparing lectures and notes, or who is orally presenting a subject to students and colleagues, is consciously considering truths that he has already come to understand, and so he is contemplating.[51]

Although anyone who is actively reflecting on any proposition, whatever its content, may be loosely said to be engaged in *theōria* with respect to that proposition, Aristotle clearly has something more exalted in mind in X.7–8. I take him to be singling out a state of mind that is the highest a human being can strive for: it is the activation of the understanding one has achieved when one has acquired *sophia*, theoretical wisdom. And we are told in Book VI of the *NE* that to have this virtue is to have understanding of the highest objects of the universe (1141a20, b3). The fact that the philosopher contemplates truths about these most knowable objects constitutes part of Aristotle's case in X.7 for the superiority of this con-

[51] Note that we would not say that someone lecturing on a given subject is at that time studying the subject. But he is engaged in *theōria*. Conversely, someone who is first learning a given subject *is* studying it, but he is not yet engaged in *theōria*.

templative activity to any other (1177a20–21). The highest object of
knowledge, he thinks, is the unmoved mover, and so he is saying in X.7–
8 that the ultimate end for human beings is to activate their understanding
of this foremost cause of the universe.[52]

In *Metaphysics* VI.1, Aristotle distinguishes theoretical disciplines from
those that are practical and productive (1025b25), and he recognizes three
kinds of theoretical disciplines: mathematics, physics, and (foremost
among them) theology (1026a18–19), which he also calls "first philosophy" (a30). What would he say about someone who has mastered only
one or both of the two lesser kinds of theoretical subjects, mathematics
and physics? More precisely, if the mathematician and the student of nature have the ultimate end of contemplating the truths of their subjects,
and they frequently engage in this activity over a long period of time,
would Aristotle say that they are leading happy lives? Or would he deny
that they are happy, on the grounds that they fail to live up to either of
the two models presented in X.7–8? They do not make moral activity
their ultimate end, and so they lack secondary happiness; and they never
strictly speaking activate the virtue of theoretical wisdom, since they do
not have an understanding of the most knowable object of the universe.
Would these theorists have been better off had they never entered upon
an intellectual career, and had become political leaders instead?

That seems an implausible way to read Aristotle, for every argument
that he gives for the superiority of first philosophy to moral activity can
also be used to show that lesser theoretical activities are superior to politics.[53] (a) Although the objects studied by mathematicians and natural
philosophers are not the most knowable there are,[54] these disciplines are
like first philosophy in that they study what is eternal and cannot be
otherwise,[55] and they thereby achieve a precision unattainable in practical
thinking. (b) The study of mathematical or physical subjects can be as
continuous as the study of the first cause. (c) Though nothing can be as
pleasant as the study of the highest causes, Aristotle himself is enthusiastic
about the pleasures to be derived from the study of nature.[56] (d) Like first

[52] See *EE* VIII.3 1249b17: the "contemplation of the god" is the finest boundary between
too many and too few natural goods. I take "the god" to refer to the unmoved mover, and
not, as some have suggested, human reason. See Woods, *Aristotle's Eudemian Ethics, Books
I, II, and VIII*, pp. 195–8, for an account of this controversy; see also Kenny, *The Aristotelian
Ethics*, pp. 174–7. See *Met.* I.2 (especially 982a23–b10, 983a5–11) for the claim that the highest form of knowledge is a divine science that studies god.

[53] The arguments I consider here are presented at (a) 1177a20–21, (b) a21–2, (c) a22–7, (d)
a27–b1, (e) b1–4, and (f) 1178b7–32.

[54] See *Met.* I.2 982a25–b10, 983a5–11, VI.1 1026a18–23.

[55] These are necessary properties of any theoretical discipline: see *NE* VI.3 1139b19–23.

[56] See *De Part An.* I.5 644b31–645a10: studying the eternal motions of the spheres pro-

philosophy, mathematics and natural philosophy can be studied even when one is by oneself. (e) These lesser disciplines are unlike practical studies in that they are loved merely for themselves, and for no further reason. (f) God exercises theoretical wisdom; similarly, the mathematician and natural philosopher have a lower kind of theoretical wisdom, whereas the politician has no theoretical wisdom. Since human happiness is ranked in terms of its similarity to the happiness of gods, one is better off being a lesser theoretician than someone who engages in no theoretical activity at all.[57]

Aristotle would therefore be in a weak position were he to insist that only those who engage in first philosophy or politics are happy. The arguments of X.7–8 are best interpreted as advancing an ideal of happiness from which one may depart to a certain degree and in various ways, without failing to be happy. The departure that Aristotle is explicitly concerned with is the political life. For he and his contemporaries are most interested in the question whether they should try to do the best they can in the realm of theory or in the realm of practice. By comparison, the question of which theoretical subjects to take up is a side issue. If one has decided in favor of the life in accordance with understanding, then of course one should want to study those subjects that are most important. Those who, for whatever reason, are restricted to the lesser theoretical disciplines are not necessarily deprived of happiness; rather, they have something less than perfect happiness, though something more than the secondary happiness of the politician. We saw earlier (1.11) that although X.7–8 compares two lives, one devoted to philosophy and the other to politics, this should not be taken to mean that a mixed life—that of a statesman and philosopher—cannot be happy. What we have now added is that the range of options is wider still, since a happy life can have something less than the highest form of theoretical understanding as its ultimate end.

The best activity for a human being is the contemplation of what is divine, but we should not take Aristotle to be saying that in the ideal human life one will always be thinking about the highest cause whenever one thinks about theoretical matters. Though mathematics and natural philosophy are lesser disciplines, that does not mean that they can or should be avoided by someone who wants to lead the best life. In order to achieve an understanding of the highest causes, it may be useful or even essential to learn these other subjects. And even after one has achieved the highest understanding, one is vulnerable to the imperfection that is part

---

vides us with greater pleasure than examining plants and animals, but the latter subject also provides extraordinary pleasures.

[57] Note the claim of *Met.* VI.1 1026a22–3 that *any* theoretical science is more choiceworthy than a practical or productive discipline.

of the human condition: we eventually tire of even the greatest pleasures, and seek variation (VII.14 1154b20–31). So the philosopher in contact with the divine will need a change from even this subject, and will then take delight, as Aristotle did, in lesser theoretical disciplines.[58]

1.20. FURTHER PROBLEMS

We have examined only a small portion of X.7–8, and have not fully considered the question of what else a philosophical life should contain, besides theoretical activity. To know what such a life is like, and why Aristotle thinks it the best available to human beings, we need to look at his other arguments on behalf of contemplation. And in examining these other portions of X.7–8, we must consider the question with which we began: can this segment of the NE be read in a way that coheres with the rest of Aristotle's practical philosophy? To settle this question, we must of course go beyond a discussion of these chapters, and consider his lengthier and more fundamental treatment of happiness in Book I. I have been assuming that he there inaugurates a search for a single ultimate end of human life, and that he locates it in some kind of virtuous activity; his defense of the philosophical life, and his claim that the political life can achieve a secondary form of happiness, build on the conception of happiness developed in Book I. This way of reading Book I and connecting it with Book X requires much more elaboration and defense.

However, before developing my reading of X.7–8 any further, and before moving on to Book I, we must come to terms with the fundamental question of whether Aristotle is an egoist. I have frequently made use of the assumption that he is not, and this nonegoistic interpretation is central to my way of connecting Books I and X. I take Aristotle to be saying that the more contemplation a life contains (above a certain threshold) the better a life it is; but if this is combined with the egoistic claim that one should always maximize one's own good, then he is saying, at least in X.7–8, that each of us should maximize the amount of time we spend

---

[58] Although the best objects to contemplate are divine, this does not mean that "a man is in the fullest sense happy *only when* he is meditating . . . on theological or astronomical propositions and their proofs," as Hardie says (*Aristotle's Ethical Theory*, pp. 337–8, emphasis added). For Aristotle does not think that we are perfectly happy only when we are actually contemplating; for example, we continue to be just as happy when we sleep. The ultimate end of human life is to engage in the highest study over a long period of time; but happiness (perfect or not) is not something that stops and starts each time virtuous activity stops and starts. And so, when someone periodically tires of thinking about divine objects, and thinks about perishable lives instead, this does not mean that he is less than perfectly happy. In fact, by pursuing these lesser branches of knowledge rather than doing something nontheoretical, he more closely approximates divine life: a greater amount of time is devoted to contemplating theoretical truths.

contemplating, come what may for others. And it is hard to see how anyone who follows this rule can have the qualities that Aristotle recommends to his readers as ethical virtues. How can I be fair to my parents, and others who have helped me in the past, if I am to maximize my own happiness, and if this is achieved by contemplating as much as possible? So it seems to me that we cannot (a) read X.7–8 in the way I advocate, (b) interpret Aristotle as an egoist, and (c) maintain the unity of the *NE*. If I want (a) and (c), I must reject (b). And the reader may rightly ask to see the case against egoism before giving further consideration to my interpretation of Books I and X. I therefore turn next to the question of whether Aristotle is an egoist.

CHAPTER TWO

_____

Self and Others

2.1. Varieties of Egoism

Many different doctrines can properly be called egoistic, so our first task must be to draw some distinctions. To begin with, there is a pure form of egoism, which holds that we should attach no independent weight to the good of others. All legitimate reasons for actions, according to pure egoism, must take this form: this act will maximize my own good. And we are to pursue this policy whatever the consequences may be for others. This of course allows one to engage in activities that benefit others, for it may be that treating others well (certain others, at any rate) is the most efficient way to maximize one's own well-being. But the pure egoist says that even when one rightly promotes the good of others, doing so has merely instrumental value, for one is never to take the well-being of others as an independent reason for action. All of one's relationships with others are to be instrumental: if one benefits them at all, one should do so only as a means to one's own optimal good.[1]

I believe that pure egoism is incompatible with the ideal of human relationships that Aristotle puts forward in his discussion of friendship. When he discusses this topic in Books VIII–IX of the *NE*, he frequently

_____

[1] Broad, "Self and Others," p. 266, defines "the extreme form of Ethical Egoism" as follows: "Each person is under a direct obligation to benefit himself as such. He is under no *direct* obligation to benefit any other person, though he will be under an indirect obligation to do this so far and only so far as that is the most efficient means available to him for benefiting himself. He is forbidden to benefit another person, if doing so will in the long run be detrimental to himself." Similarly, Frankena, *Ethics*, p. 18, takes egoism to be saying that "an individual's one and only basic obligation is to promote for himself the greatest possible balance of good over evil." Brandt, *A Theory of the Good and the Right*, p. 267, treats egoism as the doctrine that "any person ought to maximize his own welfare," and adds, p. 270: "the egoist code generally advises one to seek one's own welfare even at catastrophic cost to others." Williams, "Egoism and Altruism," p. 251, takes egoism to be "the position of an amoralist who . . . is concerned solely with his own interests." By contrast, a defender of altruism endorses "a general disposition to regard the interests of others, merely as such, as making some claim on one, and in particular, as implying the possibility of limiting one's own projects" (p. 250). Notice that pure egoism does not require us to be emotionally unaffected by the good and bad fortune of others, for such events may indirectly influence our own well-being. For example, if the good consists in health, then the pure egoist will be upset when his fellow workers are sick, because this increases the probability that he will get sick too. Similarly, if the good is contemplation, then the pure egoist will be upset at the loss of colleagues upon whom he relies for philosophical stimulation.

says that in a perfect friendship each individual wishes for and acts for the good of the other person *for the sake of that other person*.[2] Now, he does not tell us what it is to act for the sake of another, but I see no way to understand that notion other than this: when one acts for the sake of another, one is not benefiting him merely as a means to some further goal. Instead, one is taking the good of that person as something that by itself provides a reason for action.[3] And pure egoism forbids this.

Notice that this construal of "for the sake of another" leaves open the possibility of complex motivation: one may undertake an act both because it benefits oneself (one does it for one's own sake) and because it benefits someone else (one also does it for his sake). In these complex cases, one has two independent reasons for action: one is not benefiting the other person merely as a means to one's own good, but instead the good of the other person provides a further reason for action, beyond the self-interested reason one already has. And one might regard the self-interested reason as having greater weight than the "altruistic" reason; even so, one would be acting in part for the sake of the other, if the good of the other person is by itself an independent reason for acting. So to deny that Aristotle is a pure egoist is not yet to say anything about how much weight he thinks we should attach to the well-being of others, in comparison with our own happiness.[4] It merely means that he does not advocate a purely instrumental way of treating all others.

Now, even if it is conceded that Aristotle rejects pure egoism in *NE* VIII–IX, it might be thought that he reverses himself, and endorses this form of egoism, when he advocates the philosophical life in X.7–8. Or it might even be claimed that his treatment of friendship within VIII–IX is internally inconsistent. For example, he argues in IX.9 that a happy person needs friends, and this might be taken to mean that the only reason we should benefit others is that doing so will promote our own happiness. So we might conclude that parts of Aristotle's discussion of friendship are motivated by pure egoism, even though other parts are inconsistent with that doctrine. I will try to show that there is no such inconsistency in the *NE*. In this chapter, I will argue that Aristotle's emphasis on benefiting others for their sake is entirely consistent with everything else we find in his treatment of friendship. And as we will see in Chapter 3, nothing in X.7–8 abandons the conception of ideal human relationships that Aristotle proposes in VIII–IX.

There are two other kinds of egoism that I will discuss, besides pure egoism, and I will argue that neither captures Aristotle's thinking. But it

---

[2] See, for example, 1155b31, 1156b9–10, 1166a2–4.

[3] Here I follow Cooper, "Aristotle on Friendship," p. 334 n. 6, points (1) and (2).

[4] Again I follow Cooper, ibid., points (3)–(5).

will be easier to define these impure forms of egoism if I first call attention to two features of my own nonegoistic interpretation.

First, as I read Aristotle, he recognizes that the good of one person can conflict with that of others. To be more precise, let us say that such interpersonal conflicts occur when the act that maximizes A's good has consequences that prevent B from achieving as much good as he can. Conflicts of interest include those situations in which one person, A, in order to achieve his greatest good, needs the help of another, B, and yet if that help is given, then B cannot achieve his greatest good. To take our familiar examples: a son might have to give up a certain amount of time contemplating in order to benefit his father; or the son who has been specially trained might have to forgo philosophical activity altogether in order to benefit his community. In both cases, others need the son's help if they are to maximize their good, and yet if that help is given, then the son cannot maximize his good. These are not examples that Aristotle himself gives, of course. They are my ways of illustrating how a conflict of interest can come about in his system. Other examples, based on situations that Aristotle himself describes, will be given later. I will try to show that his moral philosophy allows for conflicts of interest, and that he seeks solutions to some of them.

This brings me to the second feature of my interpretation: Aristotle rejects the view that when conflicts arise, neither person should give way to the other. That is, he does not endorse the position that each should try to maximize his own good, come what may for others. For that will not be a just resolution of the conflict. Justice sometimes requires giving up a certain amount of a certain good, in order that others may also have their fair share of it. That does not provide us with a decision procedure for resolving conflicts, because there is no formula, applicable to all situations, for deciding what a just solution to a conflict is. Sometimes one person should give way to another, and sometimes both should give way to some extent. But Aristotle would have no sympathy for the view that whenever such conflicts occur, each should maximize his own good, come what may for others. Nor does he endorse other simplistic ways of resolving conflicts: for example, choosing whichever act maximizes the total amount of contemplative activity in the world (or in one's political community). Contemplation is that for the sake of which one should always be acting, but that does not mean that one is always to maximize one's own theoretical activity or the total amount of it. I will return to this point in 2.2.

Now that we have reviewed these two features of my interpretation, we are in a position to define two further forms of egoism. Each tells us to maximize our own good, and in this respect they are akin to pure egoism. Furthermore, although both allow the good of others to provide an independent reason for action (thus differing from pure egoism), each takes self-interested reasons for action to have greater weight than other-regarding reasons. In other words, they hold that one's own good is a more important reason for action than the good of others. Now, one of these additional forms of egoism, which I will call "combative" egoism, accepts the existence of conflicts of interest, and it says that when they occur, each person should try to maximize his own good, come what may for others. The second, which I will call "benign" egoism, denies that the good of one person can conflict with that of another. It tells us to maximize our own good, and it takes self-interest to be the best kind of reason for action. But it holds that pursuing one's optimal good, and attaching greatest weight to self-interested considerations, will not prevent others from maximizing their good. And so, benign egoism (unlike combative or pure egoism) cannot be characterized as the doctrine that we should pursue our own good, *come what may for others*. That phrase suggests a willingness to harm others, and the benign egoist insists that no one will be worse off if we maximize our own good and assign priority to self-interested reasons.[5]

All three forms of egoism—pure, combative, and benign—hold that we should maximize our own good; and all three agree that less weight should be attached to the good of others than to our own. But the two impure forms allow us to consider the good of others for their sake, and this can make a practical difference. For there may be no one act that is best for me; I may instead be faced with a situation in which there are a number of alternatives that are tied for best (or least bad), from my point of view. (These include circumstances in which nothing I can now do would benefit myself.) In these situations, pure egoism does not allow me to consider the good I might be able to do for others and decide among my alternatives by choosing the one that is best for those others. For it assigns the good of others no independent weight, and tells us to consider their good only when this is a means of optimizing our own well-being. By contrast, the impure forms of egoism allow us to break the tie among equally self-interested alternatives by choosing the one that is best for others. For both combative and benign egoism say that in order to take full account of the reasons we have for action, we must consider how we can promote the well-being of others, and not merely our own.

[5] Note that the impure forms of egoism accept one part of Williams's characterization of altruism, but not the other (see note 1 above). They recognize that the "interests of others, merely as such, . . . mak[e] some claim on one," but they do not accept "the possibility of limiting one's own projects." Note too Parfit's characterization of self-interest theories that are not "purely selfish": "in some cases, what will be better for me will be worse for those I love. I am self-interested if, in all these cases, I do what will be better for me" (*Reasons and Persons*, p. 5).

I have said that all three forms of egoism accept the thesis that one should maximize one's own good; but we should be careful not to label someone an egoist merely because he urges such maximization. Suppose, for example, that a philosopher begins with the idea that each person should maximize the total amount of good in the world. He then argues, on the basis of certain empirical claims, that the most effective way to bring this about over the long run is to concentrate solely on one's own good, or to give this precedence over the good of others. This philosopher is not an egoist, even though he thinks that each person should maximize his own good. For the normative theory on which he relies is not egoism: according to his theory, one's own good is just one small ingredient of the ultimate end, and each person is to concentrate solely or primarily on himself simply because this specialization of function is deemed the most effective way to promote human welfare in general. I believe that Aristotle rejects the formula "maximize your own good," but it is important to remember that egoism consists not merely in accepting this formula, but also in assigning it a basic and not a merely instrumental role in one's moral philosophy. The egoist assigns priority to the self in its relations to others, not as a matter of strategy, but because self-regarding reasons are either the best or the only kind of reason there is. Someone who thinks that the well-being of another provides just as good a reason for action as self-interested reasons is not properly called an egoist.[6]

To determine whether Aristotle is a combative or benign egoist, or no egoist at all, we will of course have to see whether he believes that one person's pursuit of his greatest good can ever leave others worse off in their pursuit of their maximal good. But I see no way to determine whether the good of individuals can conflict, according to Aristotle, unless we attribute to him some view about what the good is. And so I will

[6] However, it should be mentioned that the literature on this subject sometimes contains or implies looser conceptions of egoism than the ones I discuss here. For example, following Broad, we might take a desire to be egoistic if it is "self-referential," that is, if it is directed at the well-being of a person or group that bears a special relation to oneself. See "Egoism as a Theory of Human Motives," p. 250. In this sense, a desire for the happiness of one's own child, or one's fellow citizens, would be egoistic. And in this spirit, we could define a further form of egoism, which holds that one's actions should promote either one's own good or that of a member of one's own family or community. I am not denying that Aristotle is an egoist in this sense, but I question the value of interpreting egoism so broadly. For in this sense, egoism allows one to devote oneself to the general improvement of the human race (one's own species), even at great cost to oneself. (A similar point is made by Kavka, *Hobbesian Moral and Political Theory*, pp. 43–4.) It should be noted that Broad speaks of self-referential desires as "egoistic" only because he wants to challenge egoism (as a theory of human motives) even in its broadest form. He is not arguing that we should call the love parents have for their children "egoistic" because it is their own children that they love.

be assuming that the interpretation I began to defend in Chapter 1 is correct: Aristotle believes that both the philosophical and the political lives are happy. The first life has the ultimate end of contemplation; the second, moral activity. In each life, the more one engages in the activity that constitutes the ultimate end, the better off one is.[7]

Now, if we accept this interpretation, then it becomes hard to believe that Aristotle denied or ignored the possibility that maximizing one's own good would sometimes prevent others from maximizing theirs. If I engage in the greatest possible amount of philosophical activity, then surely I will on occasion fail to give others the help they need if they are to maximize their own good. But we will see in this chapter that conflicts of interest can occur in Aristotle's system even when we set aside his belief that contemplation is our highest good and ultimate end. For he holds that political activity is a good that equal persons must divide fairly among themselves; statesmen must not try to maximize the extent to which they engage in this second-best activity, for in doing so they would unfairly deprive others of their share of the good. In political life, as in intellectual life, Aristotle rejects the view that one should in all circumstances seek the best for oneself, and that doing so can never harm others. And so he is neither a combative nor a benign egoist: he recognizes the possibility of conflict, and does not always assign self-interested reasons greater weight than altruistic reasons. Instead, he thinks that I should accept equal relations with others, and limit my pursuit of the good, precisely because they are my equals and have as much claim on the good as I do.

The three versions of egoism that I have been discussing are all forms of "ethical egoism," a doctrine that is often distinguished from "psychological egoism."[8] Ethical egoism is a normative thesis, for it tells us how we should act: each is to maximize his own good. Psychological egoism, as its name implies, is a descriptive thesis about how human beings actu-

---

[7] I shall also assume that each person's happiness consists solely in virtuous activity of his own soul. My happiness consists in that one good, and not in a composite of virtuous activity, honor, pleasure, friends, and so on. It is sometimes said that although Aristotle is an egoist, his egoism is not as objectionable as it might seem, since each person's happiness is inclusive of all intrinsic goods, and friends are among those goods. See Irwin's translation, pp. xviii, 304, 372. In *Plato's Moral Theory*, Irwin attributes to Plato and Aristotle the view that other people's good is a component of the agent's own good. See p. 255; cf. his comment on *NE* 1169a35–b1 in his translation, p. 371. In 2.19, I argue that although Aristotle thinks that certain goods possessed by your children and friends are your goods as well, he does not think that your happiness consists in those goods.

[8] The distinction is present in Sidgwick, *The Methods of Ethics*, p. 40, although he expresses it as a contrast between ethical and psychological hedonism. See too Broad, "Self and Others," pp. 267, 269; Frankena, *Ethics*, p. 21; Brandt, *Ethical Theory*, pp. 371–2.

ally think and behave: it says that we cannot act except in a way that we think will maximize our own good. Corresponding to the normative thesis I have called pure egoism, there is the psychological claim that human beings cannot take an interest in the well-being of others for the sake of those others. Similarly, it might be claimed that we cannot avoid acting in the way that combative egoism prescribes: we must inevitably prefer our own greatest good, when this conflicts with that of others. Or even if such conflicts never occur, it might be thought that we cannot help attaching greater weight to our own good than to that of others. I will set aside these psychological theses, and concentrate entirely on the question whether Aristotle is an "ethical" egoist, in any of its three varieties. If I can show that, in his opinion, we should sometimes give up some of our own happiness for the sake of others, then it will hardly be tempting to attribute to him the view that we are incapable of making this sacrifice. He thinks that under proper conditions we are capable of ethical activity, and if such activity sometimes requires limiting one's pursuit of the highest good, then he thinks that such self-restraint is within our capacities.[9]

I should emphasize that egoism, as I construe it, is a doctrine that enjoins us to give priority to our own well-being by choosing the act that *maximizes* our good.[10] (Of course, if two or more alternatives are tied for best, then egoism says that we must choose from among this class.) It is therefore possible to deny that Aristotle is an egoist, but at the same time to take him to be saying that one should always promote one's good *to some extent*.[11] For he might believe that every act undertaken by an ideal

[9] D. J. Allan appears to read Aristotle as a psychological egoist: "Every point confirms the impression that Aristotle does not think it psychologically possible for a man to choose otherwise than in his own interest" (*The Philosophy of Aristotle*, p. 138). But notice that this statement says nothing about *maximization*. So, read strictly, Allan might be taking Aristotle to believe that everyone must choose an act that promotes his own interest *to some extent*. But I doubt that this is what he has in mind, for he goes on to say that Aristotle "is seeking . . . to say what happens when men *appear* to subordinate their interest to that of another" (his emphasis). This implies that no one can accept less happiness for himself in order to promote the well-being of others. Each of us must try to obtain as much happiness for himself as possible. For the distinction between maximizing and nonmaximizing versions of psychological egoism, see Kavka, *Hobbesian Moral and Political Theory*, pp. 38–9, 64–5. The nonmaximizing egoist holds that "the ultimate aim of every human action is to obtain some personal benefit for the agent" (p. 39).

[10] This feature of egoism is apparent in the definitions of Brandt and Frankena, cited in note 1 above.

[11] Irwin does not formulate egoism as a doctrine that requires the maximization of one's own good. Instead, he attributes to Plato and Aristotle a type of egoism he calls "moral egocentrism," which holds that "all virtue must contribute to some end valued by the agent as part of his own good" (*Plato's Moral Theory*, p. 255). But elsewhere he does seem to attribute a maximizing version of egoism to Aristotle: "the virtuous friend never 'sacrifices himself,' if that implies sacrifice of his own interests to another's" (translation, p. 371, note

agent—someone who fully understands what happiness is and how it is
achieved—will be in that agent's interest, though not necessarily in his
maximal interest. And in fact I think that this is Aristotle's view. He holds
that every virtuous act—whether it is theoretical or practical—is to some
extent desirable for the virtuous agent. For example, consider the son
who decides to give up some time contemplating in order to help his
ailing father. Though he loses some amount of happiness, he nonetheless
exercises ethical virtue, and this kind of activity is a great—though not
the greatest—good *for the agent*. So the son's act is good not only for his
father, but for himself as well.[12] It is not the act that brings him the greatest amount of good among the alternatives available, and it is not an act
that makes his life a happier one. Even so, in exercising ethical virtue, he
engages in an activity that is far better for himself than any other activity
except for those that are theoretical. When one gives up theoretical activity to undertake ethically virtuous activities, one is engaged in a better
course of action than one would be pursuing had one chosen a nonrational
ultimate end (physical pleasure, wealth, and so on).[13]

So, if egoism is the view that one should always do something that is
good from one's own point of view, then I would agree that Aristotle is
an egoist. His kind of egoism would hold that, when one decides which
kind of virtuous activity one should undertake at any given time, one
should not be guided by the principle that one's own good must be *maximized*. Instead, one should at times make a sacrifice, and do something
that is less good from one's own point of view, so that others may attain
their highest good, or at least come close to that goal. Of course, a view
that calls upon us to sacrifice our own good to some extent is not usually
called egoism. But the issue is not what word to use when we describe
Aristotle's theory, but what position to attribute to him. My aim is to
show that whether we call him an egoist or not, he cannot be accurately

---

to 1169a35–b1). This suggests that one should never, for the sake of another, pursue less
good for oneself than one might achieve.

[12] In fact, Aristotle can point out that the kind of act performed by the son is itself a form
of happiness; for secondary happiness consists in ethical activity. The son still loses on balance, since he gives up some degree of perfect happiness and replaces it with an activity that
constitutes secondary happiness. But he would lose still more if he had to give up some
degree of contemplation and replace it with a good that did not constitute perfect or secondary happiness.

[13] Recall a point made at the end of 1.19: Though thinking about the highest causes is the
ultimate end of the best life, one may not always be able to engage in this activity, and in
that case one most closely approximates the highest end by studying lesser beings. Similarly, if one must engage in practical rather than theoretical activity because of one's debt to
others, one can still approximate one's ultimate end to some extent by exercising the moral
excellences. One is doing what is good, though not best, for oneself; and one chooses this
lesser good because one wants to benefit others for their sake.

characterized as an egoist of the sort I have defined—pure, combative, or benign.[14] Taking him to be a maximizing egoist does not do justice to the complexity of his thinking about appropriate human relations.[15]

2.2. EGOISM AND INTELLECTUALISM

On my reading, Aristotle thinks that human beings, under certain conditions, develop a desire to promote the happiness of certain other human beings. In doing so, we do not treat the well-being of others as a mere means to our own; rather, we seek their happiness for their sake. At times, we rightly give priority to the well-being of others, and accept less happiness for ourselves than we might have had. Furthermore, I take Aristotle to assume that, once we have arrived at a certain conception of happiness, we should appeal to that same conception whether we are aiming at our own maximal good or that of another. And of course, on my interpretation, the good for the sake of which one should always be acting—if one fully understands the human good—is contemplation. When we do what is best for ourselves, we are contemplating, or we are in some way promoting our own theoretical activity; and when we do what is best for others, we are helping them engage in this same activity.

[14] There is another form of egoism that could be attributed to Aristotle: Just as rule-utilitarianism tells us to act in accordance with an ideal set of rules, that is, the set that maximizes the *general* good, so Aristotle might hold that we are to act in accordance with an ideal set of qualities, that is, the set that maximizes the *agent's* good. He would then be a second-order egoist: one is to act in a way that expresses the qualities that are best for oneself; and yet, it might be claimed, those qualities will not always call upon one to choose the action that maximizes one's own good. I do not regard this as a promising suggestion, for I take Aristotle to agree that in certain circumstances I should *not* develop the virtue that is best for me—theoretical wisdom—even though doing so would clearly be in my best interest. (Recall the son who has been trained to lead a political life.)

[15] Contrast Hardie, *Aristotle's Ethical Theory*, p. 329: "I suggest that the morality of altruism and self-sacrifice is consistent with the doctrine of the inclusive end but not with the more determinate doctrine of the paramount end." In other words, Hardie thinks that Aristotle wavers between a conception of happiness as an all-inclusive composite and a conception that equates perfect happiness with contemplation. To the extent that the latter view is Aristotle's, he is unwilling to say that we should give up some of our good for the sake of others. Note too that according to Sidgwick, *The Methods of Ethics*, p. 92, all of the Greek moralists take it for granted that "a rational individual would make the pursuit of his own good his supreme aim." Though he has Aristotle, among others, in mind, it is not clear that he is talking about any of the maximizing versions of ethical egoism that I have discussed here. Something can be a "supreme aim" without being a value to be maximized. Sidgwick goes on to say that if the good is equated with *eudaimonia*, well-being, or self-realization, then the form of egoism which he attributes to the Greeks is one "into which almost any ethical system may be thrown, without modifying its essential characteristics" (p. 95). I find this difficult to evaluate, since it is unclear what to count as a modification of an ethical system's "essential characteristics."

This feature of my interpretation leads to an obvious objection, which can be illustrated by means of our usual example—the philosophical son who gives up some time contemplating in order to help his ailing father. If the father is not a theoretician, then how can the son be said to be acting for the sake of *anyone's* contemplation, when he acts in a way that lessens the total amount of philosophical activity he engages in over the course of his life? He is certainly not acting for the sake of his own contemplation, for that is a good he is sacrificing to some extent. At the same time, it is hard to see how he can be said to be acting for the sake of his father's philosophical activity. By hypothesis, his father is not a philosopher, and if he is restored to good health, he will not be engaged in any theoretical work. If the son is to act in a way that promotes some good for the father, then it seems that contemplation cannot be the good in question. And so, if Aristotle is saying that one should always act for the sake of contemplation, he seems committed to the thesis that one should always be trying to maximize one's own contemplation. He would then be an egoist after all, and it would be difficult to see how he could advise anyone to do the sorts of things normally expected of an ethical person. One could try to rescue him by making all sorts of *ad hoc* empirical assumptions on his behalf: for example, one could say that if the son does not help his father, then he will inherit less money, and as a result he will have less of the leisure necessary for the philosophical life. But trying to save Aristotle in this way would be a desperate maneuver.

To solve this problem, we need to be more careful about the notion of acting for the sake of a certain end. We assumed—wrongly, I think—that if the father is incapable of contemplation, then the good for the sake of which the son acts, when he helps his father, cannot be contemplation. And this assumption is guided by normal English usage: I would not say that I am acting for the sake of someone's happiness (for example) if I take that person to be incapable of happiness. But I suggest that Aristotle has a broader notion of what it is to act for the sake of a certain goal: he thinks that when we try to come as close as we can to achieving an end, then we are acting for the sake of that end, even if we rightly believe that it is beyond our grasp. In other words, if what one wants most for a person (oneself or another) is to provide him with good A, and if one instead promotes good B because he cannot achieve A, and B is the closest approximation to A that he can achieve, then one is acting for the sake of A. For the chain of reasoning that one will invoke to justify one's action will appeal ultimately to the value of A: one seeks B for this person because A would be best for him, and by having B he comes as close as he can to having A.

So, even if the father in our example is incapable of philosophical activity, the son can still appeal to the value of contemplation when he explains what he is aiming at in promoting his father's good. He can say that he is helping his father regain his health, because he wants him to engage in ethically virtuous activity once again. And when one fully understands what the human good is, one sees ethically virtuous activity not as perfect happiness itself but as the closest most people can come to having perfect happiness. To give a complete justification of his act, the son must recognize the supreme value of contemplation, and so he is ultimately acting for the sake of that end, even though his father can only lead a life that is an approximation of the human ideal.

Why do I think that, according to Aristotle, we can act for the sake of a certain goal even when we assume that we will not reach it? Let us begin with the fact that he attributes a desire for happiness to all adult human beings. "We all do everything else we do for the sake of this [happiness]" (I.12 1102a2–3). "One might say that we choose everything for the sake of something else, except for happiness; for it is [the] end" (X.6 1176b30–31). But Aristotle does not say that everyone takes himself to be leading a happy life. In fact, he points out that when some people are ill, they think that happiness consists in health; or, when they are poor, they identify happiness with wealth (I.4 1095a24–5). Similarly, a person can say that happiness consists in virtuous activity sufficiently equipped with external goods (I.10 1101a14–15), but that because of great misfortune he has not reached this goal, or that he once attained it but later lost it (I.10 1100b35–1101a13).

Obviously, a person who is not happy can ultimately aim at that end, in all that he does. He can think that although he is not happy now, he will eventually reach that goal. But it is also possible for someone to believe, with good reason, that he is not happy now and never will be. A poor person who equates happiness with wealth might realistically believe that he will never be rich; someone who is ill, and equates happiness with health, can be perfectly justified in thinking that he will never be well again. I see no reason to say that Aristotle must deny these obvious possibilities simply because he holds that all human beings, regardless of their situation, aim at happiness. For example, he can point out that even when an ill person takes health to be unattainable, he will nonetheless try to prevent his condition from deteriorating. In this sense, he might always be acting for the sake of health. He takes the human ideal to be physical flourishing, and although he regards that end as unattainable in his own case, he always acts with the ultimate end of preventing himself from becoming further removed from that ideal. All of his actions are guided by a certain conception of happiness, even though he takes happiness to be beyond his grasp.

Similarly, the virtuous person who has fallen into misfortune will continue to do what little he can to engage in virtuous activities, and he will do this not out of force of habit but because he has a certain conception of happiness and tries to approximate that condition. He still takes happiness to consist in virtuous activity, and his desire to do what he can to act virtuously need not be based on the expectation that someday he will recover his happiness. He continues to act virtuously, making the best of his bad situation, because if he did not, he would be even further removed from happiness than he presently is. A certain conception of happiness continues to guide his actions, and he always acts in light of that conception.

Let us now return to the son who gives up a certain amount of philosophical activity in order to help his ailing father. It is at first sight tempting to say that if the son is acting for the good of his father, then that good cannot consist in his father's contemplation, since his father does not engage in this activity. But I believe this temptation should be resisted. As we have seen, someone acts for the sake of a certain good when he tries to come as close as he can to winning that good for himself. Similarly, a person can be said to act for the sake of a certain goal when the act he performs for someone else is an attempt to bring that person as close as he can come to the achievement of that goal. For example, if I believe that happiness consists in health, and if I try to prevent my father from becoming even more ill, then I am acting for the sake of health—his health, not mine. My belief that happiness consists in health does not commit me to the policy of maximizing my own possession of this good. To believe that happiness consists in health is to have a view about what the good of any human being consists in; and such a conception of happiness does not in itself make one's own health more desirable than that of others. Similarly, to hold that perfect happiness consists in contemplation is not to say that one's own theoretical activity should be maximized. Rather, it is to say what it is to act for the good of a person—whether that person is oneself or someone else. If perfect happiness is contemplation, then to benefit others is either to help them engage in this activity or to bring them as close as they can come to this ultimate end.

We saw in Chapter 1 that Aristotle ranks the goodness of a life by measuring it against a divine standard: the more a living being approximates the conditions of the gods, the better its life. The closest a human being can come to the gods is to theorize, and if one does this under favorable conditions, one will lead a life of perfect happiness. But ethical activity is a second-best way of resembling the gods, for when one always acts for the sake of moral activity, one is treating the activity of one's rational soul as an ultimate end. A life devoted to exercising the virtues of practical reason is the closest some people can come to the life of the gods. And it is important to realize this when one acts for the sake of those who are not philosophers. Though one can sometimes genuinely help others even though one has a defective conception of what human flourishing is, one will in these cases be doing the right act for the wrong reason. For example, if a son helps his ailing father because he thinks that happiness consists in health, and he wants to help his father achieve this ultimate end, then he may be performing the right act, but his reasons are very far from what they should be. Similarly, if someone thinks that the highest human good is ethically virtuous activity, and he helps his ailing father so that he can more fully achieve this good, then once again his reasons for action can be criticized, though he is much closer to the truth than the son who equates happiness with health. The ideal way to reason about this situation is to recognize that the best life for a human being is a philosophical life, and the best one can do for one's father or for anyone else is to bring him as close as he can come to that goal. If the father is not a philosopher, then the best one can do for him would be to promote his ability to lead an active life devoted to ethical activity. And if one's father does not possess the ethical virtues, then one can still try to bring him as close as he can come to the second-best life. But in any case, one's actions should always proceed from the understanding that the ultimate end we should wish for, both for ourselves and for others, is contemplation. In this sense, one should always be acting for the sake of contemplation.

Though contemplation is a better good than any other, that does not mean that if one is a philosopher one's own well-being takes precedence over the good of all others. Nor does it mean that the good of those who contemplate should always receive priority over the good of those who do not. The question of how goods should ideally be arranged within a single life is independent of the question of how one human being should treat another. We should not assume that Aristotle confused them, or that he is forced into egoism simply because he maintains an intellectualist conception of the human good.

2.3. Ostracism

I turn now to the question whether Aristotle recognizes the possibility of conflicts between the maximal good of different individuals. Does he believe that at times, if A were to maximize his good, his doing so would prevent B from maximizing his?

To begin with, we should notice that certain conceptions of human well-being make conflicts of interest unavoidable, regardless of the empirical circumstances in which we find ourselves. For example, suppose happiness were defined as the possession of a high degree of a certain good (such as virtue, status, or wealth) in comparison with other human beings. How well off one is depends on how much more one has than others. Obviously, on this conception of the good, as one person's level of well-being increases, that of others declines. It does not matter how abundant resources are, or which institutions are available for coordinating behavior: the very conception of the good makes it inevitable that human beings will be at odds with one another whenever they try to increase their happiness.

It is obvious that Aristotle's conception of the good does not have this unfortunate feature. The degree to which a life is happy is a function of the kind of virtuous activity one engages in, and the degree to which one does so. If others engage in just as much virtuous activity as you do, or more, then that does not in itself make you worse off. For happiness is not a matter of how well or poorly one is doing in comparison with others: it simply consists in one's possession of a certain nonrelational good. But even though Aristotle's moral philosophy does not make conflicts of interest *necessary*, it may still leave open their *possibility*. For empirical conditions may sometimes be such that one person's pursuit of his greatest good will have consequences that interfere with another person's maximal well-being. And the familiar examples on which I have relied (such as the son whose father is ill) show that Aristotle should have recognized this possibility. The maximal pursuit of philosophical activity does not by its very nature bring one into conflict with others, but circumstances may be such that one sometimes must choose between maximizing one's own good and helping others.

We should also remind ourselves that, according to Aristotle, we must have a certain level of resources if we are to lead good lives.[16] Even though happiness does not consist in health, strength, wealth, or other external goods, significant deprivation in these areas will diminish the level of virtuous activity (theoretical or practical) that we can engage in. And so, if the level of resources available to a group of individuals is quite low, they may not all be able to engage in as much excellent activity as each would like. For example, suppose there are too few slaves available to the political community, and as a result at least some of the citizens must engage in hard physical labor. The more manual work done by some of them, the more others can enjoy the leisure needed for political or philosophical activity.[17] This means that whoever engages in the highest possible level of excellent rational activity will be interfering with the optimal good of certain others. If one shares in the burden of supplying the community with its economic resources, one allows others to have better lives; but if one avoids this burden, one leaves others with worse lives. Since happi-

---

[16] See I.8 1099a31–b8, I.10 1101a14–16.

[17] See *Pol.* III.5 1278a20–21: "It is not possible to make a practice of the activities of virtue if one leads the life of an artisan or a laborer." So too VII.9 1328b39–1329a2: the citizens of the best polis must not be artisans, traders, or farmers, since they need the leisure with which to develop virtue and engage in politics.

ness consists in an activity that depends on external goods, shortages in those goods create situations in which the maximal good of one person interferes with the maximal good of others. If Aristotle failed to recognize this possibility, then he had little insight into his own practical philosophy.

And when we turn to the *Politics*, we find a striking case of potential conflict between a citizen and the political community. In III.13, Aristotle discusses ostracism, the device by means of which the citizens of certain Greek cities could vote to expel one of their members for a fixed period of time (often ten years), even though that citizen had violated no law.[18] And he argues that under certain conditions such an expulsion would be just. It is a device, he concedes, that can be and has been abused by corrupt regimes: in these cases, it is merely a tactic by means of which certain citizens who have no concern for the common good promote their private interest (1284b20–25). Furthermore, he says that it would not be right to ostracize a citizen who is superior to all others in virtue. Such an individual deserves permanent power, and the other citizens should be willing to obey him (b25–34).[19] When is ostracism justified, then? Evidently, Aristotle has in mind a situation in which the citizen who is being expelled does not excel all others in virtue, though he nonetheless has far more power than they, because of some superiority in external goods (wealth, friends, and so on: 1284a20–1, b27). And he defends the justice of ostracism in these cases by appealing to an analogy with the crafts: if one person has a louder or more beautiful voice than others, he should not be allowed to be a member of a chorus; in general craftsmen do not aim at making one part of their products outstandingly beautiful, to the detriment of the whole (1284b7–13).[20]

This analogy suggests that in Aristotle's opinion ostracism need not be

---

[18] Aristotle further discusses ostracism in *Ath. Pol.* 22. A brief modern account is available in Hammond and Scullard, *Oxford Classical Dictionary*, s.v.

[19] The permanent rule of a king is defended at III.13 1283b20–23 and most fully at III.17 1288a8–29. A kingship would not obviate the need for lower officeholders, and so those subject to the king's authority would not be totally deprived of political activity. Presumably Aristotle's idea is that in a kingship each member of the community engages in as much political activity as he deserves, when his abilities are compared with those of others.

[20] The example of the outstanding singer who is excluded from the chorus should not be taken to mean that any individual who exceeds all others in virtue should be expelled from the polis. The voices of the chorus must sound good together, and this becomes impossible if one singer is much better than the others. But Aristotle thinks that when one person has kingly political abilities, others will still be able to occupy lower civic posts, and they will benefit from the counsel they receive from someone with kingly wisdom. Their efforts are not undermined by the presence of a great superior. The individual who is properly ostracized prevents others from having what they deserve, just as the outstanding singer interferes with the other members of the chorus. By contrast, the rule of a genuine king does not worsen the situation of the other citizens.

justified by showing that it promotes the optimal good of everyone involved, including the person who is being ostracized. Rather, his idea seems to be that on certain occasions it is impossible to maximize the good of all individuals. Every craft is concerned with the good condition of a composite whole, and no craft can try to include every possible element within that whole, even elements that have certain attractive or outstanding qualities. Similarly, the craft of politics must concern itself with the well-being of the whole community of citizens, and if some one citizen's presence would detract from the well-being of the rest of the community, then he can justly be excluded. Whether he is better off when he is excluded is irrelevant, just as it is irrelevant whether it harms a certain singer to be excluded from a chorus. It is not always possible to consider the optimal good of all possible elements of a whole, for one such element may fail to fit in with the others. Conflict sometimes requires us to exclude the individual for the sake of the whole.

Let me state in more detail the kind of case I think Aristotle is making for ostracism. Suppose someone in a well-governed polis has far more wealth than others, and this leads to his having much more political power than any other single citizen. We can imagine him to be an ethically virtuous person, but no more preeminent in this respect than anyone else. Since he has more power than others, he has many more opportunities to exercise the ethical virtues on a grand scale.[21] He undertakes larger projects, and is given more positions of responsibility. It is just, Aristotle thinks, to require this citizen to leave: even if he did nothing wrong in acquiring so much wealth, and even though the mere possession of these riches is not in itself an injustice, his presence in the community deprives the other citizens of what they deserve. For although they are equally capable of engaging in political activities, they undertake them far less frequently than he does. His great share of political power makes their share smaller, and so they have fewer opportunities to engage in the highest form of ethical activity.

Now suppose you are participating in a meeting at which it must be decided whether any citizen is to be ostracized. You realize that if you cast your vote against a certain person, and a sufficient number of others

---

[21] See NE X.8 1178b1–3: the greater and finer an ethically virtuous act, the more external resources it requires. And the greatest acts of ethical virtue are those undertaken by political leaders, who manage the well-being of the whole community (I.2 1094b9–10, X.7 1177b16–17). The idea that larger resources create opportunities for exercising a higher level of excellence is most fully expressed in Aristotle's distinction in NE IV.1–4 between large- and small-scale virtues. A poor person can be generous (1120b7–11) but not magnificent (1122b27). So a wealthier person can have a higher degree of virtue, if he has developed the skills needed for making an excellent use of his greater resources. The same point should apply to those with different degrees of political power.

do likewise, then he will have to leave—even though it is not in his best interests to do so. For, let us suppose, he does not have philosophical ability, and so the best kind of life he can have is a political life. To lead such a life, he needs political power, and if he is exiled, he will be living in a foreign city, where he will have so little power that he will lack even the normal rights of a citizen. During the time of his exile, he will not be leading a happy life. Though he will of course still be a good person, he will lack one of the resources he needs in order to engage in the highest form of ethical activity.

Let us also suppose that you and many other citizens are not philosophers either, and that the best life you can achieve is a political life. In this case, there is a conflict of interest between your highest good and that of the person who might be exiled. His presence in the city, through no fault of his own, is depriving you of opportunities for political activity, even though all of you are equally deserving of such opportunities. So each person can rightly say that it is not only in his own best interest, but in the best interest of many others, to vote in favor of ostracism. In doing so, you are not merely promoting your own good, or the good of some faction of which you are a part. You have a general concern for the happiness of the citizens, and you correctly take happiness (that is, secondary happiness) to consist in ethical activity. If you vote for ostracism, one citizen will no longer be leading a happy life, but everyone else will benefit, and the analogy with the crafts suggests that in such situations the part must be sacrificed for the good of the whole. If the citizen being exiled deserved far more political power than others, on the basis of his greater political wisdom, then he could legitimately object to his expulsion. But in the situation imagined, Aristotle thinks that those who vote in favor of ostracism have justice on their side. Someone in this situation must be the loser—either the one individual, if he is ostracized, or all of the others, if he is not. And given this unfortunate conflict of interests, it is better that one person take the loss than that all do so.

It might be suggested that there will always be better ways to deal with imbalances of power than ostracism. For example, if a person's great wealth is what leads to the imbalance, then the community can take some of his wealth for itself. This will lead to a restoration of political equality, and the individual need not be banished. But Aristotle does not consider the idea that ostracism can always be avoided by the adoption of less severe remedies. Perhaps he thinks that once a person acquires great wealth, his great political influence will remain intact even after his wealth is diminished. The only way to reduce a person's power may be to put him out of circulation for a long period of time. And we should bear in mind that Aristotle mentions other sources of power besides wealth: for example, a person's greater influence can derive from the large number of friends that he has (1284a20–21). And there may be no better way than ostracism to diminish power that rests on personal influence.

So Aristotle's discussion of ostracism displays a certain kind of realism—a willingness to believe that circumstances sometimes require regrettable measures. It would be best, of course, if regimes could always be arranged so that such extreme measures need never be taken (1284b17–19). But when a polis is out of balance because of the excessive and undeserved power of one individual, then ostracism is a just remedy. And this realism is of a piece with Aristotle's thesis that happiness is undermined when one does not have an appropriate level of external equipment. For he says that one can be undone not only by having too few of these goods, but also by having too many (*NE* VII.13 1153b21–5). The person who is ostracized had too much power, and because this left others with too little, his fortunes are reversed. For a period of time, he becomes incapable of leading a political life, and so his happiness is diminished, or (if that period is long enough) lost.

Ostracism does not provide us with an example in which one person's greatest good *necessarily* conflicts with that of others. For in special circumstances, it can turn out that it is in someone's best interests to be excluded from the political community. Someone who has been ostracized might discover that he has philosophical ability, and he might take up residence in a community in which such activity flourishes. He can say, with Aristotle's approval, that ostracism was the best thing that ever happened to him, and he may refuse to return to his native city when the term of his banishment expires. But of course such happy results are not guaranteed. Ostracism is contrary to the interest of the person being ostracized if he is someone whose best option is to lead a political life.

Aristotle does not say that when a person is ostracized, his greatest good has come into conflict with the greatest good of others. (Nor should he say this; for as we have just seen, whether ostracism is contrary to a person's good depends on the circumstances.) Nonetheless, we can plausibly take his treatment of ostracism as evidence that he recognizes the possibility that interests may conflict. The victim of ostracism cannot lead a political life for a long period of time, and Aristotle would have to be remarkably stupid not to realize that this might not be in that person's best interests. And surely his claim that in all the crafts we look not to each individual component, but to the well-functioning of the whole, suggests that he saw the obvious: a defense of ostracism cannot rest on the claim that this will be best for the person expelled.[22]

---

[22] When ostracism is just, its victim is obeying a just command in leaving the polis. In this sense he is acting justly. Furthermore, if he has the virtue of justice, then in leaving the polis he is exercising that virtue. And if it is always good, from the agent's point of view, to exercise an ethical virtue, then leaving the city is not entirely bad. But it should not be

Before leaving the topic of ostracism, we should notice that the analogies on which Aristotle's argument relies are of a piece with his doctrine that the political community has priority over any one of its parts. Excluding a too powerful citizen is compared with omitting an eminent singer from a chorus, or with painting (however beautifully) a foot that is out of proportion with the rest of the figure. The well-being of a group similarly takes priority over that of a single individual, as several other passages in the *Politics* suggest:

> The polis is prior by nature to the household and to each of us. For the whole is necessarily prior to the part. . . . (I.2 1253a19–20)

> Since there is one end for the whole polis, clearly it is necessary to have one and the same education for all. . . . At the same time, it should not be thought that any of the citizens belongs to himself, but rather all belong to the polis, for each is a part of the polis. (VIII.1 1337a21–9)[23]

What is the community entitled to do, by virtue of the fact that it is prior to any given member? What may be required of us, by virtue of the fact that we "belong to the polis"? Surely Aristotle believes at least this much: the community may call upon its members to benefit it in various ways (through military service, political office, the education of one's children, and so on). And it may of course interfere with members who are harming it. Since the whole is prior to the part, the legitimate demands of the group take priority over the maximal good of any single member. No individual citizen can rightly resist these demands, because no one "belongs to himself, but rather all belong to the polis." And although many

---

inferred that his ostracism was after all the best thing that could have happened to him. Had he not received so many votes, the community would have allowed him to stay and retain his full power, and this would have been the better outcome from his point of view. Even if each virtuous activity is desirable to some extent, not all such activities are equally desirable. The major political activities that the ostracized citizen would have been able to undertake had he remained are more valuable from his point of view than the just act of obediently leaving the city.

[23] Aristotle refers to his whole-part conception of the political community when he discusses ostracism in *Pol.* III.17. He says that someone who is worthy to be king should not be ostracized because of his greater power, for someone who so greatly exceeds others in virtue cannot be taken as just one part of a larger whole (1288a26–8). Quite clearly, then, one of the political measures that Aristotle thinks *is* justified by the whole-part doctrine is the ostracism of someone who is equal to others in virtue, but who has far more power than is desirable from the point of view of the rest of the community. Unlike a king, such a person can be treated as just one of the many equal parts of which the polis is composed, and so when his good conflicts with that of the whole, the latter takes priority. I do not take Aristotle to be saying that when one individual excels all others in virtue and deserves to be king, the good of those ruled should be sacrificed for the good of the king. See notes 19 and 20 above. But if I am wrong about this, then there is even more room for conflict in Aristotle's system than I claim.

of the demands of the group will be in the best interests of each individual citizen, complete harmony is not guaranteed or required; for justice does not demand that the community always act in ways that promote the best interests of everyone. Ostracism provides a striking case in which the good of the polis can diverge markedly from that of one citizen. But it is not an isolated element in Aristotle's political thinking. It reflects his general thesis that the good of the whole takes precedence over that of any one individual.[24]

And this, of course, is not a position an egoist can take. If the egoist thinks that interests can conflict, then he will also say that in such situations each should try to maximize his own well-being, and should not subordinate his good to that of others. By contrast, Aristotle recognizes the possibility of conflicts, and holds that in at least some of these situations the well-being of the community takes precedence over that of the single individual. So, his political theory cannot be viewed as an expression of any of the maximizing forms of egoism that we have defined. It is not benign egoism, because the possibility of conflict is recognized. And it is not combative egoism, because it does not counsel the individual to pursue his own maximal good, come what may for others. The individual who has been rightly ostracized should leave the community, for whether or not this is in his best interests, his departure is best for the group. And if he leaves for the right reasons—namely, because this will be for the good of others—then he justifies his action in a way that is incompatible with pure egoism.

2.4. SHARING POWER

Our discussion of ostracism touched briefly upon a number of Aristotle's political doctrines that I would now like to discuss at greater length, in order to reinforce my claim that he is not a maximizing egoist. To begin with, let us consider one of his most fundamental principles: in correctly governed communities, the rulers seek the good of all citizens, and do not merely use their office to promote their own apparent good (*Pol.* III.6–7 1279a17–31). This idea plays a role in Aristotle's discussion of ostracism, for he condemns this tactic when it is a device for taking or consolidating power and is used solely to promote the apparent interests of the rulers (1284b4–5, 22–5). Ostracism is just only when the expulsion of an individual is necessary for the common good, and when it is undertaken for

---

[24] For a useful discussion of Aristotle on the citizen as a part of a larger whole, see Mulgan, *Aristotle's Political Theory*, pp. 28–35. He takes Aristotle to be saying that "the good of any individual member is less important than the good of the whole," and adds: "The democratic institution of ostracism . . . provides a good example of the general Greek view of the legitimate power of the group over the individual" (p. 33).

this reason. Now, the general principle that just regimes rule for the sake of the governed is incompatible with pure egoism. For that form of egoism must say that political leaders, like everyone else, should not benefit others for their own sake, but should help others only if this is the most effective way of maximizing their own good. Had Aristotle been a pure egoist, he would have said that ultimately all rule should be exercised for the sake of the rulers, and that regimes differ only in the ways that the rulers conceive of their own interests.[25]

A second principle that played a role in our discussion of ostracism was this: when the citizens are equal in virtue, then it is just for all to take equal turns in sharing office. Justice, construed as a specific virtue, requires equal treatment (*NE* V.1–2), and so when citizens are equally deserving of political power, they must take turns governing and being governed (*Pol.* VII.14 1332b23–7).[26] Aristotle therefore looks back with approval upon those past political systems in which the equality of citizens was recognized and offices were held in turns; nowadays, he laments, the rulers want to stay in power continuously so that they can take advantage of the benefits of office (III.6 1279a8–16). And he notes that the justice of sharing power equally among equals is independent of the question whether ruling is a good or a bad thing (II.2 1261a39–b5). I take him to mean that if it is a good, then those who are equally capable of holding office deserve an equal share of that good; and if it is a burden, then it would be unjust to avoid one's fair share of it. Of course, when the citizens of Greek cities used the device of ostracism, they presumably did so on the assumption that political power is a good, of which one individual can have too great a share. Ostracisms were not held in order to do someone a favor.[27]

By endorsing the idea that political power and office should be shared

[25] See *NE* X.7 1177b12–14: the politician promotes the happiness of the citizens, and not only his own happiness. It is clear from Aristotle's discussion of constitutions in *NE* VIII.10–12 that rulers in correct political systems seek the good of the citizens for the sake of the citizens (see, for example, 1160b1–6, 1161a10–15). Throughout these chapters, the proper relations between rulers and ruled are said to parallel family relations, and members of the same family are clearly thought to benefit each other for the other's sake (see, for example, 1166a2–6).

[26] See too *NE* VIII.11 1161a28–30; *Pol.* I.12 1259b4–6, III.16 1287a16–18.

[27] Recall the points Aristotle makes in X.7–8: The most outstanding feats of practical virtue are military or political (1177b16–17), and military activity is ranked below political activity (b6–12). The greater the acts one undertakes, the more external equipment one needs (1178b1–3), and so the most excellent acts of ethical virtue are the ones that make use of positions of greatest power. Accordingly, the person leading a political life must seek power and honor (1177b12–14). *NE* I also recognizes the instrumental value of political power (1099a32–b2), and claims that it is finer and more divine to attain the good for a whole city than for a single individual (1094b7–10). Surely those who hold the highest offices are in a better position to do this than those who are not.

equally among equals, Aristotle commits himself to the rejection of all forms of egoism: pure, combative, and benign. To see this, imagine a community of equally capable citizens who rightly take the political life to be the best they can achieve: none can develop the theoretical virtues, and so they devote their full energies to exercising the practical excellences. Since they are equal in their abilities, each can be a good general, manage the city's finances, draft legislation, judge matters of law, and so on. Now, not all offices are equal in power, and the highest positions (such as that of a general) can be occupied by only a few people at any one time. Aristotle believes that in such a situation the highest offices must be rotated among the citizens on an equal basis, since that is what justice—the equal treatment of equals—demands. But this does not mean that the citizens will regard positions of greater power as a burden or as a matter of indifference. They must think that when one is using one's high office to exercise the ethical virtues, one is better off than when one resumes the less powerful role of an ordinary citizen. Those who hold the positions of greatest power have the task of making the most important decisions; they draw upon their practical wisdom as they deliberate, and they hand down their decisions to those who temporarily have less authority. Citizens who are at the time playing subordinate roles have the task of carrying out decisions that have been made by others; and this inferior task is not one that exercises the virtue of practical wisdom.[28] Good citizenship in a community of equals requires a rotating division of labor between rulers and ruled, but for anyone who equates happiness with the exercise of practical virtue, it is better to occupy the former position than the latter.[29]

Now, just as Aristotle holds that not every contemplative life is equally happy, so he must hold that political lives too can differ in the amount of happiness they contain. The more one contemplates (above a certain

[28] See *Pol.* III.4 1277b13–30: when one is acting as a good citizen but not as a ruler, one needs only true opinion, and not practical wisdom. Of course, a good citizen must have practical wisdom, since he will need to call upon it when it is his turn to govern. But the virtue he exercises when he is following the orders of others does not require practical wisdom. In this passage, Aristotle therefore distinguishes between the justice exercised by a citizen who is being ruled and the justice of a citizen who is ruling. And he compares this to the difference between the virtues of men and those of women. Though a woman can be just, generous, and so on, the virtue she displays is of the sort appropriate to a subordinate (see I.13 1260a20–23); so too is the virtue displayed by a male citizen who is temporarily occupying a subordinate political position.

[29] So, if one polis has a much larger citizen population than another, and both require equal sharing of offices, a citizen of the less populous city is better off, since he can rule for longer periods of time. Notice too that those who want to lead political lives should be glad that some of the citizens choose not to, and decide to pursue philosophical careers instead. That diminishes the number of people with whom great political power must be shared, and increases the amount of time one can spend in office.

threshold), the more happiness one has; and those who study higher causes are better off than those who contemplate only less knowable objects of thought (see 1.19). If one aims at a certain ultimate end and takes that to be one's good, then the more one possesses that good, and the higher that good is, the better one's life. Therefore, among those who lead a political life, those who occupy high office more frequently are better off than those who do so less frequently. And the higher the office, the better off one is, for those who are more responsible for the care of the state are called upon to deliberate about matters of greater difficulty and importance. One can even say that those who are most responsible for the well-being of the community bear the closest resemblance, among political men, to the unmoved mover. For the divine is, in its own way, a cause of the goodness of the universe,[30] and the more responsible one is for the goodness of one's community, the more closely one approximates this condition.

Now, suppose one is a citizen in a community of equals that has established a system of rotating high office on an equal basis. What reason does Aristotle have for saying that one should give up one's political power when one's term of office is over? (We will continue to assume that this is a community of nonphilosophers, and so the political life is best for each citizen.) Since it is better for each to have longer rather than shorter periods of ruling activity, why should anyone leave office and let others make major decisions in his place? One answer Aristotle can give is this: the other citizens in this community will not allow one to have more than an equal share of high office. If one tries to prolong one's hold on these offices beyond the allotted time, one will be severely punished, and the likely result is that one will end up with less political power rather than more.[31]

---

[30] See *Met.* I.2 982b4–10, XII.10 1075a11–25.

[31] In *Pol.* VII.3 1325a34–b7, Aristotle considers a case in which seeking more than one's fair share of political power is contrary to one's interests. He discusses the view of a hypothetical person who favors a political life, and who holds that one should keep all others— including one's equals—from office, thus reserving the finest acts of virtue for oneself. Aristotle replies that such a policy would be best for oneself only if one assumed that "the most choiceworthy of existing things will belong to those who use robbery and force" (1325b1– 2). But he denies the assumption, and insists that the person who used these methods to deprive others of political power would depart so much from virtue that no later acts would set right what he had done. This passage does not claim that continuous officeholding is wrong in all circumstances; for Aristotle holds that if one is superior to all others in virtue, then one should be king, and others should accept their subordination. Here he is saying that when one forces one's equals into a position of political inferiority, one is acting contrary to virtue, and one will not in fact succeed in achieving the best good for oneself. The best good (apart from contemplation, as we learn in *NE* X.7–8) is to engage in ethically virtuous activity, and someone who forcibly keeps others from political office is so distant from this goal that he will never make up for this deviation by anything he does with his

But it would be a serious mistake to think that this appeal to maximal self-interest is the only argument Aristotle has for cooperating in a scheme of equal political power. For he would say, in addition, that you should give up your office to others because *they are as worthy of it as you are*. Since they are your equals, they have as much claim to political power as you do, and if you tried to prolong your stay in office, you would be unfairly depriving them of something of great value in their lives. So, these fellow citizens are owed a certain way of being treated, *whether or not treating them in that way maximizes your own interest*. And of course their recognition of their equal ability is what underlies the point made in the previous paragraph: they will not allow you to have more than an equal share of power, because they think that an equal distribution of power among equals is the only fair scheme of cooperation. Each rightly thinks that he has no worse and no better a claim on power than any other citizen. And the proper political system for individuals of this sort to establish is one that rotates offices equally. Even though each would benefit by having longer periods of rule, the system should not be tailored to the maximal interests of any one of these equal citizens. It should benefit each citizen, but should do no more good for any one of them than for any other.[32]

Egoism, as I have defined it, cannot say that a certain action would be justified whether or not it maximizes the good of the agent. And so, for reasons I have just given, Aristotle cannot be read as an egoist. He holds that since one must share power equally with equals, one must give up high office to others whether or not doing so maximizes one's interest. Of course, in a way it *is* contrary to one's greatest good to give up office; for great power gives one the opportunity to engage in the greatest acts of ethical virtue. On the other hand, when one takes into account the expectations and demands of one's equals, any attempt to prolong one's stay in office beyond the time legally permitted is likely to backfire. But these considerations of maximal self-interest can be set aside, since shar-

---

power. I take Aristotle to be saying that this power-grabbing ruler will not be able to exercise the virtues, and so will not really be promoting his own good (let alone the good of the others). He will not be able to exercise the virtues because doing so requires the willing cooperation of others. So the project of seeking permanent power in order to exercise the virtues can undermine itself, when others resist. I am grateful to Cynthia Freeland for calling to my attention the relevance of this passage to my treatment of equal power. But she may not agree with my interpretation of it.

[32] Note that when there are more than enough citizens interested in and equally capable of ruling, it will be in the interest of each to ostracize one of the others. For that will give everyone but the ostracized citizen a somewhat larger share of power. But if the citizen being ostracized has no more influence than anyone else, and is being excluded merely in order to diminish the number of competitors for office, then surely Aristotle would take his ostracism to be an injustice.

ing power with others is something one owes them in any case, when they are one's equals. And of course setting aside considerations of maximal self-interest is precisely what a maximizing egoist—whether pure, combative, or benign—cannot do.[33]

I would like to emphasize that my argument rests crucially on attributing to Aristotle a certain conception of happiness. I take him to be saying that the good of any one human being consists in the virtuous activity undertaken by that human being. Ideally, that virtuous activity should be contemplative, but if this option is unavailable it should be political; and in any case, the more such activity one engages in, the more happiness one has. Once we look at the good in this way, then it becomes obvious that, according to Aristotle, one must share opportunities to achieve it with certain others, even if this leaves one with fewer opportunities for oneself. But suppose he had held that the good of each individual consists in sharing equally in a cooperative scheme of virtuous activity. According to this conception of the good, it would not matter whether I am personally engaged in virtuous activity for six hours or two hours a day. What would matter is that I get no less and no more than my equal share of such activity; even when I am idle, I would not be worse off, if other members of my community are getting their fair share. Were this Aristotle's conception of the good, then nothing I have said about the rotation of office would show that he is not an egoist.

But I am confident that this is *not* his way of conceiving the good. As we have seen, he holds that the more contemplation I engage in, the better off I am. If I give up some of this activity, in order that others may engage in it as much as I do, then my action does leave me worse off—unless my sacrifice is merely temporary, and in the long run my concern with others leads to more philosophical activity for myself. Nothing in X.7–8 suggests that the good consists in sharing theoretical activity with others on an equal basis. Perfect happiness is contemplation, and the more one engages in this activity the more happiness one has. More generally, one's own happiness (whether perfect or secondary) consists in one's own virtuous activity, and to the extent that such activity is impeded, one is worse off, even if others benefit as a result of one's deprivation.

Of course, I have not yet completed my argument that this is how Aristotle conceives of happiness. Thus far, we have examined only a small portion of X.7–8, and many more passages in these chapters, not to mention Book I, must be discussed. We will see, however, that nothing in this new material undermines the interpretation I have put forward. For the

---

[33] It might be thought that when an equal citizen gives up office in order to have no more than his fair share of power, he is necessarily doing what is best for himself, since he is acting justly. But recall note 22 above: although exercising the virtue of justice is always good to some extent, it need not be the best good one could have achieved.

present, I am presupposing that my way of understanding Aristotelian happiness will receive further support, and I am trying to show, on this basis, that we must not read him as a maximizing egoist.

2.5. X.7–8 AND THE PRIORITY OF THE COMMUNITY

If the argument of the past two sections is correct, then Aristotle's *Politics* must be read as a work incompatible with egoism. The distinction between correctly governed and corrupt constitutions, the justification of ostracism, the priority of the community over the individual, and the rotation of office among equals—each of these aspects of the *Politics* shows that one or another form of egoism must be rejected. Nonetheless, someone might ask why this reading of the *Politics* should be brought to bear on the problem of how to interpret the *NE*. For Aristotle rejects the political life in X.7–8 of the *NE*. He urges his readers to devote themselves to philosophy rather than to the well-being of their communities. And so it might be thought that in the *NE*, or at least in this portion of it, Aristotle abandons the assumptions that guided him when he wrote the *Politics*. It may be that when he composed the latter work, he was committed to the rejection of egoism. But when he argues against the political life in X.7–8, he seems to be placing the happiness of the individual philosopher above the well-being of the community. And this seems to be a turn towards egoism: in leading a philosophical life, one is maximizing one's own good; and in rejecting the political life, one is refusing to serve others.

I believe, however, that it is appropriate to use the *Politics* as evidence when we try to understand the assumptions that lie behind the *NE*. It is good methodology to assume that Aristotle tried to think about practical matters in a systematic and consistent way, and so assumptions he makes in one work are likely to remain intact in others. We should abandon the hypothesis that he is consistent only when we have strong textual reasons against it. And of course it would be surprising to find that the *NE* is fundamentally at odds with the basic assumptions of the *Politics*. For Aristotle takes the two works to concern a single subject matter: we are told in *NE* I.2 that the field we are investigating is politics, and the closing chapter of the *NE* reaffirms the point that this treatise is a prolegomenon to further political investigations. We should not lightly assume that works so closely related in Aristotle's mind are fundamentally at odds.

Furthermore, if we read *NE* X.7–8 in a certain way, then we can defend him against the charge that these chapters are inconsistent with the *Politics*. Consistency is preserved if we attribute to Aristotle the following assumptions: In many cities and many circumstances, it does the community no harm to have within its jurisdiction a group of people who are leading philosophical rather than political lives.[34] These philosophers can be allowed to pursue their interests, and no harm will come to the community, for the city can call upon plenty of other capable citizens to fill high office and conduct the daily business of politics. These other citizens have no interest in or talent for philosophy, and so the best lives they can lead are political lives. Although the state can justifiably call upon all of its citizens to take some time away from philosophy or any other private pursuit in order to devote themselves to the affairs of the community, there is no reason why *everyone* must make political activity his main interest.

Of course, these assumptions need not hold in all cases. Think, for example, of the king's son whose community is relying upon him to take power from his father, and who must therefore reject a philosophical life. And of course there can be less extreme cases: a community may need some of its philosophers to share political office for limited periods of time, if there are few others who are capable of doing so. I do not think we should take Aristotle to be saying in X.7–8 that if you are capable of leading a philosophical life, then you should in all circumstances do so, and that you should reject all requests that you serve the community instead. Reading him in this way gratuitously brings the *NE* into conflict with the assumption of the *Politics* that the community has priority over any one of its equal members. Instead, we should take his defense of the philosophical life in the spirit of his observation that he is treating a subject that admits of much variability.[35] When he argues that the philosophical life is superior to the political life, we should take him to be saying that *if* one is free (as many people are) to pursue the former rather than the latter, then one should do so. He is not assuming that we should be concerned solely with our own good or that we should always give it priority over the good of all others. Rather, he is assuming that when we choose a career, we are free to select the kind of life that we find most attractive. His arguments in X.7–8 on behalf of the philosophical life allow him to acknowledge that there are special circumstances in which, for the sake of other people, one should not lead the best kind of human life. Though he does not say this, we need only attribute this assumption to him if we want to read X.7–8 in a way that preserves its consistency with the *Politics*.

2.6. SLAVERY

There are two different routes by which philosophers might arrive at an egoistic ethical theory. First, they might begin with a theory of human

---

[34] In fact, as we saw in note 29 above, those who lead political lives are better off if a certain number of citizens prefer to lead nonpolitical lives.

[35] For references, see Chapter 1, note 16.

nature according to which human beings cannot avoid acting egoistically. For example, it may appear to some philosophers that people are incapable of acting for any other reason than the maximization of their own well-being. And if these philosophers think that ethical theory should not demand the impossible, they would be attracted to pure egoism as the only practicable standard of human behavior. Starting with a form of psychological egoism, they would move to a related form of ethical egoism.

I believe that Aristotle's thought does not fit this pattern, and I hope to convince the reader of this by the end of this chapter. But there is a second way in which philosophers might come to adopt a form of ethical egoism. They might think that it is *inappropriate*—though possible—for any human being to place the good of others above his own. When the three forms of egoism—pure, combative, and benign—do not rest on psychological egoism, they must be based instead on this notion of proper human relations. They do not claim (absurdly) that there is some one individual whom every human being is to serve. Rather, they hold that no one should be more important to A than A himself, no one more important to B than B himself, and so on. Each person should be a kind of sovereign in his own moral kingdom, while recognizing that every other person occupies the same position of superiority in his own sphere. And this talk of importance and sovereignty is to be construed in the following way: the maximal good of others (whether one person or many) is never as good a reason for action as one's own maximal good. Pure egoism accepts an extreme version of this principle, since it holds that the good of others is never by itself a reason for action. But combative and benign egoism allow the good of others to be considered when no option can promote one's own interests, or several do so equally well; they differ in that the former holds and the latter denies that this policy involves conflicts of interest.

It is important to bear in mind, at this point, that egoism as I construe it is not merely the proposition that each person should maximize his own good. As we saw in 2.1, it is possible to accept this proposition for merely strategic reasons: one's ultimate goal might be the production of the greatest possible amount of good in the universe, but one might think that each can most effectively reach this goal by concentrating solely or primarily on his own well-being. To take a different case, suppose I want to maximize my own good only because in doing so I make myself the most effective possible servant of others, whom I view as my superiors. I am in this case taking the good of certain others to be my most basic reason for action: whenever I act for my own good, it is not because this is an end in itself, but only because it is a means to theirs. Egoism as I construe it rejects any such attitude of subordination. It urges each of us never to place the good of others above our own; either we should simply ignore their well-being (except when it is a means to our own), or we should appeal to it only to break ties between equally good or equally bad alternatives.

In previous sections, I argued that ostracism and the rotation of rule are political institutions incompatible with egoism. Each of them rests on the idea that when citizens are equal in ethical virtue, they should share equally in political power. Now just as Aristotle holds that certain arrangements are just when human beings are equal in virtue, so he holds that quite different institutions are just when they are unequal. And he thinks that the most extreme form of inequality arises when two individuals are related as natural master and natural slave. The natural slave is deficient as a practical reasoner;[36] by accepting the direction of someone who is practically wise, he will lead the best life he can achieve,[37] though it will not be a happy life.[38] And of course, the master will profit from this arrangement as well. The physical work of his household will be done by his slaves, and so he will be free to devote his time to politics or philosophy. So, when slavery is a relationship between a natural slave and a natural master, it promotes the best interests of each.

When a slave, with the help of his master, promotes his own highest good, he has two reasons for doing so, one stemming from his own well-being, and the other stemming from that of his master. For example, he has two kinds of reasons for looking after his own health: First, his own good consists in the physical activities he performs in fulfilling his role as a slave, and he cannot perform these physical tasks unless he maintains his health. Second, his master is better able to devote himself to politics or philosophy if his slaves are healthy. Now, does Aristotle think that one of these reasons has greater weight than the other? Of course, the two reasons favor the same action, but that is compatible with one of them being a more important reason. If Aristotle is an egoist, then he must think that it is inappropriate for the slave to take the good of his master to be a better reason for action than his own good. But I think a number of passages suggest that he takes the opposite view.

Consider, for example, the following remark in *Politics* III.6: "In the case of mastery, although in truth the same thing is in the interest of the natural slave and the natural master, still it rules not less in the interest of the master, but rules in the interest of the slave coincidentally. For mastery cannot be preserved if the slave is destroyed" (1278b32–7). The thought seems to be that in the master-slave relation, the good of the former has a certain primacy, even though their interests coincide. The

[36] See *Pol.* I.5 1254b16–23, I.13 1260a12.

[37] See *Pol.* I.2 1252a31–4, I.5 1254b19–20, III.6 1278b32–7. The defense of slavery is presented principally in I.5–6.

[38] See *Pol.* III.9 1280a31–4, *NE* X.6 1177a6–9.

master should be concerned about the preservation of the slave, but not because the good of the slave is one among several ends to be promoted by this relationship. Instead, the institution has one end—the good of the master—and the well-being of the slave is a means to this end. So the master should be interested in preserving his slaves solely because they are instruments by means of which he promotes his own well-being. The slave happens to benefit from his slavery, but the purpose of this institution is the good of the master, and it is an additional but unnecessary bonus that it helps the slave as well. Since the slave is inferior to the master, his good is less important than the master's, and so once it has been shown that slavery is in the best interests of masters, that is all the justification this institution needs. When Aristotle says that mastery "rules not less in the interest of the master," he means that it rules *more* in the interest of the master: the good of the master has greater weight than the good of the slave, since the latter exists for the sake of the former. If, contrary to fact, the institution were bad for slaves but good for masters, the argument for preserving it would still be stronger than the argument against it, since the interests of a superior person outweigh those of an inferior.

This way of reading our *Politics* passage receives confirmation from several remarks Aristotle makes about slavery in other works:

> Since the soul is related to the body in the same way as a craftsman is to his instrument and the master is to the slave, there is no community among these things. For there are not two, but one, and that which belongs to that one. The good is not divisible among each, but rather the good of both is the good of the one for whose sake they exist. (*EE* VII.9 1241b17–22)

> . . . That human being is free who exists for his own sake and not for the sake of another. (*Met.* I.2 982b25–6)

> The [rule] of a master over his slaves is tyrannical; for in it the advantage of the master is obtained. (*NE* VIII.10 1160b29–30)

What Aristotle means in the first passage seems to be this: We should not think that what is good for master and slave is to be divided between them, so that the master gives up something to the slave and the slave gives up something to the master. For we would not say such a thing about the relation between a man and an instrument he uses. A man should treat his tools in a way that best serves his own interests, and should not give up some of his good for the sake of an instrument. For the instrument exists for his sake.[39] Similarly, masters should treat slaves

---

[39] The slave is called an ensouled possession, and compared to an instrument, at *Pol.* I.4 1253b32–3. Cf. *NE* VIII.11 1161b4–5: a slave is an ensouled instrument, and an instrument is a slave without a soul.

in ways that are best from their own point of view. For, as the second passage implies, the slave exists for the sake of a master. And the third passage confirms this interpretation by comparing the master's rule over a slave to a tyrant's rule. As Aristotle says earlier in this chapter (1160b2–3), a tryant is distinguished from a king in that the former considers only his own interests, whereas the latter looks to the well-being of those over whom he has power. So, when Aristotle says that a master's rule is tyrannical, he means that in deciding how he should treat the slave, the master looks to his own interest, and treats the slave as an instrument for the promotion of his own good. For that is how tyrants treat others. Of course, there is a difference, in that tyrants exercise power in ways that are contrary to the interests of others, whereas the slave benefits from his subordinate position. But in neither case is there a sharing of benefits according to merit; rather, one party uses the other as a tool. Tyranny is unjust because free men do not deserve to be treated as instruments. Slavery is just because natural slaves do.

Although Aristotle speaks of the slave as a living possession, and compares the master-slave relation to that between craftsman and tool, he also insists that slaves have the ability to understand reasons for action. They lack that part of the rational soul that deliberates, but they differ from animals in that they can act on reasons.[40] And so, if they are properly trained and acquire the virtues appropriate to a slave, they are capable of seeing why they should act in certain ways.[41] They can become willing subordinates whose aim in life is to serve their masters. If they understand and accept this subordination, they will realize that the promotion of their own good is not their weightiest reason for action. The best reason for them to perform any act is that doing so will serve the interests of their master. Even if a slave does not willingly accept this subordination, Aristotle would argue that he ought to do so. In the relationship between a natural slave and a natural master, the good of another person provides a stronger reason for action than self-interest, and this remains true whether the agent realizes it or not.

Egoism, as I have defined it, is opposed to any hierarchical ordering of human interests. It holds that the well-being of others should never be treated as a reason for action that is superior to the claims of self-interest. And this means that one should never treat one's own good as something to be promoted because in doing so one will best serve a person whose good has greater weight than one's own. Egoism can endorse slavery in certain circumstances, for it may be that the best way for me to promote my own interests is to become a slave. But if I become a slave for egoistic reasons, then I am making use of this institution for my own purposes,

---

[40] See *Pol.* I.5 1254b20–23; cf. *NE* I.7 1098a4–5, I.13 1102b13–1103a3.
[41] The kind of virtue attainable by slaves is discussed in *Pol.* I.13 1259b21–1260b7.

and not because I place the good of another above my own. In this sense, egoism is a form of egalitarianism: though it does not enjoin us to treat our own good as merely one reason for action among many (as does utilitarianism), it makes each person a sovereign in his own moral realm, since it urges him never to assign the good of others priority over his own well-being. Though egoism (like utilitarianism) is in principle compatible with such antiegalitarian institutions as slavery, it is at a fundamental level opposed to subordination: no one's good is to take precedence over anyone else's. It says that each person should maximize his own good, because any other policy would constitute an inappropriate relationship between oneself and others. Aristotle's approach to human relationships, as we have seen, is utterly different. For him, it is always important to ask whether two human beings are equally capable of virtuous activity, before we determine whether the good of one should be given greater weight than the good of the other. If they are equals, then it may be appropriate for them to compromise and share the good; and if they are unequals, then one should serve the other, promoting his own interests primarily because this helps another achieve a superior way of life.

It should be recalled that there are two different ways in which philosophers can arrive at an egoistic position: they can begin as psychological egoists, and embrace ethical egoism because they think that we cannot be asked to make decisions in ways that are beyond our capacities; or they can think that it is inappropriate—though possible—for a human being to subordinate his good to that of others. We have seen in this section that if Aristotle is an egoist, then he cannot have arrived at this position in the latter way. If he is an ethical egoist at all, he must base this normative position either on the assumption that we cannot decide to benefit others for their sake or on the assumption that our nature forces us to seek the maximization of our own good. But neither of these psychological doctrines can plausibly be attributed to Aristotle. He believes that certain human beings can decide to benefit certain others for the sake of those others. And he has a conception of justice that requires an equal division of resources, whether such a division maximizes each individual's good or not. Obviously he thinks his audience is capable of acting in accordance with such a conception. More generally, he thinks that human beings, when properly educated, are capable of treating others as they deserve to be treated. And such treatment is not guaranteed to maximize the agent's happiness.

2.7. The Variety of Relationships

We have looked at two different kinds of political institutions that Aristotle defends—the sharing of power among equals, and the subordination of slaves to masters—and we have noticed that in each case the proper relationship between individuals varies according to merit. Equal citizens must recognize that each has as much claim to political office as every other, and that there is no reason why one should have more opportunities for political activity than another. In these cases, the good of a fellow citizen provides one with a strong reason for action—so strong that one should be willing to sacrifice one's own good, to a certain extent, so that others, who are equally deserving, also can share in the good. But when two human beings are as unequal in virtue as are master and slave, then the inferior individual should take the good of the superior to be more important than his own. How strong a reason one has for acting on behalf of another depends on how good that other person is; and how strong this reason is in comparison with self-interested reasons depends on whether one is that other person's equal.

Now, masters and slaves are not the only ones who form unequal relationships in Aristotle's philosophy. He thinks that although free women are capable of a higher degree of virtue than are slaves, they are nonetheless not normally the equals of free men.[42] And even among free men, there will usually be many different degrees of virtuous activity.[43] The ordinary Greek male citizen is capable of something that approximates virtuous character, but full virtue is possible only under very special conditions.[44] And children are less fully developed in character than are most adults.[45] Proper behavior between two human beings depends on their recognition of where they stand in this hierarchy. What equals owe to one another is quite different from what is owed among unequals.[46]

[42] Women, unlike slaves, have a deliberative faculty, but it is without authority (*akuros*): *Pol.* I.13 1260a13. Non-Greeks are criticized for failing to recognize the natural differences between women and slaves (I.2 1252a34–b6), and the importance of giving women an education suitable to their role is emphasized (I.13 1260b13–20). In the *NE*, Aristotle asserts that the relationships between men and women can be based on the mutual recognition of virtue, and not merely on pleasure or advantage (VIII.12 1162a25–6; cf. VIII.11 1161a22–5). When he says that the deliberative faculty of women is *akuros*, I take him to mean that it is not adequate for political decision making. For further discussion of his attitude towards women, see Fortenbaugh, *Aristotle on Emotion*, pp. 57–61.

[43] Aristotle's view that friends of good character improve each other (IX.9 1170a11–12, IX.12 1172a10–14) assumes that one can have the virtues and become still more virtuous. Greater experience over the course of one's life, when properly used, can give one a greater degree of practical wisdom (VI.11 1143b7–14). That virtue admits of degrees is also recognized at III.9 1117b9–11, IX.8 1168a33–5, and X.3 1173a15–22.

[44] See Aristotle's complaints about the many at X.9 1179b10–20. For his distinction between the virtue that would be exhibited in aristocracies and the lesser virtue achievable, under proper conditions, by most citizens of Greek cities, see *Pol.* IV.11 1295a25–40. When he says that virtue is widely shared (*polukoinon*: *NE* I.9 1099b18), he means that the male citizens of Greek cities have enough moral excellence to share in political decision making. This provides a limited defense of democracy in *Pol.* III.11.

[45] *NE* I.3 1095a2–4, VI.8 1142a14–15, VI.13 1144b1–9; *Pol.* I.13 1260a13–14.

[46] *NE* VIII.7 1158b11–28, VIII.13 1162a34–b4.

But note that Aristotle recognizes other relevant factors besides ethical virtue when he considers what is appropriate in human relationships. For example, he believes that when we have received a good from another, then we normally owe an equal return. A stranger who has lent you money should normally be repaid; the debt is owed even if he is not as good a person as you or your friends (*NE* IX.2 1164b30–33). More importantly, Aristotle thinks that even when we are adults we owe our parents a great debt, in return for the benefits of life and early training.[47] The debt is hardly canceled if one surpasses them in virtue. Even if one has friends who are better people than one's parents, that does not mean one owes the latter less than the former. A person's degree of virtue is only one factor that must be weighed when one decides how strong a reason one has to benefit that person. Kinship and benefits received can provide an even stronger reason.

Now, just as one might sometimes have to share goods with fellow citizens because they are equals, so one may sometimes have to accept less good for oneself so that one's parents may receive the treatment they deserve. Sometimes the good one gives up to others will be trivial: for example, one gives one's seat to an older person (1165a28). But there is no guarantee that the sacrifice one makes will always be so small. In the example I have frequently relied on, a philosopher gives up some time contemplating in order to help an ailing parent. In this case, one settles for less happiness in one's life because one owes it to one's father to benefit him in certain appropriate ways. Though this is not Aristotle's example, it is continuous with his train of thought. He could hardly say that one should help one's parents provided that doing so leaves one with no fewer goods needed for happiness. That would trivialize the debt he says we owe them.

Aristotle offers no formula for determining how much weight we should attach to the good of others, and what we should do to benefit them. Instead, he calls attention to the great variety of considerations to which we must be sensitive:

> . . . Should one serve a friend rather than an excellent person? Should one return a favor to a benefactor, or give something to a companion, if it is not possible to do both? Well, it is not easy, is it, to determine all such things with precision? For they have many differences of all sorts, with regard to how large or small, fine or necessary they are. (IX.2 1164b25–30)

> One should not apportion the same honor to one's father and mother, nor [should one apportion to them] that which belongs to someone who is wise, or to a general, but rather what befits a father, and similarly a mother. . . . To

---

[47] For references, see Chapter 1, note 14.

relatives, members of the same tribe, fellow citizens, and all others, one must always try to apportion what is appropriate. . . . (IX.2 1165a25–32)

The egoist, by contrast, has a simple formula: one should always treat others in ways that maximize one's own good, never allowing their well-being to outweigh one's own. All human relationships, no matter how diverse, are to be regulated by this severe stricture. It is wrongheaded to impose this formula upon Aristotle's writings, for his approach is to rec-ognize and endorse the variety of ways in which we adjust our behavior so that it is appropriate to the various relationships in which we find our-selves, or into which we voluntarily enter. In many of these relationships, he says, we act for the sake of others, and so he recognizes that the good of others can by itself provide a reason for action. To suggest that such other-regarding considerations are always outweighed by egoistic rea-sons, or that they are used only to break ties, is to impose a limitation on Aristotle's thinking that is justified by nothing in his works. As we have seen, his treatment of ostracism and the rotation of office reflects an awareness that conflicts of interest exist, and there is no reason why we should take him to believe that these cases are unique. We can plausibly take him to be assuming that in various circumstances the benefits we provide others for their sake are owed whether or not, in providing them, we diminish our own share of the good.

It should be noticed that the egoistic project of maximizing one's own good is one that looks exclusively to the present and future, and disre-gards the past. Human relationships are to be taken up and abandoned by looking to the way in which they do or will optimally promote one's interests, and so if one discovers that one is in a relationship that impedes the maximization of one's good, then that relationship is to be dropped. Such an attitude is incompatible with the idea that, because of all that someone (such as a parent) has done for me, I owe that person continuing support, even if such support requires me to sacrifice my own good to some degree. Aristotle thinks that even when we are adults we owe our parents a great debt, because of what they have already done for us, and he does not make the appropriateness of repaying this debt contingent upon the degree to which doing so will benefit us in the future.

Similarly, he recognizes that, for a time, we owe a debt to certain for-mer friends, even after they have changed for the worse:

If one accepts someone because he is good, but he becomes wicked and appears so, must one still love him? Or is this not possible, since not everything is lovable, but [only] what is good? . . . Well then, should it [one's friendship] be broken off immediately? Or should one not do so in all cases, but [only] with those who are incurable in their wickedness? When others can be set right, one should rescue their character more than their property. . . . But one who breaks off [the friendship] would seem to be doing nothing absurd, for he was not a friend of someone of this sort; and so, when the other has altered and it is impossible to save him, one keeps away. (IX.3 1165b13–22)

An egoist, who always places his maximal good above that of others, would have to calculate the costs and advantages of trying to rescue a failing relationship. He would have to drop one friend and develop another as soon as he became convinced that devoting more time to this new relationship would more effectively maximize his interests. Loyalty would not be a consideration: why should one spend time on a person who is becoming worse, when one can achieve greater gains with someone who is one's equal? But Aristotle does recognize, in the above passage, that we owe our friends a degree of loyalty. We must try to rescue a friend from moral and other forms of deterioration, simply because of what has passed between us; though there will be future gains if our relationship survives, one might have gained even more by ending the relationship and spending more time with other friends who are not in trouble. Here as elsewhere, Aristotle does not take the virtuous person to be someone who always looks to his optimal good, in order to decide how to treat others.

2.8. COMFORTING A FRIEND

Further evidence that Aristotle is not an egoist can be found in *NE* IX.11, where he discusses the comfort friends give each other when they suffer misfortunes. He points out that when one is pained by some unfortunate turn of events, that pain is to some extent lessened if one can be with one's friends and talk to them about it. But he also notes that at the same time it is painful to share one's sorrow with one's friends: "It seems that the presence [of friends] is a certain mixture of things. For the very fact that one sees them is pleasant, especially for someone who is suffering misfortune, and it helps somewhat in alleviating the pain. . . . But to see someone pained at one's own misfortunes is painful. For everyone avoids being the cause of pain in one's friends" (1171a34–b6). Misfortunes that occur only to me and not to my friends seem to create a conflict of interest: For my own good, I want to tell my friends about my ill fortune; my pain is to some extent lessened when I share it with others. But for altruistic reasons, I don't want to tell my friends about what has happened to me; their pain is to some extent increased when I share the news with them. In addition, the pain I cause them may to some extent impede the important activities—political or philosophical—in which they are engaged. Though they will of course try to comfort me if I ask them to do so, it is better for them if they can continue to engage in the highest forms of practical or theoretical activity. On the other hand, the pain caused by my misfortunes may be interfering with my own virtuous activities, and it will be best for me if I alleviate that pain by seeking the comfort of my friends.

If Aristotle were an egoist, then we would expect him to think about this dilemma in the following way: Each time I suffer a misfortune, I should share it with my friends. That will lessen my pain, and though it will increase theirs, egoism (of any form) tells me always to attach more weight to self- than to other-regarding reasons. The only problem for me is that if I share my misfortunes with them, that might lead them to share their misfortunes with me; and then I will have to be pained by news that might otherwise have been kept from me. If there is some way of telling how vulnerable my friends are to misfortune, then I should share my misfortunes with those among them who are less likely to need comfort from me.

But when we look at the text, we see that Aristotle's approach to this conflict of interest is just the opposite. He assumes that in these situations, the interest of the friend should receive more weight than one's own. For he says that we should be reluctant to share our pain with others, even though this will lighten our own burden; and we should be eager to comfort our friends, even though this will cause us pain:

> Therefore those who have a manly nature are reluctant to share their pain with their friends, and unless one is excessively insensitive to pain, one does not put up with the pain that comes to them. And in general one does not allow fellow mourners to approach, because one is not oneself the sort to mourn. (IX.11 1171b6–10)

> Therefore it would seem that one should eagerly call one's friends when one has good fortune, for it is fine to be someone who does good. But one should shrink [from calling one's friends] when one has bad fortune. For one should share bad things as little as possible, whence comes the saying, "What I have of misfortune is enough." One should call them to one's side most of all when they would be inconvenienced a little but would benefit one a great deal. Conversely, it is presumably fitting that one go, without being called and eagerly, to those who suffer misfortunes. For it is the mark of a friend to do good, especially to those who are in need and who do not expect it. (IX.11 1171b15–22)

The assumption Aristotle makes here is that a friend willingly endures a certain amount of pain for the sake of others. He keeps misfortune to himself and forgoes opportunities to have it lightened, in order that his friends may suffer less. But he would like his friends to share their burdens with him, because even though that will cause him pain, it will alleviate theirs. Aristotle recognizes the conflict of interest but thinks that it should usually be resolved in favor of the other person. His recognition of conflict shows that he is not a benign egoist, and his way of resolving it shows that he is not a combative egoist. And of course, if he were a pure egoist, then the misfortunes of friends would never in themselves provide one with a reason for action.

2.9. MORAL COMPETITION

Thus far, I have been treating the question of Aristotle's egoism in a one-sided way: I have tried to show how much evidence there is against the egoistic interpretation. But it must be admitted that I have been looking at only part of the picture. For there are passages that seem to point in the opposite direction, and they must now be considered.

Paradoxically, the passage that seems to provide the strongest possible evidence in favor of an egoistic reading is contained within Aristotle's discussion of friendship. For the main thesis of *NE* IX.8 is that self-love should have a certain primacy over one's love of others. This chapter opens with the observation that "it is a puzzle whether one should love oneself most of all, or someone else" (1168a28–9), and as Aristotle's treatment of this puzzle proceeds, it becomes clear that in his opinion, if self-love is construed in the right way, it is oneself that one should love most of all (see especially 1168b29–31, 1169a2–3). And that certainly seems to commit him to the kind of egoism that we have been considering: all three forms of egoism agree that we should always assign greater weight to our own good than to the good of others. Egoists—whether pure, combative, or benign—can all join in saying that one should love oneself more than others, and since Aristotle agrees, we might infer that he too is an egoist. Perhaps he is not a pure egoist, since he does think that in the best friendships, at least, one person benefits another for the sake of the other. But he may still be a combative or a benign egoist: he would allow that the good of others may in itself provide us with a reason for action, but he would be saying, in IX.8, that we should always give priority to our own good. And what he says in this chapter must be given a great deal of weight in our overall assessment of whether he is an egoist. For in the other passages we have considered thus far, he does not directly raise the question of how strong one's love of oneself should be, in comparison with one's love of others. Here in IX.8, he does tackle that issue, and the fact that he argues for the priority of the self is a serious stumbling block for anyone who believes that he should not be read as an egoist.

We must therefore look more closely at the thesis that we should love ourselves most of all, to see what Aristotle means by this, and why he believes it. I will try to show that when we look at the arguments he uses to defend this thesis, it will not turn out to be a form of egoism, as we have defined that doctrine. Everything he says in this chapter is compatible with the view that the optimal good of individuals can conflict, and that in such situations the proper course of action is sometimes to do what is less than best for oneself so that others may benefit. In fact, I will suggest that this chapter is best understood if we take him to be accepting this antiegoistic thesis.

To defend the thesis that we should love ourselves most of all, Aristotle makes a distinction between two different attitudes that might be called "self-love." As that term is usually used, it applies to those who compete for such things as money, honors, and physical pleasures (1168b15–25). These people consider such goods to be the best there are, and they try to get as many of them as they can for themselves. When self-love takes this form, Aristotle says, it is rightly criticized. But he then claims that there is a different form of self-love: the term can also apply to someone who tries to outdo others in the realm of ethical action (1168b25–1169a11). And this form of self-love, he claims, is admirable: "For if someone is always eager that he, more than all others, should perform just and temperate actions, and do everything else in accordance with the virtues, and if in general he always secures what is fine for himself, no one would say that such a person is a self-lover, nor will anyone blame him" (1168b25–8).[48] Though such an individual is not usually called a self-lover, Aristotle thinks that he has a better claim to that title than does the person who competes with others for more and more external goods. For, he says (1168b29–1169a6), someone who tries to outstrip all others in ethical activity loves a certain part of himself—his understanding—whereas the so-called self-lover, who competes for wealth, honor, or physical pleasure, loves something other than himself, namely, his body or some external good.

We will examine at a later point Aristotle's doctrine that understanding is the true self. What is important to notice immediately is that when he defends the genuine self-lover, he does so by appealing not only to that person's good but also to the good of the whole community. His claim is that when individuals compete with one another in the moral arena—each striving to be a better person than every other—then everyone benefits and no one loses: "When all compete for the fine and exert themselves to do the finest things, then all will be as it should for the community, and each individual will have the greatest of goods, since that is just what virtue is. Therefore the good person must be a self-lover, for he himself will profit from doing fine things, and he will benefit the others"

[48] Other passages in which Aristotle writes approvingly of moral competition are IV.3 1124b9–15 and VIII.13 1162b8–13

(1169a8–13). I take Aristotle to be saying that moral rivalry differs from other forms of competition in precisely this respect: normally, when people try to outdo one another, one person's gain is another's loss; but when virtuous individuals "compete for the fine" then everyone benefits in some way or other. One person wins the competition, but in a way (to be explained), no one loses.

The following example, I suggest, captures the sort of situation Aristotle has in mind. Imagine a number of solo musicians who come together one evening to compete against one another. Each takes a turn, and tries to play in a way that will be judged best when the evening is over. The better each plays, the more likely he is to win, but at the same time, everyone else benefits by the fact that each is striving to do his best. For one thing, the harder each tries to win, the better the music sounds, and all get more enjoyment from listening to better performances. For another thing, the spirit of competition encourages each to strive harder than he would in a more relaxed and noncompetitive atmosphere. When one sees how hard the others are trying, one puts more effort into one's own performance, and the closer one comes to performing at one's peak, the more one enjoys one's activity. So the passive and active benefits of music making (listening and playing) are increased by the fact that a competition is being held. Each musician wishes the others well; each wants the others to do the best they can. But at the same time, each would like to be the one who is judged best.

Though Aristotle does not spell out his notion of moral competition in this much detail, I suggest that he is thinking along the same lines. For in the passage just cited, he defends such competition by claiming that everyone is better off when each tries to outdo the others: when each tries to outperform the others, then each "will have the greatest of goods, since that is just what virtue is" (1169a10–11). Here Aristotle points to the active benefits that accrue to each individual who competes with others: in this way, one becomes a more virtuous person, and gains the greatest of goods. And he also has the passive benefits of competition in mind, when he says that the self-lover will not only "profit from doing fine things" but also "benefit the others" (a12–13). So he is saying that when I try to outdo others in the moral arena, then I benefit from my heightened activity, and others benefit because of what they receive from me. Now, he does not raise the question of why these benefits might not be equally available to those who merely try to be one another's equals. But since he is emphasizing the mutual benefits of a competitive spirit, it is obvious why he thinks this superior to a situation in which each, in an unaristocratic spirit, sees to it that he is not the best member of a group. If I make sure that I am not better than every other person, then my character will not be as outstanding as it might be, and others will not be the recipients of my outstanding activities. If others are equally careful not to strive for too great an excellence, the whole community will suffer. We are all better off if each tries to be better than all the others. This of course does not mean that each hopes the others will make moral mistakes, or fail to fulfill their potential: that way of wanting to be best is incompatible with a good person's desire to see others flourish. The kind of competition Aristotle must have in mind is one in which each tries to be the best, but no one wants someone else to be worse than he can be.

We will be looking at other points that Aristotle makes in *NE* IX.8, for it might be thought that his egoism emerges only in passages that have not yet been discussed. But we can ask whether anything Aristotle has said thus far, in his defense of self-love, commits him to egoism, and surely the answer is no. He argues that one should love oneself more than one loves anyone else, but we have thus far seen no reason to equate this with egoism as we have defined it. To love oneself most of all in the proper way is to have a complex attitude: one would like to excel all others in virtuous activity, and one tries to approximate this goal as best one can; but at the same time one does not want others to be less virtuous than they can be. This is not at all the attitude advocated by combative or benign egoists: they hold that we should always assign greater weight to our own good than to the good of others. Still less is it the attitude, endorsed by pure egoism, which accords the good of others no independent weight at all. Though Aristotle endorses the priority of the self, this is a different kind of priority from the one that egoists have in mind.

Furthermore, Aristotle's way of justifying moral competition does not commit him to any form of egoism. He argues that when people strive to outdo one another in this friendly way, each is better off than he would be in the absence of such competition. So there are two kinds of reasons why I should try to outstrip others in virtue: (a) I will benefit (both as agent and as recipient), and (b) others will benefit (both as agents and as recipients). A pure egoist would deny that (b) has any independent weight, while combative and benign egoists would say that (a) gives me a stronger reason than (b). But Aristotle simply cites both sorts of reasons, without saying that one is stronger than the other. He therefore leaves open the possibility that there may be situations in which your maximal good conflicts with that of others, and that in these cases you should sometimes give way to them. We have seen that such conflicts are possible, since resources (such as political power) are limited, and nothing he says in his defense of self-love requires him to deny this.

Aristotle's defense of self-love commits him to the view that there is a good that everyone should try to acquire, but that only one person can have—the good that consists in being the most virtuous member of one's community. In this limited sphere, one person's victory is everyone else's loss. In wanting to have this good for myself, I want it to go to me rather than to you. But it would be ludicrous to generalize from this peculiar case and infer that Aristotle would say the same about every type of good. For it is crucial to Aristotle's argument in favor of this peculiar kind of competition that everyone benefits from it, and he would hardly say the same of all conflicts. For example, as we have seen, he thinks that opportunities for political office should be shared among equals: it would be wrong to strive to have as much of this good as one can for oneself, because such a competition would deprive others of equal opportunities for political activity. When competition for a good would diminish the happiness of others, it should be shared on some fair basis; but when competition would enhance the happiness of all, by encouraging greater efforts, then Aristotle endorses it. Such an attitude towards conflict with others hardly betokens a commitment to egoism.

It is important to bear in mind that for Aristotle happiness does not consist in having a quantity of goods that compares well with the quantity that others have. Whether or not one is happy depends solely on one's own level of virtuous activity, and so if others are doing better than I am, that fact does not make me worse off. The comparative good for which a true self-lover strives—the good that consists in being best—is not among the goods in which happiness consists. And this fact is in harmony with the interpretation for which I shall be arguing throughout this study: happiness is not inclusive of all intrinsic goods, or even all compossible intrinsic goods. So, when Aristotelian agents compete with one another to be best, each places far more emphasis on doing as well as he can than on doing better than others; each takes happiness to consist in exercising the virtues, and not in exercising them more fully than others. In arguing for the legitimacy of self-love, Aristotle is claiming that the feeling of competition that lies behind so much human behavior can be put to good use, and need not be repressed. For even though this is a competition that nearly everyone loses, the proper conception of happiness reveals that what one gains by competing is far more important than one's loss.

2.10. Heroism

It might be objected, at this point, that the competition among the good, described in IX.8, is more pernicious than I think. Consider the following passage, in which Aristotle describes the virtuous person's willingness to die for his friends and fatherland:

> He will give up money and honors and in general the goods that are fought over, gaining what is fine for himself. For he would choose to have great pleasure for a short time rather than little pleasure for a long time, to live his life in

a fine way for a year rather than take potluck for many years, and to engage in one fine and grand action rather than do lots of little things. This is presumably true of those who die in defense of others. They choose a great and fine thing for themselves. They would give up money on condition that their friends get more, for the friend gets money but [the virtuous person] gets what is fine. So he assigns the greater good to himself. (IX.8 1169a20–29)

Although the battlefield hero benefits others, it sounds as though he is the sort of person who always wants to emerge as the winner when goods are divided between himself and his friends. He makes sure that they receive the lesser goods, and he reserves for himself the greater good that consists in courageous activity. Rather than equally dividing opportunities for virtuous activity with his friends, he assigns as many as possible to himself. And of course his friends, being virtuous people, adopt the same competitive strategy. When they are all faced with a situation in which only one can perform a great moral act, and the others merely gain lesser advantages, then each strives to be the hero, and to avoid getting the smaller goods. And so they are all combative egoists—though of a high-minded sort. Each wants to maximize his own good, and when this policy prevents others from maximizing their good, self-interest prevails.

But there is a high price to be paid if we read our passage in this way. For as we have seen, Aristotle believes that political offices should be shared among equals. Having greater political power involves having greater opportunities for political activity, and because political activity is the highest form of ethical activity, Aristotle thinks that such opportunities should be shared equally among equals. It would be incomprehensible for him to approve of the rotation of offices and at the same time to urge virtuous individuals to rob their friends of opportunities for virtuous activity. The need to share such opportunities is what lies at the bottom of his belief that offices should be shared.

Furthermore, if a virtuous person is someone who takes opportunities for fine action from his friends so that he can have more for himself, then it becomes difficult to make sense of Aristotle's treatment of friendship in *NE* VIII–IX. For he contrasts virtue-friendships with advantage-friendships by saying that the latter but not the former are marred by quarrels and accusations (VIII.13 1162b5–8, 16–21). Those who are friends for the sake of advantage are always trying to have the larger share of advantages, and complain that the other party has given up too little or has received more than is right (b16–21). But if virtue-friends are competing for opportunities to perform heroic actions, then why should they not have as much hostility towards each other as advantage-friends? If you equate happiness with virtuous activity, and your ultimate aim is to maximize your own happiness, come what may for others, then you are going to be quite upset if your "friend" tries to beat you to the punch whenever opportunities for virtuous activity present themselves. True, you will receive certain other goods because of his virtuous activity; after all, your friend might say, he is acting for your sake. But those lesser benefits are not the ones you equate with happiness. If your friend is really acting for your sake, he will sometimes let you have your chances for virtuous activity, rather than always treat you as the passive recipient of lesser goods.

Aristotle says that virtue-friendships are characterized by trust (VIII.3 1156b28–9, VIII.4 1157a21–4); such friends help each other develop in character (IX.9 1170a11–12), correct each other (IX.12 1172a12), and confer in difficult situations (III.3 1112b10–11). But it is difficult to understand why any of this should be true if one sees a friend as a competitor in the struggle for great moral achievements. For example, wouldn't such competitors occasionally try to take advantage of each other by deliberately giving bad moral advice? Suppose a friend seeks your counsel, and wants to know whether he should undertake a certain project, or whether it is not worth his energies. You feign sincerity, and tell him to wait for a finer occasion; then, having convinced him, you go off and do it yourself, explaining to him later that circumstances forced you to accept an opportunity that he rightly turned down. Such behavior is not at all what Aristotle expects of virtue-friends, but it is hard to see why it would not occur among egoists who struggle against each other to gain opportunities for moral achievements.

I suggest, therefore, that we are misreading Aristotle's description of battlefield heroism if we take him to mean that the virtuous person always wants to get the best kind of good whenever a division of goods is called for. We do not have to take him to be saying, in this passage, that whenever opportunities for courageous activity present themselves, the virtuous person sees to it that they fall to him, rather than to his friends. Instead, he may be thinking of situations in which only one person is presented with a chance to exercise courage. Suppose, for example, that you are on a military campaign, and are standing guard while your friends are asleep. Suddenly you see the enemy's soldiers approach, and you realize that if you don't risk your life and fight them, then your friends may be killed in their sleep, and the chances of winning the war will be reduced. If you try to get a fellow soldier to take your place and face the enemy, then you will both be killed. And so the heroic act you perform is not one that your friends could have performed instead. You are not competing with them to fight the enemy, and in holding your ground you do not deprive them of a good they might otherwise have had.

My suggestion is not that Aristotle has these precise details in mind when he discusses the virtuous person's willingness to die. Rather, my example merely shows that there are situations that call upon one person and no others to act courageously. And so we should not assume that whenever Aristotle discusses a virtuous act undertaken for others, he must be thinking of a case in which it was open to all to perform that act. The important point is that we not misinterpret him when he says, of those who courageously die for others: "They would give up money on condition that their friends get more, for the friend gets money but [the virtuous person] gets what is fine. So he assigns the greater good to himself" (IX.8 1169a26–9). This does not say, and should not be taken to mean, that those who rightly die for others have robbed those others of their opportunities for virtuous activities. Instead, Aristotle is merely pointing out that the good attained by engaging in a courageous act is greater than the goods others may receive as a result of this action. We should not infer that the courageous person arranged the situation so that he rather than others would have the chance to receive this greater good. The situation called upon him to act courageously, and we simply read too much into the passage if we think that in so acting, he was depriving others of their opportunities.

What Aristotle is emphasizing is the difference between the good of heroic activity and the lesser goods received by passive beneficiaries. The person who fights courageously thereby gains one great good (the virtuous act), though he may lose all others (money, honors, office). Those who are saved by his heroism and eventually return home can continue to enjoy wealth, honor, and office. What the hero gives his friends through his courageous activity are the material conditions—wealth, honor, office—that they need for their own virtuous activity. His heroism does not itself cause them to be heroes, but is done in the hope that, through such acts of courage, the enemy will be defeated, and peacetime activities (whether political or philosophical) will resume. Others, who do not have opportunities for courageous activity, will passively receive the benefits of his protection, but how much they profit from his act depends on what they do on their own.

This explains why the hero thinks of himself as profiting more from his action than his friends do. He does not think of them as people who equate happiness with external goods, or as people who prefer a long and undistinguished life to a shorter period of outstanding ethical activity. It is not as though, in dying for his friends, he were giving them what they most want (safety, longevity, money), but insisting that what he wants most (courageous activity) is better. Nor is he claiming that the whole of his short life will be happier than the whole of theirs. If his friends go on to lead lives of outstanding virtue and suffer no major misfortunes, then they will have a long and happy life, which is better than having a short and happy life. None of these points are denied by Aristotle in our passage. He is merely saying that courageous activity is a greater good than the passive rewards reaped by those who are protected by such activity. Since the virtuous person realizes this, he also realizes that when he acts courageously, his "friend gets money but he gets what is fine. So he assigns the greater good to himself" (1169a27–9). We should not infer from this that the virtuous person is someone who always tries to structure situations so that his friends always gain lesser goods, and he comes out the winner. There is no reason why Aristotle should not say that opportunities for virtuous activity should be shared among equals: that is why he endorses the rotation of office, and surely intimate friends who regard one another as equals will be no less fair, in sharing benefits, than citizens who regard one another as equals.

We must be quite careful, therefore, when we acknowledge that according to Aristotle virtuous individuals view one another as competitors. As we saw in the preceding section, the good that they are competing for is relational: each wants to be better than all the others, or to come as close to this ideal as possible. But they are not competing for opportunities to engage in virtuous activity, for if each were trying to maximize such opportunities, come what may for others, then they could not remain friends. There is, among equally virtuous individuals, a complex pattern of cooperation and rivalry: they equally divide opportunities for virtuous activity, but as each takes his turn, he tries to outperform the others.

2.11. ENLARGING THE PIE

I now want to consider a remark Aristotle makes near the end of the passage describing the virtuous person's willingness to die for his friends and fatherland. Having said that such a person "assigns the greater good to himself" (1169a28–9), Aristotle then adds: "He might also give up actions to his friend, and it might be finer to become the cause of his friend's action than to do it himself. So, in everything praiseworthy, the excellent person is seen to assign more of the fine to himself" (1169a32–b1). It is possible to read this as a kind of joke: Aristotle would be saying that when you and your friends are in danger, no one should volunteer to be the hero, but each should try to talk someone else into risking his life. By persuading a friend to protect you by risking his life, you become responsible for his heroism, and that is finer than actually facing the risk yourself. But I doubt that Aristotle is engaging in sly humor at this point. He is deadly serious about the value of courageous behavior, and any suggestion that evading risks is actually nobler than courage on the battlefield would probably not strike him as funny.

How then should we construe this remark? Aristotle is saying that situations having these three features are possible: (a) one causes a friend to engage in some virtuous activity; (b) one could have undertaken that virtuous activity in one's friend's place, but chose not to; (c) the act by which one creates an opportunity for one's friend is more virtuous ("finer": 1169a33) than the act one would have performed had one not ceded the opportunity to him. Suppose, for example, that you think that your friend is capable of supervising major civic projects, but that he has had too few opportunities to show his worth. You discuss the matter with public officials who oversee such projects, and you prepare your friend so that he is ready to take on this responsibility. In preparing your friend and securing this opportunity for him, you are acting in accordance with virtue—so much so, that you are doing something finer than you would have done had you ignored your friend's good and undertaken this civic project yourself.

Now, Aristotle says of the person who helps his friend in this way: "he assigns more of the fine to himself" (1169a35–b1). I suggest that in saying this he is comparing acts performed by two different individuals: if A has virtuously caused B's virtuous action, then A has done something finer than B. For throughout this passage, Aristotle has been saying that the good attained by the virtuous agent is superior to the goods received by his beneficiaries. His point, in our present passage, is that one of the goods received by beneficiaries might be opportunities for virtuous activity, but that even so the act performed by the creator of such opportunities is superior. Just as the courageous person who defends the external goods of others assigns the greater good to himself (1169a26–30), so too the friend who enables others to increase their level of virtuous activity.

But we must not be misled by this talk of "assigning more of the fine to oneself." It would be a mistake to think that, according to Aristotle, there are a fixed number of opportunities for virtuous activity, and that each virtuous agent tries to get the largest amount, leaving smaller shares for others. For Aristotle recognizes that the pie to be divided increases in size when one kind of virtuous act is the cause of others. Of course, as we have seen, there is a sense in which each virtuous person is trying to outdo the others: each would like to be best. And so someone who creates opportunities for others will be conscious of the fact that he has performed an act that is finer than theirs. Though he is glad to be helping them (because he seeks their good for their sake), he is also glad to be outperforming them (because they compete to be best). But this does not mean that he is willing to take opportunities for virtuous action away from others so as to have them for himself. Nothing Aristotle says in IX.8 conflicts with the view that if, in certain situations, opportunities for virtuous activity are limited, then they must be shared on the basis of merit.[49]

2.12. HARMONY OF INTERESTS

In the past three sections, I have examined three passages from *NE* IX.8 and have denied that they commit Aristotle to any of the maximizing forms of egoism defined earlier. He argues that everyone will do best when each strives to surpass the others in moral competition. He affirms the superiority of ethical activity to the external goods passively received by beneficiaries. And he claims that when someone causes another to engage in moral activity, the first person's act is finer than the second's. But none of this suggests that other-regarding reasons should be given no independent weight, or less weight than self-regarding reasons. The priority of the self endorsed by Aristotle is not the kind of priority I have identified with egoism.

Nonetheless, it might be thought that IX.8 provides evidence of Aristotle's egoism because it seems to claim that the good of human beings, properly understood, cannot conflict. In his endorsement of moral competition and praise of self-love, he says nothing about the possibility of conflict between one person's self-interest and another's. On the contrary, his idea seems to be that when one strives to do the best one can for oneself, one will inevitably produce the best results for all others as well: "When all compete for the fine and exert themselves to do the finest things, then all will be as it should for the community, and each individual will have the greatest of goods, since that is just what virtue is" (1169a8–11). If this means that the pursuit of maximal self-interest (properly understood) can never bring one into conflict with the best interests (properly understood) of others, then we could plausibly take Aristotle to be a benign egoist. Since he says that one should love oneself most of all, we could infer that he assigns greater weight to self-interest than to other-regarding reasons. He would be saying that this assignment of priority is unobjectionable, since no one will suffer because of it. Happily, when we make decisions about how to act, self- and other-regarding rea-

---

[49] We should note the connection between the passage discussed in this section and Aristotle's high regard for political activity. He says here in IX.8 that the best ethical acts are those in which one causes others to act virtuously. And of course such causal power is greatest among outstanding political leaders. When a private person creates an opportunity for a friend to exercise his virtue, he is thereby outperforming his friend; political leaders do this on a grand scale (and their accomplishment is therefore more difficult and more desirable) when they oversee the education of the citizens and thereby foster their moral development.

sons always point in the same direction: whatever is best for myself is best for others, and vice versa.

But such an interpretation is highly implausible. To see why, let us ask whether, according to Aristotle, practical reasoners are ever faced with a decision in which they must resolve conflicts between two or more persons other than themselves. Surely he would have been blind not to recognize that such conflicts are commonplace: jurors are always faced with them, as is anyone who must vote for one of several competing candidates. And Aristotle himself mentions a number of conflicts that occur outside the political arena: Sometimes one must decide whether to benefit a friend or some other excellent person who happens not to be a friend; or one must decide whether to repay a debt or to use the money to help a friend in need (IX.2 1164b25–33). In these cases, doing what is best for one person is incompatible with doing what is best for another. That is what makes them hard cases. Aristotle gives no formula for their resolution, but instead thinks that the weight of competing considerations can vary from case to case. He never suggests that when we deliberate about such cases correctly, all reasons will point in the same direction, so that what is best for one person will also be best for all others.

Now, if it is agreed that Aristotle recognizes such conflicts as these, then why should we think that, in his opinion, the matter is entirely different when a practical reasoner must take into account his own best interests as well as those of others? If he realizes that we are sometimes faced with a conflict between the good of two other individuals, then surely he recognizes that in different circumstances such a conflict can also occur between one's own good and another's.

Nor do I think that IX.8, when properly interpreted, provides any evidence that Aristotle is denying the existence of such conflicts. What he does claim is this: when someone strives to perform the finest actions, then he gains the greatest good for himself, and others benefit from his performance as well (1169a8–13), so that they will make no complaint about his attempt to benefit himself in this way (1168b25–8). I have argued that in making these assertions, Aristotle assumes that virtuous individuals compete with one another *fairly*. That is, they do not rob one another of opportunities for virtuous activity, or deceive one another so as to get a larger share of the pie for themselves. Since each regards his friends as equals, each wants the others to have equal opportunities for virtuous activity, and each hopes that the others, for their sake, will make the most of those opportunities. So the competition among virtuous individuals to be best is a competition among individuals who observe decent limits; each wants to be best, but will undertake only such actions as will leave others with their fair share of opportunities for moral activity.

No virtuous person wants to be best if this turns his equals into people who are predominantly passive recipients of his moral feats.

It is true that Aristotle does not discuss this danger in IX.8, but there is no reason why we should take him to be blind to its existence. As we have seen, he thinks that offices should be equally shared among equals, and he would presumably say the same about all other opportunities to engage in virtuous activity. So IX.8 must be read against the background of Aristotle's other writings. It does not discuss the need to share the highest good, for that is not its aim. Aristotle is pointing out a way in which each person can justifiably love himself most of all: when I strive against others in fair moral competition, the person I want most of all to win is of course myself. But we can see from what he says elsewhere that, in his opinion, we may sometimes have to settle for less of the good for ourselves so that others can have their fair share.

In IX.8, Aristotle resolves the conflict between those who approve and those who condemn loving oneself most of all by distinguishing two forms that this phenomenon can take. The person who loves himself most of all is usually thought to be someone who assigns himself the larger share of external goods or physical pleasures (1168b15–19), and this is rightly condemned. But, Aristotle holds, the term "self-lover" would be more rightly applied to those who compete for the best good, and this kind of self-regard would lead to no complaints from others (b25–8). Now, it is possible to be misled by his way of handling this issue, and to think that he here commits himself to criticizing only one way of placing one's own good above that of others: he can object *only* to the person who tries to maximize the number of external goods he has. And, it might be thought, he is prevented from condemning someone who maximizes the degree to which he possesses the good properly understood.

In my opinion, however, there is no reason to think that his hands are tied in this way. He discusses the "materialistic" self-lover in IX.8 because this is the kind of self-love that he and his contemporaries are most familiar with, and it is this that has given self-love a bad name. But Aristotle's failure to discuss any other bad form of self-love does not require him to hold that it is the only possible bad form. In his treatment of ostracism, he recommends that if someone's great power deprives his equals of their fair share of political opportunities, then he should be removed from the community. And he is committed to saying that anyone who tries to acquire such great power over his equals is to be condemned simply because he is seeking to deprive them of their fair share. Such a person could not successfully defend himself by saying that he wants power not for its own sake, but only because he needs it in order to engage in virtuous activity of a high order. He would still be guilty of a form of self-love that harms others. This high-minded way of placing one's own good above that of others is not mentioned in IX.8, but there is no reason to think that this single chapter contains everything that Aristotle has to say about the proper relation between oneself and others. Once we place *NE* IX.8 within the context of Aristotle's other writings, it neither provides evidence of egoism nor undermines my claim that, in his opinion, one person's maximal good can conflict with another's.

2.13. The Real Self

There are other parts of the *NE* besides IX.8 that we must examine to determine whether Aristotle is an egoist. But before we move away from his defense of self-love, one further feature of this chapter must be discussed. When he argues that the ethically virtuous person rightly loves himself most of all, he claims (1169a3) that there is one part of the soul that such a person loves more than any other—his understanding (*nous*: 1168b35). As the context indicates, *nous* here refers to the part of the soul that enables someone to deliberate and make choices: someone's understanding is in control when he is continent, and loses control when he is incontinent (1168b34–5). Though *nous* sometimes refers to the part of the soul that engages in *theoretical* reasoning (X.7 1177a13, 1178a7), in IX.8 it refers to *practical* reason. And in IX.8 Aristotle says that this practical understanding is the part of the soul that the ethically virtuous person loves most. Furthermore, he makes the mysterious claim that each person "is or most of all is" this part of the soul (1169a2).

I take his meaning to be this: When we say that someone is in control of his appetites or passions, we are referring to one part of the soul— practical reason—and identifying the person with this one part. We do not mean by this that all there is to a person is practical reason; although we view the soul as a complex whole, we make statements (for example, "he is not in control of his appetites") that identify the person with the part of that complex whole that should be dominant. Similarly, when Aristotle says that the ethically virtuous person loves himself, he thinks he can justify this statement by picking out that same part of the soul— practical understanding—as the one the good person loves. To love your *self* is to love your practical reason, or to love it more than any other part.

Why does Aristotle conceive of an ethically virtuous person as someone who loves his practical reason most of all? I take him to be assuming that a person loves a capacity of the soul whenever he loves the activity he engages in by virtue of having that capacity. For example, someone who loves to make music more than anything else would most love the part of his soul that enables him to engage in this activity. Similarly, if someone chooses philosophical activity above all others, he loves his theoretical understanding above all. And so, when Aristotle says that the ethically virtuous person loves practical reason above all, I take him to be basing this claim on the assumption that a good person likes to think about and solve ethical problems. Practical problems of the highest order—that is, political problems—are the ones that he loves most of all, and so the favored activity of those who love practical reason is political activity. Such activity, for Aristotle, is not to be treated as a mere means to something else; rather, deliberating with others about what laws to pass and how to put them into effect is a reasoning process that is to be enjoyed and desired partly for its own sake. And as we saw in 1.16, the reasoning activity of the politician is what makes him akin to the unmoved mover: though the statesman cannot achieve perfect happiness, the goodness of his life depends on the degree to which he approximates the divine, and he achieves a secondary form of happiness by making the exercise of practical reason his ultimate aim.

In Chapter 6, I will try to give a fuller defense of this way of reading Aristotle. For now, we must turn to a seeming incompatibility between what he says in IX.8 about the self and what he says later when he defends the philosophical life. In X.7, after giving several arguments to show the superiority of contemplation to moral activity, he claims that each person is his *nous* (1178a2), or is this part most of all (a7). And the context clearly indicates that he is identifying a human being with *theoretical*, not practical, understanding. So there appears to be a conflict between IX.8 and X.7: the former identifies a person with practical reason, the latter with theoretical reason.

But I think that the contradiction is merely apparent: though there is a verbal conflict, it does not reflect incompatible beliefs or a change of mind. For it is hard to believe that when IX.8 speaks approvingly of the person who loves practical reason "most of all" (1169a3), Aristotle means that one should love practical reason even more than theoretical reason. Similarly, when he speaks of ethically virtuous acts as the finest and best there are (1168b28–9, 1169a9–11), it is implausible to take him to be saying that they are finer and better than contemplation. For Aristotle never claims, in any of his writings, that ethical activity is superior to theoretical activity. When he considers what our highest goal should be, he says that it is contemplation, and nothing in his treatment of friendship suggests that he is reversing himself. The only passage in the *NE* that compares the merits of theoretical and practical reason is X.7–8, and it is a mistake to read IX.8 as though Aristotle were implicitly making that comparison and favoring practical *nous*.[50]

---

[50] According to our familiar example, the son who gives up some philosophical activity in order to help his father is—barring unusual circumstances—choosing a lesser good for

I therefore suggest that we read IX.8 in the following way: Aristotle is simply leaving theoretical reason out of the picture, and writing as though the soul consisted solely of practical reason and other parts that should be under its control. To take theoretical reason into account at this point, and to assert that each person is that part most of all, would call for arguments he is not yet prepared to give. Instead, he confines himself to a comparison between the ethically virtuous person and those who love such goods as money, honors, and physical pleasure. Within this group, he says (1168b28–9), the person who strives to act virtuously is the one who has a better claim to be called a self-lover. For what he loves—*nous*—is the self, or is the self most of all. Now, when Aristotle fills out his conception of happiness in X.7–8, and finally addresses the question of whether the political or the philosophical life is best, he commits himself to a more complex conception of self-love than the one he had given in his treatment of friendship. The comparison he now needs to make is between (a) the lover of theoretical intellect, (b) the lover of practical intellect, and (c) the self-lover as most people think of him, that is, the person who seeks larger shares of external goods. And when the contrast drawn in IX.8 between (b) and (c) is supplemented and revised by the contrast drawn in X.7 between (a) and (b), the following result emerges: The person who loves himself most of all is the philosopher, since a person is theoretical reason most of all; but the person leading a political life is still more of a self-lover than is the ordinary grasping person, since the former loves his understanding most of all, and the latter does not. In a way, both the philosopher and the statesman can be called self-lovers: each loves *nous*, the highest part of the soul, the part that is the person most of all. But if we distinguish parts of the soul more finely, then it is only the philosopher who should be called a self-lover, for he alone loves the best part of the soul, namely, theoretical understanding.

Which is the right way of speaking, according to Aristotle? Should we, after reading X.7, continue to say that the good person who is not a philosopher loves himself? Or should we say this only of the philosopher? Once we see that this is only a question of how finely we should distinguish parts of the soul, it becomes verbal and insignificant. For Aristotle, the important point is to understand why theoretical reason is best, and to see why one should lead a philosophical life. And for us, as interpreters of Aristotle, the important point is that we not take IX.8 and X.7 to re-

---

himself. For he is actualizing the lesser of two virtues. However, some may wish to cite IX.8 1168b28–9 and 1169a9–11 as evidence against this interpretation: since ethically virtuous acts are the best one can do for oneself, the son who gives up some theoretical activity in order to treat his father justly is really doing what is best for himself. But if IX.8 is read in a way that makes it consistent with X.7–8, this objection to my interpretation loses its force.

flect conflicting comparisons between the theoretical and the practical lives. Whether we say that the statesman is a self-lover or not, we should take Aristotle to be claiming that the philosopher is the paradigm of a self-lover, and that the politician is a self-lover to the extent that he approximates that model. He does not present this paradigm in IX.8, but this is not because he there rejects the conception of happiness eventually defended in X.7. There is a much simpler way to explain the discrepancy between these two chapters: rather than defend the philosophical life in IX.8, Aristotle postpones that issue, and presents a model of self-love that is later revealed to be a second-best approximation of the ideal.[51]

2.14. FROM SELF-LOVE TO FRIENDSHIP

I now turn to another chapter—IX.4—in which Aristotle asserts that the self has a certain kind of primacy over others. I will argue that here too we find no evidence of egoism. The opening lines of this chapter read: "The features of friendship that extend to one's neighbors, and by means of which friendships are defined, seem to have come from the features of friendship that extend to oneself" (1166a1–2). What does this mean? Aristotle explains himself by enumerating five features by means of which friendship is defined (a2–10). In any friendship between two different people, X and Y:

(1) X wishes goods for Y, for the sake of Y.
(2) X wishes Y to be alive, for the sake of Y.
(3) X spends time with Y.
(4) X makes the same choices as Y.
(5) X has the same pains and pleasures as Y.

Aristotle then argues that these statements also hold true when X and Y are the same person, and that person is virtuous. But we should notice that even if we grant him this conclusion, that by itself will not establish the claim made in the passage quoted above. For he says there that friendship towards others "comes from" a relation one has to oneself. Whatever "comes from" (*elēluthenai*) means here, Aristotle's point is that this self-directed attitude has a certain kind of priority over the corresponding

---

[51] For further discussion of the self in IX.8, see Cooper, *RHGA*, pp. 169–175. He emphasizes the contrast between this chapter and X.7–8. Cf. Nussbaum, *The Fragility of Goodness*, p. 376, point 7. My argument for the consistency of Aristotle's two treatments of self-love depends in part on material to be presented in later chapters. If other apparent inconsistencies between X.7–8 and earlier portions of the *NE* are merely apparent, then so is the "conflict" between his conception of the self in Book IX and his conception in Book X. For further discussion of Aristotle's identification of each person with theoretical reason, see Chapter 6, note 34.

other-directed attitude. Merely arguing that (1)–(5) hold true of a virtuous person's relation to himself does not establish this priority.

What kind of priority is this, and how can Aristotle establish it? I suggest that what he has in mind is this: when we consider each of the five relations mentioned, we find that a single virtuous person exhibits them (in relation to himself) more fully than do any two separate individuals (in their relation to each other). For example, consider the third relation: X spends time with Y. Obviously a good person spends more time with himself than he does with even the closest of friends. Similarly for the fourth relation: someone who has the virtues is never at odds with himself in the choices he makes (1166a13–14), whereas two different individuals will sometimes make different choices, even when they are close friends. (This does not mean that one of them must at least sometimes think the other is making a bad choice; the point, rather, is that since their circumstances sometimes differ, they do not always face the same alternatives, and so they will not always make the same choices.) And when we turn to the fifth relation, we find Aristotle claiming in IX.4 that it applies more fully when X = Y than it does when they are two different individuals. He says of the virtuous person: "he shares pain and pleasure most of all with himself" (1166a27); and though this statement is not supported here, he does go on to defend it in IX.11. As we saw earlier (2.8), he thinks that a good person will be reluctant to share his misfortunes with friends, and will do so only in unusual circumstances.

If this is how Aristotle defends the priority self-love has over two-person friendships, then we can say what that priority amounts to. Friendship towards others "comes from" self-love in the sense that the latter provides the paradigm case of the attitudes characteristic of the former. Or, as Aristotle puts the point in IX.4, the virtuous person is a "standard (*metron*) of each thing" (1166a12). The excellent person's attitude towards himself provides the model for good relationships with others, and this ideal is nearly matched by the perfect friendships of two virtuous individuals. Confirmation that this is Aristotle's point can be found in IX.8:

> They say that one must love most of all the person who is most of all one's friend, and he is most of all a friend who wishes good things for the sake of the other person, even if no one will know about it. And these things belong most of all to a person in relation to himself, and so do all the remaining features by which a friend is defined. For it is said that all the features of friendship that also extend to others proceed from oneself. (1168b1–6)

When Aristotle makes this claim, he is not saying that self-love is temporally prior to our love of others, or that self-love causes friendship. His point is simply that the five marks of friendship are most fully instantiated by the attitude virtuous individuals have towards themselves. To support this claim of priority, he could point out that when a person has certain relations to himself—the ones described in (1)–(5)—and when he has those relations in an almost equal degree to someone else, then that other person is called "another self."[52] In these close relationships, one's self-love and lack of self-distance are almost matched by one's strong feeling for and frequent association with another.

If this is correct, then we can see how Aristotle's fuller discussion of self-love in IX.8 clarifies and supports the thesis of IX.4 that friendship towards others "comes from" a good person's attitude towards himself. For in that later chapter, Aristotle shows how we can accept the seemingly objectionable statement that one ought to love oneself, and not someone else, most of all (1168a28–30). That sounds offensive, he argues, only if we associate self-love with a grasping attitude towards external goods. But since those with such an attitude do not really love their *selves*, it is better to take the self-lover to be someone who loves his understanding more than any other part of the soul (1168b33–4). Similarly, we should take the person who loves himself most of all to be someone who tries to outdo everyone else in the sphere of virtuous action (1168b25–8, 1169a8–11). When we recognize that loving oneself most of all can take this public-spirited form, then we can see why the first two relations mentioned in IX.4 apply more to the good person's self-regard than to friendship with others:

(1) X wishes goods for Y, for the sake of Y.
(2) X wishes Y to be alive, for the sake of Y.

Consider the first relation: Why should Aristotle think that it holds to the highest degree when X = Y and that person is virtuous? If my earlier treatment (2.9–12) of IX.8 was correct, then he must be thinking of the phenomenon of moral rivalry. Each good person considers virtuous activity to be the highest good, and each strives, within the bounds of fair competition, to outperform every other. That highest good is what happiness is, and so, in wanting the most outstanding virtuous agent to be me, I want to be the person whose life turns out to be happiest. So (1) applies most of all to the virtuous person's self-love not because he wishes to have the greatest share of *every* good, but because the one good for the sake of which he acts is something he would like to have most of all for himself.

Relation (2) can be treated in the same way. There is one person whom one should most of all want to remain alive, and that is oneself. The person who is happiest is, appropriately, the one who most of all wants to continue living (III.9 1117b9–13, IX.9 1170a25–9). And just as it is justified to want to be happiest (if one interprets this in the right way), so it is right for one's wish to remain alive to be stronger than one's wish for

---

[52] IX.4 1166a31–2, IX.9 1170b6–7. The latter passage is discussed more fully in 2.16.

anyone else to remain alive (if, again, one interprets this in the right way). This greater love for oneself must not be taken to mean that one would choose oneself over every other person if one had to decide between one's own life and someone else's. My desire that I continue living may be stronger than my desire that my father or daughter or closest friend remain alive—and appropriately so—but that does not mean that if I had to choose between us, then I would sacrifice the other person in order to remain alive. For I might decide in certain circumstances that the right thing to do is to give up my life for others; recall that Aristotle applauds such a choice (IX.8 1169a18–29). My desire to act virtuously is the one that should be given priority when I take action, and not my desire, however strong it is, to go on living. Similarly, although Aristotle would say that I should want the most virtuous and therefore the happiest person to be myself, he does not think that this desire should be expressed in ways that make others worse off. His defense of self-love is always qualified by the proviso that it be expressed in ways that would incur no objection from others (1168b28).

When Aristotle says that one should love oneself most of all, and when he claims that "X wishes goods for Y for the sake of Y" and "X wishes Y to be alive for the sake of Y" are most fully instantiated when X and Y are a single good person, it is easy to be tempted by the thought that he is an egoist. But if we take into account the context of these remarks, and the kind of defense Aristotle gives them, we see that this temptation should be resisted. It is wildly implausible, for example, to take Aristotle to be saying that when you or another person must die, then each should strive to make sure that it is the other person. His defense of death on behalf of others forbids such a reading. More generally, the primacy he gives to the self in IX.4 and IX.8 should not be confused with the kind of primacy advocated by the combative egoist, who is willing to make others worse off in order to maximize his own good. Aristotle's doctrine, as we have seen, is far more complex, and pays far more attention to the good of others.

My conclusion, then, is that IX.4 no more shows that Aristotle is an egoist than does IX.8. The former claims that friendship derives from self-love, and the latter helps Aristotle establish this claim, but neither chapter suggests that one should always seek to maximize one's own good.

2.15. Self-interest and Friendship in IX.9

In IX.9, Aristotle tries to show why friendship is a necessary ingredient of a happy life. Some or all of the arguments he gives may contribute to the impression that he is an egoist. Let us consider what he says, in order to see why this impression is misleading.

When Aristotle argues that a happy individual needs friends, he relies on the conception of happiness that he defended in Book I. We have not fully discussed his treatment of *eudaimonia* in that book, but I will argue that there, and throughout the *NE*, he takes both political and philosophical lives to be happy. Someone leading either life takes goods to be arranged in a hierarchy, with virtuous activity at the pinnacle; in the philosophical life contemplation is the topmost good, whereas in the political life moral activity is the ultimate end. But in IX.9, Aristotle does not explicitly or implicitly rely on the thesis, eventually defended in X.7–8, that the philosophical life is happier than the political life. The business of IX.9 is not to show that a philosopher, because he is a philosopher, needs friends; rather, it is to show that an ethically virtuous person, because he has the ethical virtues, needs friends. Since (as I will later try to show) Aristotle assumes that the ethical virtues are possessed not only by those who lead political lives but by philosophers as well, his arguments in IX.9 are intended to show that *any* happy person, because he possesses the ethical virtues, needs friends. He does not confine himself to the far narrower thesis that those who are *perfectly* happy need friends.

So Aristotle's question in IX.9 is: Why does someone who has the ethical virtues need friends? He concedes that such a person has no need of a friend who is merely useful or merely pleasant (1169b22–7). And he claims that the virtuous person's lack of interest in these highly imperfect relationships has misled certain thinkers, who infer that the happy person in fortunate circumstances needs no friends of any sort (b27–8). He then goes on to show why a happy person does need a certain kind of friend, namely, someone else who has the excellences of character. His arguments, as I have said, are not tailored to the specific needs of philosophers, but concern the needs of anyone, philosopher or not, who possesses the ethical virtues.

Now, at least some of these arguments are straightforward appeals to the self-interest of the ethically virtuous person. That is, they are attempts to show that such a person will be better able to engage in virtuous activity if he has friends. Aristotle's argument is not that by having friends, you are better able to do good to other people, and so it is for their sake that you should become their friend. Rather, it is that *you* are better off if you have friendships with others, and this is why you should develop these relationships rather than isolate yourself. You need friends because, if you understand your own happiness correctly, you will want to have and exercise the ethical virtues; and friends, properly conceived, are the sorts of people who will help you accomplish these goals.

This is clearly what Aristotle has in mind when he says that "one can

get a certain training in virtue by living with those who are good"
(1170a11–12): an ethically virtuous friend is someone who offers you valuable advice, and in many other ways helps you develop your character
and improve your moral skills (VIII.1 1155a14–16, IX.12 1172a10–12).
And a self-interested reason for having friends is also advanced in the following passage: "It is thought that someone who is happy must live
pleasantly. But for the solitary person, life is hard, for it is not easy to be
continuously active when one is on one's own. But when one is with
others and acts in relation to them, it is easier. Therefore, one's activity
will be more continuous . . ." (1170a4–7). The kind of activity Aristotle
is talking about here is of course the ethically virtuous activity of a good
person. So his claim is that if you lack friends of good character, you will
engage in this activity less often, since continuous action will be difficult
to achieve on your own. Once again, friendship is being promoted as
something one needs for one's own good: you want *your* activity to be
continuous and pleasant, and so you should form the right sorts of relationships with other good people, rather than remain alone. It is not for
their sake that you should develop these relationships.

Now, as we have seen, one of the main ideas that Aristotle relies on in
his treatment of friendship is that in good relationships individuals benefit
each other for the other person's sake. Is this thesis compatible with the
arguments we have just considered? That is, if Aristotle's only arguments
for forming friendships are appeals to self-interest, then can he consis-
tently describe these relationships as ones in which we act for the sake of
the other person? I see no difficulty here, but we must be careful not to
avoid the difficulty in a confused way. It might be suggested that, according to Aristotle, whenever we benefit others for their sake, we should
always have a deeper reason for being motivated in this way, and this
deeper reason should be self-interested. In other words, he might be
taken to be saying: "it is for one's own sake that one should benefit others
for their sake." In this way, he might be portrayed as a philosopher who
seeks an egoistic foundation for altruism. But I do not think that this
thought—"benefit others for their sake for your own sake"—is intelligible, and I see no reason to attribute it to Aristotle. There is a far better
way of showing that his altruistic conception of friendship is compatible
with his arguments that a happy person needs friends.[53]

[53] My remarks here are a reaction to some statements made by Charles Kahn in "Aristotle
and Altruism." He says: "there is probably some truth in the frequently expressed view that
in Greek moral philosophy it is taken for granted that egoism or the pursuit of one's own
interests is somehow fundamental. . . . It is a kind of reversion to the Greek model when
Hobbes takes the individual desire for self-preservation as the premise in an argument
whose conclusion is a version of the Golden Rule. And this logical priority of egoism over
altruism is not unknown even in the orthodox Christian tradition, where the love of one's

Imagine the following conversation:

A: What was your reason for acting in a way that benefited him?
B: I did it for his sake.
A: But what was your reason for benefiting him *for his sake*?
B: I benefited him for his sake for my sake.

It is not clear what to make of A's second question and B's second reply. B does not take A to be asking, "What was your reason for benefiting *him* for his sake?" For an answer to that question would appeal to certain features of the beneficiary, or some special relation between him and B. Instead, B seems to be saying that he had a deeper reason for benefiting someone *for his sake*: he did it ultimately for his own sake. But how can benefiting another person for your own sake provide a reason for benefiting him for his sake? Your own good can of course provide a reason for benefiting another person—but it cannot provide a reason for benefiting that person *for his sake*. To benefit another for his sake is to take his good as something that *by itself* provides a reason for action. But if one takes the good of another as a reason for action because promoting his good serves one's own, then one does not in fact take his good as something that *by itself* provides a reason for action. If one says, "I did it for his sake for my sake," the last three words undermine the claim made in the first part of the sentence.

The problem would not arise if the first question and reply were followed by:

A: But did you have any other reason for benefiting him?
B: Yes, I also benefited him for my sake.

For of course an act can be done for two independent reasons: to benefit others and to benefit oneself. What is unintelligible is that one of these considerations should provide a further reason for the other. One can have a self-interested reason for helping another, but not for helping another for his sake.

Assuming that we want to avoid this confusion, let us return to our earlier problem: if Aristotle appeals only to self-interested reasons for having friends, then can he also describe such relationships as ones in which we benefit others for their sake? It seems to me that there is no conflict between these two ideas. Aristotle shows that a happy person

---

neighbor may be recommended as the path to one's own salvation" (p. 23). Kahn then goes on to label this "the rational priority of egoism," according to which "an argument for altruism may take self-love or self-interest as a premise" (p. 23). Now, Kahn correctly uses "altruism" to designate "a concern for the interests of others for their own sake" (p. 21). So he seems to be saying that, according to Aristotle, we should be altruistic—we should benefit others *for their sake*—because doing so is ultimately in our own interest.

needs friends by considering an ethically virtuous person without friends, and pointing out why the deficiencies of this situation would be remedied if he were to join together with other like-minded individuals.[54] Although the considerations that motivate such a change of status are appeals to self-interest, this does not mean that these are the only or the strongest reasons for action that exist when a person is involved in friendships. (Recall that once a friendship is formed, we cannot dissolve it just because our friend has begun to change for the worse, even though such disloyalty may open the way to forming better friendships; see IX.3 1165b13–25, discussed above in 2.7.) We can meet the needs of our friends for their sake, even though when we began to develop these relationships, we were acting only for our own sake. To initiate a friendship is to set one's motivation into flux, so that self-interested reasons are eventually supplemented by, and sometimes outweighed by, altruistic reasons. And that is why Aristotle can argue that one needs friends for the sake of one's own happiness without committing himself to the unintelligible thesis that it is for one's own sake that one should benefit others for their sake. His claim, instead, is that if one is isolated, then it is for one's own sake that one should develop relationships in which one will come to have a strong reason to benefit others simply for their sake. This should not be confused with the claim that whenever one acts for the sake of others, one's reason for acting *for their sake* is that this will benefit oneself.

Aristotle might nonetheless be criticized for placing too little emphasis on altruistic reasons. That is, one might think that an important reason for developing friendships is other-regarding. If we do not have these close ties, we are in a worse position to meet the needs and promote the well-being of others; the isolated person should develop friendships not just for his own sake, but also for the good of others. But whatever we make of this criticism, we should not confuse it with the claim that Aristotle is committed to a maximizing form of egoism. I am not trying to show that he gives the appropriate weight to other-regarding considerations; and in any case, it would be exceedingly difficult to determine what that weight should be. My claim is only that the way in which IX.9 provides a self-interested basis for friendship is compatible with the rejection of egoism.

Our discussion shows how important it is to avoid a certain confusion: I have been assuming that, according to Aristotle, when one acts for the sake of certain other persons, one takes their good to be a sufficient reason for action. Whether or not one also promotes one's own good, the fact that one benefits those other individuals is already a good enough reason

---

[54] We will see that this pattern is not followed in all of the arguments in IX.9. See especially note 56 below.

to ground one's action. But I am not taking Aristotle to be saying that the mere fact that an action would benefit some person or other (no matter whom) provides a reason for action. He thinks that the individuals whose well-being one should promote for their sake must have some special connection with oneself (parents, siblings, fellow citizens, and so on); or they must have something special to offer oneself (they are virtuous individuals whom one needs for one's own happiness). The good of others does by itself provide a reason for action—but only on condition that those others are of a certain sort. This should be distinguished from the view, which I do not attribute to Aristotle, that everyone has a reason to perform any act that would benefit someone or other.

Once again, it is possible to complain that Aristotle is not altruistic enough: it might be objected that he gives no weight to the well-being of other human beings as such, whether they have some special relationship to oneself or not. Furthermore, if egoism is defined as the doctrine that one should benefit others only when they have something to offer in return, or when they are closely tied to oneself, then it may be that Aristotle is an egoist after all. The philosophical criticism—that Aristotle is not altruistic enough—is important, but I will not consider it here. On the other hand, the verbal point—that Aristotle can be considered an egoist of sorts—is merely verbal. I do not deny that one can concoct some sense of "egoist" that will allow him to bear this label. My claim is that he is not a maximizing egoist, since he believes that in some circumstances one should promote the good of others whether or not this is in one's own best interests.

2.16. THE OTHER SELF

I now want to consider the argument in IX.9 (1170a13–b19) to which Aristotle devotes his greatest attention. My interest in it is twofold. First, if we are not careful, we may take his way of arguing as evidence that he treats happiness as a composite of all intrinsic goods. This mistaken interpretation must be resisted. Second, this argument deserves attention in its own right, for it follows a different pattern from the ones we have examined thus far.

According to the two arguments discussed in the previous section, an ethically virtuous person needs virtuous friends in order to be happy, because such friends are instrumental to the achievement of his own ends. A good person profits by having friends because they make his virtuous activities more continuous (1170a4–8) and he learns from them (a11–13). Friends are tools we need in order to do the best we can in our moral activities. Of course, Aristotle does not mean that friends should be treated only as tools: they are individuals whose good we promote for their sake. But when he asks why one needs friends for one's own sake, two of his arguments show why the lack of friends would diminish one's ability to engage in virtuous activity on a regular basis.

Now, it seems to me that we suffer a different kind of loss when friends die. However useful they have been by helping us to engage in our favored activities, we suffer a loss simply because we can no longer take pleasure in their presence and in the perception of their merits. This is not to deny that we grieve at their death partly because *they* have incurred a great loss, if their lives have less happiness as a result of their death. But we are sad also because *we* suffer a loss; and part of the reason for this is that we once enjoyed seeing them, and can no longer do so. So, any account of why our friends are good for us must recognize not only their instrumental value, but the pleasure we get from them. Aristotle's fullest attempt to show why we need our friends is an attempt to do justice to this aspect of friendship.

The initial segment (1170a13–b5) of this long argument describes the attitude of a virtuous person towards himself: he recognizes his own goodness, takes pleasure in this recognition, and because of this self-awareness is glad to be alive. Having established these points, Aristotle then applies them to the virtuous person's attitude towards a good friend:

> . . . As the excellent person is related to himself, so is he related to his friend, for a friend is another self. Therefore, just as one's own being is choiceworthy to oneself, so is that of one's friend, or nearly so. To be is choiceworthy because of the perception of one's own goodness, and such a perception is pleasant in itself. Therefore, one must also perceive that one's friend exists; and this would come about through living with him and sharing in conversation and thought. . . . Whatever is choiceworthy for oneself, one must possess, or else one will be in need, in this respect. Therefore, one who is to be happy needs excellent friends. (1170b5–19)

One of the premises on which Aristotle relies here is that a happy person must have everything that it is desirable for him to have. If he lacks any such good, then he is to some extent deficient; and to be happy is to have a life that is free from deficiency. So, if Aristotle can show that it is desirable for a virtuous person to have good friends, then he can also reach his conclusion that a virtuous person needs such friends.

This is the part of his argument that may mislead us into thinking that happiness is a composite of all intrinsic goods. We may fail to notice the difference between (a) the claim that a happy person has every type of good and (b) the claim that happiness itself is a composite good, containing within it all other intrinsic goods. (a) is compatible with the view that our ends should be given a hierarchical structure, and that happiness should be identified only with the one type of good at the pinnacle of the hierarchy. But (b) would commit Aristotle to the view that if there are many types of intrinsic goods, then happiness cannot be identified with any one of them, however desirable it is, or with any subclass of them. It is clear, however, that his present argument rests on (a) rather than (b). He says that a happy person must have everything that is choiceworthy, but this does not entail that the good he is looking for, when he seeks our ultimate end, must be an all-inclusive composite.[55]

Now, how does his argument purport to show that it is desirable for a good person to have excellent friends? The crucial implicit premise seems to be this: If a certain feature makes X desirable for someone to perceive, and Y has that same feature, then Y is also desirable for him to perceive. Relying on this premise, Aristotle moves from the fact that perceiving one's own being is desirable (if one is virtuous) to the conclusion that it is also desirable to perceive the being of one's friend. For a friend is another self: the attractive qualities one sees in oneself, which make one glad to be alive, are also qualities one has learned to recognize in one's friends. And just as it is reasonable to be glad that one is alive and to take pleasure in the perception of one's own goodness, so it is to the same extent reasonable to be glad that one's friend is alive and to take pleasure in perceiving his goodness. Should one's friend die, one will be losing something one needs, simply because it is desirable from one's own point of view to observe (through conversation and thought: 1170b12) his good qualities, and this is no longer possible. Of course, as Aristotle points out in his two earlier arguments, there are other reasons for taking the loss of friends to be the loss of something one needs: the level of one's virtuous activity will diminish, and one will no longer learn from them. But it is important to realize that the main emphasis of IX.9 is on the way in which one needs one's friends apart from their usefulness as means.[56]

[55] When Aristotle says that the happy person must have everything that is choiceworthy for him (1170b17–18), he is clearly relying on his definition of self-sufficiency as that which "when taken by itself makes life choiceworthy and in need of nothing" (I.7 1097b14–16). The happy person must be in need of nothing because happiness makes one's life in need of nothing. But notice that Aristotle's definition does not say that happiness itself contains all goods. We will see (5.11) that a single good (such as contemplation) can by itself make a life choiceworthy and in need of nothing, even when that good is not all-inclusive.

[56] My treatment of Aristotle's argument should be contrasted with that of Cooper in "Aristotle on Friendship." He takes this argument to be "abortive" (p. 320) because it "assumes, altogether without explicit warrant, that a good man will have friends" (p. 318). I agree that Aristotle makes this assumption, but I do not see that as a defect. To begin with, it seems a perfectly reasonable assumption. Second, making this assumption does not beg the question being asked throughout IX.9: does a happy person *need* friends? The fact that we have something leaves open the question of whether we need it, that is, whether it is *desirable* for us to have it. The most that Cooper can claim is that if all of Aristotle's arguments took this form (that is, if they all assumed that virtuous individuals have friends), then he would merely have shown that those who have friends need friends. And surely we

Nonetheless, these three arguments have something in common. Each tries to show why friends are good from one's own point of view, and none suggests that a person lacking friends should cultivate such relationships in order to do more good for others. On the other hand, once a friendship between equals has been formed, neither of the individuals thinks that his optimal good has priority over that of his friend. Though there is rivalry in such relationships, it is not a cutthroat competition, in which each robs the other of opportunities for virtuous activity. For various kinds of reasons, each regards his friend as a good he needs for his own happiness, but this does not commit Aristotle to saying that in such relationships there is no need to limit one's pursuit of one's own good, or that each individual treats the other only in ways that maximize his own happiness.

2.17. CONTEMPLATING OTHERS

For the sake of completeness, I now want to discuss the remaining argument Aristotle gives in IX.9 for the conclusion that a happy person needs virtuous friends. It begins with the premise that happiness is a certain activity (1169b29–30), and continues as follows: "We are able to contemplate our neighbors more than ourselves, and to contemplate their actions more than our own. And the actions of excellent friends are pleasant to those who are good. . . . So the blessed person will need such friends, since he chooses to contemplate decent actions that are his own, and such are the actions of one who is a good friend" (1169b33–1170a4). In I.10, Aristotle had characterized the virtuous person not only as someone who loves doing virtuous acts, but also as someone who loves to contemplate such acts (1100b19–20). Just as an athlete or musician enjoys observing athletic or musical performances, so someone who has the virtues of the rational soul likes to observe the exercise of these moral skills. Not only is it good to act virtuously, but it is also good to see such actions done. And, Aristotle thinks, if a virtuous action is our own, then there is a special pleasure attached to observing it, simply because it is our own (1169b33). But, he says in the above passage, we are better able to observe

---

would like to know whether those who do not have friends also need them. Some of Aristotle's arguments do show this: if one's aim is to engage in ethically virtuous activity, then one needs good friends, whether one has them or not; for such friends enhance one's ability to engage in this activity. But there is no reason why every one of Aristotle's arguments must show how friends are useful instruments. In connection with this, it should also be noticed that Aristotle would be in a great deal of trouble if the premises of his second-self argument were so strong that they led to the result that the unmoved mover needs friends. The unmoved mover may perceive its own excellence, but Aristotle wants to avoid the conclusion that it must live with others in order to be happy. He can avoid this result if he takes the second-self argument to be applicable only to those who have friends.

our friends' actions than our own. Moreover, he seems to be counting the actions of one's friend as, in a way, one's own. Since it is good to observe one's own virtuous actions, and one is better able to do this when one contemplates the actions of one's friends, it is desirable to have friends.[57]

Two questions arise: First, why does Aristotle take the actions of one's friends to be one's own? Second, why does he think we are better able to observe our friends than ourselves?

Help with the first question is provided by Aristotle's remark that when our friends accomplish our goals for us, their doings are in a way our own (III.3 1112b27–8). I take him to be saying that if I ask a friend to do something for me, then in a way his action is done *by* me, since I initiated it. As he says at 1112b28, in such cases "the starting point is in us." Now, a friend is someone whose character I have helped shape, over the course of our long association. For this reason, there is a sense in which "the starting point" of whatever he does, when he expresses his character, is in me. What he does is in a way my doing as well, because his actions flow from the character that I influenced. Although the virtuous actions of a friend are not activities of one's own soul, they are, in an extended sense, one's own actions. And as we will soon see, Aristotle similarly believes that the good fortunes of your friends and children are among the goods you have, even when you are no longer alive (I.10 1100a17–30, I.11 1101b5–7). Their success is something that should be partly credited to you, and so it is your good, and not theirs alone.

But what of the second question: why does Aristotle think that we can contemplate our friends' actions better than our own? His idea, I suggest, is that too much self-consciousness about the performance of an activity undermines its chances of success. To exercise one's skills in the solution of a practical problem, one must focus on the problem itself, and not reflect on those skills. The musician, for example, must think about the notes to be played, and not about his virtues as a musician. Similarly, the courageous person thinks about how to win this particular battle, and is too engaged in this activity to step back and enjoy the observation of a courageous man in action. The political leader justly resolving a conflict between other citizens must be thinking about the details of their dispute, whereas an admiring friend can observe his skills as a negotiator. When we enjoy seeing our friends use their moral skills, we are seeing something of ourselves, since we have much to do with their accomplishments. This oblique perspective on our "own" actions gives us a better

---

[57] Like the longer argument discussed in the preceding section, this one turns on the pleasure we take in observing our friends. But there are obvious differences as well. The present argument is unique in its claim that we can observe others better than we can observe ourselves. And Aristotle's fuller argument attempts to give a deeper grounding to the claim that we take pleasure in perceiving ourselves.

view of moral activity than we can achieve through direct self-observa-
tion.[58]

2.18. EGOISM IN *NE* I?

We have found that Aristotle's discussion of friendship in the *NE* does
not commit him to pure, combative, or benign egoism. These doctrines
hold that, in all circumstances, self-regarding reasons should take precedence over other-regarding reasons; but we have seen that Aristotle's theory cannot be fit into this narrow mold. His treatment of friendship defends self-love and shows why we need virtuous friends in order to be
happy, but these aspects of his theory should not be confused with egoism in our sense. Both in the *Politics* and in the *NE*, he recognizes the
possibility of conflicting interests, and he believes that such conflicts
should be resolved in ways that reflect the legitimate claims of the various
parties. For example, those who want to lead a political life should share
office with their equals, and should not try to hold positions of power for
as long as possible; friends should similarly share opportunities for virtuous activity with their companions; and children should support their
parents, in return for the great goods they have received from them. In
such cases as these, we should act for the sake of others because they
deserve our aid, whether or not, in giving this support, we are choosing
the optimal act from our own point of view.

My reading of Aristotle conflicts with the idea that he places a person's
own happiness at the center of all practical reasoning. More precisely, it
is sometimes thought that, according to the *NE*, we should always act for
the sake of our own happiness, and if one act brings us more happiness
than any other, then it is the one we should choose. Now, if there is any
textual basis for this interpretation, it is presumably to be found in *NE* I,

---

[58] Cooper gives a very different account of the argument in "Aristotle on Friendship," pp.
320–24. He takes Aristotle's idea to be that we must study the actions of others because if
we did not, we would not know whether we ourselves are virtuous. Though Aristotle does
not actually say this here in *NE* IX.9, there is a parallel passage in *MM* II.15 (1213a10–26)
according to which self-knowledge is attained by looking to the moral features of our
friends. But I am not persuaded that Aristotle's argument in *NE* IX.9 is an attempt to convey the same idea. The passage in IX.9 concerns the pleasure we get from observing our
friends, and it says that we can observe them better than we can observe ourselves. By
contrast, the *MM* passage concerns the difficulties of knowing oneself, and it takes the observation of friends to be a mere means to the acquisition of self-knowledge. There is not a
word in *MM* 1213a10–26 about the pleasure to be had simply in observing one's friends. So
it is implausible to take the passages to be making the same point. (The authenticity and
date of the *MM* are a matter of dispute. Its authenticity is defended by Dirlmeier, *Aristoteles,
Magna Moralia*, passim, and by Cooper, "The *Magna Moralia* and Aristotle's Moral Philosophy." See too Rowe, "A Reply to John Cooper on the *Magna Moralia*"; Kenny, *The Aristotelian Ethics*, pp. 215–220, 225–230.)

for that is where Aristotle makes happiness the focal point of practical reasoning. But I shall argue that when we look carefully, what we find him saying is this: happiness is the ultimate end for the sake of which one should always act. That is quite different from the claim that *one's own* happiness is the ultimate end of one's actions.[59] Aristotle's idea, as I want to construe it, is that whether we act for our own sake, or for the sake of others, or both, happiness (our own or another's) is the good we are ultimately trying to attain. He never says, in Book I, that one's ultimate end should simply be one's own happiness, and that the happiness of others should be promoted only as a means to one's own. Such an instrumentalist attitude towards others would of course conflict with his idea that in the best relationships we seek the good of others for their sake. Aristotle's conception of friendship makes it clear that the happiness of certain others should, by itself, provide us with a reason for action. And so we should not read Book I in a way that conflicts with this. In saying that our ultimate end is and should be happiness, Aristotle must be taken to mean that ultimately we are and should be aiming at *someone's* happiness, whether our own or another's.

The *NE* opens with the observation that every craft and decision aims at some good (1094a1–2), but it does not claim that every craft and decision aims at the good of the craftsman or the decision maker. On the contrary, it is obvious from the examples Aristotle uses that crafts typically aim at the good of someone other than the craftsman. Medicine aims at health (a8); this does not mean that the doctor's task is to promote his own health, and that he ministers to others as a means to an ultimate end that is self-interested. Aristotle's point in I.1, which I will discuss more fully in Chapter 4, is that ends can be arranged in a hierarchy; it is not that the hierarchy always terminates in one's own good.

The question of where this hierarchy ends is broached at the beginning of I.2, where Aristotle claims that if there is some terminus to the hierarchy of goals (and surely, he says, there is), then we must examine what it is. That passage too will be explored more fully in Chapter 4, but for now we should notice that it contains no claim that we should try to attain that ultimate end only for ourselves:

> If there is some end of actions that we want because of itself, and we want the others because of this, and we don't choose all things because of something else

[59] W. D. Ross says: "For the most part Aristotle's moral system is decidedly self-centered. It is at his own *eudaimonia*, we are told, that man aims and should aim" (*Aristotle*, p. 230). If the second sentence is meant to support the first, then Ross must mean that it is *only* or *primarily* "at his own *eudaimonia* . . . that man aims and should aim." But there simply are no passages to support this, and Ross cites none, despite his claim that this is something "we are told."

(for they would thus proceed without limit, and desire would be empty and vain), it is obvious that this would be the good and the best. Well then, with a view to living, wouldn't knowledge of it have great weight, and wouldn't we, like archers, have a target, and be better able to strike where we should? (1094a18–24)

If we know what lies at the top of the hierarchy of ends, then that will and should have a profound impact on how we lead our lives. It will provide us with a target at which we should aim, in all we do. Now, suppose the target turns out to be physical health (a conception of happiness mentioned at I.4 1095a24). Nothing in the above passage suggests that, in that case, each of us should make our own health the ultimate end and pursue the health of others only as a means to our own. Rather, to equate happiness with health is to say what it is, ultimately, to benefit a person, whether yourself or another: it means that your highest aim, when you promote your own good, should be health; and your highest aim, when you promote the good of others, should also be health. Similarly, when Aristotle concludes that happiness consists in virtuous activity, that provides a standard at which one should always be aiming, whether that activity is one's own or that of others.

Several lines after the above passage, Aristotle assigns the study of the good to the political craft, and takes the politician to be godlike because of his concern for the good of the whole community (1094b7–10). The *NE* is a treatise on politics because it guides the statesman's decisions about how to promote the happiness of all the citizens: there is no suggestion, in Book I or elsewhere, that the politician should be concerned only with his own happiness, or that he seeks the well-being of the other citizens only as a means to his own. Aristotle thinks that the politician is appropriately concerned with both his own happiness and that of others (X.7 1177b14), and never says that his self-interested concern should always take priority over his concern for the rest of the community. The *Politics* and the *NE* are incompatible with this form of egoism. Accordingly, the claims Aristotle makes in *NE* I about the centrality of happiness should not be misread as an assertion of the priority of one's own happiness over that of others.

As we have seen, Aristotle argues in IX.9 that a happy person needs virtuous friends, and this may contribute to the mistaken impression that Book I is to be read in an egoistic way. That is, we might take him to be assuming that the appropriate place to start, when one approaches ethical theory, is with one's own happiness. The question whether one should have friends, and act for the sake of anyone besides oneself, is treated as a matter for investigation: if extending one's range of concern in this way maximizes one's own happiness, then one should do so, and otherwise not. Eventually one sees, for reasons given in IX.9, that in order to be happy, one needs friends; and since a friend is someone whose well-being is taken as a reason for action, it turns out that, for the sake of one's own happiness, one should act for the sake of others.

But, for reasons given in 2.15, I am mystified by the notion that one's own good can provide a reason for benefiting others *for their sake*. And we have seen how to read IX.9 without invoking this obscure idea. In any case, there is no textual basis for thinking that, according to Aristotle, ethical theory should begin with the assumption that maximizing one's own good is reasonable, whereas wanting to promote the good of others for their sake is a questionable attitude whose merits need to be established. For Aristotle thinks that for one to become a good person, one's emotional nature must be trained at an early point in one's childhood, so that one is eventually ready, as an adult, to harmonize the reasoning and nonreasoning parts of one's soul (X.9 1179b23–35). And no doubt the love a child has for his parents, siblings, and others who have helped him is part of the early experience that prepares the way for the more reflective life of an adult. Since friendship plays such an important role in a happy life, the childhood emotions that attach us to the good of others should be cultivated and rewarded. And so, when someone who has been properly brought up starts thinking about the topics discussed in the *NE*, he will not be concerned solely with his own good, and will not subscribe to the opinion that his own optimal well-being always takes precedence over that of others. These are not attitudes Aristotle tries to justify by means of ethical theory, nor are they attitudes he thinks the student should bring to ethical theory. Instead, he takes his audience to be directly concerned with others besides themselves. When they try to determine what happiness is, this will have a great bearing on their lives, because when they understand what this target is, they will be better able to promote their own well-being and that of all others with whom they are appropriately concerned.

There is another way in which one might arrive at the view that, according to the *NE*, each person should maximize his own good. Aristotle is often thought to equate happiness with a composite of all the types of intrinsic goods there are. Since friendship is desirable in itself (VIII.8 1159a26), having friends is taken to be a component of my own happiness, and so my acts of friendship are always undertaken not only for my friends' sake, but also for the sake of my own happiness. If, for example, a friend is ill, and I take time away from philosophy in order to help him, I am both helping him and doing what is best from my own point of view. For my own good consists not just in contemplation, but in friendship as well, and on certain occasions the mixed nature of the good requires me to give up a certain amount of philosophical activity for the sake of my friendship.[60]

But I will argue that, according to Aristotle, happiness consists in just one type of good—virtuous activity. It is not a composite of virtuous activity and friendship, or any other composite; for the passages on which such an interpretation rests have been misread. Our discussion of contemplation in X.7–8 has led to the conclusion that, according to Aristotle, the more contemplative activity a life has, the better a life it is. Accordingly, the choice between contemplation and helping a friend is a choice between an act that maximizes my own good and one that maximizes the good of another person. The reason one should help a friend in certain circumstances is that the optimal good of others sometimes has priority over one's own. Without this widely accepted assumption, Aristotle's defense of the philosophical life would require a rejection of the kind of behavior typically expected of virtuous individuals.[61]

2.19. SHARED GOODS

On my interpretation, a boundary of sorts separates the happiness of each individual from that of every other: My happiness consists entirely in my level of virtuous activity, and your happiness consists entirely in your level of virtuous activity. The happiness of an individual is not a composite of goods possessed by that individual and goods possessed by others.

[60] This is Irwin's view. In the introduction to his translation, p. xviii, he considers the objection that Aristotle's moral theory rests on "an immoral and objectionable version of egoism" and replies that this criticism "rests on a mistake about the relation between happiness and other intrinsic goods," citing his notes to 1097b3 and 1170b5. The former note says that happiness is inclusive of all intrinsic goods, and the latter says that "having friends is a part of my happiness."

[61] There is a further argument that is sometimes used to show that Aristotle is an egoist. He says that a person who has practical wisdom can deliberate well "about the things that are good and advantageous for himself" (VI.5 1140a26–7). Hardie, *Aristotle's Ethical Theory*, p. 215, takes this as evidence of an "egoistic account of practical activity," and connects this passage with Aristotle's view that the ultimate end is contemplation—another doctrine that commits Aristotle to egoism, in Hardie's opinion (see note 15 above). But 1140a26–7 does not say that the person of practical wisdom thinks *only* of his own good, or that he always places his good above that of others. Aristotle thinks that, in order to arrive at a proper conception of one's own good, one must have a general conception of the good for all human beings; anyone who has this is equipped to promote the good of others, and not just his own. This point is made explicit at 1140b7–10: people like Pericles are credited with practical wisdom because they contemplate what is good for themselves and for human beings. I take Aristotle to be rejecting the view (discussed at VI.8 1142a1–9) that politicians are mere busybodies and that practical wisdom should be attributed only to those who keep to themselves. After all, he takes the political life to be second only to the philosophical life. At 1142a9–10 he distances himself from those who say that a political life is incompatible with practical wisdom.

Of course, this does not mean that human beings are or should be un-affected by the lives of others. For one thing, the way other people treat us has a great causal influence on the degree to which we can engage in virtuous activities. If they deny us opportunities for political activity, or prohibit the study of theoretical subjects, then obviously our chances of leading happy lives are diminished. Furthermore, as we have seen, Aris-totle believes that we should not be concerned solely with our own hap-piness; instead, the misfortunes of our parents or friends may require us to take time away from our own projects. A good person not only feels pain when he learns of the misfortunes of friends, but also acts in ways that alleviate those misfortunes, even if doing so is not optimal from his own point of view. So when my family or friends suffer in various ways, and their lives are less happy, my own happiness will diminish as well, if I am aware of what has happened to them, and have the appropriate amount of concern for their well-being.

Still, their well-being and mine do not consist in the same individual goods. As I have said, my happiness consists in my virtuous activity; their happiness consists in theirs. The fact that my happiness is not a composite of an activity of my soul and the activities of other souls does not imply that I have no concern for anyone's good but my own. And although I may share in the good and bad fortune of my friends, this talk of "shar-ing" must be interpreted in causal terms: learning of their misfortunes brings me pain and causes me to alter my plans in appropriate ways. But I do not share in their fortunes in the sense that their happiness is a com-ponent of my own; their loss of happiness is not *in itself* a loss of happiness for me as well, apart from its effect on me.

Although my own happiness consists solely in the degree to which I have one type of good—virtuous activity—there are many other goods that I need as well. To engage in this activity over the course of a lifetime, I must have such other goods as health and strength. These goods are mine simply because the body that has these properties is mine. Now, I take Aristotle to be saying in I.9–11 that some of the particular goods that belong to one person can also belong to another person, by virtue of the fact that the two individuals are closely related. My child's success in his virtuous activity, for example, can be a good that I have. It belongs to him because it is a feature of his soul, and it belongs to me as well simply because he is my child. If some great good fortune has befallen my child, then whether I realize it or not, I have been fortunate as well. Even if I am no longer alive, it is good for me that my child is doing well. And yet, the good I have by virtue of my child's success is not a component of my happiness, for my happiness consists in the activities I undertook when I was alive, and it cannot be increased or diminished by anything that be-falls others after I die. So, in addition to the goods that are normally taken to be mine—goods of my soul, goods of my body, honors I have received, friends I have made—there are goods that are mine because they belong to others to whom I am closely related. My happiness is not a composite of two or more of these goods, but consists only in the virtuous activities of my own soul.

I think support for this interpretation can be found in the discussion of good and bad fortune in I.9–11. In these chapters, Aristotle takes up Solon's dictum that no one should be counted happy until his life is over (1100a10–21). That piece of advice is based on the assumption that the future may bring many reversals of fortune, and so even if someone seems to be faring well thus far, it may turn out that his life is not a good one. Solon infers that it is only after someone has died that a secure judgment can be made about his life. But Aristotle points out (a18–31) that if one follows Solon's line of reasoning to its limits, postmortem judgments may also require revision. A person can receive goods and evils after he has died: for example, he may be honored or dishonored, and his children (and their children) may do well or suffer misfortunes. If Solon has a good argument for withholding eudaimonistic judgments about a person's life until his death, then that same argument would require us always to withhold judgment. And that conclusion is absurd. But, Aristotle thinks, it is also absurd to claim that, once you are dead, the fortunes or misfortunes of your descendants have nothing to do with you (a29–31).

He agrees with Solon that we should make judgments about a person's happiness only if those judgments are relatively secure (1100b1–12), but points out that his own conception of happiness gives these judgments the requisite degree of stability (b7–22). Virtuous activities are likely to endure, and a person who has developed the virtues will be stymied in his activity only if he suffers misfortunes that are far greater than ordinary (1100b22–1101a13). If we correctly and justifiably believe that someone's life has been going well, then it is unlikely to change so much that we would want to revise our judgment. For whether or not someone is happy (that is, is engaged in virtuous activity) does not depend on whether he is lucky or unlucky in small matters. And even when great misfortunes do occur, depriving the individual of the resources he needs for the regular exercise of virtue, we can still say that he was happy for a certain considerable period of his life.[62]

---

[62] I take 1101a6–16 to be saying that a period of happiness can be succeeded by one of unhappiness, which can in turn be followed by a new period of happiness, and so on. But 1101a16–21 proposes that judgments about a person's present happiness contain an implicit prediction about the future, in which case later misfortunes can undermine the present claim that a person is now happy. It is unclear whether Aristotle accepts this proposal. See Irwin's translation, notes to 1101a16–21. This issue is more fully discussed in his "Permanent Happiness: Aristotle and Solon."

But what about the fortunes of descendants, and their potential for undoing a person after he has died? In I.11, Aristotle returns to this puzzle, and provides the following solution: Good and bad fortune vary greatly in magnitude, and the time when they occur has a bearing on this difference; events that occur after death are less important than those that occur while one is alive (1101a28–34). Accordingly, the admission that the dead share in good and evil requires no reversal in our judgments of *eudaimonia*: "If anything penetrates to them, whether it is good or the opposite, it is something feeble and small, either in itself or for them, and its quantity and quality do not make happy those who are not, nor does it take blessedness away from those who are" (1101b1–5). What underlies this solution is the claim, which Aristotle emphasizes throughout I.10, that happiness is an activity.[63] Since the dead are no longer active, their former happiness or unhappiness is a settled matter, even though they can continue to accumulate goods and evils. For happiness does not consist in possessing the sorts of goods that we can have even after we die. I take Aristotle to be saying that although our happiness is affected by the fortunes of our friends when we and they are alive, this is no longer true when one dies and one's friends (or family) remain alive. When all are alive, the good fortune of the others can causally affect one's virtuous activities; but when one dies, these activities cease, and they cannot be impeded or enhanced by the fortunes of others.

Notice that when you, your friends, and your children are all alive, the good fortune of one is also a good for all the others, whether they know about that good fortune or not (1100a19–21): just as it is a good for a dead parent when his children fare well, so too it is a good for a living parent when his children fare well, even if he is not aware of their success. But the goods we share in by virtue of our close relations with others are not components of our happiness, even when we are alive. And therefore goods we receive after we die can make no difference to our well-being. Judgments about someone's happiness are fairly stable while he is alive, and absolutely stable once his life is over; and this is compatible with the admission that good things and bad things can happen to you even when you do not realize it—even when you are dead.

Suppose Aristotle had opted for the view that a person's happiness consists not only in certain goods of his soul, but also in the happiness of other people with whom he is closely connected (such as friends, parents, and children). He would then have to face a number of serious problems. For example:

(1) If one of the goods that A possesses is B's happiness, then A should

[63] See 1100a14, 1100b10, 1100b13, 1100b19–20, 1100b30, 1101a14–15. Some of these passages will be more fully discussed in Chapter 4.

be at least as happy as B. But suppose A dies and B continues to live a good life. Why not say that A is still happy, even though he is dead? He can still possess goods after he is dead, and one of the goods he continues to possess is the happiness of B. And by having the happiness of B as one of his goods, he should be at least as happy as B. How can Aristotle maintain his position that the term of one's happiness does not extend beyond one's life?

(2) Suppose a woman has a son who leads a happy life. If his happiness is among the goods she possesses, then she should be at least as happy as he is, even though she leads a sheltered life that contains no philosophical or political activity. How can Aristotle defend his view that in order to be happy one must fully develop the ethical virtues and lead a political or intellectual life?

(3) If a son's philosophical activity is among the goods his father has, then why should a son diminish that activity in order to minister to his father's physical needs? The son's contemplation is the best good he has, and if that good belongs to his father, then it is the father's best good too. So it seems that the son will make his best contribution to his father's well-being by simply continuing to contemplate, and ignoring his father's weak physical condition. If Aristotle accepts this, then his conception of proper behavior among parents and children is radically at odds with conventional opinion. And yet, when he discusses the proper relations among family members, he relies on common opinion.

(4) If, because of our close connection, I have all the goods you have, and you have all the goods I have, then we are equally happy, even if one of us engages in more outstanding activities than the other. But, according to Aristotle, virtuous individuals rightly have a desire to outdo each other in moral competition. If one of us is going to excel the other in virtue, then I want that higher level of virtue to be mine, not yours. But if my happiness includes both my level of virtuous activity and yours, then it should not matter to me whose level is higher.

All of these problems are easily solved by the same levelheaded principle: a person's happiness consists only in his own activity, and is not a composite of the activity of several individuals. This allows Aristotle to hold that we are not happy when we are dead, and that women should not be considered happy simply because of their love of their children. Traditional family obligations are preserved because Aristotle recognizes that what is best for parents need not be best for their children. Even though a child's successful pursuit of a theoretical life may be a good possessed by his parents, it is not a good in which their happiness consists, and his debt to them is not discharged by simply carrying on with his work. Finally, moral competition makes perfect sense if each person's level of happiness depends solely on the level of his own accomplishment.

In a sense, friends share in one another's success, since the accomplishments of one are a good possessed by all. But happiness consists in exercising the moral or intellectual skills of one's own soul, and is not a composite of accomplishments.

2.20. CONCLUSION

We have seen that maximizing egoism is too simple a theory to impose on Aristotle's moral thought. He clearly believes that the good of one's family, friends, and fellow citizens by itself provides a reason for action. So reading him as a pure egoist is out of the question. But it is almost as implausible to read him as a combative egoist. He does not condone harming others as a means to one's own good. Even when he defends self-love, he insists that those who properly love themselves most of all will give others no grounds for complaint. So, if he is any kind of maximizing egoist, he must be a benign egoist. In that case, he would take it to be an ultimate principle that each person should maximize his own good. He would be saying that reasons of self-interest always have greater weight than other-regarding considerations. And he would be assuming that when we have a proper conception of our self-interest, we can never come into conflict with others. In light of his defense of self-love in IX.8, it is understandable that such a doctrine should be attributed to him.

I have argued, however, that there is a good deal in Aristotle that does not fit this picture. To begin with, he has a conception of the good that allows for the possibility of conflict between individuals. If happiness consists in the fullest amount of philosophical or political activity, then maximizing my good would in many circumstances bring me into conflict with others. Aristotle recognizes that attaining happiness requires at least a moderate level of material resources, and nothing guarantees that one person's possession of the most desirable amount will always leave as much for others as they could profitably use. Furthermore, a number of his political doctrines cannot easily be reconciled with maximizing egoism. For example, his defense of slavery implies that when a slave properly serves his master, his other-regarding reasons have greater weight than his self-regarding reasons. Similarly, his defense of ostracism and his belief that the polis has priority over any one of its equal members suggest that conflicts of interest are possible, and should be reconciled in the community's favor. He believes that we owe certain other individuals—such as our parents and fellow citizens—an appropriate form of behavior, and the rightness of such treatment does not depend on its maximizing one's good. We should help our parents when they are old, whether this fosters our philosophical and political careers or not.

In light of these facts, it seems best not to impose a simplistic maximizing formula on Aristotle's conception of human relations. Although he does claim that one should love oneself most of all, his arguments show that he is endorsing *fair* moral competition, and so he is not committed to denying the possibility of conflict between the optimal good of different individuals. I conclude that *if* Aristotle equates an individual's happiness with the virtuous activity of that individual, and not with some larger composite of goods, then he is not a maximizing egoist. Of course, this way of understanding Aristotelian happiness requires further support. In Chapter 3, we must look once again at Aristotle's defense of the philosophical life, and then, in Chapters 4–6, we must see how that defense flows from the conception of happiness put forward in *NE* I.

CHAPTER THREE

Philosophy and Other Goods

3.1. AN OVERVIEW

In this chapter, I return to Aristotle's conception of the philosophical life, and to the problem of how it is tied to his treatment of happiness in Book I of the *NE*. In particular, we need to consider several portions of X.7–8 that might mislead us into thinking that this late segment of the *NE* is radically at odds with the rest of his work. As I see it, when Aristotle argues on behalf of contemplation, he does not turn his back on the goods and psychological assumptions that play an important role in the rest of the *NE*. To support my reading, I will consider a number of those goods—pleasure, friendship, ethical virtue—and explain why they are included within the philosophical life. Our treatment of these topics will lead us through several of the arguments Aristotle gives in defense of contemplation. We will thus move beyond the narrow focus of Chapter 1, which considered only one argument (the argument from divinity: X.8 1178b7–32) for equating perfect happiness with contemplation.

But I will not yet try to give a full explanation of why Aristotle thinks that the best human life is devoted to theory: that will be possible only after we have examined the function argument of *NE* I.7. Nor will this chapter address all legitimate doubts about whether the discussions of happiness in Books I and X can be made consistent. For we must still determine whether Book I treats happiness as a composite of all intrinsic goods. Instead, my aim at present is to propose a way of integrating Aristotle's two treatments of happiness, and the material that falls between them. By a series of small steps, I will try to argue for this synoptic interpretation, and to disarm some objections to it. Once the reader has this larger picture of the *NE* in mind, we can turn to the heart of Aristotle's conception of human well-being, in Book I.

On my reading of the *NE*, Aristotle thinks that the ideal life for human beings is one in which we engage in theoretical activity on a regular basis. Furthermore, I take him to be saying that there is no such thing as too much philosophy for one's own good. The more such activity a life has, the better a life it is. But I also believe that, according to the *NE*, we must have many other goods besides contemplation if we are to lead a life in which we are regularly occupied with theoretical studies. Though perfect happiness consists in contemplation alone, that good is just the pinnacle of a large hierarchy of goods, each of which plays a role in promoting the philosophical life. To contemplate over a long period of time, we need not only theoretical wisdom, but the ethical virtues, friends, physical pleasure, honor, health, financial resources, and so on. Human beings are not gods, for we can engage in contemplation over an extended period of time only if we recognize the normal features of the human situation: we can attain our good only by uniting together in communities, and only by providing ourselves with various material resources. Without physical security, health, and like-minded friends, the philosophical life of any normal human being becomes difficult at best.

To what extent should these subordinate ends be pursued? According to the interpretation I shall be defending, Aristotle thinks that the best a person can do for himself is to pursue each subordinate good to the extent that it contributes to his own perfect happiness. In other words, a person's good is optimized when contemplation is pursued without limit, and all other goods besides this should be promoted to the extent that they contribute to contemplation. There are upper and lower bounds to the value of all other goods besides theoretical activity, and this good alone is valuable without limit.

For example, consider a person who cuts back on the amount of philosophical activity he engages in, because he wants (for his own sake) to engage in feats of outstanding ethical virtue. As I read Aristotle, he would say that such a person attaches too much weight to ethical and too little to philosophical activity. He is making his life less happy by cutting back on the best activity in order to make room for one that is inferior. Of course, there may be excellent reasons for setting aside one's theoretical work and engaging in ethical acts instead: the well-being of others may vitally depend on it. But in these cases, one's act is justified because it is sometimes appropriate to benefit others for their sake, even if this diminishes one's own happiness to some extent. The best amount of ethical activity to engage in, from one's own point of view, is the amount that will best promote one's theoretical interests. This does not mean that there is some one right number of ethical acts. Rather, it means that we have a guideline for establishing the best upper and lower limits for engaging in this kind of activity. And similarly for all other goods: physical pleasure promotes one's happiness to the extent that it facilitates the intellectual life; the right number of friends to have is the number that best promotes one's theoretical activities; the best level of wealth is the one that frees one for intellectual work without burdening one with unnecessary financial responsibilities; and so on.

It should be remembered, however, that Aristotle has an account of what the second-best human life is: if one cannot engage in theoretical activity, or if one owes it to others not to do so, then one should devote oneself instead to the cultivation and full exercise of the moral virtues. If a life must be devoid of theoretical activity, then the best one can do is to engage in ethical activity as much as possible. And this too provides a standard for determining the extent to which lesser goods should be pursued: for such a person, the right number of friends, the right amount of physical pleasure, and so on is the amount that best promotes the ethical life. Notice that the upper and lower limits set by ethical activity and those set by philosophical activity may sometimes be the same: for example, the best number of friends to have may be any number between two limits, whether one is leading a philosophical or a political life. But this will not be true in all cases. If one is leading a political life, then one will need far more political power than it would be advisable for a philosopher to have.

It should also be noticed that these two standards—philosophical and ethical activity—can be applied to one's treatment of others, as well as to the design of one's own life. The ideal way to promote the good of others is to help them arrange their lives in such a way that they contemplate as much as possible. But Aristotle assumes that the number of people who are suited to such a life is small, and so in most cases one best promotes the good of others by using virtuous practical activity as a standard. The best one can do to help most people is to promote their ability to lead an ethically virtuous life; all of their other goods should be arranged in a way that facilitates their achievement of this second-best end. Accordingly, a political leader will adjust the level of resources in a community so that they are neither too great nor too small: crafts, drama, wealth, and so on should be regulated with a view to their effect on the citizens' ability to develop and exercise the ethical virtues.

So, whether one leads a philosophical life or not, one should always appeal to some form of virtuous activity (theoretical or practical) as one's standard in determining how to promote the good of a human being. And these standards should be used both when the human being in question is oneself and when he is someone else. Such a standard does not tell us how much weight to attach to one person's good as opposed to that of others. Aristotle does provide some general guidelines for dealing with interpersonal conflicts: for example, we owe a great debt to our parents and friends, and they should receive more attention than strangers. But contemplation and virtuous activity are not proposed as goods to which we should appeal in resolving conflicts between different individuals. Aristotle is not saying that since philosophical activity is the highest good, the well-being of a philosopher always takes precedence over the good of a nonphilosopher. Similarly, he does not believe that if one owes a debt to a person of middling character, but a person of superior virtue can make better use of the money, then one should help the latter, rather than repay one's debt (IX.2 1164b30–34). The superiority of contemplation and ethical activity to all other goods is a fact to which we should appeal when we are trying to decide what will be in a person's best interests. What to do when there is a conflict between the good of several individuals is a further question.

3.2. Too Much and Too Little

The interpretation sketched in the preceding section can be defended only by means of a thorough discussion of *NE* I and its connection with X.7–8. I will undertake that task in Chapter 4. For now, I will try to explain what motivates my reading, and why I think it is viable.

I will argue that in Book I Aristotle identifies happiness with only one type of good—virtuous activity. I take him to mean by this that happiness consists either in excellent theoretical activity or in excellent practical activity. That is, to lead our lives well, we should make one of these goods our ultimate end, and all other goods should be sought for the sake of one of these highest goals. In Book I, Aristotle leaves aside the question of whether one of these ultimate ends is a better choice than the other, but in X.7–8 he argues that a life lived for the sake of philosophical activity is superior to one devoted to moral activity. Accordingly, the best among happy lives is that of a person who regularly contemplates and who chooses all other goods for the sake of contemplation. The second-best life is that of a person who regularly engages in political activity and who pursues all other goals with an eye to *this* ultimate end.

Now, since Aristotle thinks (I.12 1102a2–4) that everything we do is and should be done for the sake of happiness (our own or another's or both), his identification of happiness with virtuous activity alone commits him to a certain attitude towards other types of good: we should pursue them only to the extent that doing so promotes our ability to engage in virtuous activity. Since happiness is virtuous activity, and we should act only for the sake of happiness, there is no reason to have more other goods than are needed in order to sustain a virtuous life. And of course we should not have so few of these subordinate goods that our ability to lead such a life is impaired. So, Aristotle thinks that once we recognize what the ultimate end of our lives should be, this provides us with the appropriate standard for determining the extent to which lesser goods should be pursued. If we are to engage regularly in virtuous activity—of whichever form—over a long period of time, then, as Aristotle puts it, we must be "sufficiently equipped" with other goods besides this: "What then prevents us from saying that a happy person is someone who is active in accordance with perfect virtue and who is sufficiently equipped with external goods, not for some chance period of time, but for a perfect life?" (I.10 1101a14–16). What Aristotle means here by "perfect virtue" is an important and difficult question, which we will discuss in Chapter 4. Setting that problem aside for the moment, it is reasonable to take him to be saying here that when it comes to external goods, the question of how much is enough is to be answered by determining the contribution they make to perfect virtuous activity. To have too few external goods is to have so few that one's pursuit of virtuous activity is impaired. Similarly, to have more than one needs is to have more than is necessary from the point of view of such activity. And Aristotle believes (X.8 1179a1–9) that a moderate supply of external goods is all we need in order to lead the philosophical life. In any case, when it comes to goods other than virtuous activity, there is no such thing as an appropriate amount, apart from the question of how these goods are related to virtuous activity. It provides the standard for determining the extent to which they should be pursued.

Another passage that suggests this same picture can be found in the discussion of pleasure in Book VII. After asserting that a virtuous person will no longer be happy if he falls upon great misfortunes, Aristotle notes that our vulnerability to chance has misled some into identifying happiness with good fortune: "Because fortune is needed in addition, it seems to some that good fortune is the same as happiness. But it isn't, for even it is an impediment when it is excessive, and perhaps it is no longer right to call it good fortune. For it is in relation to happiness that it has a limit (*horos*)" (VII.13 1153b21–5). To see whether a chance occurrence is good for a person, and how good it is, we must determine how it has affected his virtuous activity. If it increases his level of wealth, for example, it may provide him with the resources he needs in order to carry out some outstanding project for the community; and by enabling him to engage in this virtuous activity, it will increase his level of happiness. On the other hand, an increase in wealth may make no contribution at all to a person's well-being: since an increase in wealth is not in itself an increase in happiness, a windfall may do one no good. And Aristotle suggests that great resources can even detract from one's level of virtuous activity. Ostracism, as we saw in Chapter 2, provides him with one example, but he may be thinking of other cases as well. Perhaps, if one is leading a life devoted to theoretical studies, too much wealth brings attentions or responsibilities that impede one's favored activities. In any case, when Aristotle says that happiness provides a limit to good fortune, he means that we should wish for only that level of fortune that enhances our virtuous activity. More generally, the right level for any good other than happiness is the level at which it best contributes to one of the ultimate ends in which happiness consists.

This concern with quantitative questions—how much of any good is the right amount?—begins with a remark Aristotle makes in I.2. Having posed the question of what the ultimate end is, he argues that the science devoted to the study of this question is politics. And to defend this connection between politics and the ultimate end, he takes note of the authoritative position of politics with respect to other pursuits. "It determines which of the sciences are needed in cities, and what sorts of things each person should learn, and to what extent (*mechri tinos*)" (1094a28–b2). To determine the extent to which music, drawing, gymnastics, or any other subject should be studied, politics must look to the ultimate end of human life. How large a role they should play depends on the value of the goods they provide, and these goods are in turn assessed by the contribution they make to virtuous activity. So, in looking for an ultimate end, Aristotle is looking for a way to determine, for any given good, how much is too much and how little too little. Since ethically virtuous activity is the highest end that *all* citizens are capable of, the goal of politics is to foster the practical virtues and to regulate all other ends and pursuits so that they contribute to this goal.

Aristotle's conception of politics rests on the assumption that no specialized craft has the resources for understanding how worthwhile its end is, and that such normative questions can be properly answered only by undertaking a study of human happiness. The doctor's study of health can tell him what physical condition it consists in, and how it is most effectively attained or safeguarded, but it does not tell him how good it is or why it is good. Medical science just assumes that health is a good and carries on from there. To determine how large a role health should play in human life, we must ask what our ultimate end should be: does it consist partly or wholly in health, or is health instead valuable because it promotes some further good? Similarly, the trained musician does not learn, by virtue of that training, how large a role music should play in human life. No study that bypasses the question of what human well-being consists in can assess the worth of its own goal. And since Aristotle argues that the ultimate end of every political community and every individual should be some form of virtuous activity, he must say that health, music, and all other goods should be valued and pursued to the extent that they make some contribution to philosophical or moral activity.

These points are made explicit in *Politics* VII.1, where Aristotle sketches the conception of happiness that will guide his construction of an ideal state. Like any instrument, external goods have a limit (*peras*) beyond which they are of no use and may even do harm (1323b7–10); happiness consists not in them, but in goods of the soul, for the more we have of these goods, the better off we are (b10–11). And just as in *NE* X.8 Aristotle appeals to the activity of the gods to support his conception of happiness, so in *Politics* VII.1 he tries to justify his conception of happiness by pointing out that the gods lack external goods without suffering any loss in happiness (b23–6).[1] Accordingly, the degree to which we are happy is the degree to which we possess the goods of the soul (b21–3), and external goods are important only to the extent that they promote these further ends.

In searching for an answer to the question of how much of any good is the right amount, Aristotle seems to be looking for a mean between extremes, and this of course puts us in mind of his famous doctrine of the mean. But precisely what does that doctrine amount to, and how is it connected with his search for an ultimate end? I will turn to these questions in Chapter 6. For now, I will simply note that Aristotle wants his notion of a mean to provide substantive answers to quantitative questions. Having organized his treatment of the ethical virtues in Books II–IV around the mean, he complains at the beginning of VI that what he has said so far is too weak:

> In all the states mentioned, as well as others, there is a certain target to which the person who has reason looks as he tightens or relaxes; and there is a certain *horos* [limit, standard, boundary, definition] of the mean states. . . . To say this is true, but not precise. . . . If one had only this, one would be none the wiser. For example, [one would be none the wiser about] what sorts of things must be applied to the body if someone were to say: whatever medical science prescribes, and as the one who has this [science applies them]. Therefore, this also holds for the states of the soul: one must not only say this thing truly, but one must also determine what the right reason is and what is its *horos*. (VI.1 1138b21–34)[2]

He offers to remedy this weakness in the remainder of Book VI by discussing the virtues of the rational soul, but it is not clear how that discussion makes the doctrine of the mean a more substantive guide to action. According to the interpretation I shall defend, Aristotle's idea is that his

---

[1] Note that Aristotle here violates the rule that, according to Nussbaum, he imposes on himself throughout his practical works (with the sole exception of *NE* X.7–8). She takes him to believe that practical philosophy must not draw any conclusions about how humans should live from information about how the gods live. "The life of a divine being might be ever so admirable; but the study of this life, insofar as it lies beyond our capabilities, is not pertinent to the practical aim of ethics" (*The Fragility of Goodness*, p. 293). This does not accurately represent Aristotle's view in the *NE* (as X.7–8 shows) or in the *Politics* (as VII.1 shows). Nussbaum's idea that Aristotelian ethics must be insulated from theology is based on false inferences from the texts cited in Chapter 1, note 43.

[2] Aristotle here takes up a thread left hanging at II.2 1103b31–4. Though *NE* VI is also one of the books of the *EE*, *NE* II is not common to the two treatises, and it explicitly calls for further clarification of "the right reason." Because of this connection between *NE* II and VI.1, we cannot take the questions raised in the latter chapter to belong solely to the *EE*.

treatment of practical and theoretical wisdom, and his assessment of their relative worth in X.7–8, will give us a far more precise idea of how to lead our lives. Once we know what practical and theoretical wisdom are, and once we decide which is the superior virtue, we will have developed our conception of happiness so that it is precise enough to tell us how much honor, wealth, pleasure, and so on is too much and how little is too little. If we simply know that we should not have too many or too few of these goods, we have no standard for decision making. But when we take our ultimate aim to be the exercise of either theoretical or practical wisdom (integrated with the ethical virtues), then we can strengthen the doctrine of the mean so that it has real substance: we should pursue the lesser goods, and adjust our emotions, in such a way that we are best able to lead the philosophical life or, if that option is unavailable, the political life.

3.3. The Problem of Intrinsic Goods

One of the many objections that can be made to the interpretation I have just outlined is that it takes Aristotle to be treating all goods other than virtuous activity as though they had purely instrumental value. On my reading, he believes that every good other than virtuous activity should be pursued only to the extent that it promotes that activity. But it is uncontroversial that, according to Aristotle, other goods besides virtuous activity are desirable in themselves (see, for example, I.7 1097b2–4). And it may be thought that, in his opinion, our decision making should be sensitive to this difference between goods that are desirable in themselves and those that are not: the fact that a good is intrinsically good should give it greater weight than it would have if it were desirable only as a means. Since a purely instrumental good is one that is desirable only to the extent that it promotes something else, an intrinsic good must be one that has some value beyond any instrumental worth it may have. And decision making that ignores that additional source of value is defective.

Accordingly, in order to decide how to act, we must assess each good at its true worth, apart from its role in promoting other goods. We must develop a sense of how important virtuous activity, pleasure, honor, friends, and so on are, and we must not pursue any of these goods merely to the extent that it promotes one or more others. The proper level of physical pleasure, for example, must be greater than the level that would be appropriate if it were merely a means to virtuous activity.[3] Accord-

---

[3] This is explicit in Cooper, *RHGA*, pp. 109–110. He says that Aristotle assigns to physical pleasures "a value of their own, albeit a small one, and treats them as worth giving up some amount of thinking in order to enjoy" (p. 109). More generally, he holds that Aristotle's discussion of the ethical virtues is "constructed on the assumption that there is a plurality of independent values which it is the function of the moral virtues to support, each

ingly, Aristotle must believe that happiness consists in all such intrinsic goods. He thinks that we should always act for the sake of happiness, and there will be times when we should pursue physical pleasure just for itself, even though our doing so does not contribute to virtuous activity or any other good. On those occasions, we will be pursuing pleasure just because it is one of the components of happiness.

My arguments against this widely accepted picture of the *NE* are yet to come. I will try to show in Chapter 4 that Aristotle identifies happiness with virtuous activity alone, even though he realizes that other goods besides this are desirable in themselves. And in Chapter 5, I will argue that the "inclusivist" conception of happiness put forward in the preceding paragraph lacks sound textual support. There simply is no good evidence that in the *NE* Aristotle identifies happiness with a composite of virtuous activity and other intrinsic goods—though there is one passage, cited in the Introduction, that has led many readers to this misinterpretation (I.7 1097b14–20).

But I believe that this common misreading of the *NE* is encouraged by a preconception of what Aristotle must mean when he says that certain goods are desirable in themselves. That preconception is the one just described: if a good is desirable in itself, then it must be given more weight in decision making than it would appropriately receive if it had merely instrumental value. To think otherwise is in effect to collapse the distinction between goods that are desirable in themselves and goods that are not. This preconception about intrinsic value is not based on anything Aristotle says, but is simply our own prejudice about what he must mean if he is to make sense. And the way to rid ourselves of this prejudice is to examine the text and let it determine the meaning of Aristotle's distinction between intrinsic and instrumental value. This is a task I will undertake later (see 5.12–14). What I will do now is consider two goods that he takes to be desirable in themselves: amusements and friends. The right amount of amusement, he believes, is the amount that best promotes virtuous activity. And similarly the right number of friends to have is the number that we need for such activity. So he sees no incompatibility between saying that a good is desirable in itself and saying that it should be

---

at its appropriate level" (p. 110). I think that part of this is perfectly correct: Aristotle believes that physical pleasures and certain other goods are "independent values," in the sense that each is desirable in itself. But I do not accept Cooper's inference (not based on anything in Aristotle) that they must be "worth giving up some amount of thinking in order to enjoy." Notice that this interpretation by itself makes X.7–8 inconsistent with the rest of the *NE*. Those chapters hold that more contemplation is always better than less, and this means that one should *not* give up a certain amount of theoretical activity in order to make more room in one's life for physical enjoyment. Of course, in *RHGA*, Cooper accepts this inconsistency.

pursued to the extent that it contributes to some other good. If we make the a priori assumption that these claims are incompatible, then we will inevitably misunderstand what Aristotle is doing.

3.4. AMUSEMENT

In *NE* X.6, Aristotle returns to the topic of happiness and restates some of the main ideas of his earlier treatment in Book I. Happiness, he reminds us, is an activity rather than a state (1176a33–b2), and it is an activity that is choiceworthy in itself (1176b2–5). Now, although his own view is that happiness consists in virtuous activities (b7–9), he first considers a rival thesis, before he takes up the question of which virtuous activities are best. According to this thesis, happiness consists in pleasant amusements (b9–10). Advocates of this view would point out that they engage in such activities for no further end. And so, in their opinion, amusements meet two of the conditions Aristotle himself has laid down: they are activities, and they are desirable in themselves.

Aristotle makes several diverse points about this conception of happiness: The fact that many people are considered happy because they amuse themselves is no argument in favor of this conception, for they have experienced nothing better than these pleasures, and choose their end out of ignorance (1176b16–27). Furthermore, if these sorts of pleasures are to be equated with happiness, then a good life is available to anyone at all— even a slave; and yet no one would say that a slave's life is happy (1177a6–9). But for our purposes, the most important point Aristotle makes is the one that reveals his own view about the proper role of amusement in a happy life. He reminds us that happiness is the end for the sake of which everything is to be done (1176b30–31), and insists that it is "extremely stupid and childish" to take that ultimate end to consist in something frivolous rather than something serious (b32–3). Those who identify happiness with amusement have reversed the proper relationship between the serious and the amusing: the latter is for the sake of the former (b33–4). For amusements are a form of relaxation, and we need relaxation because we cannot engage in serious work continuously (b34–5). Even when we enjoy serious pursuits, we cannot go on enjoying them indefinitely; as Aristotle points out in VII.14 (1154b20–31), we eventually grow tired of what we are doing, and need to change the object of our attention. So for a while we turn to less demanding pursuits, until we are ready to return to the activities we prefer.

I suggest that this attitude towards amusement commits Aristotle to a certain way of determining how much of it is appropriate. If the purpose served by amusement is the restoration of our ability to engage in more serious undertakings, then the proper amount of time to devote to amusement is whatever amount—no more and no less—that serves this purpose. To be consistent, he can take no other view, given his thesis that more philosophical activity is always better than less, and the parallel thesis that, contemplation aside, more ethical activity is always better than less. A person who undertakes less virtuous activity than he might, because he wants to spend more of his time on amusements, leads a less desirable life than he could: he is needlessly devoting less time to what is important in order to make more room for what is frivolous. Conversely, it is possible to underestimate the amount of relaxation we need, and by returning to serious pursuits before we are ready to carry them out with skill and pleasure, we may undermine our own purposes. Of course, it is not possible to decide precisely how much time is needed for relaxation before we are ready to return to more important activities. To put Aristotle's guidelines into effect requires a certain amount of self-knowledge, but guesswork cannot be entirely eliminated.

An alternative reading of Aristotle would take him to be saying that we should amuse ourselves even more than we need to in order to return to more serious work. According to this interpretation, amusements have a certain intrinsic value, and so we must to some extent curtail our more serious pursuits in order to have some fun. Even when we want to continue with our philosophical or political work, even when we are fully enjoying it and are fully exercising our skills, we must sometimes cut our activity short, and give amusements the amount of time that reflects their intrinsic worth.

Part of what this interpretation asserts may be true: Aristotle may believe that amusements are desirable in themselves. (We will soon investigate this question.) But the rest of the interpretation is obviously undermined by what he says in X.6–8. Amusements are for the sake of more serious activity, and have no proper place in our lives beyond the contribution they make to whatever it is that happiness consists in. If we read him in any other way, we do so not on the basis of any text, but simply because we assume that intrinsic goods must play a larger role than this.

If I have given a correct account of how much time Aristotle thinks should be devoted to amusement, we can turn to the next question: Does he think that this good is desirable in itself? Or does he take it to be desirable *only* for the sake of the more serious activities that it promotes? In X.6 (1176b9–10), he points out that pleasant amusements are chosen for themselves, but this does not commit him to saying that they are *rightly* chosen for themselves. He argues that they are not at the pinnacle of the hierarchy of goods, but instead occupy some lower position. This allows for the possibility that they are both desirable in themselves and desirable for the sake of virtuous activity. But in X.6 he does not commit himself to that possibility.

Nonetheless, in view of what Aristotle says elsewhere, a plausible case can be made that he takes certain amusements—the ones chosen by a virtuous person—to be good in themselves. He says that amusements are necessarily pleasant (*Pol.* VIII.5 1339b15–16), and pleasure is a good that he and his audience desire for itself: "Honor, pleasure, understanding, and every virtue we choose because of themselves (for if nothing resulted we would choose each of them), and we choose them also for the sake of happiness, since we assume that because of them we will be happy" (I.7 1097b2–5). These lines need further discussion, for it is unclear what Aristotle means when he says that pleasure is desired for the sake of happiness. We will turn to that question in Chapter 4. In any case, it is clear from this passage that he and his audience take pleasures to be good in themselves, apart from their contribution to happiness. Similarly, the discussion of pleasure in X.1–5 suggests that Aristotle takes it to be good in itself. Without objection, he records Eudoxus's point that pain is in itself to be avoided, and that correspondingly pleasure must be desirable in itself (X.2 1172b19–23). Once we know that something is painful, we already have a reason to reject it; and similarly, once we know that something is pleasant, we do not need a further reason for pursuing it. Aristotle takes these and other arguments to be too weak to show that pleasure is *the* good (b26–35), but he never challenges the claim that pain is in itself bad and pleasure in itself good. Accordingly, since amusements are pleasures, they are desirable both for their own sake and also because they restore our ability to engage in more difficult activities. If we could take a tasteless pill that had the same restorative powers as amusing activities, that pill would be a mere means; but the pleasantness of amusing activities makes them desirable in themselves.

Now, Aristotle believes that not all amusements are equally worthwhile (IV.8 1128a19–25), and that some will be completely avoided by a virtuous person (a29–32). Such activities may appear to be pleasant to an inferior person, but that does not show that they really are pleasant. Presumably Aristotle would not want to say that these amusements are desirable in themselves; the person to whom they seem pleasant may want them for their own sake, but since they are not really pleasant, he is wrong to want them for that reason (X.5 1176a10–24). They are desired for themselves, but are not desirable in themselves.

Accordingly, Aristotle believes that the amusements chosen by a virtuous person are genuinely pleasant and therefore good in themselves; yet at the same time he thinks that such activities should be pursued only to the extent that they restore our ability to engage in virtuous activities. Whether or not we take these to be inconsistent claims, Aristotle makes them both.

3.5. How Many Friends?

If Aristotle were to make a list of the various external goods that some particular person has, then the names of that person's friends would be on the list. For he takes a person's friends to be among his external goods (I.8 1099a31–b1, IX.9 1169b9–10). Furthermore, if the list of external goods were split into three—those desirable merely as means, those merely good in themselves, and those that have both intrinsic and instrumental value—then that person's friends would be included within the latter group. For in the *Rhetoric*, when Aristotle makes a list of the various items that are goods, he says that a friend is choiceworthy in himself, besides being productive of many things (I.6 1362b19–20). In other words, he holds that the desirability of friends is not exhausted by their instrumental value. Even if we already had the various good things that friends bring us, and did not need them for their instrumental value, it would still be good to have friends. And Aristotle makes the same claim in the *NE*: "Presumably it is absurd to make the blessed person solitary. For no one would choose to be by himself and have all the goods" (IX.9 1169b16–18).[4] That is, even if we could have all other goods besides friends, we would still want friends. For they are in themselves worth having.

But how many friends (that is, friendships based on character) is it desirable for one to have, from one's own point of view? Aristotle raises this question in *NE* IX.10, and argues that although there is no single right answer, upper and lower limits exist (1170b29–33). The smallest possible number, of course, is one, and although Aristotle does not urge his readers to have only one friend, neither does he argue that one is always too few. As he points out, the friendships commemorated in verse are those that exist between just two people (1171a15). But what of the upper limit? Here, he argues that it would be a mistake to try to have as many friends as possible. To begin with, when friendship is based on character, the individuals involved devote a considerable amount of time to each other; and to have such relationships with more and more people makes it difficult to continue the friendships already established (a2–6). Furthermore, since friends share each other's joys and sorrows, larger and larger circles of friends are increasingly vulnerable to a certain conflict: one may need to share the joy of one friend while sharing the sorrow of another (a6–8).

What criterion should one look to, then, in deciding how many friends

---

[4] Notice that this statement does not commit Aristotle to the view that friends are components of happiness. It only commits him to the claim that no human life can be happy if it is devoid of friendship. Friends are necessary for happiness, but are nonetheless subordinate to the ultimate end, which consists solely in virtuous activity. For the connection between friendship and virtuous activity, see 2.15–17, 3.6–8.

would be too many and how few too few? Aristotle's formula is that one should have "as many as are sufficient for living together" (1171a9–10). Now, to live together with someone else is not necessarily to reside together in the same house, as one does with one's children, parents, or spouse. Living together is a matter of jointly participating in some common activity on a regular and frequent basis. But as Aristotle points out elsewhere, the interests that unite people and provide the focus for common pursuits are diverse:

> Whatever existence is for each person, or whatever it is for the sake of which he chooses to live, this is what he wants to pursue with his friends. Therefore, some drink together, others play dice together, others do gymnastics together and hunt together, or philosophize together. They spend their days together in whatever it is that they love most, of all the things in their lives. For since they want to live together with their friends, they do these things, and share in the things by means of which they think they live together. (IX.12 1172a1–8)

No one would take this to mean that it doesn't matter what one does with friends, so long as one pursues one's favored project with like-minded individuals. Aristotle is simply pointing out that many different kinds of favored activities can lead people to want to spend their time with others. Some people like drinking more than any other activity, and so they pursue this interest with friends who have the same preference. This should not be taken to mean that such friendships are based on character. For as Aristotle has said in a previous chapter, individuals united together in that superior kind of relationship live together in order to "share in discussion and thought" (IX.9 1170b11–12). Those who spend their days together in order to play dice or hunt or drink have friendships based on pleasure rather than character.

So, one should have as many friends as are "sufficient for living together" (1171a9–10), and one lives together with others in order to pursue one's favored activities. In other words, to decide how many friends one should have, one must first determine what is most worth pursuing; the right number of friends is the number that will best enhance one's pursuit of this activity. Now, Aristotle obviously believes that the activity most worth pursuing is philosophy, and so the right number of friends to have is the one that would best facilitate the achievement of philosophical understanding. As he points out, there may be no single number that is uniquely correct (1170b32–3). And he leaves open the possibility that one very close philosophical friend may be best for a certain sort of person. But he rejects the idea that the more such friends one has the better off one is. For at some point a circle of philosophical friends becomes too large to serve its purpose. Though he does not explain why this is so, he is presumably thinking of the fact that the opportunity to share in conversations diminishes as the conversational group grows. Accordingly, the best number of friends to have falls within the intermediate range, whatever it is, that best promotes one's philosophical understanding and activity. Of course, on my reading of the *NE*, Aristotle also believes that if one cannot or should not make contemplation one's ultimate end, then one should instead devote one's life to ethical activity. In this case, one uses a second-best standard to determine how many friends one should have: one chooses one's friends solely on the basis of their practical virtue, and the number that is best to have is whatever number will best promote one's own moral development and activity. The number of friends that is best for philosophers could be the same as the number of friends best for statesmen. But since they live together for different purposes, they look to different standards to determine how many friends are "sufficient for living together."

The upshot of our discussion is this: Aristotle believes that (a) the friends one has are among the goods that are desirable in themselves, and (b) one should have as many friends as will promote some further end, namely, either of the two ultimate ends. He sees no incompatibility between (a) and (b). And this parallels the point made in the preceding section: though amusements are desirable in themselves, we should pursue these pleasures only to the extent that they are needed for the sake of virtuous activity. So, the fact that Aristotle takes something to be desirable in itself does not show that he sets its appropriate level higher than the level that best promotes some further good. Of course, we have not yet said what Aristotle's distinction between purely instrumental and intrinsic goods comes to. What does he mean by saying that a good is desirable in itself? What is the practical significance of classifying a good in this way? These are questions I will address in Chapter 5. The only point I have tried to establish is that certain intrinsic goods have a property in common with purely instrumental goods: they should be pursued to the extent that they lead to something else.

One further observation is in order. In the last chapter of the *EE*, Aristotle raises a problem that parallels the one posed in *NE* VI.1: some limit (*horos*) is needed so that we can determine the proper amount of such natural goods as honor, wealth, health, and good fortune (1249a21–b3). We cannot say "as reason prescribes," and leave it at that. For that would be like saying that the healthy amount of food is whatever medical science prescribes: though this is true, we need a more precise standard (1249b3–6). And then Aristotle gives the following answer: "Whatever choice and possession of things good by nature will most of all produce contemplation of the god—[whether it be goods] of the body, or money, or friends, or the other goods—this is best, and this is the finest limit. But whatever, either through deficiency or through excess, hinders us from serving and contemplating the god, is inferior" (b16–21). I take this to mean that just as we should have enough money to lead a philosophical life, but not so much as would impede this activity, so too with friends. In a roundabout way, then, the *NE* arrives at the same practical result as the *EE*: we should have as many friends as are sufficient for living together, and we should live together with friends in order to further our common interest in philosophy.[5]

3.6. SELF-SUFFICIENCY

I believe that throughout the *NE*, Aristotle accepts the point that he makes most fully in IX.9: in order to lead good lives, human beings need friends. In X.7–8, he does not abandon this view, but instead provides a criterion for determining how many friends it would be best to have. We live together with others in order to pursue common interests (IX.12 1172a1–8), and should have as many friends as are needed to do so (IX.10 1171a9–10). Since philosophy is the most important common interest, the number of friends it is best to have is the number that most contributes to one's philosophical understanding. However, a remark Aristotle makes in X.7 might be taken to suggest that, if one leads a philosophical life, one can be happy even if one lacks friends. To demonstrate the superiority of contemplation, he argues that those who have theoretical wisdom are more self-sufficient than those who have the practical virtues. And to support this point, he says: "The theoretically wise person is able to contemplate even while he is by himself, and the more theoretical wisdom he has the more he is able to do so" (1177a32–4). This does not say in so many words that the practically wise person can be *happy* even if he is isolated and has no friends. It says only that he can *contemplate* even when he is by himself. But it might seem that Aristotle is committed to the further statement. If perfect happiness consists in contemplation, and

---

[5] For a different interpretation of this passage, see Cooper, *RHGA*, pp. 135–143. On his reading, Aristotle is allowing that the proper amount of natural goods (friends, wealth, and so on) might be quite different from the amount that would best promote contemplation. Instead, the right level is to be determined through a two-stage process: (a) Have as many natural goods as one needs in order to fulfill all of one's moral requirements; (b) then add whatever additional goods are needed so that one can contemplate as fully as possible. Intellectual goods "are to be pursued single-mindedly, and preferred to any amount of other goods, once the requirements of the moral virtues are met" (p. 142). By contrast, on my reading, Aristotle provides a simpler standard: have as many natural goods as will promote contemplation. I think he is assuming that the level of natural goods, as determined by this standard, will never be so high or low as to make it impossible to be an ethically virtuous person. Cooper's more complex reading is based on the fact that, according to this passage, the natural goods, when chosen by a fine-and-good person, are fine (1249a5–14). I do not think this is evidence for a two-stage standard.

if one can contemplate even when one is by oneself, then isn't he in effect saying here that the philosopher can be happy without friends?

Before we answer this question, we should recall a point made in I.7; we cannot determine whether a person is happy by looking at a small temporal segment of his life—an hour, a day—and seeing what he is doing at that time. "One swallow does not make a spring, nor does one day; so too, one day or a short time does not make someone blessed and happy" (1098a18–20). So, from the fact that a person is contemplating on a given day or during any other short period of time, we cannot infer that Aristotle would count him happy. For nothing in X.7–8 suggests that these chapters abandon the temporal proviso mentioned in I.7; in fact, Aristotle reaffirms that proviso (X.8 1177b25). Furthermore, as I argued in 1.18, according to the *NE* happiness consists in *regular* activity over a sufficiently long period of time: someone who suffers from a sleeping sickness for thirty years (for example), and who engages in virtuous activity only on rare occasions during that time, does not have enough activity in his life to qualify as happy. And there is no reason to think that this assumption is operative only in Book I and dropped in Book X; for, as I have just noted, Aristotle says in X.8 (1177b25) that happiness consists in contemplation only if that activity endures over a sufficiently long period of time.

This means that we would be wrong to infer that the philosopher can be happy without friends. Aristotle does not have to move from the fact that (a) one can contemplate without friends, to the conclusion that (b) one can be happy without friends. He can continue to uphold his view that human beings cannot be happy without friends (IX.9 1169b16–19) by insisting that although a theoretically wise person can engage in a certain amount of contemplation even if he has no philosophical companions, that activity will not be lengthy enough. Human beings cannot regularly engage in philosophical thought over a long period of time unless they join together with like-minded colleagues; living in isolation, the best one can achieve is occasional philosophical reflection.

We should note that in IX.9 Aristotle adopts the view that *any* human activity is unpleasant and susceptible to interruption if it is carried out in isolation from others: "It is thought that someone who is happy must live pleasantly. But for the solitary person, life is hard, for it is not easy to be continuously active when one is on one's own. But when one is with others and acts in relation to them, it is easier. Therefore, one's activity will be more continuous . . ." (1170a4–7). The context indicates that Aristotle is talking about ethical activity in particular, but nothing in his argument restricts it to that activity. Accordingly, although he is saying in X.7 that a person of theoretical wisdom can think in isolation, whereas the practical virtues cannot be exercised when one is by oneself, this should not be taken to mean that the isolated person's contemplation will be pleasant, easy, or long-lived. There is no reason to think that in X.7 he is trying to reverse or restrict the point he had made in IX.9 about the disadvantages of isolated activity. In fact, immediately after he says that the philosopher can contemplate in isolation, he adds that "it is presumably better to have co-workers" (1177a34).[6] Clearly, he does not think that whether the theoretician is isolated or works with others is a matter of indifference. And his reason for thinking that it is better to have philosophical colleagues must be the one put forward in IX.9: activity is unpleasant and susceptible to interruption when it is not carried on with others.

Further evidence that the person who identifies perfect happiness with contemplation will not want to live in isolation can be found in X.8: in a remark to be discussed more fully later in this chapter, Aristotle says that the philosopher, being a human being, lives together with a larger group (1178b5). This means not that it is impossible for the philosopher to be isolated, but rather that he does not choose to be, if he can avoid it. And surely one of the reasons why he would regard isolation as a misfortune is that "it is . . . better to have co-workers."

We should also remember (see 1.19) not to be misled by the term "contemplation" into thinking of *theōria* as a meditative withdrawal from social activity. A person engages in *theōria* whenever he brings to mind the already discovered truths of some theoretical discipline, and this focusing of attention is something that occurs whenever one engages in discussion with others about appropriate subjects. I think Aristotle is making sensible observations when he says that although one can contemplate even when one is by oneself, this activity will be more continuous when it is carried on with others. We can think over truths we have learned even when we are alone, but we are not likely to do this on a regular basis unless we are members of an intellectual group in which discussion is a common activity. Someone who has grasped a subject is more inclined to think it through again if he teaches it to others, or draws on it when he continues his research with colleagues. For Aristotle, contemplation is not inherently a social activity (the gods contemplate in splendid isolation), but given the social nature of human beings, it is for us an activity that is seriously impeded if it must be carried on in isolation over a long period of time. Accordingly, he can say that a philosopher whose friends have died, and who must therefore carry on his theoretical work alone, is not leading a happy life. He can contemplate, but in the absence of an

[6] The word *isōs* (translated here "presumably") can also mean "perhaps." But Aristotle frequently uses it when he makes points of which he is confident. See, for example, 1095b3, 1098b32, 1102b27, 1169a25, 1169b16, 1171a8, 1171b20.

intellectual community he will not do so on a regular basis for a long period of time.

It may nonetheless be objected that even if as a rule human beings need the stimulation of colleagues to carry on with their intellectual work, there may be exceptions. Couldn't there be an unusually self-sufficient philosopher who is able to continue contemplating just as much as he did before even after his fellow workers have died? Doesn't Aristotle himself have to concede this possibility, in light of his remark that the more the-oretical wisdom one has the more one is able to contemplate in the ab-sence of others (1177a33–4)? And if he does concede this possibility in X.7–8, then he must retract his claim (IX.9 1169b16–19) that human beings cannot be happy unless they have friends. For on my interpreta-tion perfect happiness consists in contemplation, and if someone regu-larly engages in that activity over a long period of time, he is leading a happy life—even if he has no friends.

I do not think that Aristotle needs to deny the possibility of such cases. The individual under consideration is a cross between gods and human beings: like humans, he has a body that grows, requires nurture, and dies; like gods, he is not made better off by spending his time with others, since he has an extraordinary degree of wisdom and self-sufficiency. Aristotle can say that part of what makes someone human is a certain limitation in wisdom and self-sufficiency, and therefore any good *human* life is the life of someone who engages in activities with friends. He would gladly ad-mit that this half-divine and half-human being has a life superior to ours; since such an extraordinary individual is wiser and more independent than we are, he can engage in more contemplation, and so he more closely approximates the condition of the gods. The possibility of such demigods would make no difference to the question of how we human beings should lead our lives. We are far more dependent on the society of others, and if we tried to have a more contemplative life by cutting our-selves off from like-minded friends, we would be defeating our own pur-poses.[7] For us, "it is presumably better to have co-workers" (X.7 1177a34). And, having developed friendships with like-minded col-leagues, we (unlike gods) will promote the happiness of others, and not merely our own. The gods provide us with models of what is best for a single human life, but since they do not form a community, we can learn nothing from their example about how to resolve conflicts among human beings.

A question still remains: If Aristotle assumes in X.7–8 that philoso-phers need friends, then why does he bother making the point that it is

---

[7] See too *EE* VII.12 (especially 1244b1–15, 1245b14–19), where Aristotle argues that a self-sufficient life for a human being is not asocial, even though the gods need no friends.

possible to contemplate even when one is by oneself? What difference does it make that we can contemplate even when we are isolated, if there is no happiness for a normal human being who lacks like-minded friends over a sizable period of time? I take his point to be this: In weighing the different advantages of competing ways of life, we should consider not only what each offers when all goes well, but also what each offers when things go badly. For no one can be sure that misfortunes will not occur, and it counts in favor of a way of life that even in unfortunate circumstances we can salvage something. Now, in Book I, when Aristotle tries to confirm the conclusion of I.7 that happiness consists in virtuous activity, he claims that no matter what misfortunes befall an ethically virtuous person, he makes the best of circumstances, and will therefore never sink to the depths of human misery (I.10 1100b33–1101a8). Though such a person is not invulnerable to bad luck, he is less vulnerable than others, because he always retains a great good: the virtues he has acquired enable him to do what is most appropriate, even in highly unfavorable circumstances. By contrast, if someone takes happiness to be honor, or health, or wealth, or any other external good, then he is identifying his well-being with a good that he may entirely lose. If the worst happens, then he himself will have to admit that his life is miserable.

When read against this background, Aristotle's observations about the greater self-sufficiency of the philosophical life make good sense. The more external goods a life needs, the more vulnerable it is to misfortune. For example, if it is an advantage for the political leader but not for the philosopher to have great wealth, then a change from great to moderate wealth would be a misfortune for the former but not the latter. The circumstances that can impede the well-being of the theoretician are fewer than those that can impede that of the statesman. And Aristotle's remark about our ability to contemplate without friends should be understood in the same spirit. For reasons I have given, he should not be taken to be denying that the loss of friends would be a great misfortune for a philosopher. Rather, his point is that such a misfortune would not be as great for a philosopher as for someone leading the political life. Since the philosopher can still on occasion contemplate the truths he has discovered, he can continue to engage in his favored activity to some extent; by contrast, if ethical activity must always be undertaken in conjunction with others, the loss of others is a more severe blow. So, when we ask what the philosophical and political lives are like when things go badly, the former has an advantage over the latter.

Even if these points are accepted, a legitimate question can still be raised about self-sufficiency: When Aristotle argues in X.7 for the greater self-sufficiency of the philosophical life, is his notion of self-sufficiency different from the one he employed in Book I? In I.7, he says: "The self-sufficient we posit as that which when taken by itself makes life choiceworthy and in need of nothing" (1097b14–15). And as I noted in the Introduction, this is often taken to mean that the self-sufficient good contains all of the others: it makes life in need of nothing by containing every good within it. By contrast, when Aristotle argues for the greater self-sufficiency of the contemplative life, he seems to be treating that concept in an entirely different way. Surely contemplation is not more self-sufficient than ethically virtuous activity by being a larger composite; it is not a composite at all.

As I have said, however, I think that these lines about self-sufficiency in I.7, and those that follow them, have been widely misunderstood. We will discuss them in Chapter 5, and although we will see that there is a shift in the way I.7 and X.7 treat self-sufficiency, the difference is not as great as might be thought. More important, we will see that in X.7–8 Aristotle has not changed his mind about how life is to be lived. The supremacy of the intellectual life is a conclusion for which he lays the groundwork in Book I.

3.7. PHILOSOPHICAL FRIENDSHIP

If, as I have argued, Aristotle thinks that philosophers lacking superhuman qualities will benefit from having friends, then we should go on to ask what kind of friendships these will be. Books VIII and IX of the *NE* distinguish three main kinds of relationships: (a) friendships among those who have good character, and who seek the other person's good because that other person is virtuous; (b) friendships among those who merely want to receive pleasure from each other, and who enjoy each other's company because of this common aim; (c) friendships among those who only seek some advantage from the other.[8] The first kind of relationship is the one that deserves most of all to be called a friendship. Those who associate with each other on the basis of ethical virtue will enjoy each other's company, and will profit from their friendship. So this kind of relationship exhibits all three features: virtuous treatment of others who are virtuous, the enjoyment that comes with spending one's days with others in common pursuits, and the advantages of having friends who promote one's good (VIII.3 1156b13–17). Friendships based solely on pleasure have one of these features: the individuals like spending their time with each other. And friendships based solely on advantage also have

---

[8] For this threefold division, see especially VIII.3, which in turn relies on the distinction made at VIII.2 1155b18–19. Unlike Cooper, "Aristotle on Friendship," pp. 308–315, I do not take Aristotle to be saying that in each of the three types of friendship, the individuals benefit each other for the sake of the other person. But nothing in my interpretation depends on whether Cooper's reading is right or wrong.

something in common with those based on virtue: each individual receives some good from the other. It is because these lesser relationships bear some resemblance to the primary kind of friendship (the one based on character) that each can be called a friendship of sorts.[9]

Now, as we have seen, Aristotle thinks that those who lead a philosophical life will and should live together with others; they need fellow workers with whom they share their theoretical interests. Does this kind of relationship fall into any of his three categories, or is it *sui generis*? And if it does fit into the scheme of VIII–IX, which kind of friendship is it? I think that the most plausible answer to these questions is this: Aristotle assumes that the sort of friendship that philosophers will and should form with each other is the best kind—a friendship based on character. For he clearly thinks that the other kinds of relationships are seriously defective, and it is implausible to suppose that in his opinion the best human life (that is, the philosophical life) is one marred by serious problems in one's relationships with friends. The best human life is one that we cannot improve upon, but if our relationships with friends are highly imperfect— as they would be in pleasure- or advantage-friendships—then there is room for significant improvement. And it is uncontroversial that, according to Aristotle, these lesser forms of friendship are deficient in various ways. Advantage-friendships are the least satisfactory: they are the relationships that are most filled with quarrels and mistrust (VIII.13 1162b5– 21), and since the individuals involved do not necessarily get pleasure from each other, they sometimes provide no companionship (VIII.3 1156a27–8). Those who are friends because of the pleasure they give each other do spend their days together (VIII.3 1156b4–5), and so these relationships (unlike those based on advantage) possess the most characteristic feature of friendships.[10] But even though pleasant relationships are closer to being real friendships than are merely advantageous associations (VIII.4 1157a12–14, VIII.6 1158a18–20), they are still highly defective. Pleasure-friendships merely provide pleasure, whereas friendships based on virtue are both advantageous and pleasant (VIII.6 1158b7–8). Only in virtue-friendships can the individuals be confident of each other's trust, and these are the only relationships that can be expected to endure (VIII.4 1157a20–25, VIII.6 1158b8–10).

Since a life of perfect happiness will be one in which one's relationships with friends are the perfect kind of relationship, Aristotle is evidently assuming that philosophical friendships are formed among those who have both the practical and the theoretical virtues. It is because these individuals possess and highly value the practical virtues that their relationships

[9] See VIII.4 1156b33–1157a3, 1157a25–36, VIII.6 1158b5–8.
[10] See VIII.5 1157b19, VIII.6 1158a8–10, IX.10 1171a2.

are based in part on character. In looking for friends, they seek individuals who are just, generous, courageous, and so on; and when they benefit these individuals for their sake, they do so partly because their friends have these fine qualities. But since those leading the best life do not merely value and possess the practical virtues, but esteem the theoretical virtues even more, they value their friends not merely because of their good character, but also because of their theoretical skills.

If we take Aristotle's defense of the intellectual life to be consistent with the rest of the *NE*, then he cannot be saying, in X.7–8, that we should be indifferent to the ethical virtues discussed in Books II–V, and should cultivate the theoretical virtues *instead*; he must mean that we should cultivate the latter virtues *in addition*. And if this is the way we read X.7–8, then our understanding of Aristotelian friendship must follow suit: we must say not that Aristotle has *abandoned* his view that friendship among good people is the best sort there is, but instead that he has *supplemented* it. If perfect friendships are those in which people of good character join together to pursue the good for whose sake they lead their lives (IX.12 1172a1–8), and if the best choice for such a good is contemplation, then the best kind of perfect friendship is one in which ethically virtuous people engage in joint philosophical activities as much as they possibly can. As Aristotle says, those who are happy want to live together with others by "sharing in discussion and thought" (IX.9 1170b11–12). And if the best subjects to talk about are the ones discussed by those who study theoretical subjects, then philosophy is the best common interest around which human friendships can be organized. This of course does not mean that it is the only common focus that friends leading good lives can have, for the philosophical life is not the only kind of good life. Those who do not acquire theoretical interests and skills will devote themselves to moral activity, and in their friendships they will deliberate together about common political projects.

My argument for this interpretation is not yet complete, for I must still defend my view that *NE* I and X.7–8 should be read together as a coherent defense of two kinds of lives (the philosophical and political lives), each possessing a single ultimate end. What I have claimed in this section is that if this reading can be defended, then Aristotle's conception of friendship as put forward in VIII and IX should be extended in a natural way to cover the material added in X.7–8. As we have seen, he does not take isolation to be a condition conducive to human happiness. The philosopher who lacks superhuman wisdom is best off if he has fellow workers, for otherwise his theoretical activity will be intermittent at best. And if the *NE* is a coherent whole, then it is reasonable to assume that the philosopher and his fellow workers will have not only the theoretical virtues, but the practical virtues as well. Furthermore, if the relationships among these people were mere advantage- or pleasure-friendships, they would be highly imperfect, because of their instability and lack of trust. And since a perfect life cannot be defective, we must think of the ideal life as that of a person who has all the virtues (theoretical and practical) and who regularly engages in the best activities with like-minded friends over a long period of time.

3.8. Moral Equipment

I believe that, according to Aristotle, there is a causal relationship between the two kinds of virtues—theoretical and practical—that those leading the best life have. His idea, as I understand it, is that to be well equipped for the theoretical life, one needs certain habits of character, and not merely skills of pure thought; the ethical virtues, in other words, are desirable in part because they help one lead the philosophical life. If one is to acquire theoretical wisdom and lead a life in which one regularly engages in philosophical activity over a long period of time, then one's deepest desire must be to discover, understand, and reflect on the truth. And to succeed in this project, it is necessary or at least desirable to be free from various defects of character: for example, one should not have an excessive love of money, or of physical pleasure. For strong desires in these directions would make it difficult or impossible to spend one's life undertaking the kind of research that brings no rewards beyond itself. Accordingly, it is no accident that the relationships among those who lead a philosophical life are friendships based on character. To be well prepared for the life of the mind, each of these individuals needs the moral excellences, and not merely the theoretical virtues. And each will not only want to have the ethical virtues himself, but will also look for philosophical co-workers who have these same social skills. For each wants to work with individuals who will treat others fairly, generously, and so on. So, defects of character create motivational disturbances that impede the philosophical life, and they also detract from one's ability to form the sort of human relationships that will best promote one's intellectual activities.

I suggest that these and kindred assumptions are what lie behind an obscure but crucial claim that Aristotle makes when he comes to the close of the function argument in I.7. Having argued that happiness consists in activity of the soul in accordance with virtue, he cryptically adds: "and if there are many virtues, in accordance with the best and most perfect" (1098a17–18). He does not explain what he means by that phrase, or which virtue is best and most perfect, but I will argue that he should be understood in the following way: One good is more perfect than another if the first is desirable for the sake of the second, where "for the sake of" is to be taken in part as a causal relationship. For example, since wealth is for the sake of various ends (that is, should be used to promote those ends), it is less perfect than they. And similarly, Aristotle assumes at 1098a17–18, certain virtues of the soul are less perfect than others: the less perfect virtues are desirable in part because they facilitate the development and exercise of the virtues that are more perfect. On my reading, the most perfect virtue turns out to be theoretical wisdom, and the practical virtues are less perfect than it because they are to be desired in part because of their causal relationship to that supreme virtue. Aristotle assumes, in other words, that if we have various defects of character this will impede the theoretical life. Since more philosophical activity is always better than less, it would be undesirable to have the strong desires for amusement, honor, or wealth that are possessed by those who lack the ethical virtues. As Aristotle says in X.7, activity in accordance with the practical virtues is desired for the sake of other goods to which it leads (1177b2–4), whereas theoretical activity is for the sake of no other good (b1–2, 20). All goods are to be located in a hierarchy constructed out of the for-the-sake-of relation, and since theoretical activity alone is desirable for the sake of nothing further, the ethical virtues must be desirable in part because they promote the philosophical life.

Let me spell out more fully the assumptions I take Aristotle to be making. For every ethical virtue, we can ask whether it would contribute in some way or other to the success of a philosophical life. More precisely, we can compare the qualities Aristotle takes to be ethical virtues with those he takes to be vices, and ask whether he thinks that one is better equipped for the philosophical life if one has the virtue or the corresponding vices. According to my interpretation, he assumes in each case that someone who plans to engage in philosophical activity on a regular basis over a lifetime would do better to develop and exercise the virtue than to develop and exercise the vice.

To be more specific: Temperance is the virtue that hits the mean in matters having to do with certain physical pleasures. If one takes the best life to be one that has the greatest amount of philosophical activity, then having too great a desire for physical pleasure is an impediment to the fulfillment of one's plans. On the other hand, a lack of normal physical appetites would also be an impediment. Suppose someone gets no pleasure from such activities as eating and drinking, and feels no pain at the absence of food and drink. Such a person is in serious physical danger: he lacks a natural mechanism that induces him to take the nourishment he needs for his health. If he does eat, he takes no pleasure in doing so, and therefore he cannot rely on the loss of pleasure as a signal to stop eating. For a short while, he may engage in philosophical activity more than anyone else: he continues to contemplate even when doing so undermines his health (a possibility Aristotle envisages at VII.12 1153a20). But over the long run, it is surely better for a philosopher with a normal human body to be equipped with a moderate level of appetite. Similar arguments can sustain the idea that one should have a moderate sexual appetite. Children are especially needed for support in one's later years,[11] and it is easier to engage in the appropriate amount of procreative activity if one has the right level of sexual desire.

Courage is the virtue that enables one to master one's fear on the battlefield and to determine when it is necessary to fight. Now, the philosophical life is no different from any other, in this respect: to be free to lead the kind of life one chooses, one must live in favorable political circumstances. Tyrannical regimes must be opposed, and foreign enemies who seek one's death or enslavement must be resisted. When one is sent to the battlefield to help accomplish these purposes, one's effectiveness in defending the life one leads will be impeded if one lacks the emotional and physical skills of a courageous fighter. A disabling fear of death would undermine one's efforts to defend oneself. But on the other hand, someone who never experienced fear at the prospect of dying would be disabled in other ways: apathy in dangerous situations would deprive him of a useful warning signal that special caution is needed. Susceptibility to a certain level of fear serves a useful purpose, whether one leads a philosophical life or not.

Since co-workers enhance philosophical activity, and since philosophical groups need good relations with the larger political community, it will be helpful for the philosopher to have the skills and attitudes that enable him to hit the mean in matters having to do with wealth, honor, and justice. Too great a concern for wealth will impede one's ability to focus on intellectual activity; but if one is indifferent to wealth and allows one's resources to slip away, one will lack the equipment one needs to lead a leisurely and philosophical life. Similarly, a great love of honor would only distract one from one's theoretical interests; but indifference to the good opinion of one's friends and the larger community would endanger the good social relations one needs. Fairness and an ungrasping nature also enable one to live with others on terms that are acceptable to them: if one takes what others deserve, or fails to reciprocate when reciprocation is rightly expected, one will not be accepted as a decent member

[11] See, for example, Isaeus, *On the Estate of Menecles* 10. In Athens, children who did not provide food and housing for their parents were liable to prosecution. See MacDowell, *The Law in Classical Athens*, p. 92. No doubt obedient children would also provide many other types of benefits for their parents. The desire to have children because of the advantages they offer is consistent with genuine love of one's children, just as the advantages of equal friendship are consistent with genuine altruism. Recall the discussion of *NE* IX.9 in 2.15.

of the community, and will be deprived of the benefits that come with living together with others.

Of course, if you manage to escape detection, then certain injustices might bring you more contemplation rather than less. For example, if you ignore the needs of your parents, and no one finds out about this neglect, then your standing in the community will not suffer, and you will have more time for theoretical activity. My interpretation does not attribute to Aristotle the assumption that such cases cannot occur. But I do take him to be assuming that *for the most part* unjust actions become known to others, and that when this is taken into account it will be more in a philosopher's interest to have the virtue of justice than the vice of injustice. This is an assumption that Plato makes in Book X of the *Republic*: those who commit injustices are usually found out in the long run and are punished, while those who act justly are normally appreciated by the community and enjoy the rewards of virtue (613b–e). I take Aristotle to accept this point, and this lies behind his assumption that those who are best equipped to lead the philosophical life have the virtue of justice rather than the vice of injustice. This does not mean that in his opinion one should think only of oneself, and act justly only when doing so maximizes one's own good. On occasion, the acts one should undertake for others may not be the ones that are best from one's own point of view. Nonetheless, on most occasions, the just acts performed by the philosopher will not only be good for others, but because of their publicity will be best for himself as well.

In the *Republic*, Plato tries to show that even if we set aside the rewards of justice, it is still in our interest to be just. And he thinks that it is important for us to recognize that this is so: otherwise, we might believe that justice is not good in itself, but desirable only for the sake of its consequences. I will argue that something similar can be found in the *NE*. Aristotle holds that even if we set aside the ways in which the ethical virtues support the philosophical life, it still can be shown that it is desirable to have those qualities. For it is possible to lead a happy life even if one does not engage in philosophical activity: the political life is happy in a secondary way, and in such a life everything is done for the sake of ethical activity. Aristotle, as I understand him, has an argument to show why these virtues should occupy this high position in the hierarchy of ends, and I will discuss that argument in Chapter 6.[12] So we should not be misled by the fact that he takes the ethical virtues to contribute to the philosophical life. His belief that they are good for their consequences

---

[12] Contrast Urmson, *Aristotle's Ethics*, p. 3. He says that Aristotle simply accepts Plato's conclusion that we need ethical virtues in order to be happy, and provides no arguments of his own.

does not prevent him from saying that they are also desirable in themselves. In fact, on my interpretation, it is not enough to say that ethical virtue and moral activity are desirable in themselves; for that merely puts them in the same category as such other goods as honor, friends, and pleasure. The special value of ethically virtuous activity can be brought out only by noting its unique status in Aristotle's hierarchy: no life can be happy if it lacks these qualities, and every other good (except for contemplation and theoretical virtue) is desirable for its sake.

In this section, I have put forward a number of assumptions I take Aristotle to be making, but I have not tried to show that we must interpret him in this way. In Chapter 4, I will argue that he takes the ethical virtues to bear a causal relationship to theoretical activity; that is how I will construe his reference (I.7 1098a17–18) to the virtue that is "best and most perfect." If my understanding of this phrase is accepted, then we cannot avoid the question: why does Aristotle believe that the ethical virtues promote contemplation? I do not think this is an impossible question to answer. Plato holds that one needs a training in virtue in order to become a genuine philosopher (*Republic* 485a–487a), and Aristotle has all the materials he needs to arrive at the same conclusion.

3.9. Unphilosophical Friendship

My way of connecting Aristotle's ideas about friendship and philosophy is an attempt to mediate between opposite interpretations. At one extreme, it might be held that in defending the contemplative life he rejects the conception of human nature that is so prominent elsewhere in his writings: we are social creatures who must find our good by joining together with others in common activities. This way of making X.7–8 discontinuous with the rest of the *NE* must be rejected, since Aristotle emphasizes our social nature even while he is arguing on behalf of contemplation (X.8 1178b5). At the other extreme, it might be held that the connection between friendship and theoretical activity is far closer than I realize: according to this rival view, Aristotle would be saying that character-friendship must be based on a mutual interest in philosophy. So far from claiming that philosophers have no need of friends, this interpretation takes *NE* VIII–IX to mean that character-friendship exists *only* among philosophers. By contrast, I take Aristotle to believe that although philosophers will profit from forming character-friendships, this sort of friendship can exist among nonphilosophers as well.

There are, however, a few passages that might be taken to mean that character-friendships exist only among those who share theoretical interests. For example, when Aristotle comes to the end of his lengthiest argument for the conclusion that a happy person needs good friends (IX.9

1170a13–b19), he claims that character-friends live together by sharing in "discussion and thought" (1170b11–12). If he is thinking specifically of philosophical conversations here, then he is assuming that an ethically virtuous friend must be a theoretician. Note that several chapters earlier (IX.4 1166a26–7), he had described the ethically virtuous person as someone whose mind (*dianoia*) is well stocked with "things to contemplate" (*theōrēmata*). Furthermore, he says that such a person is a self-lover because he loves the thinking part of his soul, and this is what each person is (IX.4 1166a14–17). Since the *NE* eventually goes on to argue that each person is his theoretical intellect (X.7 1178a2–7), should we not infer that a genuine friend must be a philosopher? To enter into friendships, one must love oneself (that is, one's theoretical intellect), and accordingly one will have many philosophical subjects to contemplate and to talk about with like-minded friends.

I think that such a reading of the *NE* would be extremely farfetched. Aristotle's explicit doctrine in Books VIII–IX is that the best kind of friendship is one that is based on character, that is, on ethical virtue. It is never said that one must have theoretical wisdom in order to enter into these relationships. Furthermore, as I argued in Chapter 1, according to the *NE* two different kinds of lives can be happy. That is, although the philosophical life is best, those who regularly exercise the ethical virtues and are sufficiently equipped with external goods over the course of a lifetime are happy to a secondary degree—even though they do not engage in philosophical activity. If this interpretation is accepted, then Aristotle must be taken to believe that one must have character-friends whichever of the two good lives one leads. For his argument in IX.9 is intended to be perfectly general: his claim is that in *any* happy life one needs friends. Since it is possible to lead a nonphilosophical life and still live well, and since any good life must be lived with ethically virtuous friends, Aristotle must believe that such relationships are possible for those who lack theoretical wisdom.

How then are we to read the passages cited above, in which the genuine friend seems very much like a philosopher? He lives together with others by sharing in discussion and thought, reflects on many objects of contemplation, and identifies himself with the thinking part of his soul. These passages show that any ethically virtuous person is in certain ways *like* a philosopher, but they do not show that he actually *is* a philosopher in the strict sense, that is, someone who has the virtue of theoretical wisdom and contemplates the eternal truths of the theoretical sciences. I have argued (1.14) that the politician who leads a good life must, like every other living creature, bear some resemblance to Aristotle's gods, and the passages under discussion should be read in this spirit. The conversations in which character-friends regularly engage need not be philosophical discussions: those character-friends who are also philosophers will discuss metaphysical and scientific topics, whereas those who have chosen the political life will talk about matters that affect the well-being of their fellow citizens. Similarly, just as theoreticians contemplate theoretical truths and the objects of the sciences, so those leading a practical life have their own special subject to contemplate—taking "contemplate" in the loose sense.[13] And just as theoreticians will love their theoretical reason more than any other part of their soul, so those who lead the second-best life will most of all love their ability to engage in excellent practical reasoning.

Another point made earlier (2.13) should be kept in mind: The self-lover described in IX.8 is someone who loves his *practical* reason most of all (1168b31–1169a3). And so Books VIII–IX can hardly be saying that a good friend is necessarily someone who loves his *theoretical* reason most of all. It would be a mistake to read VIII–IX as though it contained a secret doctrine—only philosophers can be character-friends—at which Aristotle occasionally hints. But it would also be implausible, as I argued in 2.13, to take VIII–IX to be at odds with X.7–8, the former proposing practical reason as the highest part of the soul, the latter proposing theoretical reason. We should instead take Aristotle to be simplifying in VIII–IX, because of his desire to postpone the question whether it is better to lead a practical or a theoretical life. Since theoretical reason is what we most of all are (X.7 1178a2–7), it is this part of the soul that we should love most. Philosophical friendships are the best among friendships based on character, because they are based on the highest activity, and therefore arise from the best kind of self-love. So far as I can see, this is the only way in which X.7–8 requires a modification in Aristotle's treatment of friendship. Certainly it is better to bring the topics of friendship and philosophy together in this way than to adopt either of the two extreme views considered in this section. For the text shows that in X.7–8 Aristotle continues to assert the social nature of human beings, and that the perfect friendships discussed in VIII–IX need not be based on common philosophical interests. The best way to make sense of all of this material is to acknowledge that two kindred lives—one philosophical and the other political—can be happy, each devoted to a different activity of the reasoning part of the soul, and each shared with others through a mutual interest in discussion and thought.

3.10. Living a Human Life

I now want to consider a remark Aristotle makes in X.8 that seems to undermine the way in which I have connected philosophical activity and

---

[13] See Chapter 1, note 2.

the other goods. Recall that, on my interpretation, he thinks that there is no such thing as too much philosophical activity for one's own good: the more contemplation a life has (above a certain threshold), the better a life it is. The textual support for this reading comes from X.8 (1178b7–32), where Aristotle argues that contemplation is the sole activity of the gods. Since they are assumed to have unsurpassably happy lives, they provide a standard by means of which the well-being of all other animals can be measured; the more closely a living creature approximates their condition, the better off it is. Accordingly, "as far as contemplation extends, thus far happiness extends, and those who have more contemplation also have more happiness" (1178b28–30). And this provides a standard for determining the level at which it is in one's best interest to pursue other goods: the best amount to have, for one's own sake, is the one that allows for the fullest amount of philosophical activity.

The passage that seems to conflict with this reading occurs just before the argument from divinity. The general context is this: After recognizing the secondary happiness of the political life, Aristotle insists once again (X.8 1178a23–b7; cf. X.7 1177a27–b1) that this second-best life has a greater need for external equipment than does the philosophical life. He concedes, at least for the sake of argument, that the philosopher and the politician need the necessary goods to an equal degree (1178a25–7; cf. 1177a28–9). To live well, each must stay alive, and so they both need food, shelter, health, and so on (1178b33–5). Nonetheless, he insists that the politician needs more external goods to engage in his characteristic activity than does the philosopher to engage in his. To act generously one needs money; to be brave one needs power; and to exercise temperance one needs freedom (1178a28–33). And the grander the actions a politician undertakes, the larger his resources must be (1178b1–3).

After making these points, Aristotle turns to the very different situation of the philosopher: "For someone contemplating, there is no need of any of these, at least regarding that activity. Instead, one could even call them impediments, at least regarding the contemplation. But insofar as he is a human being and lives together with a larger group, he chooses to do the things that are in accordance with virtue. Therefore, he will need such things in order to live a human life" (1178b3–7). This could be taken to mean that if the philosopher wanted to contemplate as much as possible, then he would have no use for the goods mentioned: money, power, freedom. Aristotle would then be saying that the need for such goods in a philosophical life derives from the fact that the philosopher does not and should not want to contemplate as much as possible. To lead the best possible life, he should want only so much contemplation (Aristotle does not say how much) and no more; he should cut short his philosophical activities and engage in ethical activities to a certain extent. And to engage in these activities, he needs a certain amount of money, power, and freedom. Possessing these goods to the right extent actually impedes his philosophical activity, but that is a "sacrifice" he chooses to make, because it leads to the best balance of moral and theoretical activity.[14]

There are three reasons for rejecting this interpretation. First, it leaves Aristotle with no answer to the question "What is the right level of philosophical activity?" That is, it takes him to be saying that a certain amount of theoretical activity is too much for one's own good, but it leaves him with nothing to say about what that amount is, and how we can tell when we have reached it. Second, this interpretation brings the above passage into direct conflict with the one that immediately follows it. For, as we have seen, the "argument from divinity" commits Aristotle to the view that nondivine lives are increasingly happy as they more closely approximate the life of the gods. He cannot accept this and at the same time hold that we should, for the sake of our own happiness, contemplate less, in order to leave more room for ethical activity. Third, it is hard to believe that, according to Aristotle, a philosopher who wanted to maximize theoretical activity would best do so by having no money, no power, and no freedom. For he says in X.8 that in order to lead a philosophical life we should provide for our physical needs. Speaking of the philosopher, he says: "He will also need external prosperity, since he is a human being. For his nature is not self-sufficient for contemplation; rather, he needs his body to be healthy, and he needs to provide it with nourishment and other care" (1178b33–5). This certainly implies that the philosopher needs other external goods besides the ones mentioned. Without money, for example, it would be difficult or impossible to remain well nourished and healthy. Could Aristotle be denying this, when he says that money is an impediment to contemplation? How could he think that health is needed for philosophical activity, but that money is not?

To arrive at a more satisfactory interpretation, we need to ask what Aristotle is getting at when he says, with reference to money, power, and freedom: "For someone contemplating, there is no need of any of these, at least regarding that activity. Instead, one could even call them impediments, at least regarding the contemplation" (1178b3–5). I suggest that he is making the following contrast between the philosopher and the statesman: Someone who is engaged in generous, courageous, or temperate activity needs the external goods to which these virtues are related, just as any craftsman needs certain tools in order to carry out his work. The flute-player cannot make music without his flute, and similarly the

---

[14] This seems to be the way Whiting reads our passage. See "Human Nature and Intellectualism in Aristotle," pp. 91–3.

political leader cannot achieve his end without money, power, freedom, and other goods. By contrast, philosophy as Aristotle conceives it is an activity that needs no tools. Once one has acquired theoretical wisdom, one need only focus one's thoughts on a certain system of truths, and one is thereby contemplating. This claim is perfectly compatible with a further statement Aristotle makes (b33–5): since we are human beings, we will not be able to continue contemplating for very long if we neglect our health. Contemplation itself does not need external equipment, for otherwise the gods could not contemplate; no contemplator, considered merely as a contemplator, needs external goods. But since we are not merely contemplators, we must attend to the conditions that best promote philosophical activity. Someone who ignored his status as a human being and merely contemplated, neglecting all other goods, would not have a good life, for he could not regularly engage in philosophical activity over a long period of time.

I think that this gives a plausible explanation of why Aristotle says, "For someone contemplating, there is no need of any of these [money, power, freedom, and so on], at least regarding that activity" (1178b3–4). When we read him in the way I suggest, we can avoid the three problems mentioned above: he tells us what the best level of philosophical activity is, he says nothing to undermine the "argument from divinity," and he acknowledges that the philosophical life must be equipped not only with health but with a moderate amount of money and other external goods. But how are we to understand the line that immediately follows: "Instead, one could even call them impediments, at least regarding the contemplation" (b3–5)? The interpretation I reject takes this to mean that if one wants to have as much philosophical activity as possible, one should have no money, since this is an impediment to contemplation. Instead, I take Aristotle to be saying that at the time one is contemplating, having money and other external equipment can interfere with one's activity. He does not explain why this is so, but presumably he is thinking along these lines: Having goods other than contemplation can make it more difficult to focus one's attention. Instead of thinking about philosophical subjects, one's mind may wander, and one may ask, "Do I have enough equipment? Do I have too much for my own good? Who most deserves my support?" and so on. The gods have none of these problems, and so nothing in their lives impedes contemplation. By contrast, since we are complex beings—we have bodies, emotions, families, friends—we must attend to many other goods besides contemplation. This does not mean that we would in the long run be able to contemplate more if we ignored these other goods: they are not impediments in that way. Rather, it means that while we are contemplating, our possession of other goods can distract us and lead to an interruption in our activity.

If my reading of these lines is accepted, then Aristotle's remark that external goods can be called impediments to contemplation should not be construed as a piece of advice about how we should lead our lives. He is not saying that to lead a philosophical life we should have only such other goods as are physically necessary for staying alive. Surely he believes that in addition to health, the philosopher needs enough wealth to sustain his leisure, enough friends to foster philosophical conversations, enough children to support him in old age, and so on. His point that these resources also impede contemplation is not an argument for rejecting them, but is intended only to emphasize that contemplation itself is an activity for which no equipment is needed: so far from needing such tools, contemplation can even be interrupted because one has them. Aristotle thinks that this further supports his point that the philosopher is more self-sufficient than the politician. The more external goods a life needs, the more vulnerable it is to misfortune; and the philosopher's smaller dependence on such goods is highlighted by the fact that contemplation not only needs no tools, but can even be impeded by them. The philosopher, as Aristotle points out near the end of X.8 (1179a1–13), needs only moderate supplies of external goods, whereas those who lead a political life, and who therefore aim at large-scale projects on behalf of the whole community, need them in much larger quantities. The point Aristotle makes in Book I—that to lead good lives, we need adequate supplies of external goods (see, for example, I.10 1101a14–16)—is made more precise in X.7–8: how much we need depends on which of the two lives we choose.

After noting that external equipment can impede contemplation, Aristotle reminds us that the philosopher is not *just* a contemplator, and that his need for resources derives from this complexity in his nature: "Insofar as he is a human being and lives together with a larger group, he chooses to do the things that are in accordance with virtue. Therefore, he will need such things in order to live a human life" (1178b5–7). If my reading of X.7–8 is accepted, then this should not be taken to mean that leading a good life requires striking some balance between what is divine in us (our capacity for contemplation) and the rest of our interests. For in that case Aristotle would be saying that the divine part could get a larger share than it merits, and we might engage in too much philosophical activity for our own good. Rather, I take him to be saying that if we had a divine nature and nothing more, then we would not seek the company of others, virtuous activity would not be in our interests, and external goods would be unnecessary. For this reason, the presence of a divine component in our nature does not by itself explain why we do or should seek these other ends. We want these other goods because our capacity to contemplate is not all there is to us: we are not simply contemplators, but are instead contemplators who have bodies that eventually perish, emotions that can obstruct or aid reason, and so on. The fact that we are complex in these ways does not by itself tell us how much weight to assign to each of the different goods that plays a role in human life. Aristotle's proposal, as I understand it, is that a human being makes the best use of his complex nature if he pursues subordinate goods to the extent that they promote what is divine in us. This is not a recommendation that we ignore the fact that we are human beings, and pretend that we are gods. Lacking super-human wisdom and self-sufficiency, we would fail to lead good lives were we to follow that advice. Rather, his claim is that our lives are best when we neither underestimate nor overestimate the importance of merely human goods: we overestimate them if, for our own sake, we engage in less philosophical activity than we might; but we can also underestimate the way in which health, wealth, friends, ethical virtue, and so on contribute to a life that has theoretical research as its ultimate end.

So Aristotle insists that we are human and not solely divine; leading one's life in the best way requires attention to this point. But we must not misunderstand the lesson he thinks we should learn from this. We should give expression to the human side of our nature by adopting a divine end—contemplation—and pursuing it in a way that befits our human limitations. With good fortune, such a life will contain all that human beings rightly desire: friends, moral activity, physical pleasure, and so on. But there is no need to limit oneself even further and to pursue, for one's own sake, a complex ultimate end, in which divine activity is cut short to make room for some lesser good. If we did this, we would give expression to our complex nature by having a complex ultimate end, but as a result we would have a less desirable life than we might have had, for no good reason. Instead, we should try to live like gods as much as we possibly can—recognizing that we will fail miserably if we do not see how large a contribution human goods must make to this project.

3.11. USELESS THEORIZING

I have been gradually developing my argument that X.7–8 coheres with the rest of the *NE*. These late chapters do not reject the ethical virtues, communal life, or friendship based on character. Instead, Aristotle can be taken to mean that all of these goods will be included in the life devoted to philosophy, because each has a causal contribution to make to the development and exercise of theoretical wisdom. The only "conflict" we have found thus far is this: in IX.8, persons are identified with practical reason, whereas in X.7, they are instead identified with theoretical reason. And I have claimed that this apparent inconsistency is superficial. Aristotle wants to postpone his treatment of the philosophical life until all aspects of the ethical virtues have been discussed, and so he allows himself an oversimplification in his treatment of self-love. X.7 shows how IX.8 must be modified: when theoretical reason is left aside (as in IX.8), then we are to be identified with practical reason; but when theoretical reason is brought into the picture, the arguments for the superiority of contemplation show that we should instead identify ourselves most of all with this highest part of the soul. Just as the political life is a second-best choice, so the conception of self-love put forward in IX.8 is eventually shown to rest on a second-best conception of the self.

There is, however, another problem that must be confronted by any attempt to find a unified conception of happiness in the *NE*. For one of Aristotle's arguments on behalf of contemplation seems to conflict with his belief that many different kinds of ends are desirable in themselves. At one point in X.7, he says about contemplation: "And it alone seems to be loved for itself.[15] For nothing comes to be from it apart from the contemplation, whereas from practical activities we profit apart from the action, to a greater or smaller extent" (1177b1–4). Similarly, some fifteen lines later, he says that political and military activities "aim at some end and are not choiceworthy for themselves" (b18); by contrast, contemplation does not "aim at any end beyond itself" (b20). Now, these remarks seem to be at odds with statements Aristotle makes throughout the *NE* and in other works as well. In I.7, for example, he says that "we choose honor, pleasure, understanding, and every virtue" both for themselves and for the sake of happiness (1097b2–5). Earlier, in I.5, he treats wealth as a less plausible candidate for happiness than honor and virtue, since the latter are loved for themselves (1096a8–9). And when he resumes his discussion of happiness in X.6, he says that "doing fine and excellent actions is among the things choiceworthy for themselves" (1176b8–9); the context (see, for example, b24–6) indicates that ethically virtuous actions are being included within this group.[16]

---

[15] Here there is a significant difference between my translation and that of Irwin: he has Aristotle saying that *theōria* "seems to be liked because of itself alone." That way of reading the Greek carries no implication that contemplation alone is in the category of things loved for themselves. Contrast Ross and Ostwald, whose translations are similar to mine. I am grateful to Elizabeth Asmis for discussion. I would also depart from Irwin's translation of 1177b18: the Greek says that excellent practical activities are not choiceworthy in themselves. (Contrast Irwin: such activities are "choiceworthy for something other than themselves.") As the reader will see, I take Aristotle to be speaking elliptically at 1177b1–2 and b18, and so in the end my understanding of these lines comes to the same thing as Irwin's. But his translation masks the problem raised by these lines.

[16] The conflict is noticed by Cooper, *RHGA*, pp. 156–7 n. 12. He takes it to be "highly significant" that Aristotle claims in X.7 that only *theōria* is loved for itself. For he takes X.7–8 to be saying that "the man bent on contemplation as his ideal does *not* love anything for its own sake except *theōria*" (p. 157), and he takes those chapters to be advocating this ideal.

So Aristotle's usual view is that other types of good besides virtuous activity are desired (and desirable) for themselves, and that anything within the general category of virtuous activity is desired (and desirable) for itself. Why should he suddenly reverse himself, and declare that only one type of good—contemplation—is loved for itself? Such a claim is badly in need of argument, since it conflicts with the general consensus that many types of goods are desirable for their own sake;[17] and as we have seen, it contradicts the position Aristotle himself adopts in many other passages. Nothing in X.7–8 explains why he would change his mind without argument.[18] Furthermore, it is hard to understand why these chapters would allow a secondary form of happiness to consist in ethical activity, if they insist that such activity is—like wealth—desirable only as a means to other goods. If X.6 reaffirms Aristotle's belief that happiness consists in something that is desired for itself (1176b4–5), how can X.7–8 go on to claim that (a) ethical activity is a form of happiness, even though (b) it is not desired for itself?

At this point, it becomes natural to suspect that we are misreading the text cited above if we take it to be at odds with the rest of the NE. How can we make Aristotle more intelligible, and restore consistency to his project? I suggest that although his normal practice in much of the NE is to place goods into one of three categories, X.7–8 works with a simpler scheme, and places goods into either of two groups. The usual threefold distinction is the one mentioned in I.7 (1097a25–b6):

(a) Goods desired for the sake of something else but not for themselves: for example, wealth, instruments;
(b) Goods desired for the sake of something else and also for themselves: for example, honor, pleasure, understanding, and every virtue;
(c) Goods desired for themselves and not for the sake of anything else: for example, happiness.

But there is nothing inconsistent about collapsing the first two categories, and drawing the following contrast:

(d) Goods desired for the sake of something else;
(e) Goods desired for themselves and not for the sake of something else.

Nussbaum, *The Fragility of Goodness*, pp. 375–6, cites our passage as evidence that X.7–8 conflicts with the rest of the NE.

[17] Evidence for the existence of this consensus is provided by *Rhet.* I.6 1362b10–28; *NE* I.6 1096b13–19, I.7 1097b2–4. Cf. Plato, *Republic* 357b4–c3.

[18] Cooper's explanation in *RHGA* is that Aristotle adopts a new theory of personal identity in X.7–8, according to which the person consists solely in theoretical intellect. For criticism, see Whiting, "Human Nature and Intellectualism in Aristotle." Cooper withdraws from this position in "Contemplation and Happiness: A Reconsideration."

And in fact, this simplification may serve a useful purpose. For if perfect happiness must consist in something that falls into category (c), then the contrast between (a) and (b) is irrelevant, and the similarity between (a) and (b) becomes more salient. Goods in both (a) and (b) are desirable for the sake of something else, and in X.7–8 Aristotle assumes that anything that has this characteristic is a poor candidate for perfect happiness. Accordingly, he collapses (a) and (b), and works with a twofold distinction between (d) and (e). Furthermore, he expresses the contrast between (d) and (e) in the following compressed way:

(f) Goods desired for the sake of something else;
(g) Goods desired for themselves.

The assumption that all goods must fit into one or the other of these two groups should not be treated as a rejection of the threefold distinction between (a), (b), and (c). In other words, Aristotle is not now mysteriously denying or forgetting that a good can be desired both for itself and for the sake of its consequences. Asking whether a good goes into (f) or (g) is simply an abbreviated way of asking whether it goes into (d) or (e), which in turn represent merely a regrouping of (a), (b), and (c).

Let us now look again at the passage that created our difficulty. Speaking of contemplation, Aristotle says: "And it alone seems to be loved for itself. For nothing comes to be from it apart from the contemplation, whereas from practical activities we profit apart from the action, to a greater or smaller extent" (1177b1–4). If we take Aristotle to be working with the threefold distinction of I.7, this makes no sense: from the fact that practical activities are desired for the sake of other goods, it does not follow that they are not loved for themselves. And as we have seen, Aristotle says elsewhere that other goods besides contemplation are desired for themselves. It is far more plausible to take him to be regrouping his categories and naming them in the simplified manner of (f) and (g): a good is either desired for the sake of something else or desired for itself. (More fully expressed: it is either desired for the sake of something else or desired for itself and not for the sake of something else.) Once we take Aristotle to be distinguishing goods in this way, rather than in the threefold manner of I.7, his claim in the above passage makes perfect sense, and it coheres with everything else in the NE.[19]

3.12. USELESSNESS AND HAPPINESS

Suppose it is agreed that X.7–8 requires no radical revision in the list of intrinsic goods; Aristotle still believes that honor, pleasure, the virtues,

---

[19] My interpretation of 1177b1–2 is in agreement with that of Hardie: "what he ought to say, and must mean, is that it [contemplation] alone is loved for its own sake alone" (Aristotle's Ethical Theory, p. 356).

and so on are desired (and desirable) for themselves. Even so, an important puzzle remains: how can a reasonable person believe, as I claim Aristotle does, that it is a point in favor of contemplation that it produces no further goods? According to the interpretation I am defending, he is saying in X.7–8 that although moral and philosophical activity are both desirable in themselves, the latter differs from the former in that it merely has intrinsic value, whereas practical activity has both intrinsic and instrumental value. We can understand how this contrast might be used in favor of ethical activity: whatever its intrinsic worth, its overall value is increased by the fact that it leads to other goods. And we can understand how the unproductiveness of contemplation might be viewed as one of its disadvantages: although it is desirable in itself, that is all that can be said in its favor. It seems bizarre for Aristotle to take the opposite point of view, and to argue on behalf of contemplation that it has no instrumental value. Can we make sense of this?

I think we can, if we recognize that X.7–8 completes a project begun in Book I. As we shall see in Chapter 4, Aristotle's initial discussion of happiness takes the form of a search for a good that has three characteristics: (a) it is desirable in itself; (b) all other goods are desirable for its sake; and (c) it is not in turn desirable for the sake of anything further. Accordingly, when he claims in X.7 that contemplation "alone seems to be loved for itself" (1177b1–2) and that it aims at no end beyond itself (b20), he is trying to show that contemplation satisfies the first and third conditions. Since it produces nothing further, it cannot be desired for the sake of further goods; by contrast, we do hope and normally expect to gain further goods through our ethical activities. Accordingly, contemplation passes a test that ethical activity fails: theoretical activity meets condition (c), whereas practical activity does not.[20]

Now, it might be objected that, so far from helping, this only makes matters worse. For now we must make sense not only of Aristotle's bizarre way of defending contemplation in X.7, but also of the whole project undertaken in the *NE*. Why should anyone think that everything we do is desirable for the sake of some single intrinsic good—one that has no instrumental value? That question can be answered only after we have examined Aristotle's hierarchical ordering of ends (Chapter 4), and his

---

[20] For a different solution to the problem, see Korsgaard, "Aristotle and Kant on the Source of Value," especially pp. 490–95. She does not take 1177b1–2 to be saying that contemplation alone is in the category of goods desired for themselves (and not for the sake of other goods). Instead, she argues that Aristotle is making a different distinction—one between conditional and unconditional ends—and putting contemplation alone in the latter category. Conditional ends are valuable in themselves, given the circumstances of human beings; by contrast, an unconditional end is what makes it worthwhile to be a human being. Korsgaard believes that this distinction can be found in *NE* I.7, but I disagree. Furthermore, I take Aristotle to believe that ethical activity, as well as theoretical activity, is something that makes it worthwhile to be a human being.

argument that contemplation should be placed by itself at the top of that hierarchy. What I can do now is explain why the defense of contemplation in X.7 is perfectly reasonable once we connect it with the rest of the NE in the way I propose.

The important point is that Aristotle, as I understand him, is not claiming that the unproductiveness of contemplation is *by itself* a reason for pursuing it. The fact that an activity leads to no further good is not being proposed as a good-making characteristic of that activity. For example, Aristotle can perfectly well agree that if someone is piling stones on top of one another, and his activity leads to no desirable end, then that lack of instrumental value does not count as a reason in favor of piling up those stones. To think otherwise is bizarre indeed. Aristotle is not committed to this crazy idea, because the tacit assumption of X.7–8 is that when the unproductiveness of contemplation is combined with two of its other features, then it can be equated with happiness. Anything that is an ultimate end—anything that meets conditions (a), (b), and (c)—is the highest end at which we should aim. Pointing out that contemplation meets condition (c) is not in itself an attempt to give a reason why we should engage in that activity. And it does not commit Aristotle to the insane idea that lack of instrumental value is by itself a good-making characteristic, or a reason for action. Once we see that the NE is looking for an ultimate end, then the argument of X.7 on behalf of contemplation is perfectly reasonable: the topmost end, by definition, must not be desirable for the sake of any further good, and since contemplation leads to no further good, it meets this condition. If contemplation were not only desirable in itself but also productive of further goods, it would not be the most desirable good there is, but would instead be less desirable than that for the sake of which it is pursued. When X is for the sake of Y, then Aristotle takes Y to be more desirable than X (I.1 1094a14–16).

Of course, it may be complained that in X.7–8 Aristotle does not argue as fully as he should to convince his audience that perfect happiness consists in contemplation. He needs to show that all of the other goods are desirable for the sake of contemplation, and he does not attempt to do so. But the lacuna is smaller than it might first appear to be: Aristotle does say in X.7 that we will contemplate more if we do so with fellow workers (1177a34); he points out that since the philosopher must live with others, he chooses to act in accordance with the ethical virtues, and therefore needs a moderate amount of external equipment (1178b5–7, 1179a1–13); health and physical needs must also be met, if we are to engage in philosophical activity over a long period of time (1178b33–5). Furthermore, we should recall that in X.6 Aristotle makes a place for amusement in any well-lived life, and earlier in Book X, he points out that when we take pleasure in any activity, we become better at it (X.5 1175a31–6). When we read X.7–8 carefully, and connect it with preceding material, we can see that Aristotle in not inattentive to the point that an ultimate end must be the good to which all others make a contribution. And if my reading of "the most perfect virtue" in I.7 (1098a17–18) is correct, Aristotle believes that each of the ethical virtues is desirable in part because it contributes to philosophical activity. We can with good reason complain that X.7–8 does not spell out the way in which they make this contribution: Aristotle should explain how temperance, courage, justice, and so on facilitate the intellectual life. Admittedly, he does point out, as we have seen, that the practical virtues are desired for the sake of other goods. But he should be more specific, and say why contemplation is among the goods promoted by excellent practical activity. In 3.8, I have tried to show how this part of his argument might go. The fact that he himself does not spell out these important details suggests that he expects no challenge from his audience: they do not need to be persuaded that ethically virtuous activity leads to many other goods, and they have no reason to doubt that contemplation is among them.

Suppose we do not take X.7–8 to be arguing that contemplation should be our ultimate end. We might instead take Aristotle to mean that happiness is a composite of many goods, and his arguments on behalf of contemplation would then be attempts to show that it is the most desirable element in that complex whole. According to this interpretation, Aristotle is using the following argument (among others) to show that contemplation is more desirable than any other good: this activity is loved merely for itself, and leads to no other good. But surely we should question Aristotle's good sense, if this is how we read him. For why should the fact that one activity is less productive of good than a second be taken to show the superiority of the first? Is uselessness a good-making characteristic? If we refuse to take X.7–8 to be saying that our ultimate end should be a single good—contemplation—then it is hard to make sense of Aristotle's defense of this activity.

But, it may be objected, his defense will disappoint us no matter how we read it. For example, one of his arguments on behalf of contemplation is that it is more continuous than any other activity (X.7 1177a21–2); another claims that it is more pleasant than any other virtuous activity (a22–7). How can any sensible person believe that these points, even if accepted, give us reason to make contemplation our ultimate end? Even if that activity is better than every other, why shouldn't our ultimate end be a composite good, of which contemplation is the most desirable component? If we want to make good sense of the arguments that refer to contemplation's great continuity and pleasantness, hadn't we better restrict Aristotle's conclusion to the only one that these arguments can support—namely, that contemplation is more desirable than any other good?

True, if this is his conclusion, then he uses a bad argument for it when he says that contemplation is unproductive of further goods. But perhaps we will minimize the number of bad arguments we attribute to him if we take him to be trying to show, not that contemplation *is* the ultimate end, but that it is the best component of the ultimate end.[21]

My reply is that the arguments used in X.7–8 to defend the philosophical life cannot be understood unless we know how to connect them with the treatment of happiness in Book I. In Chapter 6, I will try to show how the function argument of I.7 takes Aristotle a large part of the way towards the conclusion he eventually reaches in X.7–8: perfect happiness consists in contemplation. Once we read X.7–8 in light of the material that precedes it, we will realize that the greater continuity and pleasantness of contemplation are not meant to provide self-contained arguments for making that activity our ultimate end. Rather, Aristotle takes the function argument to give a reason for making some virtuous activity— whichever virtuous activity turns out to be best and most perfect—our ultimate end. When he claims that theoretical activity has greater continuity and brings more pleasure than moral activity, he is supplementing the function argument by giving reasons for taking theoretical virtue to be superior to practical virtue. Once we read X.7–8 in conjunction with Book I, we can make good sense of the arguments in defense of contemplation, and we can take the conclusion of these later chapters to be that this activity should be our ultimate end. On this interpretation, Aristotle will not be saying that an activity's lack of instrumental value is by itself a point in its favor.

[21] This is the approach adopted by Keyt, "Intellectualism in Aristotle," pp. 376–382.

CHAPTER FOUR

The Hierarchy of Ends

4.1. An Overview

The remainder of this study concerns the conception of human happiness that Aristotle presents in Book I of the *NE*. I will try to show that this part of his treatise develops an account of the good that is both internally consistent and continuous with his later defense of contemplation. Before entering into details, however, it may be useful to give an overview of how I read Book I, and how my interpretation differs from one that is widely accepted.

I take this book to have the following structure: In I.1–2, a certain problem is posed: what is the good? That is, what is such that (a) it is desired for itself, (b) it not desired for the sake of any further good, and (c) all other goods are desired for its sake? In I.3–6, Aristotle discusses alternative ways of answering this question, and rejects most. Finally, in I.7, after further clarifying the nature of his question, he argues that the human good consists in "activity of soul in accordance with virtue" (1098a16–17). And most of the remainder of Book I (chapters 8–12) tries to confirm this answer. So, this part of the *NE* can be divided into three unequal parts: first (I.1–6), a question is posed—what is the good?—and several inadequate answers are canvassed; second (I.7), Aristotle defends his own answer: the good is virtuous activity; and third (I.8–12), he gives further reasons for accepting that answer.

Controversy arises, however, because I.7 does not say *merely* that the good consists in virtuous activity. More fully, the conclusion of the function argument reads as follows: "The human good turns out to be activity of soul in accordance with virtue, and if there are more than one virtue, in accordance with the best and most perfect" (1098a16–18). Some scholars take "the best and most perfect virtue" to refer to theoretical wisdom, and I will argue that they are correct.[1] But I do not infer from this that according to *NE* I there is just one kind of happy life for human beings—the theoretical life discussed in X.7–8. For I take those late chapters to be

---

[1] See Cooper, *RHGA*, pp. 100–101 n. 10; Gauthier and Jolif, *L'Éthique à Nicomaque*, comments on 1097a30, 1098a17; Hardie, *Aristotle's Ethical Theory*, pp. 23, 25. Cooper gives further support to his reading in "Contemplation and Happiness: A Reconsideration." On the other side, see Ackrill, "Aristotle on *Eudaimonia*," pp. 27–9. Hardie replies to Ackrill in "Aristotle on the Best Life for a Man," pp. 38–40.

saying that although perfect happiness consists solely in contemplation, one can also be happy (to a secondary degree) if one lives a life devoted to ethical activity as one's ultimate end. Accordingly, I read the above statement as an approximation that is later made more precise. Aristotle's fuller meaning is this: perfect happiness consists in exercising theoretical wisdom (the most perfect virtue), while a less than perfect happiness consists in exercising the practical virtues (the ones that are not most perfect).

Accordingly, on my reading, there are two good ways of leading one's life, but in both of them one is to take one's ultimate end to consist in a single kind of activity, and other ends are to be pursued to the extent that they promote that highest goal. Whether one leads a philosophical or a political life, all goods are to be arranged in a hierarchy: each lower end is for the sake of some better end, which may in turn be desired for the sake of a still higher end. But each of the two hierarchies terminates in a single end, and in fact the two termini are of the same type: they are activities of the part of the soul that has reason. So, I take the *NE* to be saying that every other type of good (everything that is not virtuous activity) is to be desired for the sake of just one type of good—virtuous activity. In Book I, Aristotle leaves aside the question of which sort of virtuous activity— theoretical or practical—is best. He need not decide that question just yet, for no matter which of the two goals one adopts as one's ultimate end, one will lead a good life—if one is adequately supplied with other goods, so that one can regularly engage in virtuous activity over the course of a lifetime.[2] But if Aristotle had failed to compare the two kinds of virtues, and to say which is most perfect, his treatment of happiness would have been radically incomplete. He would not have discussed a major question faced by many of his readers: should I lead a philosophical or a political life?

According to the reading of the *NE* that I shall oppose, Aristotle is saying that happiness is a composite of all the goods that are desirable for themselves: it is not to be equated with virtuous activity alone, for that is not the only good that is desirable for itself. For example, as we have seen, he says that we desire pleasure and honor for themselves (I.7 1097b2–3); and no doubt he approves of this attitude. A passage in I.7, cited in the Introduction, is often thought to commit Aristotle to this all-inclusive conception of happiness:

> The self-sufficient we posit as that which when taken by itself makes life choiceworthy and in need of nothing. Such we think happiness to be. Furthermore, it is the most choiceworthy of all, without being counted in addition— being counted in addition, it is obviously more choiceworthy [when taken]

---

[2] And of course he *cannot* determine which virtue of the rational soul is best until he has examined them all.

with the least of goods. For what is added on is an increase of goods, and of goods the greater is always more choiceworthy. (1097b14–20)

If happiness needs nothing and cannot be made more choiceworthy because it is composed of all that is desirable in itself, then it cannot be equated solely with virtuous activity, and it would be even more wrongheaded to identify it with just one type of virtuous activity (contemplation). But I shall argue in Chapter 5 that this is not what Aristotle is saying here. Because these enigmatic lines will receive a full discussion there, the present chapter will take no further notice of them.

One point should be emphasized, however, before we move on: Although there is divided opinion about how the conclusion of the function argument should be understood, that conclusion clearly equates the human good with virtuous activity and with that type of good alone. Recall Aristotle's formula: "The human good turns out to be activity of soul in accordance with virtue, and if there are more than one virtue, in accordance with the best and most perfect" (1098a16–18). Aristotle is not saying here that virtuous activity is just one good among many; after all, the same could be said about pleasure, honor, friendship, and so on. No special argument would be needed if he were simply trying to show in I.7 that "activity of soul in accordance with virtue" is *a* good. Clearly, he needs a special argument—the "function argument"—because he is singling out virtuous activity and giving it a special status: it is not just *a* good but also *the* human good. And as I have said, the function argument of I.7 is Aristotle's attempt to answer the question that has been raised in I.1–2: what is the intrinsically desirable end for the sake of which all others are pursued, but which in turn is not desirable for the sake of any other? When we connect I.1–2 with the function argument in this way, we must conclude that he takes the ultimate end to be just one type of good—virtuous activity.

Now, it might be argued, against my interpretation, that he does not want to narrow his equation any further: on this rival view, Aristotle would be saying that the ultimate end of the best life consists not just in contemplation, but in a composite of many different types of virtuous activities. Although I shall reject that interpretation, it should be emphasized that even if it is accepted, the function argument is still equating the human good with virtuous activities and with no other type of good. Accordingly, we must pay a high price if we also take I.7 to be treating human happiness as a composite of all intrinsic goods. On such a reading, Aristotle is contradicting himself within a single chapter: first (1097b14–20) he says that happiness is an all-inclusive composite, and then (1097b22–1098a18) he equates it solely with virtuous activity. In Chapter

5, we will see how that contradiction can be avoided by reinterpreting the first of these two passages.

4.2. FOR THE SAKE OF

There are many different types of human endeavor, we are told in *NE* I.1, each aiming at a different good. The doctor seeks health; the builder makes a ship; the general tries to achieve victory; the head of the household maintains its wealth. But Aristotle does not think that our activities and goals are equal in value; on the contrary, he assumes without argument that some things are superior to others. For example, he expects his audience to agree with him that the physical objects produced by a craftsman are superior to the activity by which they are produced (1094a5–6). Having a ship that is already made is better than the activity of making the ship. No argument is given for this claim, but presumably Aristotle is relying on the following idea: If we had to choose between (a) having the products of the crafts without going through the process by which they are made and (b) going through the process but not having the products, we would surely prefer (a) to (b). The activity of making something is undertaken for the sake of having the product, and the activity is less desirable than its outcome.

Furthermore, Aristotle assumes that certain crafts are subordinate to others, and that if pursuit A is under the direction of pursuit B, then A's end is less choiceworthy than B's (1094a9–16). For example, various crafts (such as bridlemaking) produce equipment for horses, and so they are subordinate to horsemanship. This in turn (along with other crafts) is subordinate to the study of military strategy. The process of making the bridle is inferior to the finished product, which is in turn inferior to the good pursued by the expert rider, which is in turn inferior to the goal— victory—pursued by the general. Each lower good is desirable for the sake of some higher end, "lower" and "higher" indicating different degrees of desirability.

Aristotle is here introducing, by way of example, a relation that is of the utmost importance to his conception of happiness—the relation two things have when one is pursued for the sake of the other. He gives no definition of this "for-the-sake-of" relation, and expects his readers to have no trouble grasping it by means of the examples presented in I.1. Notice that the relation is a causal one, at least in part. The process of making the bridle causes the product to come into being; the bridle is then used as an instrument that facilitates the activity of riding; and riding in battle is a means of defeating the enemy and achieving victory. But it should also be kept in mind that the for-the-sake-of relation has a normative component: when A is pursued for the sake of B, then B provides a norm that guides A. The bridlemaker decides how to treat his raw material by looking to a paradigm of the finished product, and the proper design of his product is determined by the expert rider. The horseman tells the bridlemaker what sort of bridle he needs; so the activity of riding provides a standard for determining how bridles should be made. And in turn the military leader tells his cavalry which sorts of maneuvers they need to master. The bridlemaker puts himself at the service of the rider, who puts himself at the service of the general; each lower discipline plays a causal role in the pursuit of each higher discipline, and the higher disciplines in turn provide the norms for the proper pursuit of lower disciplines. The for-the-sake-of relation is accordingly a mixture of causal and normative elements.

It should be noticed that this relation is asymmetrical: If A is desirable for the sake of B, then B cannot also be desirable for the sake of A. For, Aristotle holds, when A is for the sake of B, B is more desirable than A (1094a14–16). And if B is more desirable than A, then A cannot also be more desirable than B. The asymmetrical nature of the for-the-sake-of relation does not prevent Aristotle from recognizing that certain goods promote each other. For example, skill in riding may help secure victory in battle, and victory allows one to go on exercising that skill; a certain degree of strength enables one to lift certain weights, and that activity enables one to sustain that level of strength. These sorts of examples do not prove that, in committing himself to the asymmetry of the for-the-sake-of relation, Aristotle is guilty of confusion. For that relation is not one that is purely empirical and causal (in our sense of "causal"). To say that lifting weights is desirable for the sake of maintaining strength is to say that we should regulate that activity by looking to the good it produces: we should choose our exercises by seeing how they contribute to strength, and we should choose the amount of exercise that will best promote this good. And although the strength we achieve will help us engage in these exercises, that does not show that strength is for the sake of exercise. To determine which goods are for the sake of which others, we must go beyond purely causal questions about which goods produce which others; we must ask what the appropriate norms are for regulating our activities.

This shows that a skeptical reader could challenge Aristotle even at this early point in the *NE*. It might be asked, for example: why should generalship be placed over horsemanship? Those who love to ride for the sheer pleasure of it might say that battles should be fought and won so that the citizens can go on enjoying themselves in this way. It is true that riding helps win battles, but even so, it might be the case that victory in battle is desirable for the sake of exercising the skills of horsemanship.

Another question can be asked: Is Aristotle being naive when he assumes that every craft aims at some good? Consider someone who makes a burglar's tools: surely Aristotle would not want to say that what the practitioner of this craft aims at is a genuine good. Would he try to avoid this result by denying that such a toolmaker practices a genuine craft? In that case, he needs to tell us how to determine which objects produced by human activities are goods and which are not. So he is assuming a great deal as he begins his treatise: he takes only certain objects (bridles, ships) to be goods, and he takes certain goods to be more desirable than others. Can he say anything to defend these assumptions?

I believe he can, once he is allowed to develop his theory more fully. For I take Aristotle to be saying, at a later point, that the hierarchy of goods that he began to explore in I.1 has a single terminus: every lower good is desirable for the sake of activity of the reasoning soul in accordance with virtue. If he can defend this conception of the human good, then he can return to the assumptions he made in I.1 and explain why the objects of the crafts are genuine goods, and he can justify the hierarchy of disciplines there taken for granted. Certain human pursuits will be genuine crafts and their products will be genuine goods because they contribute to the ability of citizens to engage in virtuous activity; ships, buildings, bridles, and health presumably pass this test, whereas a burglar's tools presumably do not. Similarly, if virtuous activity—rather than the exercise of riding skill—is the final end to be pursued, then Aristotle can justify his claim that the horseman should be subordinate to the general. If riding is not the final end, then its place in the hierarchy of goods is to be determined by seeing how it will best contribute to that ultimate goal; and it will make its best contribution if it supplies able riders to the general who is protecting citizens so that they can go on engaging in virtuous activity. So, although Aristotle assumes his readers will raise no objections at this early stage in his argument, he is prepared to say more, at a later stage, if pressed.

An important methodological remark in I.4 suggests that we are on the right track:

> Let it not escape our attention that arguments from starting points differ from arguments towards starting points. For Plato too did well to be puzzled about this, and to ask whether we are proceeding from starting points or towards starting points, just as on a racecourse one proceeds from the judges to the boundary, or back again. For although we should begin with what is known, things are known in two ways: known to us, and known without qualification. Presumably we at any rate should begin with what is known to us. For this reason, one must be trained in fine habits if one is to listen in a satisfactory way [to what is said] about what is fine and just, and about political matters in gen-

eral. For the starting point is the [fact] that [something is so], and if this is sufficiently apparent, one will not also need the reason why. (1095a30–b7)

The student of practical philosophy need not approach the subject already having an answer to the question "What is the good?" That is a matter for investigation. But at the same time, it is necessary to make some initial assumptions, and in I.1 we see that among these assumptions are certain beliefs about the crafts and their hierarchical arrangement. We take certain things—bridles, health, victory—to be good; and we take some of these goods to be inferior to others. If a student begins with no beliefs at all about what is worthwhile, or if he makes assumptions that do not let Aristotle's arguments get off the ground, then he is not well suited to learn the subject presented in the NE. On the other hand, those students who agree with Aristotle's initial assumptions will eventually reach a different kind of starting point: having understood the ultimate end of all goods, they will see why they were right to assume from the start that certain crafts are needed, and why they should be subordinate to other disciplines.

4.3. THE TERMINUS

We have seen that NE I.1 introduces, by way of example, the notion that certain goods are pursued for the sake of others, and that this for-the-sake-of relation has both causal and normative elements. We will soon return to this chapter, for it has been claimed that it invokes a second kind of for-the-sake-of relation as well. Rather than turn to that issue immediately, I want to move on to NE I.2, for the main ideas of that chapter are continuous with the ones we have begun to explore.

Having pointed out in I.1 that some ends are subordinate to others, which are in turn inferior to still higher ends, Aristotle naturally shifts his attention, in I.2, to the question of what is at the top of this hierarchy. And he argues in a well-known passage that the chain of goods, each desirable for the sake of something higher, must come to an end: "If there is some end of actions that we want because of itself, and we want the others because of this, and we don't choose all things because of something else (for they would thus proceed without limit, and desire would be empty and vain), it is obvious that this would be the good and the best" (1094a18–22). I take him to be saying that we must choose between two alternatives: either the chain discussed in I.1 goes on forever, or it does not. If the first alternative is correct, then desire is empty and futile. Since desire is not empty and futile, the chain must come to an end.

But why must it end in something that we desire for itself? Aristotle is assuming that if the topmost good were desired, but not desired for itself, then it would be sought for the sake of some still better good. In that case, however, it would no longer be the topmost good; it would instead be inferior to the good that it promotes. Accordingly, whatever is at the top of the hierarchy of ends must be something we desire for itself.

It should be evident that Aristotle discounts the possibility that the chain of ends might avoid going on forever by turning back on itself: in such a circle, A would be desirable for the sake of B, which would be desirable for the sake of C, which would be desirable for the sake of A. His reason for rejecting this possibility is contained in his assumption that the for-the-sake-of relation is asymmetrical: if A is desirable for the sake of B, then B cannot be desirable for the sake of A. In a circular chain connected by this asymmetrical relation, each of two ends would be more choiceworthy than the other. So, given the asymmetry of the for-the-sake-of relation, and the other assumptions Aristotle makes, he can conclude that the hierarchy of ends must terminate in something that has these three properties: (a) it is desirable in itself, (b) it is not desirable for the sake of something else, and (c) everything else is desirable for its sake. The hierarchy of ends cannot continue indefinitely in a linear direction—for then desire would be empty and vain. The hierarchy of ends cannot turn back on itself—for then some good would be both more and less choiceworthy than some other good. So it must terminate somewhere, and it must terminate in something that is desirable only for itself, and not because of some further good.

Even so, a familiar objection can be raised: thus far, Aristotle has given his readers no good reason to think that the hierarchy of ends must terminate in a single point. For all he has said, the hierarchy might turn out to have this structure:

$$A \quad B \quad C$$

$$M \quad N \quad O$$

$$X \quad Y \quad Z$$

Suppose that X is desirable for the sake of M, which is in turn desirable for the sake of A. And suppose that Y-N-B and Z-O-C are similar chains, each lower good in a column being desirable for the good above it. And let A, B, and C be goods that are desirable in themselves. In that case, there would be no circles, and the hierarchy of ends would eventually terminate in something desirable for itself, but that something would not be a *single* good. There would be no one end for the sake of which all subordinate goods are pursued, except in the trivial sense in which we could say that everything else is desirable for the sake of A-B-C. But A, B, and C could be quite diverse: they might be physical pleasure, contemplation, and health. To speak of them as a single end, and to say that everything else is done for the sake of some one good, would be quite artificial.

Has Aristotle tried but failed to produce an argument that the structure of ends cannot take the form depicted above, but must instead terminate in some single unified ultimate end? I think there are three good reasons for resisting this interpretation. First, as others have pointed out, he does not assert here that there is a unitary ultimate end. He says that *if* there is some single end for the sake of which all others are pursued, *then* this will be the good.[3] He gives a reason for thinking that the chain of ends cannot be infinite, and we can understand why he assumes that it is noncircular and that its starting point must be desired for itself. But he makes no attempt to show that there is only one such starting point, and the conditional form of his sentence can be taken to mean that, in his own eyes, he is only formulating a hypothesis to be explored, rather than stating a conclusion for which an argument has been presented.[4]

Second, I shall argue that in *NE* I.7 Aristotle still holds open the possibility that the ultimate end does not consist in just one kind of good, but is a combination of several diverse ends. That is, he recognizes that the topmost part of the hierarchy of ends might consist in a row of ends, each of which is desired only for itself: this is the possibility depicted in the above diagram. It is only when he introduces the function argument that he starts to close off this possibility, and opts for a theory in which all subordinate ends are desired for the sake of some single unitary goal. If I am right about this, then Aristotle cannot be trying to show in I.2 by means of a purely formal argument that the hierarchy of ends must terminate in a single point, rather than in a row of diverse goods. For in I.7 he takes himself to have not yet shown this.

Third, we have already seen that Aristotle's method involves making assumptions that are justified only at some later point in his argument. As he says in I.4, we begin with starting points for which no reasons are given, but we eventually discover something more basic, which can in turn help us better understand our initial assumptions.[5] It would not be surprising, then, if I.2 is only putting forward the hypothesis that there is a single ultimate end: Aristotle is confident that the hypothesis will prove fruitful, because he already sees the direction in which his argument is heading. Virtuous activity will turn out to be the ultimate end, and so the

---

[3] See Hardie, "The Final Good in Aristotle's *Ethics*," p. 297; Cooper, *RHGA*, p. 93.

[4] Ackrill, "Aristotle on *Eudaimonia*," pp. 25–6, dissents. I discuss his alternative in 4.7.

[5] Aristotle does not explicitly say in I.4 1095a30–b7 that our initial starting points (the ones that are at first better known to us) are eventually better understood, after they are connected to the more basic starting points of a science. But he implies that those more basic starting points give us "the reason why" (1095b7) our initial assumptions are true.

proposal that there is only one will eventually be vindicated. Just as we
cannot expect Aristotle to show why certain products are good and certain disciplines superior merely by means of the materials he has assem-
bled in I.1, so we cannot expect him to establish in the first few lines of
I.2 that the ultimate end is unitary. We must take seriously his plea that
we not seek justification right from the start, but patiently wait for his
argument to unfold.

In fact, on my reading, we have to wait until X.7–8 until we fully understand why the ultimate end should not be a multiplicity. For even if
we agree with Aristotle that happiness consists solely in virtuous activity,
we can ask why we should not regard theoretical and practical virtue as
equally desirable, and take our ultimate end to consist in equal parts of
intellectual and moral activity. Aristotle's argument against taking our
highest good to consist in this particular mixture is postponed until Book
X, and in Book I he rests content with a more modest conclusion: the
ultimate end is not a composite of honor, pleasure, virtuous activity, and
other goods that are desired for themselves. It consists in virtuous activity
alone. But of course, that is hardly a conclusion we can expect him to
reach at the beginning of I.2. To show why the good should be conceived
in this narrow way, more work is needed, and there is every reason to
think that Aristotle realizes this.

My proposal, then, is that we read the *NE* in the following way: Aristotle takes himself to have shown in I.2 that the hierarchy of ends terminates, and he proposes that we find out what lies at the top of that structure. The possibility that there might be more than one end at the top is
kept open, but in I.7 he begins a defense of two closely related kinds of
lives, each having one ultimate end. The defense of one of those lives—
the life devoted to ethical activity—is continued throughout the remainder of Book I, and the defense of the life devoted to theoretical activity is
taken up in Book X. Both lives are happy, though the political life has
certain defects that prevent it from being one of perfect happiness. But
none of this should be taken to mean that Aristotle is committed to the
thesis that if someone leads a philosophical-political life—a life that seeks
to balance these two activities—then he is not living well (see 1.11). And
it should be noticed that even this mixed life is still devoted to one kind
of good, namely, virtuous activity. Even so, nothing important hangs on
the question whether we describe this mixed life as one that has one ultimate end (virtuous activity) or two (ethical and intellectual activity).
What is important is to recognize that a life can be a good one if it has just
one ultimate end—provided that this end is some form of virtuous activity—and that a life cannot be the best that is possible for us unless it is
devoted to a single ultimate end (contemplation). That complex conclu-

sion is one for which Aristotle is preparing us in I.2, but at that point he still has a long way to go.

4.4. THE TARGET OF POLITICS

As I read the opening lines of I.2, Aristotle *argues* that the hierarchy of ends must have a terminus, but he *assumes* that it will terminate in a single good. Now, as soon as he says that this single ultimate end will be "the good and the best" (1094a22), he emphasizes the practical importance of determining what it is. Like archers, we are more likely to hit the right mark if we have an understanding of the good for the sake of which all others are desirable (a23–4). But even if we provisionally accept his assumption that the ultimate end will be a single good, we might wonder whether he is overemphasizing its importance, and undervaluing the need to study the subordinate goods as well. In other words, why not say that our target should be the whole hierarchy of ends, or at least those among them that are desirable in themselves? The single end at the top (assuming that there is just one) will no doubt be more desirable than everything beneath it. Even so, it is just one of our ends. Since nothing prevents subordinate goods from being desirable in themselves, it might turn out that those subordinate goods, when combined, are far more desirable than the single topmost good. In that case, even though it is important to determine what lies at the pinnacle of the hierarchy, it will be even more important to study the intrinsic goods that fall below it.

For example, suppose our ends take this form:

$$A$$
$$M \quad N \quad O$$
$$X \quad Y \quad Z$$

A is good in itself and not desirable for the sake of anything else. M, N, and O are both desirable in themselves and desirable for the sake of A. X, Y, and Z are merely means to goods in higher rows. Even though A must be more desirable than each of the other goods, it may not exceed their value by much. In leading our lives, we would have to give the greatest weight to A, but we would still need to know how much more weight we should assign to it than to the other goods. Furthermore, it may be that M is very close in value to A, while N and O are far less desirable in themselves. In that case, we would want to lead a life in which A and M get nearly equal weight and N and O receive far less emphasis. It would be appropriate to say that our target is the right balance between A, M, N, and O.

Now, some scholars would argue that my question is a bad one, for it rests on the assumption that a good can be desirable in itself and yet fail to be located in the top row of Aristotle's hierarchy. According to their interpretation, the good is a composite of all the goods we desire for themselves. And once we read Aristotle in this way, then it becomes obvious why our target should be the good for the sake of which all else is desired: everything desirable for the sake of that all-inclusive end is a mere means. It would be crazy to balance the good in the top row against anything that falls below it, since those subordinate goods are desirable only to the extent that they contribute to something in the top row. And they are desirable only to this extent because they are not good in themselves; if they had intrinsic value, they would be in the top row, not beneath it.

I will soon argue that there is no good textual support for this alternative interpretation. In this section I am setting it aside and raising a question that my own interpretation takes to be a legitimate one: Since goods that are not at the pinnacle of Aristotle's hierarchy can be desirable in themselves, why does he say that our target is simply the topmost good? Why not say that each good that is desirable in itself—even those that are subordinate to some other—should be assigned a certain weight, and that our target should be this whole composite?

I think Aristotle would reply that there simply is no way to make such an assignment of weights. We can say, for example, that honor and pleasure are desirable in themselves, but we have no way of comparing them and saying how much more desirable one of them is than the other, when they are considered just in themselves.[6] This does not mean, however, that there is no way of deciding how large a place they should occupy in our lives. We can do so by asking whether they are desirable for the sake of some further good, and if they are, we can determine how large a contribution they make to that more desirable good. And that is why it is so important to determine which good—if there is just one—occupies the topmost position in the hierarchy of ends. The only way to make decisions about the relative weights of various ends is to use that highest good as the target of all our actions. So it is not merely the best of all goods—it is also the standard by which we fix the value of all else.

Of course, in I.2, Aristotle has not yet shown that there is anything that deserves to play this role in our decision making. The good he is looking for must not only be more desirable than all others; it must also be a good that all others contribute to in some way. For the extent of their contribution will determine the extent to which they should be pursued. One such good, he will argue, is activity in accordance with ethical virtue; an even better one is contemplation. We can look to either one, and

---

[6] Recall *Pol.* III.12 1282b36–1283a15, discussed in Chapter 1, note 17.

determine the extent to which subordinate goods should be pursued. And in using them as standards, we will see why the goods we take for granted—friendship, pleasure, honor, and so on—are truly desirable. This is the project Aristotle carries forward throughout the rest of the *NE*.

We should recall at this point a remark I made earlier (3.2) about *NE* I.2: Aristotle says in this chapter that politics is the science that studies the ultimate end of human life, and in arguing for this claim, he is mindful of the politician's need to answer quantitative questions. Politics "determines which of the sciences are needed in cities, and what sorts of things each person should learn, and to what extent" (*mechri tinos*, 1094a28–b2). Those who lead political lives must decide not only what must be learned, but also how much weight should be assigned to various studies and pursuits. And they can answer these questions correctly only if they have a defensible conception of the ultimate end for all citizens. For example, if they make the mistake that Aristotle thinks the Spartans made, and take the ultimate end to be military victory, then the city will overemphasize the importance of physical training, and citizens will spend far more time on this than they ought.[7] The question of how much physical strength one should strive for depends on what one uses it for, and so too for all goods subordinate to the ultimate end.

Aristotle, as I read him, takes politics to have the same relation to subordinate disciplines that any superior craft has to those subjects that come within its jurisdiction. The expert on horsemanship is to be governed by the general, whose concern is victory in battle; and the general is in turn subordinate to the rulers who decide when war should be waged. The line of thought that proceeds from I.1 to I.2 is continuous, and there is a single kind of relation that holds between any subordinate end and that for the sake of which it is desirable. In each such case, it is a causal-normative relation: lower ends facilitate higher ends, and the higher ends provide a norm for the lower ends. This relation holds whether the ends in question are mere means or not: boats are for the sake of something higher, and so too are victory and health. Whether or not these last two ends are good in themselves, the for-the-sake-of relation they bear to a further end is the same for-the-sake-of relation that mere instruments bear to their ends. And in each case the norm provided by the higher end settles quantitative questions about the lower ends. How many ships or bridles should be produced depends on how many are needed to serve higher goals. So it should be no surprise to us that politics, by looking to its special end, determines the extent to which subordinate crafts and sciences should be pursued. Every discipline that regulates others does so by

[7] See *EE* VIII.3 1248b37–1249a16, *Pol.* VII.2 1324b5–9.

looking to its peculiar end, and asking how the subordinate crafts can best contribute to that end.

But it may be asked: Is Aristotle saying, on my interpretation, that contemplation is the ultimate end to which political leaders should look as they make decisions about how to govern the city? Should these leaders try to turn the citizens into philosophers, and should they develop an educational curriculum that will prepare young people for the philosophical life? I see no evidence for reading Aristotle in this way. When he discusses education in *Politics* VII–VIII, he recommends that the city provide some common training to all citizens (VIII.1 1337a21–30), but nothing suggests that they are all to become philosophers. I take him to be assuming that even in ideal circumstances only a small portion of any citizenry will be intellectually equipped to develop the virtue of theoretical wisdom. So the single ultimate end to which the political leader should look when he makes decisions affecting all citizens is activity in accordance with ethical virtue. But at the same time, he should realize that this ultimate end is an imperfect approximation of the one that should ideally govern a person's life. He should look upon his own life—the political life—as one that is less than ideal for a human being, even though it may be the best he can achieve in his circumstances. And when he promotes the well-being of the citizens by looking to the development of ethical virtue, he should realize that even though this is the best contribution he can make to their lives, they can do even better if they exercise other virtues that he does not himself instill in them—the theoretical virtues.

Aristotle's claim, then, is that everyone benefits from undertaking the study of politics, for this is the subject that investigates the ultimate end. But after having examined this subject, some do best to devote their lives to the understanding of other subjects: they take to heart the conclusion that the best life is philosophical, and they have the ability to lead such a life. Others do best to stay with politics, pursuing the questions investigated in Aristotle's other practical writings and exercising civic leadership in light of his conclusions. In either case, one will be pursuing a single ultimate end. And the ultimate end that the political leader seeks for himself and for others is not contemplation but moral activity—not because moral activity is better, but because it is the highest good that all citizens can achieve.

4.5. PART AND WHOLE

It is time to start looking at a way of reading *NE* I that differs from my own. The rival interpretation I have in mind is one that has been mentioned several times already: it holds that in Book I, at least, Aristotle takes happiness to be a composite of all goods that are desirable in them-

selves. On this reading, the good is not to be identified with contemplation or with virtuous activity in general. Instead, Aristotle thinks that
contemplation and every other single end should be chosen for the sake
of happiness. That all-inclusive good is better than every one of its components, no matter how valuable any single component may be. For the
whole is more desirable than any one, or any subset, of its parts.

J. L. Ackrill has done more than anyone else to persuade the current
generation of scholars that this is the way to read Book I.[8] The most important evidence he cites is drawn from I.7, and we will eventually consider his way of reading that chapter. But Ackrill also thinks that his reading finds support in I.1–2, and in the next few sections I will examine his
treatment of these first two chapters. I believe that he misreads them, and
that this seriously weakens his attempt to show that in I.7 Aristotle takes
happiness to be an all-inclusive composite.

But before we look at the text, let us more fully consider the way individual goods are related to happiness, on Ackrill's reading. He says:

> One may think of the relation of putting to playing golf or of playing golf to
> having a good holiday. One does not putt *in order to* play golf as one buys a club
> in order to play golf. . . . It will be "because" you wanted to play golf that you
> are putting, and "for the sake of" a good holiday that you are playing golf; but
> this is because putting and golfing are *constituents of* or *ingredients in* golfing and
> having a good holiday respectively, not because they are necessary preliminar-
> ies. . . . Now the idea that some things are done for their own sake and may
> yet be done for the sake of something else is precisely the idea Aristotle will
> need and use in talking of good actions and *eudaimonia*. . . . That the primary
> ingredients of *eudaimonia* are for the sake of *eudaimonia* is not incompatible with
> their being ends in themselves; for *eudaimonia* is constituted by activities that
> are ends in themselves.[9]

Notice that the for-the-sake-of-relation that Ackrill is trying to explain
here is quite different from the one we discussed in 4.2. That causal-normative relation is illustrated by means of the examples Aristotle uses in
I.1: certain activities are pursued for the sake of the products they yield,
and those products in turn are desired for the sake of further ends they
promote. But the for-the-sake-of relation that Ackrill is talking about is
a relation between part and whole. Happiness is the whole for the sake of
which each of its components is desired, and to say that one good is desired for the sake of another, in this sense, does not mean that it causally
contributes to that further good. Contemplation is—in this new sense—

---

[8] Ackrill, "Aristotle on *Eudaimonia*." This paper contains the fullest defense of inclusivism
known to me, and it is frequently cited by those who presuppose inclusivism as a basis for
their own research.

[9] Ibid., p. 19, Ackrill's emphasis.

for the sake of happiness, without causing it to come into being. And if I am asked why I want this good, then I should reply, according to Ackrill's reading, that I want it both for itself and because it is one of the goods of which happiness is composed. Ackrill does not hold that this for-the-sake-of relation is the only one present in the *NE*. His claim is that both sorts of relations can be found in Aristotle's work. Intrinsic goods are for the sake of happiness in one way, and mere means are for the sake of their ends in another.

I find the for-the-sake-of relation that Ackrill invokes a mysterious one. My perplexity arises from the fact that, on his reading, the various components of happiness seem to be a mere aggregate; they need have no connection to one another in order to be included within *eudaimonia*. Honor, pleasure, virtue, friendship, and so on are parts of the all-inclusive whole simply because each is good in itself: more such goods are better than fewer, and so the best good is the one that is most inclusive, regardless of whether this optimal composite has any internal principle of organization or not. Now, if there need be no connection between any one component of happiness and any other, then there is no explanatory value in the statement that some single good is desirable *for the sake of* the larger whole. If I asked you why you pursue A, and you replied that it is both desirable in itself and desirable for the sake of the whole that consists of A and some unrelated good, B, my reaction would be one of puzzlement. For B explains nothing about why you want A. When one thing is desired or desirable for the sake of a second, there must be something about the second that helps us understand why wanting the first is appropriate. And this holds as much for Aristotle's *heneka* or *charin* as for the English expression—"for the sake of"—by which they are translated. But this demand is not met when the for-the-sake-of relation is read in the way Ackrill suggests, and the parts of happiness are included in the larger whole merely because more goods are better than fewer.[10] Since that re-

[10] When parts do bear a causal relation to one another, then of course they can be desirable for the sake of the whole in a nonmysterious way. For example, the eyes are desirable in part because of the contribution they make to the proper functioning of the rest of the body. The body is not a mere aggregate of parts, and this allows us to understand how each of them operates for the sake of the unified whole. Similarly, the various steps of a dance, or the moves in a game, may be undertaken because they are parts of a larger whole: one wants to dance or to play, and doing so consists in these steps or these moves. Here the appeal to the whole (the dance, the game) has explanatory value to the extent that one understands the connection between the various parts. Dances and games are not mere aggregates; instead, their components bear complex relationships to the larger unity of which they are a part. But no one would hold that the many intrinsic goods alleged to be components of happiness (friends, honor, virtues, pleasures, and so on) are related to the larger whole as are parts of the body, or steps in a dance, or moves in a game. Appealing to such examples would not answer the question I am raising: if happiness is the largest possible aggregate of

lation is mysterious, we should not attribute it to Aristotle without strong textual reason for doing so.[11]

4.6. Two Kinds of Ends

Aristotle never says that in some cases, when A is for the sake of B, A is a part of B. All of his examples in which A is desired for the sake of B are cases in which A bears a causal relation to B, and B provides a norm for the pursuit of A. Nonetheless, Ackrill holds that there is much indirect support for his interpretation. There are several passages, he thinks, that can only be understood, or are best understood, if we take Aristotle to be assuming that the for-the-sake-of relation connects part and whole.

The first piece of evidence he cites in support of his view is a distinction Aristotle draws in the opening remarks of I.1. Let us see what that distinction is, and then consider the use Ackrill makes of it. The first few lines of *NE* I.1 read as follows: "Every craft and inquiry, and similarly every action and choice, seems to aim at some good. Therefore, it has been well said that the good is what all things aim at. But there seems to be a certain difference between ends: [a] some of them are activities, while [b] others are certain products beyond these activities" (1094a1–5). Aristotle then goes on to make some points about (b) which we have already discussed: the product is better than the process of production, and the ends of supervisory disciplines are more choiceworthy than the ends of the disciplines they control (a5–16). Having introduced the for-the-sake-of-relation in this way, he then completes his first chapter by returning to (a)—the activities that do not issue in products—and making the following remark: "It makes no difference whether the ends of actions are the activities themselves, or whether they are some other thing beyond these

---

goods, none of which need have any bearing on any other, then what is being explained when we are told that one of them is desirable for the sake of the entire composite?

[11] A related point is made by Ackrill himself, "Aristotle on *Eudaimonia*," p. 22: "It is not necessary to claim that Aristotle has made quite clear how there may be 'components' in the best life or how they may be interrelated. The very idea of constructing a compound end out of two or more independent ends may rouse suspicion. Is the compound to be thought of as a mere aggregate or as an organized system? If the former, the move to *eudaimonia* seems trivial—nor is it obvious that goods can be just added together. If the latter, if there is supposed to be a unifying plan, what is it?" When Ackrill says that "the move to *eudaimonia* seems trivial," I take him to mean that if happiness is an aggregate of A, B, C, . . . , then it is trivial to say that all goods are desired for the sake of happiness. But if this is his point, it would be better expressed by saying that the move to *eudaimonia* seems nonexplanatory. The other question Ackrill raises (but leaves unanswered) here is also important: "if there is supposed to be a unifying plan, what is it?" Aristotle's answer to the question "What is happiness?" cannot be a mere list of goods, containing no specification of their relative importance. On my reading, he does tell us what the "unifying plan" is, since the single ultimate end enables us to organize all other goods into a system.

activities, as is the case in the sciences that have been mentioned" (a16–18). I take this to mean that the point made about (b) applies equally to (a). But what is the difference between (a) and (b), and what point made about (b) can be transferred to (a)?

It is uncontroversial that the distinction Aristotle makes here is the same one he later draws in VI.4–5, where he discusses the differences between craft-knowledge and other states of the rational soul. He takes the crafts to be involved in production (*poiēsis*) rather than action (*praxis*); and he says that the end of production is some further thing, whereas the end of action is good action itself (1140b6–7). Now, how should this distinction between producing and acting be understood? It is tempting to think that producing always yields a physical object, and that Aristotle's distinction turns on this fact. The builder produces houses or ships; the doctor seeks a certain balancing of elements in the body; the horse trainer puts his animals into good physical condition; and so on. But Aristotle does not in fact say that the product (*ergon*) of a craft must be some arrangement of physical elements, and one of the examples he gives in I.1 does not easily fit into this category: the general aims at victory (1094a9), and the art of the general is included among the endeavors that aim at ends beyond themselves (a17–18). Victory is an outcome or result that the general aims at as he engages in strategic thinking and issues orders, but it is difficult to conceive of it as a physical product. What then unites the general with the builder, and makes them both producers of some end that is separate from their activity? And what is it for an activity to have an end that is not separate in this way?

I take Aristotle to be making the following claims: The craftsman engages in a process that is worth undertaking only on condition that it leads to some further result or product that lies at the end of the process. The baker mixes his ingredients only because he assumes that a cake will eventually emerge from the oven. Similarly, the general thinks strategically and issues commands only because he hopes that these activities will eventually lead to victory. But matters are quite different when we consider the exercise of higher rational skills. Someone who activates the virtue of courage, for example, does not think it desirable to stand firm in battle only because this will lead to victory. Of course, he hopes for that outcome, and his mastery of fear increases its likelihood. But he also thinks that exercising this mastery—this integration of emotion and reason—is desirable in itself, even apart from the contribution it makes to his success in subduing the enemy. Similarly, someone who exercises the virtue of generosity looks forward to certain results: the person he has aided now has better chances of leading a good life. But even if that result is thwarted by misfortune, the generous person rightly takes his action to have been desirable in itself. To act in accordance with the ethical virtues is in this sense to have an end which consists in the action itself: the action need not terminate in some hoped-for end in order to be desirable; rather, the end sought by the agent is the ethical act itself. Similarly, the end for the sake of which the contemplator acts is not some expected outcome of his thought process. Both contemplation and ethical activity fall into category (a) of *NE* I.1: each endeavor aims at an end, but their goodness does not depend on some further result, and in this sense the end is the activity itself.

Notice that in this account of Aristotle's distinction, I have not said that when an end falls into category (a), then the activity in question has no further result or product. On the contrary, ethical activities typically do give rise to further results—victory in battle, the well-being of a friend, and so on. And we have seen that Aristotle emphasizes this feature of moral action in X.7 (1177b2–4, 18). An end falls into category (a) when the activity having that end does not depend for its value on its reaching further results; and so when the activity has such results, that does not remove its end from this category.

Now that we have considered Aristotle's distinction between the two kinds of ends, we can ask what he means by his final observation in I.1: "It makes no difference whether the ends of actions are the activities themselves, or whether they are some other thing beyond these activities, as is the case in the sciences that have been mentioned" (1094a16–18). He is of course claiming that some point he has made about ends in category (b) applies equally to ends in category (a). And surely the point he wants to transfer is that just as some ends in category (b) are for the sake of others in that same group, so too with ends in category (a). As we have seen, even though actions (unlike productions) do not depend on further results for their value, nothing prevents at least some of them from being undertaken for the sake of something better. And the interpretation I am defending allows us to see what Aristotle is getting at. For I take him to be saying in X.7–8 that ideally the ethical virtues should be exercised for the sake of contemplation (see 3.8); and I will argue that his distinction between more and less perfect virtues (I.7 1098a17–18) depends on the assumption that ethical virtue is to be desired in part because it promotes theoretical virtue. If this way of reading the *NE* can be defended, then the remark cited above should be taken as an allusion to the fact that certain virtuous activities occupy a lower position in the hierarchy of ends than do others.

It should be noticed that my reading of I.1 allows Aristotle to operate with a single for-the-sake-of relation, and that this is precisely the relation he has been illustrating throughout that chapter. Ethically virtuous activity causally promotes contemplation, and the latter end provides a norm by means of which one can determine how much ethical activity it is desirable to have in one's life. By contrast, Ackrill thinks that in order to understand Aristotle's remark in I.1, we must attribute to him a new for-the-sake-of relation. How does he arrive at this interpretation? First, he alerts us to a difficulty: "Commentators have not been sufficiently puzzled as to what Aristotle has in mind. It is after all not obvious what is meant by saying that one action or activity is for the sake of another, in cases where the first does not terminate in a product or outcome which the second can then use or exploit."[12] Ackrill is here asking: if we take "for the sake of" to be a causal relation, then how can A be for the sake of B when A does not yield any "product or outcome" which promotes B? Naturally, his answer is that it cannot. And so he suggests that Aristotle must be invoking a different kind of for-the-sake-of relation: "What immediately suggests itself instead is a relation like that of part to whole, the relation an activity or end may have to an activity or end that includes or embraces it."[13] And he then goes on to propose that individual ends are related to happiness as playing golf is related to having a good holiday.

I suggest that Ackrill's move to a new for-the-sake-of relation rests on a misreading of Aristotle's distinction in I.1 between two kinds of ends. As I have argued, we need not take his two categories to be (a) pursuits that have no "product or outcome" and (b) those that do. Rather, he is drawing a distinction between (a) ends that are activities and (b) ends that are the further results for which activities are pursued. When an end is an activity, rather than something beyond that activity, it is worth pursuing whether or not it yields further results; but its presence in category (a) does not mean that it has no such results. And so the puzzle Ackrill raises—how can A be for the sake of B when A does not promote B?—is a false one. An activity that falls into category (a) can perfectly well be for the sake of another such activity, because activities in this category can lead to other goods. Though their presence in category (a) requires that they be desirable in themselves, this does not prevent them from also being desirable because they promote some further good.

So, a second for-the-sake-of relation is never mentioned in I.1, and there is no need to invoke it in order to understand what Aristotle is saying. We should also recall (see 4.5) the problematic nature of this relation: it is not clear whether anything is explained by saying that A is desired for the sake of A and some unconnected B. The for-the-sake-of relation construed as a relation between part and aggregate is a puzzling one, and we should attribute it to Aristotle only if there is strong reason to do so. Furthermore, the conclusion towards which Ackrill is driving is one that lands Aristotle in inconsistency: according to the function argument,

[12] Ibid., p. 18.
[13] Ibid., p. 19.

happiness consists in virtuous activity (I.7 1098a16–18), and is not a composite of this and every other intrinsic good. So we do not make the *NE* a more coherent treatise if we take I.1 to be invoking a for-the-sake-of relation that exists between individual goods and the all-inclusive whole of which they are a part.

One further point should be made: I.1 prepares the way for the argument of I.2 and for the whole program initiated by that second chapter. In I.1, we are introduced to the for-the-sake-of relation, and to the idea that when A is for the sake of B, B is more choiceworthy than A. In I.2, Aristotle says that this chain of ends must have a terminus, and announces the importance of discovering what it is. In proposing that there is some one end *because* (*dia*) of which we want the other things (1094a19), he means that there is one good *for the sake of* which all others are pursued. Now, if he has introduced two different for-the-sake-of relations in I.1, then it is not at all clear what he intends to search for in the remainder of Book I. He might be looking for some good that bears a causal-normative relation to all others, or he might instead be looking for some good that bears a whole-part relation to all others. And the reader of I.2 who thinks both of these relations are present in I.1 would have no way of knowing which of these two possible targets Aristotle is seeking.

I see no reason to think that Aristotle has embarked upon his project in such a confusing way. He mentions only one kind of for-the-sake-of relation in I.1, and we can understand the distinction he makes there between two kinds of ends without invoking any other such relation. And when we read him in this way, then we can take him to be asking a single clear question in I.2: What lies at the top of the hierarchy of ends, each of which is related to some other by means of the for-the-sake-of relation illustrated in chapter 1?

4.7. AN ALLEGED FALLACY

Let us now consider a second passage that Ackrill uses to support his interpretation. Recall the opening lines of I.2, which were discussed in 4.3: "If there is some end of actions that we want because of itself, and we want the others because of this, and we don't choose all things because of something else (for they would thus proceed without limit, and desire would be empty and vain), it is obvious that this would be the good and the best" (1094a18–22). Ackrill thinks that this argument commits a fallacy: Aristotle is moving from the claim (a) that every activity aims at some end, to the conclusion (b) that there is some one end aimed at by every activity.[14] (This is the same fallacy that would be committed by

---

[14] Ibid., pp. 25–6. Cf. Anscombe, *Intention*, sec. 21, p. 34: "there appears to be an illicit

someone who argued that, since everyone has a father, there is some one person who is the father of everyone.) As he reads this passage, Aristotle is not merely saying, in these lines, that *if* there is some end for the sake of which all others are desired, *then* this would be the good. For the next thing Aristotle says in I.2 is that knowledge of this good has great importance, and that we must determine what it is. And so, as Ackrill reads I.2, Aristotle is taking himself to have shown that there is some one good for the sake of which all others are pursued.

Now, how does this provide evidence that, according to Aristotle, individual goods are desired for the sake of the all-inclusive whole of which they are parts? Ackrill's idea is that although it is "impossible to acquit" I.2 of fallacy, we can "explain and excuse" Aristotle once we realize that he is thinking in terms of this for-the-sake-of relation.[15] The excuse takes this form: "For the fallacy would disappear if an extra premise were introduced—namely, that where there are two or more separate ends each desired for itself we can say that there is just one (compound) end such that each of those separate ends is desired not only for itself but also for *it*."[16] I take Ackrill to be saying that Aristotle mistakenly thinks he does not need this extra premise, and for that reason does not state it. As a result, he commits a fallacy. But once the extra premise is introduced, then Aristotle can reach the conclusion he wants: there must be some one end of all the things we do, for even if there are many of them, we can say that

---

transition in Aristotle from 'all chains must stop somewhere' to 'there is somewhere where all chains must stop.' " It might be thought that Aristotle is making this "illicit transition" in the opening lines of the *NE*: "[a] Every craft and inquiry, and similarly every action and choice, seems to aim at some good. [b] Therefore, it has been well said that the good is what all things aim at" (1094a1–3). But instead, I think we should take Aristotle to be saying that although (a) provides some basis for (b), further argument is needed before (b) is accepted. After all, he does go on to provide that further argument: although the various crafts and actions aim immediately at their own peculiar goods, there is an ultimate end upon which they all converge (happiness), and this ultimate end can be identified with a single type of good (virtuous activity). The idea of the opening lines is that if *each* craft, inquiry, and so on aims at *a* good, then it would be appropriate to say something stronger about something aimed at by *every* craft, inquiry, and so on—namely, that it is *the* good. On this reading, Aristotle realizes that if his inference is to be fully justified, he must produce an argument to show that there is some one ultimate end. Notice that in a way contemplation is the end at which all crafts, inquiries, actions, and choices aim. Just as plants and animals are imitating the unmoved mover, without realizing it (for discussion see 1.14), so craftsmen, by exercising lower rational capacities, are coming as close as they can to the supreme reasoning activity. Even the choices made by human beings with highly defective conceptions of the ultimate end are, in this way, aiming at contemplation. For example, if they aim at physical pleasure, then they are imitating the way lower animals imitate the unmoved mover. (See VII.13 1153b25–32: since there is something divine in all creatures, they all pursue the same pleasure, though the pleasure they are pursuing is not always the one they think it is.)

[15] Ackrill, "Aristotle on *Eudaimonia*," p. 26.

[16] Ibid., Ackrill's emphasis.

they form a compound, and that each of its parts is desired for the sake of that compound.

I do not find this an appealing way of reading our passage. If Aristotle can "prove" that everyone aims at some one end by assuming that, no matter how diverse one's projects are, "we can say" that they form a compound, then his conclusion is completely uninteresting. For there is no real unity in this compound. Suppose someone has many different goods at the top of his hierarchy: he wants physical pleasure, honor, and contemplation for themselves, and desires none of them for the sake of any other good. Someone who says that he has a single ultimate end—that is, the compound of physical pleasure, honor, and contemplation—is simply using "single" in an unusual way, and is not really disagreeing with those who speak more plainly and say that this person has several ultimate ends. In effect, then, I think that Aristotle would be sinning in two ways if Ackrill's interpretation were correct: the argument he actually gives would be a fallacious one, and the argument he has in reserve would be of no significance, since the conclusion it reaches is merely a new way of using words.

Suppose someone tries to prove that some one person is the father of everyone, and offers as his premise the fact that everyone has a father. And suppose he holds a further thesis, though he does not think he needs to state it to make his argument work: if A is my father and B is your father, then there is a father that we both have, namely, the compound of A and B. We can see how his adherence to this further thesis helps explain why he gives a fallacious argument. His unusual way of talking about fathers explains why he thinks there is one father of everyone, and his acceptance of that thesis encourages mental laxity: having already accepted the conclusion that there is a superfather, he thinks he can support it by means of a premise (everyone has a father) that we all accept. But obviously the person who reasons in this way is extremely confused. And if we read Aristotle in the way Ackrill advocates, then we have to say that the confusion in I.2 about ends is as horrendous as this confusion about fathers.

Ackrill's interpretation of I.2 would of course be helped if it could be shown that in I.1 Aristotle relies on the notion that diverse goods are desirable for the sake of the compound of which they are parts. But we saw in the preceding section that I.1 needs no such idea. The only for-the-sake-of relation that is discussed there, and the only one Aristotle relies on, is the causal-normative relation that we have examined. And so this must be the relation that Aristotle invokes in I.2: we are looking for some end for the sake of which all others are desired, and they are for the sake of that end in the way that bridles are for the sake of riding, and riding for the sake of victory.

We should therefore stick to the interpretation adopted in 4.3: Although Aristotle argues in I.2 that the hierarchy of ends must have a top—it cannot go on forever—he does not take himself to have shown that the top consists in a single type of good. He says that *if* there is some end of the things we do, because of which all other ends are desired, *then* that would be the good. The protasis would be false if we chose everything because of something else and the hierarchy continued endlessly; and although Aristotle rejects the possibility of such an endless hierarchy, there is no reason to take him to be saying that therefore the protasis must be true. He proceeds by asking what the one highest end is, but carrying on such an investigation is a fruitful activity even if it leads to the negative result that there is no such single end. And we will see that in I.7, before Aristotle presents the function argument, he is still allowing for the possibility that the best life will have diverse ultimate ends.

One further point should be made: Aristotle's audience was far less suspicious than we are of the idea that a well-lived life is organized around some one final end. This point emerges when he goes on in I.4 to say that people generally call the highest good *eudaimonia*, but differ about what *eudaimonia* consists in (1095a14–20). He then gives a sample of the various things said about happiness: some identify it with pleasure, others with wealth, still others with honor (1095a23); and in I.5, he considers a further candidate: virtue (1095b30–1096a2). None of this commits Aristotle or his readers to the view that happiness must consist in some single good,[17] but it does suggest that in fact it was common to equate happiness with some one end. And surely this helps explain why Aristotle asks in I.2: what is the one good that is at the top of the hierarchy? Although he does not take himself to have proved that only one good is at the top, he and his audience treat that as a natural and widespread assumption. Since it is a belief that Aristotle eventually tries to confirm, we have every reason to acquit him of fallacy in I.2. He rejects the possibility of an endless hierarchy, draws on his audience's willingness to believe that some one good is at the top, and focuses our attention on the question of what that good is.

4.8. The All-embracing Science

Let us now consider a third way in which Ackrill uses *NE* I.1–2 to support his reading. I.2 argues that politics is the discipline that studies the good, and, according to Ackrill, the way Aristotle characterizes politics in this chapter reflects his commitment to an inclusivist conception of the good.

---

[17] See *EE* I.1 1214b4–5, where Aristotle leaves open the possibility that happiness may consist in two or more of the candidates frequently mentioned.

More specifically, Ackrill calls our attention to two points Aristotle makes about politics: first, it is more of a ruling (*architektonikē*) craft than any other (1094a27); second, "its end embraces (*periechein*) the ends of the other [crafts]" (b6).[18]

It is hard to see, however, why the first point should be taken to mean that the ultimate end is a composite of many different intrinsic goods. In I.1, Aristotle uses the term *architektonikē* when he describes the relation between two crafts one of which is subordinate to the other: he says that the end of a ruling (*architektonikē*) craft is more choiceworthy than those of the crafts that are beneath it (1094a14–15). The bridlemaker is subordinate to the horse trainer (a10–11), and the latter is in turn subordinate to the general (a11–13). The notion of one discipline ruling another is introduced by means of the same examples that illustrate the for-the-sake-of relation between ends. That is, one craft rules another when the end of the subordinate craft is desirable for the sake of the end of the superior craft. And so, when Aristotle says that politics is a discipline that is more of a ruling craft than any other (a27), nothing in his use of the term *architektonikē* suggests that politics must have an end that is a composite of all goods desired for themselves. For one subject can be more of a ruling discipline than another even though each has its own single end. The general, for example, is in charge of the horse trainer, although the art of the general has just one end (victory). So, when Aristotle says that politics is the craft that is most of all a ruling craft, he means merely that, whatever it is for one craft to rule another, politics bears that relation to all other crafts. The fact that it has that authority over all other subjects does not tell us whether the end it studies is a single good or a composite.

It should be emphasized that the notion of one discipline ruling another and the notion that some ends are desired for the sake of others are introduced by means of the same examples. For this suggests that Aristotle is envisaging a single hierarchy of ends, each of which is related to some other by means of a single relation—namely, the causal-normative relation that we are supposed to grasp by means of the examples used in I.1. In that chapter, he calls our attention to the way in which certain crafts have authority over others, because of the superiority of the ends they pursue; then, in I.2, he asks what lies at the top of that chain of command, and assigns the study of this question to politics. Just as the general has authority over the horse trainer because the latter's goal is desirable for the sake of the former's, so politics has authority over all other subjects because all other ends are desirable for the sake of the ultimate end studied

---

[18] Ackrill, "Aristotle on *Eudaimonia*," p. 26. In citing these passages as evidence of an inclusive-end conception of happiness, Ackrill follows Hardie, "The Final Good in Aristotle's *Ethics*," p. 300.

by politics. All crafts are being linked together in a single chain of command, and so the for-the-sake-of relation that underlies the architectonic relation among crafts must be of just one sort: it is the causal-normative relation that Aristotle introduces in I.1.

So I think that the first point about politics to which Ackrill appeals—its status as the most authoritative science—provides support for my interpretation rather than his. But it might be thought that the second point does favor Ackrill's interpretation. For Aristotle says that the end of politics embraces the ends of the other crafts (1094b6), and this seems to provide Ackrill with just the evidence he needs. According to his interpretation, the ultimate end is not a single good, but a composite. And is this not what Aristotle means when he says that the end of politics embraces the others?

Before we decide whether Ackrill's reading receives some support from 1094b6, we should ask ourselves which "others" Aristotle has in mind there. I suggest that he is referring to *all* the ends mentioned in I.1–2, together with the ends of *all* other crafts: he is saying that the end of politics embraces health, ships, victory, wealth (1094a9), and all such goods. For politics is a master discipline that has authority over *every* other pursuit (1094a26–b2); even such highly esteemed capacities as generalship, household management, and rhetoric are subject to its commands (b3–4).[19] And so, when Aristotle says that the end of politics embraces the ends of the others, he means that it embraces health, ships, victory, wealth, persuasion, and so on. And once we realize that this is what he means, we also realize that this passage does *not* support Ackrill's interpretation. For Ackrill does not take happiness to be an ultimate end that includes all other ends whatsoever; rather, he claims that it is a composite of all goods that are desirable for themselves.[20] Since Aristotle says

---

[19] At 1094b4 there is a textual difficulty, but I do not think it undermines my point. Reading Bywater's text, we have (a) "It uses the other sciences . . ." But Bywater brackets *praktikais*; if this word is restored, we have (b) "It uses the other practical sciences . . ." Furthermore, one of the manuscripts omits *loipais*; with this omission, and retaining *praktikais*, we have (c) "It uses the practical sciences . . ." For our purposes, the chief question raised by these variant readings is this: If Aristotle wrote *praktikais*, and therefore (b) or (c) is correct, then which nonpractical sciences are being excluded from the jurisdiction of politics? The best answer to this question is that politics does not govern the theoretical sciences. For *praktikos* sometimes contrasts with *theōrētikos* (see VI.2 1139a27–8, X.7 1177b3, 6), and we are told at 1145a8 that practical wisdom (the same state as politics: 1141b23–4) does not use theoretical wisdom. (See 4.23 for further discussion.) In any case, it is quite clear that the end of politics embraces ends that are not desirable in themselves (such as bridles, ships, and wealth); therefore *praktikais* at 1094b4 cannot be construed so as to exclude the crafts devoted to these instrumental goods. The end of politics embraces the ends of all sciences over which it exercises legitimate control, and obviously it legitimately controls bridlemaking, shipbuilding, and so on.

[20] Ackrill, "Aristotle on *Eudaimonia*," especially pp. 21–2.

that wealth is not (and should not be) loved for itself (I.5 1096a7–9), and puts all instruments in this same category (I.7 1097a25–b6), the class of ends desired for themselves is considerably smaller than the one Aristotle refers to in I.2. For as we have seen, he is saying in this chapter that the political end embraces every other, including wealth and all instruments.[21]

It might now be claimed that both Ackrill's interpretation and my own are undermined by 1094b6. For on my reading, Aristotle identifies the good with just one type of end, namely, virtuous activity; but at 1094b6, the good—that is, the end of politics—is said to embrace or include every other end. So, it could be argued, Ackrill and I are both wrong: it turns out that happiness is a composite of all intrinsic and instrumental goods; it is neither a narrower composite (Ackrill's view) nor a single kind of good (my view). However, the new interpretation now being proposed—that the good includes all ends whatsoever—cannot be taken seriously. For Aristotle has proposed at the beginning of I.2 that the good is an end which is desired for itself and for the sake of which other ends are desired (1094a18–19). This means that there are other ends besides the ultimate end; and so the ultimate end cannot be inclusive of all intrinsic and instrumental goods.

Where does this leave us? We know that the end of politics embraces all other ends, but that Aristotle is not identifying the end of politics with a composite of all other goods. To understand this, we must now turn our attention to the verb *periechein*, which Ackrill translates as "embrace." Our question is: why does Aristotle use this word to describe the relation between the political end and all other ends? The Greek word is a compound of *peri* ("around") and *echein* ("to hold"), and it frequently designates a spatial relation: one thing *periechei* a second when the first surrounds, encompasses, contains, or confines the second. If Aristotle is drawing on this sense, then he is speaking metaphorically: he is saying that the political end is related to the other ends as a surrounding object is related to the objects it surrounds. But why would he think this a suitable figure of speech?

In answering this question, we should bear in mind that *all* other ends are "embraced" by the political end. And we should ask ourselves how Aristotle has reached that conclusion: why doesn't he think that the end of politics embraces some ends, but fails to embrace others? Surely the answer is that he has placed politics at the top of the hierarchy of crafts, and has identified its end as the one for the sake of which all others are

---

[21] Or at any rate the end of politics embraces the ends of the *practical* sciences (see note 19 above). Henceforth I will not mention the possibility that theorizing is the one good not embraced by the political end.

desired. In other words, the end of a controlling discipline embraces the ends of however many crafts are subordinate to it: the end of the general embraces the end of the horse trainer; the latter's end embraces the end of the bridlemaker; and so on. Whatever the spatial metaphor means, it is applicable not only to politics, but to all disciplines that supervise the work of others; what is special about politics is not that its end embraces other ends, but that it embraces *all* other ends. So, our question about *periechein* is a general question about ends: what makes it appropriate to say that the end of any supervisory craft *periechei* the ends of the crafts it governs?

Aristotle, I suggest, is drawing on the idea that a surrounding object limits the elements it contains and prevents them from increasing in size. He is saying that just as some physical objects impose spatial boundaries upon others, so the ends of supervisory crafts set limits to the pursuit of subordinate ends. For example, the end of the flute-maker is confined to what the flute-player needs for the pursuit of his end: he should make a kind of flute that will serve the flutist well, and should produce only as many as are needed. But the kind of music to be played, and the occasions on which such music is appropriate, are issues to be decided by those who govern the political community. In the same way, the proper degree to which any other end is to be pursued is a matter that is determined by looking to the highest end; and it is the task of the political craft to determine what that ultimate end is. The end of politics "embraces" all others (alternatively: it contains them, or confines them) in the way in which a container "embraces" the objects within it: the inner objects can only be of such a size and nature as is allowed by the surrounding element. And this point about politics is one that Aristotle makes in I.2, before he uses the term *periechein*: it determines "to what extent" (*mechri tinos*) each subject should be learned (1094b1), and it tells us what we must do and what we must refrain from (b5–6). Since he has stressed the limiting role politics plays, it is entirely natural for Aristotle to portray its end as one that contains, confines, or surrounds all others.

When we read *periechein* in this way, we can easily understand why Aristotle thinks that the end of politics *periechei* all others, even though he does not identify the good studied by politics with a composite of all other ends. A surrounding object is not identical with or composed out of the other objects contained within it, and similarly the end of politics is something other than the goods Aristotle mentions in I.1–2: it is not the end of the general, or the household manager, or the rhetorician (1094b3), nor is it a composite that includes victory, wealth, and persuasion. Quite clearly, Aristotle takes the end of politics to be something that has not yet been mentioned in I.1–2. It is only when we turn to the function argument in I.7, and the continuation of that argument in X.7–8, that we discover what the ultimate end is: the best choice for such an end is contemplation, and the second-best is ethically virtuous activity. In either case, our target will be an activity of the rational soul, and aiming at this target will give us a way of determining the extent to which all other goods should be pursued. Taking contemplation as an end, we have a way to limit our other pursuits to their appropriate levels; and ethical activity gives us a second-best measure. In this sense, either of the two ultimate ends contains or embraces the ends of all the disciplines subordinate to it.[22]

So, Aristotle's remark (1094b6) that the end of politics *periechei* all others creates no difficulty for the interpretation I am advocating. An ultimate end can embrace all others even if it is a single end. By contrast, if we were to take *periechein* to be a relation between whole and part, as Ackrill does, then we would have to say that the ultimate end has all goods as its parts, including goods that are not desired for themselves. And this is not what Aristotle means.

4.9. THE STRATEGY OF I.5

I now want to move beyond *NE* I.1–2, and look briefly at what Aristotle does in I.5. We have seen that only one for-the-sake-of relation is at work in these first two chapters, and that it is illustrated by means of examples drawn from the crafts. Aristotle begins his search for the good by asking what lies at the top of the hierarchy of ends: what is it, for the sake of which all other goods are to be desired? In I.4, he says that it is happiness, but notes that there is no general agreement about what happiness consists in (1095a14–22). Then, in I.5, he argues against certain candidates for this ultimate end. He tells us here (1095b17–19) that there are three prominent views about what kind of life it would be best to lead: people generally favor the life of pleasure, or the political life, or the theoretical life. The bulk of this chapter is then devoted to a discussion of the first two choices, and treatment of the theoretical life is postponed (1096a4–5).

One point I would like to emphasize is that here, as in I.4 (1095a22–5), we are told that happiness is generally identified with some single good. Those who lead the life of pleasure equate happiness with just one thing—pleasure (1095b16). After rejecting this ideal, Aristotle turns to the political life, and once again he takes those who favor this kind of life to equate happiness with some single end. At first, he takes this end to be honor (b23), but after presenting several arguments against identifying happi-

---

[22] For my explanation of the sense in which contemplation is the end at which politics aims, see the last two paragraphs of 4.4.

ness with this external good, he considers a revised account: perhaps those who lead the political life have virtue as their end (b30–31). Once again, however, he argues that this is deficient as a conception of happiness. And finally, he takes up a candidate for happiness that is not associated with one of the three most favored lives: wealth (1096a5–7). This too is dismissed, on the grounds that it is sought only for the sake of further goods. In this respect, Aristotle says, the other goods mentioned—pleasure, honor, and virtue—are more plausible candidates for happiness, since they are loved for themselves. Even so, in the last line of I.5, he says that all of the candidates examined in this chapter should be dismissed.

Another point deserves emphasis: In I.5, Aristotle never argues against a conception of happiness in the way we would expect if Ackrill's interpretation of I.1–2 were correct. That is, if Aristotle takes happiness to be a complex good that has every intrinsic good as a component, then he can reject any single-end conception of happiness by means of the same argument: he could simply say that many different goods are desired for themselves. For example, he could say that happiness cannot consist in pleasure alone, because we choose pleasure for the sake of the larger composite to which it belongs. And the same argument could be given against honor, virtue, and any other good desired for itself: each is not only desired for itself but (according to Ackrill) desired for the sake of a larger composite that includes it. There would be no need to examine each particular good on its merits and decide whether it has defects that make it unsuitable as a conception of happiness. All single-good conceptions of happiness could thus be defeated with a single stroke.[23]

The fact that Aristotle does not use such an argument is easily explained, on my interpretation. He is looking for a single good to which all others bear the for-the-sake-of relation, where this is taken to be the causal-normative relation that links craft activities to their ends. Conceptions of happiness that identify it with a single end are therefore perfectly in order: their success or failure will depend on the kind of good they propose as the ultimate end. This does not mean that some single good must succeed: it may turn out that all single goods are poor candidates for the ultimate end, and that happiness must instead be identified with a complex combination of goods. But the best way to find out whether this is true is to examine the leading single-end candidates, and see whether any can plausibly be regarded as the ultimate end.

Later, we will examine the arguments Aristotle gives in I.5 against

[23] Such a strategy would work only if Aristotle's audience is already convinced that there is more than one intrinsic good. But clearly this is their assumption: Aristotle simply points out that we choose many goods for themselves (I.7 1097b2–4), and gives no indication that his audience needs an argument for this position. See too *Rhet.* I.6 1362b10–28.

pleasure, honor, and virtue. For now, we should merely note that if we have understood I.1–2 correctly, then his strategy in I.5 is a reasonable one. He cannot dismiss single-end conceptions of happiness with a single stroke, but must instead examine them one by one.

4.10. Some Preliminaries in I.7

NE I.5 and I.6 reach negative results: we see in the former that the single ends often identified with happiness are inadequate in one way or another; in the latter, Aristotle argues that the good he is seeking should not be equated with the Platonist's Form of the Good. And then, in I.7, he makes a new beginning, eventually arriving at a conception of happiness that he thinks will survive scrutiny. The main conclusion of this chapter is defended by means of the function argument, which we will examine later. In order to understand the conclusion of that argument—with its reference to the best and most perfect virtue (1098a17–18)—we must first consider a distinction Aristotle makes in I.7 between three kinds of ends: those that are not perfect, those that are perfect but not most perfect, and one that is most perfect (1097a25–b6). For our notion of what Aristotle means by "the most perfect virtue" will be affected by the way we understand his distinction between ends that are perfect to different degrees.

We will turn to this distinction in the next section. First, let us look at the important preliminary material Aristotle provides in the first few lines of I.7 (1097a16–24). He starts out by reminding us of the main idea presented in I.1: the good in each action and craft is that for the sake of which it pursues everything else. In medicine it is health, in generalship victory, in house building a house; and in general it is the end of the activity or craft (a16–21). Of course, Aristotle is not suggesting that the ends mentioned—health, victory, houses—are conceptions of happiness that are now to be examined. He is not here looking for further candidates for happiness, but is instead reminding us of the for-the-sake-of relation that is to be grasped by reflection on crafts and their ends. His terms for this relation occur twice in these lines (*charin*: a18; *heneka*: a21), and the good he is looking for is the one to which all others bear this relation.

But now Aristotle makes a remark that explicitly allows for the possibility that the hierarchy of goods linked by the for-the-sake-of relation will not terminate in a single point: "And so, if there is some end of all actions, this would be the good achievable by action; but if there are many [it would be] these" (1097a22–4). Here Aristotle cannot be saying that one possibility, still to be investigated, is that there are many different kinds of ends. For that is no longer an open question; he has already said that the end of each craft is different, and since there are many crafts, there must be many ends. When he says "if there are many," he must be talking about the top of the hierarchy. He is trying to determine where this hierarchy terminates, and is admitting that this highest level might be a row of several goods rather than some single end. Evidently, he did not intend to prove in I.1–2 that the hierarchy of goods has just one end at the top. That is a conclusion he has yet to reach.

Two further points should be made about the beginning of I.7: First, though Aristotle reminds us here of the way in which craft activity is for the sake of an end, he says nothing about a second kind of for-the-sake-of relation. Second, it would be difficult to make sense of the possibility he is allowing for in this chapter if we construed the for-the-sake-of relation in the way Ackrill proposes. Aristotle says, ". . . if there is some end of all actions, this would be the good achievable by action; but if there are many [it would be] these" (1097a22–4). But what sense would it make to wonder whether "the good achievable by action" is some single end or many if that highest end were a composite of all goods that are desirable for themselves? How can there be many different ends each of which contains all intrinsic goods? What would distinguish these various all-inclusive composites from one another? Perhaps these questions could be answered, but Aristotle is not concerned with them, and the remark just cited makes perfect sense when we read it in context: The for-the-sake-of relation illustrated by means of the crafts links all ends together in a single system, and that system terminates in one of two ways: there is either one end at the top of the hierarchy, or more than one. In either case, the good achievable by action is whatever occupies that top row.

4.11. THREE KINDS OF ENDS

After pointing out that "the good achievable by action" might be one or many, Aristotle tries to clarify matters further by making a distinction between three kinds of ends. We may divide his statement of the distinction into the following components:

(1) Since the ends seem to be many, and we choose some of them (for example, wealth, flutes, and instruments in general) because of something else, it is obvious that not all ends are perfect (*teleia*). But the best good seems to be something perfect.

(2) Therefore, if there is only a single one that is perfect, this would be what we are seeking, while if there are many, it would be the most perfect of them.

(3) Now, we say that what is in itself worth pursuing is more perfect than [what is worth pursuing] because of something else.

(4) And what is never choiceworthy because of something else [is more

perfect than] those things that are choiceworthy both in themselves and because of it.

(5) And so what is always choiceworthy in itself and never because of something else is perfect without qualification. (1097a25–34)

Consider (1): Aristotle does not explicitly say here that such ends as wealth, flutes, and instruments are desirable *only* as means; he merely claims that they are chosen because of something else. But earlier, in I.5, he contrasted wealth with pleasure, honor, and virtue by saying that the latter are loved for themselves (1096a7–9). I take him to be saying in I.5 that wealth is chosen and pursued only on condition that it leads to something further, whereas pleasure, honor, and virtue are desired for themselves. In light of this, it is plausible to take him to be saying in (1) above that wealth, flutes, and instruments in general are desired not because of themselves but only because of other goods. Such ends are not perfect. And once we read (1) in this way, it is reasonable to take (3) to be drawing a contrast between ends that are pursued for themselves and ends that are pursued not for themselves but only for the sake of something further.

So read, (1) and (3) invoke a distinction between two types of ends: those that are not desired for themselves, and those that are. The former are not perfect; the latter are more perfect than the former. In (4) and (5), Aristotle adds a further distinction: if A, B, and C are desired in themselves, but B and C are desirable for the sake of A, whereas A is not desirable for the sake of anything further, then A is more perfect than B and C, and is perfect without qualification. Presumably, he believes that all of them—A, B, and C—are perfect, but that A is the most perfect among them.

We have, in other words, a hierarchy with three types of goods occupying three rows:

$$A$$

$$M \quad N$$

$$X \quad Y \quad Z$$

The lowest row contains goods that are desirable not in themselves but only because of other goods. The middle row contains goods that are desirable both in themselves and for the sake of A. And A has the three properties of an ultimate end: it is desirable for its own sake, it is desirable for the sake of nothing else, and everything else is desirable for its sake. Furthermore, I take it that each good on a lower row is linked to at least one good on a higher row by means of the for-the-sake-of relation. Wealth, instruments, and the objects of any subordinate craft are pursued *because of* other goods in that they are chosen *for the sake of* those higher ends. The less perfect ends help bring about those that are more perfect, while the more perfect ends serve as norms for the proper pursuit of ends that are less perfect. In making this threefold distinction, Aristotle is not introducing new material, but merely trying to give a clearer picture of the scheme he has been working with.

We will shortly look at a different way of reading this passage, proposed by Ackrill. Before we do so, however, something should be said about the second segment of our passage:

(2) Therefore, if there is only a single one that is perfect, this would be what we are seeking, while if there are many, it would be the most perfect of them. (1097a28–30)

In reading this, one may wonder what has become of the point Aristotle had made several lines earlier: "And so, if there is some end of all actions, this would be the good achievable by action; but if there are many [it would be] these" (a22–4). Here Aristotle realizes that the top of the hierarchy may consist in a row of goods, but in statement (2) he seems to ignore this possibility and to assume without argument that some one good must be most perfect. Why can't there be several goods that are equally perfect, instead of one that is most perfect?

It would be implausible to suppose that in (2) Aristotle has forgotten the possibility mentioned a few lines earlier. Instead, I suggest that, as he writes, he does not continue to remind us of this possibility, because it will turn out, on his own account, that happiness *does* consist in a single type of good. That is a conclusion that he reaches within I.7, for the function argument shows that the human good consists just in virtuous activity. Admittedly, there are many types of virtuous activity, but Aristotle will go on to argue, in X.7–8, that a single type of virtuous activity—contemplation—occupies the highest point in the hierarchy of ends. And because his own theory will show that there is a single perfect good, he does not think it important to acknowledge once again, prior to the function argument, that happiness could turn out to consist in a variety of diverse goods.

4.12. ACKRILL'S READING

After Aristotle distinguishes three kinds of ends—nonperfect, perfect, and most perfect—he goes on to locate happiness and other goods within this scheme:

We always choose it [happiness] because of itself and never because of something else, but we choose honor, pleasure, understanding, and every virtue because of themselves (for if nothing resulted we would choose each of them), and we choose them also for the sake of happiness, since we assume that because of them we will be happy. But no one chooses happiness for the sake of these, nor in general because of anything else. (1097b1–6)

Happiness is the most perfect good, and the other goods mentioned—honor, pleasure, understanding, and every virtue—are not perfect without qualification, since they are chosen for the sake of something else. They occupy a higher position than wealth and instruments; for the latter ends are not perfect, whereas honor, pleasure, and so on are. Nonetheless, they are not at the top of the hierarchy of goods, and so happiness must consist in something else.

But Ackrill rejects this way of reading Aristotle's threefold distinction among ends. He proposes instead that this passage treats happiness as the end that includes all goods desired for themselves. Translating *teleios* as "final" rather than "perfect," he says: "the *most* final end is that never sought for the sake of anything else because it includes all final ends."[24] In other words—to switch back from "final" to "perfect"—one end is more perfect than another by being more inclusive than the other. That is why happiness is the most perfect end: it has every intrinsic good as a component. And Ackrill takes this to be a conceptual point: "that *eudaimonia* is inclusive of all intrinsic goods" is true "by definition."[25] Similarly, he argues that Aristotle is making a conceptual claim when he places honor, pleasure, and so on in the category of ends that are perfect but not perfect without qualification. As he says: "Surely Aristotle is here making a clear conceptual point, not a rash and probably false empirical claim. To put it at its crudest: one can answer such a question as 'Why do you seek pleasure?' by saying that you . . . seek it as an element in the most desirable sort of life; but one cannot answer . . . the question 'Why do you seek the most desirable sort of life?' . . . [P]leasure [is] an element in *eudaimonia*."[26] And Ackrill would make the same claim about honor and virtue: in this passage, Aristotle makes and needs no assumptions about whether these goods are desirable partly because they help promote some further good. The conceptual point he is making is that they are just single goods. This is what makes them less perfect than happiness.

But if the arguments I have given in the preceding sections are accepted, then we must reject Ackrill's way of reading Aristotle's threefold distinction among ends. According to those arguments, there is no evidence that the for-the-sake-of relation is sometimes treated as a relation between individual goods and a larger composite that includes them. In

[24] Ackrill, "Aristotle on *Eudaimonia*," p. 23, his emphasis.
[25] Ibid., p. 22.
[26] Ibid., p. 21.

fact, as we have seen, Aristotle takes seriously the possibility that happiness might be one of those individual goods. In I.5, he examines several of these candidates on their merits, and rejects none of them on the grounds that it is merely a single good. Furthermore, we have seen how Aristotle leads up to his trichotomy of ends in I.7 by reminding us of the way each craft is focused on a single good: in each case, the good of a craft is that for the sake of which all craft-activity is undertaken (1097a18–19). So, the only for-the-sake-of relation mentioned in Book I prior to the division of ends into three kinds is the causal-normative relation that figures prominently in I.1. And on my interpretation, this is the relation that Aristotle has in mind when he makes his division: wealth is desirable for the sake of further goods, and is desirable only if it leads to them; honor is also desirable for the sake of some further good, but would still be desirable in any case; and happiness is not desirable for the sake of anything further. It is hard to believe that Aristotle's trichotomy is based on a for-the-sake-of relation that has not yet been mentioned or explained; and if my way of reading I.1–2 is correct, his arguments do not need such a relation.

Three other points about Ackrill's interpretation should be kept in mind: First, he will have to say that there are two different more-perfect-than relations, just as there are two for-the-sake-of relations. Instruments and wealth are less perfect than honor and pleasure, which in turn are less perfect than happiness. But the way in which instruments are less perfect than intrinsic goods has nothing to do with the way in which intrinsic goods are less perfect than happiness. Accordingly, there will be two different ways in which a good can be most perfect: it can be at the top of a causal-normative chain, or it can be all-inclusive. So, even if the part-whole relation Ackrill finds in Book I were really there, we would have to accuse Aristotle of ambiguity about a crucial point: in which of the two ways is the good we are seeking most perfect?

Second, we should recall Aristotle's admission in I.7 that happiness does not have to turn out to consist in a single good: "And so, if there is some end of all actions, this would be the good achievable by action; but if there are many [it would be] these" (1097a22–4). As we saw in 4.10, Aristotle's point here would be a mysterious one if he were taking "the good achievable by action" to be, by definition, the composite of all goods desirable in themselves. For it is not clear how there can be a plurality of such composites: what would distinguish them? We decided, however, that Aristotle's remark makes perfect sense when taken in context. He is talking about the crafts and the hierarchy of goods linked by a causal-normative relation, and he is admitting that, although this hierarchy must have a terminus, that highest level might be occupied by many goods. Now, surely Aristotle would identify "the good achievable by action" mentioned in this passage with the most perfect good mentioned later in I.7: it is happiness, whether happiness consists in one good or many. And so I.7 equates happiness with the top point or top row in a causal chain, even though some of the goods subordinate to it may be desirable in themselves. This chapter cannot also identify happiness with a composite of all intrinsic goods, regardless of where they occur on the causal chain.

Finally, we should recall the way in which Aristotle argues for the superiority of contemplation: one of the points he makes is that nothing results from contemplation, whereas ethical activity is desirable for the sake of something further (X.7 1177b1–4, 18). Clearly, in seeking a good that is perfect happiness, he is looking for some single good which is not a means to something further. And so, if we want to read the *NE* as a coherent unit, we have no reason to resist the natural way to construe his threefold distinction in I.7: here too, he is looking for the highest end, and he takes an end to be most perfect when it is not a causal means to anything else.

4.13. ACKRILL'S OBJECTION

As we have seen, Ackrill takes the *NE* to be "making a clear conceptual point" when it says that we choose honor and several other goods for the sake of happiness (1097b1–6).[27] And one reason he gives in favor of his reading is that the alternative is so unpalatable: if Aristotle is not making a conceptual point, then he is making "a rash and probably false empirical claim."[28] I take Ackrill's idea to be that, since Aristotle is a careful thinker, he is unlikely to have made assumptions that fly in the face of empirical facts available to him and his contemporaries. But that is just what he would be doing, according to Ackrill, if he were saying that honor, pleasure, and virtue *promote* some further good. Accordingly, he thinks that we should not treat the for-the-sake-of relation as a causal relation when Aristotle says that we choose honor and so on for the sake of happiness.

On my interpretation, of course, Aristotle *is* making certain empirical assumptions. I take him to be saying that he and his readers choose the ends in question—honor, pleasure, understanding, and every virtue—partly because these ends help them attain some other good or goods. In other words, Aristotle thinks these ends are part of a causal chain leading to happiness, and he expects his audience to agree with him that whatever happiness turns out to be, it will not consist in these ends, but in something better, which they promote. Is Ackrill right to think that Aristotle

[27] Ibid.
[28] Ibid.

is unlikely to be making these empirical assumptions, and expecting his audience to agree with him?

First, consider honor. Although Aristotle acknowledges in I.5 that honor is loved for itself (1096a8–9), he argues there against those who equate it with happiness. One of his arguments appeals to the motives of those who choose a political life: "They seem to pursue honor in order to persuade themselves that they are good; at any rate, they seek to be honored by those who have practical wisdom, and by those who know them, and on the basis of their virtue. It is obvious therefore that, according to them, at any rate, virtue is superior" (1095b26–30). And then he immediately turns to the question of whether this further good—virtue—might be happiness. I take Aristotle to be saying here that although his contemporaries love honor for itself, their attitude towards this good reflects the fact that they also seek it for the sake of virtue. They don't just want honor—they want to be honored for their virtue by those in a position to assess their character. In other words, even though they may not realize it, they love virtue even more than they love honor, and they seek honor as an indication that they have succeeded in their efforts to become virtuous. If they are honored by the right people and for the right reasons, then they can be more confident that they really do have the virtues, and no adjustments are needed in the way they lead their lives; if they are not honored in these ways, then they need to ask whether they really are virtuous. So they take honor to promote virtue. Just as a mirror is a useful instrument for someone who wants to have certain virtues of the body, so, they think, we are better able to acquire the virtues of the soul when we know what attitude certain other people have towards us.[29]

Does Aristotle agree? It is plausible to assume that he does. For he is arguing that happiness should not be equated with honor, and he is appealing to the beliefs of those who love honor to support his claim. Surely he is not trying to give an argument that is merely *ad hominem*; rather, he wants to use plausible and widely accepted assumptions that lead to the conclusion that since honor is desirable for the sake of further goods, it is not what happiness consists in. And of course he himself agrees that we should not seek honor from every source, but only from those who are virtuous (IV.3 1124a5–11), and only on the basis of our virtue (IV.3 1123b35). Presumably, then, he agrees that honor should be desired partly because it helps us develop the virtues.

We can now return to the objection Ackrill makes to the sort of interpretation I am giving: he says that I.7 cannot mean that we desire honor

---

[29] Of course, honor is not causally sufficient for virtue, just as a mirror is not causally sufficient for good looks. My claim is only that, according to a common opinion, honor makes a causal contribution of some sort to the acquisition and continued possession of virtue.

and various other goods as a means to something else, because these empirical claims would be "rash and probably false." But surely this objection has no force, at least in the case of honor. For we have just seen that in I.5 Aristotle rejects honor as a candidate for happiness by pointing out that it is a means to something else (virtue). He notes that those who equate happiness with honor pursue the latter good in order to assure themselves that they really have the virtues; and he apparently agrees that this is a good reason for seeking honor. So, Aristotle himself takes honor to be desirable in part because it helps achieve some further good. Even if this empirical belief is "rash and probably false," it is nonetheless one of his beliefs. And, for that matter, why should we take such a dim view of this empirical assumption? The good opinion of certain other people surely does reassure us that we have the skills for which we are honored.

Let us consider another one of the goods that is said in I.7 (1097b2–6) to be desired for the sake of happiness: virtue. Does Ackrill's objection have force in this case? Is it implausible, in other words, to take Aristotle to be saying that he and his audience choose virtue in part because of the empirical connection between this and some further good?

To answer this question, we must remember that Aristotle is quite careful in Book I to make a distinction between virtue and activity in accordance with virtue. The former is a good that is considered in I.5 and rejected as a candidate for happiness. But the latter is the good that Aristotle goes on to identify with happiness at the end of the function argument. Having virtue is compatible with being asleep or inactive throughout one's life, and this is why Aristotle thinks that this good should not be equated with happiness; only those who are going all out to defend a thesis would consider such a life happy (I.5 1095b30–1096a2). But he thinks that his own candidate for happiness escapes this objection: if one engages in virtuous activity over the course of a lifetime (I.7 1098a16–21), then of course one cannot be asleep or inactive throughout one's life. And in I.8, Aristotle points out that his own conception of happiness is invulnerable to the objection made against virtue in I.5: Olympic prizes go to those who actually compete and win, and are not awarded on the basis of one's physical condition; similarly, happiness should be equated with using the virtues, and not merely with having them (1098b31–1099a7).

Now consider the question whether virtue is desirable in part because it promotes some further good. Surely Aristotle's answer is yes, and again we should not accuse him of saying something "rash and probably false." Just as having physical strength is a necessary causal condition of exercising that strength, so one must have a virtue in order to use that virtue. And so it is perfectly plausible to take Aristotle to be saying in I.7 that we want to have understanding and all the virtues both because they are good in themselves and because they contribute to some further good.

What that further good is, we soon find out: it is activity of the rational soul in accordance with virtue.[30]

There is one remaining good that I.7 (1097b2–6) says we desire both for itself and for the sake of happiness: pleasure. Now, notice that pleasure has something in common with honor and virtue—the other two kinds of goods that are said in I.7 to be perfect but not most perfect: all three of these goods have been shown in I.5 to be deficient candidates for happiness. This strongly suggests that Aristotle's list in I.7 is not randomly chosen: if he is going to say of a certain good that it is desired or desirable for the sake of happiness, he must choose a good that is not to be equated with happiness. For a good that *is* happiness is not desirable for the sake of happiness. If it were desirable for the sake of happiness, it would be less choiceworthy than happiness. And if A is B, it cannot be less desirable than B.

If I.7 is discussing those perfect ends that have already been rejected in I.5 as candidates for happiness, then the pleasure in question in I.7 must be physical pleasure. For this is clearly the sort of pleasure that is considered in I.5: the life of pleasure is rejected because it is appropriate for slaves and cattle, not for human beings (1095b14–20). (Of course, Aristotle is not saying that we should avoid all physical pleasure; he is merely rejecting the view that our ultimate end should be this kind of enjoyment.) Now, it is reasonable to take I.7 to be making the same sort of claim about pleasure that it is making about honor and every virtue: we are said to choose each of these goods for the sake of happiness, and "for the sake of" must mean the same thing in each case. And we have seen that Aristotle is saying nothing rash and implausible if we take him to be making an empirical claim about honor and virtue. Each causally contributes to some further end, and that end is eventually identified as virtuous activity. But do we not run into difficulty when we apply this interpretation to physical pleasure? How does it contribute to virtuous activity? At least in this case, is Aristotle not saying something quite dubious if we read him in the way I suggest?

Pleasures of the body are not all of the same type, but there is at least one kind that Aristotle clearly takes to be a means to virtuous activity. When he discusses the place of amusement in a good life (X.6), he clearly has physical pleasures in mind (1176b20–21, 1177a6–7), and he says that we should pursue such amusements because they relax us and restore our ability to engage in more serious and demanding pursuits (1176b28–1177a1). The pleasures of relaxation, in other words, are a means to happiness. And in saying that these sorts of enjoyments promote our ability

[30] See too *EE* II.1 1218b37–1219a13: the virtue of a thing is desirable for the sake of the function that is performed by means of that virtue.

to pursue some further good, Aristotle can hardly be accused of making an implausible empirical claim.

Of course, not all pleasures of the body are amusements, and the *NE* never claims they are. Eating and drinking, for example, are not always forms of relaxation: at times, we seek food and drink because we are hungry and thirsty, not because we have been working hard and need to do something easier for a while. Can Aristotle believe that the sorts of pleasures we get from these activities promote virtuous activity? He can and does. For he takes the pleasure associated with any activity to affect the way we engage in that activity. For example, if we get pleasure from building things, we become and remain better builders than we would be if we were indifferent to this activity, or if we found it painful (X.5 1175a28–b1). If we apply this empirical generalization to eating and drinking, then Aristotle's claim would be that we are better at nourishing ourselves if we take pleasure in these activities than if we are pained by or indifferent to food and drink. And this is a perfectly sensible point to make. Someone who doesn't care about these physical activities, and gets no pleasure from them, suffers from a disability that endangers his health. He has to remind himself and force himself to eat. And when he starts eating, he can rely on no natural signals that tell him when to stop; he cannot eat until he is satisfied, because he gets no satisfaction from eating. Being a good eater facilitates the project of maintaining good health, which is of course a means to many other goods, including virtuous activity.

This does not mean that, according to Aristotle, whenever we enjoy a physical pleasure, we should consciously be thinking of the way in which this promotes virtuous activity. On the contrary, the whole point of engaging in certain pleasures—those that relax us—is to stop thinking about more serious undertakings. Aristotle is saying that if we are asked why we want a life in which we have these and other kinds of physical pleasures, we should not simply reply that these are choiceworthy in themselves, but should add that they make an indirect causal contribution to our ultimate end. Reading the *NE* in this way does not saddle it with implausible empirical claims, and so there is no good reason for adopting the alternative interpretation that Ackrill proposes.

4.14. THE CONCLUSION OF THE FUNCTION ARGUMENT

After Aristotle distinguishes between imperfect, perfect, and most perfect ends, he describes the self-sufficiency of happiness (1097b6–16) and the special way in which it is the most desirable good (b16–20). And then he develops the most important single argument in his treatment of happiness—his attempt to show that human beings have a proper function, and to determine what that special function consists in. Important though this material is, I want to postpone discussion of it until Chapters 5 and 6. For now, I would like to focus on the conclusion of the function argument: "The human good turns out to be activity of soul in accordance with virtue, and if there are more than one virtue, in accordance with the best and most perfect" (1098a16–18). I want to ask two questions: First, what is Aristotle saying about activity of the soul in accordance with the best and most perfect virtue when he equates it with the human good? Second, which virtue does he think is "best and most perfect"?[31]

I think there is only one plausible way of answering the first question: when Aristotle says that activity in accordance with the best virtue is *the* good, he is saying that it should be our ultimate end. He is not merely saying that it is *a* good; it is *the* good, and this means that it has the three properties of an ultimate end: it is desirable in itself, it is not desirable for the sake of anything else, and every other end should be desired for its sake. We have seen that in Book I Aristotle is searching for an end that has these characteristics, and there can be no doubt that the function argument is an attempt to specify what this end is. He is saying that a certain virtuous activity is at the top of the hierarchy of ends.[32]

[31] A third question can be asked: what is it for an activity to be *in accordance with* (*kata*) virtue? I assume that an activity is in accordance with virtue when it makes use of or actualizes that virtue. For example, to act in accordance with theoretical wisdom is to engage in philosophical thinking, and to act in accordance with courage is to exercise the mastery of reason over fear in life-threatening situations. Contrast the way "in accordance with" is sometimes used in English: any lawful act one performs is in accordance with the law, and in this sense any morally permissible act I perform may be said to be in accordance with virtue. In this broad sense, when I sleep, or amuse myself, or think philosophically, I am acting in accordance with ethical virtue, so long as I am acting as a virtuous person would. I do not think this broad sense of "in accordance with virtue" captures Aristotle's use of *kat' aretēn*. For one thing, on my interpretation, his phrase covers both theoretical and practical virtue; and surely it is implausible to take activity in accordance with theoretical virtue to include anything permitted by theoretical wisdom (whatever that would mean). For another, Aristotle thinks that the activities that are in accordance with ethical virtue merit admiration because of their outstanding qualities. They do not include such humdrum activities as sleeping, amusing oneself, and walking—even when these acts are permissible and, in this sense, in accordance with virtue. Activities that are genuinely in accordance with moral virtue are a special subset of the acts that would be done by an ethically virtuous person. For evidence that supports this reading, see 1099a11, 1099a29–31, 1099b29–32, 1100b12–17, 1177a9–18.

[32] On my reading, the virtuous activity equated with the human good in the function argument is virtuous activity of the reasoning part of the soul. It is not a composite of this activity and excellent activity of lower parts of the soul (the nutritive soul, the perceptive soul, and so on). Of course, we need these lesser excellences too if we are to live as well as we can; but activities of these lower capacities are not themselves components of happiness. This reading is supported by I.7 1098a3–10 and 14, and confirmed by I.13 1102b11–12: the excellence of the nutritive soul has no place in Aristotle's study, since it is not a specifically human virtue, that is, it is shared by lower forms of life. If virtuous activities of subrational

My reply to the second question is that, according to Aristotle, theoretical wisdom is the best and most perfect virtue. Accordingly, I take him to be saying here—though he does not spell this out until X.7–8—that the good is contemplation. For contemplation is the activity of the soul in accordance with the virtue that he takes to be best and most perfect.

I will soon say why I think the conclusion of the function argument should be read in this way. But first, I want to consider an objection that will surely be made against my reading. The objection says that if my interpretation is right, then the conclusion of the function argument implies that happiness does not consist in activity of the soul in accordance with the *ethical* virtues. In fact, on my reading, moral activities are not even components of the good; rather, the good consists in intellectual activity and nothing else. But, the objection continues, this reading simply does not fit the context of Book I. For after he has completed the function argument, Aristotle continues to discuss happiness in a way that suggests that it consists at least partly in ethically virtuous activity. For example, in I.8, he tries to confirm the conclusion of the function argument by showing that the good life as he conceives it will include pleasure (1099a7–21); for, he says, a just person is someone who enjoys just action, and a generous person enjoys acting generously (a18–20). If I were right about the function argument's conclusion, then what business would Aristotle have appealing to facts about the *ethically* virtuous person? If he means to say that happiness consists in intellectual activity, then how is

---

parts of the soul were components of human happiness, Aristotle would hardly dismiss them in this way. Furthermore, if all of these various kinds of virtuous activities were included within the human function, then Aristotle would need some further argument to show that exercising reason is more choiceworthy than exercising some subrational faculty. But he presents no such argument—presumably because he takes the function argument to be precisely the argument he needs in order to show the superiority of reason over other faculties of the soul. The good consists in exercising this part of the soul, rather than others, because this is what sets us apart from plants and other animals. (I will expand on this point in Chapter 6.) My interpretation should be contrasted with that of Irwin: "If x can do A, B, and C, and nothing else can do C, but other things can do A and B, we might describe x's peculiar function either as 'doing A, B, and C' or as 'doing C.' Now it is fairly clear that Aristotle understands the peculiar activity of man in the first, inclusive way" ("The Metaphysical and Psychological Basis of Aristotle's Ethics," p. 49). According to this suggestion, the function of human beings is to engage in activities of the reasoning part of the soul *and* to do many other things besides. But this trivializes Aristotle's argument: everything we can do becomes part of the human good, and no organization is imposed upon our ends. Irwin's interpretation is viable only if there are passages in which Aristotle equates human happiness with a composite of all the activities we engage in (or at least the ones that are desirable in themselves). But we will see that there are no such passages. Certainly the text of the function argument (1097b22–1098a20) does not itself provide evidence of an all-inclusive conception of human happiness.

his conclusion confirmed by the claim that a just and generous person enjoys acting from these virtues? An opponent of my interpretation could also point to I.13, where Aristotle proposes that, in the light of his account of happiness, a study of virtue is needed (1102a5–6). It is clear from the rest of this chapter, and from the way the NE continues from Book II onward, that Aristotle takes both practical and theoretical virtues to require further study. And surely that means that his function argument identifies the good with something more than theoretical activity. He must be saying that happiness consists in a composite of theoretical and practical activity.

My response to this objection begins with a reminder that in X.7–8 Aristotle makes a distinction between perfect happiness and a secondary form of happiness. He says that the former consists in contemplation, but that by exercising the practical virtues the politician can also be happy. In arguing for the superiority of the philosophical life, the NE finally resolves an issue that it left hanging in I.5: it tells us that both the philosophical and the political lives can be well lived, but that only the former can be a life of perfect happiness. What I would like to suggest is that if we bring this distinction between perfect and secondary happiness to bear on the function argument, we can better understand its place in Aristotle's thinking. When he concludes in I.7 that the good consists in a certain kind of virtuous activity, he should be taken to mean that the ultimate end is contemplation; he identifies the good with activity in accordance with the most perfect virtue, and that turns out to be theoretical activity. But we should also take him to be assuming that the function argument supports a further conclusion: though the good does not consist in moral activity, the function argument can help show that such activity is an approximation to the good. To use the language of X.7–8: the function argument is the beginning of an argument that perfect happiness consists in theoretical activity, and it is also the beginning of an argument that a secondary form of happiness consists in practical activity. The conclusion of the function argument does not tell us of this double role, but the way Aristotle proceeds after I.7 indicates that his explicit conclusion—the good consists in activity of soul in accordance with the most perfect virtue—is not the only one he wants to draw.

So, on my reading, Aristotle is in a way denying that happiness consists in ethical activity. But the point can be put less misleadingly if we say that he denies that *perfect* happiness consists in such activity. And there is unambiguous evidence for this interpretation in X.7–8. On the other hand, he also says that happiness does in a way consist in ethical activity; more precisely, he believes that to be happy to a secondary degree, one must lead a life in which all other ends are pursued for the sake of activity in accordance with ethical virtue. It is perfectly correct, then, to say that the function argument does not commit Aristotle to the thesis that happiness consists in contemplation alone. Contemplation is the only activity being referred to when he speaks of "the best and most perfect" virtue, but we should not infer from this that, in his opinion, no other kind of good should be identified with happiness.

We will soon see that, according to Aristotle, the function argument entitles him to draw a conclusion that differs slightly but importantly from the one that he states in I.7: he says several times that happiness consists in exercising *perfect* virtue.[33] The function argument, by contrast, tells us that the good consists in activity in accordance with *the most perfect* virtue. Why the discrepancy? I shall argue that the virtues that are perfect without being most perfect are the practical virtues of temperance, generosity, practical wisdom, and so on. And on my reading, Aristotle's several references to perfect virtue reflect his belief that he can use the function argument to show that secondary happiness consists in exercising the moral virtues. He holds that happiness consists in using the most perfect virtue, and that happiness consists in using perfect virtue. These two doctrines are to be unpacked in the following way: perfect happiness consists in exercising the most perfect virtue, whereas secondary happiness consists in exercising virtues that are not perfect without qualification.

I have claimed that the function argument plays a dual role: it begins Aristotle's defense of the philosophical life as well as his defense of the political life. But I have said nothing about how it provides such a defense. To do that, we will have to examine the details of the argument. For now, I hope I have convinced the reader that unacceptable consequences do not follow from the identification of the best and most perfect virtue with theoretical wisdom. Once we see how the function argument is supposed to work as a defense of two lives, we will understand why Aristotle feels entitled to draw two conclusions from it—the one stated immediately (the good is exercising the most perfect virtue), and the one stated later (happiness is exercising perfect virtue).

4.15. THE MOST PERFECT VIRTUE

Let us now ask what Aristotle means by "the most perfect virtue." He gives no explanation of this phrase when he uses it at the conclusion of the function argument, and he says nothing about which virtue is most perfect. But surely it is significant that, just prior to this passage, he discusses the way in which ends differ in degrees of perfection. The most perfect end, we are told, is the one for the sake of which all others are chosen (1097a25–34). This account of perfection is the only one that Ar-

[33] See I.9 1100a4–5, I.10 1101a14–16, I.13 1102a5–6.

istotle offers in Book I, and it would be absurd not to use it in our attempt to understand what the most perfect virtue is.[34] If ends have more or less perfection depending on where they stand in a hierarchy, then Aristotle must mean that virtues too can be arranged in a hierarchy. Accordingly, a virtue that is not perfect is one that is desirable only on condition that it promotes some further virtue. A virtue that is perfect is one that is desirable in itself. And the most perfect virtue is the one that is not desirable for the sake of any other, though all of the other virtues are desirable for its sake.

In arriving at this conclusion, I have used the same methodology as Ackrill, for he too believes that we should appeal to Aristotle's threefold distinction among ends in attempting to understand "the most perfect virtue." He therefore takes that highest virtue to be a composite of all the virtues: it is not just theoretical wisdom, but rather a whole composed of all theoretical and practical virtues.[35] But this is a conclusion we cannot accept, since we have rejected his way of understanding Aristotle's trichotomy of ends. There is no justification for taking the most perfect virtue to be a composite of all virtues, unless Aristotle has already introduced the idea of a composite good, and has treated degrees of perfection in terms of greater inclusiveness. And this he has not done.

The interpretation I am defending needs to be spelled out more fully, of course. According to my scheme, there are virtues that are perfect and yet not most perfect: which ones are they? Similarly, I must say which virtues are not perfect. But before I turn to these questions, I would like to say more about the virtue that is best and most perfect. I take this to be a single virtue, not a composite, and I think that Aristotle eventually identifies it with theoretical wisdom. Accordingly, the good turns out to be activity of the soul in accordance with theoretical wisdom; it is, in other words, contemplation. Several considerations support this way of reading the conclusion of the function argument, apart from the fact that it allows us to explain "the most perfect" virtue by appealing to Aristotle's earlier discussion of degrees of perfection.

First, if Aristotle had wanted to say what Ackrill takes him to be saying—that the good consists in exercising *every* virtue of the soul—then he would have chosen a far more straightforward and less misleading form of expression. He need only have said: ". . . and if there are more than one virtue, then in accordance with all of them." The fact that instead he says ". . . in accordance with the best and most perfect" naturally suggests that he is singling out one virtue. This of course does not commit

---

[34] The point is implicit in Gauthier and Jolif, *L'Éthique à Nicomaque*, comments on 1097a30 and 1098a17. See too Cooper, *RHGA*, p. 100 n. 10, point (3).

[35] Ackrill, "Aristotle on *Eudaimonia*," pp. 28–9.

him to the view that someone leading the best human life needs only one virtue. Rather, his claim is only that the activity at the pinnacle of human goods is the exercise of some one virtue; many other virtues and goods are needed, but they occupy lower positions in the hierarchy.

Second, as W.F.R. Hardie observes, a passage in I.8 reinforces the suggestion of I.7 that some one type of virtuous activity is being identified with happiness.[36] Aristotle here (1099a27–8) refers to the Delian inscription according to which justice is the finest thing, health the most beneficial, and attaining what one loves the most pleasant. Against this, he claims that all three properties—finest, most beneficial, and most pleasant—belong to a single type of good, namely, the best activities. And then he adds: "And these, or one of them—the best—we say is happiness" (a29–31). It would be implausible to take this to mean: "And these, or one of them—namely, all of them—we say is happiness." For "these" and "one of them" are being contrasted, and we would lose this contrast if "one of them" were then taken to refer to all of them. The only way to read Aristotle's remark is to see it as a reflection of the function argument's conclusion. He has tried to show that the good consists in activity in accordance with the single best virtue, but he thinks the same argument shows that if we act in accordance with a less perfect kind of virtue, we will also be happy. That is why he says in I.8 that happiness consists in the best activities, or in one of them—the one that is best. His meaning emerges more clearly in X.7–8, when he distinguishes perfect and secondary happiness: the former consists in the one best activity, the latter in a second-best activity.

Third, the way in which X.7 begins Aristotle's defense of the contemplative life suggests that he is returning to the conclusion of the function argument. For he opens the chapter with this statement: "If happiness is activity in accordance with virtue, it is reasonable that it is in accordance with the best" (1177a12–13). The function argument says that the human good consists in activity in accordance with the best virtue, and so the line just quoted can only be read as a repetition of that basic point. As Aristotle soon goes on to say, the activity in accordance with the best virtue is contemplation. Now, since X.7–8 takes some one virtue—not a composite—to be best, it is reasonable to read Book I in the same way, if such a reading fits the context. Since we are trying to see how the discussion of happiness in Books I and X can be joined together into a coherent unit, it would be foolish to overlook the way in which X.7 completes the thought Aristotle had initiated in I.7. And we should bear in mind that in

---

[36] Hardie, *Aristotle's Ethical Theory*, twice (pp. 23 and 25) alludes to this passage in connection with his view that the "most perfect virtue" of 1098a17–18 is theoretical wisdom. See too his "Aristotle on the Best Life for a Man," p. 39, and Cooper, "Contemplation and Happiness: A Reconsideration," p. 200.

X.7–8 Aristotle argues for the superiority of contemplation by pointing out that it alone is loved for itself and that nothing comes from it (1177b1–2). He must believe, then, that the virtue we exercise when we contemplate is not desired for the sake of any further virtue. It is, to use the terminology of I.7, the most perfect of the virtues. And so X.7–8 not only tells us what the best virtue is, but argues for its perfection in a way that assures us of the continuity between I.7 and these later chapters.

I conclude that the virtue Aristotle refers to at the conclusion of the function argument—the one that is "best and most perfect"—is some single virtue, whose superlative nature consists partly in its relation to the other virtues: all other virtues are desirable for its sake, and though it is desirable in itself, it is not desirable for the sake of any other virtue. Aristotle does not say which virtue it is, because he has postponed discussion of the contemplative life. But he can hardly be blamed for not saying which virtue is best until he has had a chance to discuss them all. By referring to some one virtue that is best, he alerts us to the fact that some ranking of the virtues will be required before we can determine which life is best.

4.16. Complete Virtue

I would now like to consider several statements in Book I that connect happiness with activity in accordance with *perfect* virtue:

> For as we have said, one must have both perfect virtue and a complete life.[37] (I.9 1100a4–5)

> What then prevents us from saying that a happy person is someone who is active in accordance with perfect virtue, and who is sufficiently equipped with external goods, not for some chance period of time, but for a complete life? (I.10 1101a14–16)

> Since happiness is a certain activity of soul in accordance with perfect virtue, it is necessary to examine virtue. (I.13 1102a5–6)

One feels like protesting: "But you said in the function argument that the good consists in activity in accordance with *the most perfect* virtue. Now, without explanation, you have changed your formulation. Instead of 'most perfect virtue,' you say 'perfect virtue.' Do these two expressions mean the same thing? And if there is a difference, what justifies the switch from one to the other?"

One way to answer these questions—a mistaken way, I think—is as

---

[37] Here, with "complete life," I revert to the conventional translation. See Chapter 1, note 46.

follows: The term "perfect virtue" in the statements cited above means "complete virtue," and complete virtue of the rational soul is a composite of all the virtues of that part of the soul.[38] Accordingly, when Aristotle says that "happiness is a certain activity of soul in accordance with perfect virtue" (I.13 1102a5–6), he means that it consists in activity in accordance with every virtue of the rational soul. Among these virtues are theoretical wisdom, practical wisdom, justice, temperance, and so on. Happiness does not consist merely in exercising one of these virtues—rather it consists in exercising all of them. And so, there is no one virtuous activity for the sake of which all other goods are to be desired.

Now, if we read Aristotle in this way, an obvious question arises: How can this conception of happiness be reconciled with the one that Aristotle adopts as a result of the function argument? We have seen that in I.7 he singles out some one virtue—though he does not say which it is—and says that the human good consists in exercising *it*. Once we accept that interpretation of the function argument, it would be bizarre to read Aristotle's later statements in Book I as equations of the good with the exercise of *all* the virtues. Why would he identify happiness with the use of some one virtue in I.7, only to draw back from that conclusion in the rest of the book?[39] Why would he begin by referring to a single most perfect virtue, and then act as though he had identified happiness with complete virtue, that is, a composite of them all?

It might be suggested that the way out of this difficulty is to employ the distinction between perfect and secondary happiness made in Book X. We might then say that in the function argument, Aristotle identifies *perfect* happiness with contemplation, but that in the later three statements he identifies *secondary* happiness with exercising all the virtues of the rational soul. The best life, in other words, is one in which all goods are pursued for the sake of one ultimate end, contemplation; the second-best

---

[38] Thus Ackrill, "Aristotle on *Eudaimonia*," pp. 28–9; Cooper, "Contemplation and Happiness: A Reconsideration," p. 198. Cooper's position (p. 199) is that "most perfect" at 1098a18 must be understood by reference to Aristotle's threefold distinction among ends earlier in I.7, but that we need not appeal to that distinction when we interpret the three later statements about "perfect virtue" (or, as he says, "complete virtue").

[39] Cooper's reply is that I.7 does *not* identify happiness with the exercise of some one virtue, even though "the best and most perfect" virtue is nothing other than theoretical wisdom. He takes 1098a17–18 to mean: "if there are more than one human virtue happiness is activity of all of them, including most particularly activity of the best among the virtues" ("Contemplation and Happiness: A Reconsideration," p. 202). I agree that the function argument leaves a place for the less perfect virtues in an account of happiness; more precisely, secondary happiness consists in exercising those virtues. But I take 1098a17–18 to be preparing the way for Aristotle's eventual conclusion that perfect happiness consists in contemplation. If this is correct, then these lines should be taken to mean that the good (that is, perfect happiness) consists in exercising the single best virtue, *rather than* a composite of that and other virtues.

life is one in which all virtuous activities, including contemplation, share a place at the top of the hierarchy. In this life of secondary happiness, every other good is desired for the sake of some virtuous activity, but no virtuous activity is desired for the sake of anything else.

But then we would have to take Aristotle to be saying in X.7–8 that the two best lives are both philosophical lives, and that the difference between them is that one is more fully devoted to philosophy than the other. And this is a reading that we rejected in 1.12. If Aristotle believes that the more contemplation a life has the happier it is, then it would serve no useful purpose for him to present his readers with two model lives that differ only in the degree to which they are devoted to contemplation. Since he implies in Book I that each of the three most prominent lives is devoted to a different ultimate end, it is best to take the difference between the political and the philosophical lives to turn on the different ultimate ends around which they are organized. Accordingly, the second-best life contains no philosophical activity, and all subordinate ends are pursued for the sake of the highest kind of ethical activity. And the statements of Book I that equate happiness with activity in accordance with perfect virtue cannot be taken to mean that *secondary* happiness consists in exercising *all* the virtues.

Where does this leave us? We want to know what Aristotle means by "perfect virtue" in the three statements cited at the beginning of this section. And we have been running into trouble by assuming that "perfect virtue" of the rational soul refers to the composite of all such virtues. The obvious step to take next is to reject this hypothesis, and to explore the possibility that the word "perfect" here means what Aristotle tells us it means when he distinguishes three kinds of ends. We have already seen that there is good reason to take the phrase "most perfect virtue" in this way: the most perfect virtue is the one that is desirable in itself and for the sake of which the other virtues are desired. And since Aristotle uses the for-the-sake-of relation to distinguish between perfect and imperfect ends, he presumably looks at perfect and imperfect virtues in the same way. An imperfect virtue of the rational soul is one that is desired only on condition that it promotes some further virtue: in this respect it is like such imperfect ends as wealth and instruments. By contrast, a perfect virtue of the rational soul is one that would be desired even if it did not promote any further virtue: it is analogous to honor and pleasure. And among perfect virtues, the one that is most perfect is that for the sake of which the other virtues are desired, but which is not in turn desired for the sake of any further virtue.

But is there any textual basis for saying which virtues go in which categories? Does anything in I.7 suggest that Aristotle has such a distinction in mind? And if we understand perfect and imperfect virtue in the way I propose, can we make sense of the fact that Book I first identifies happiness with exercising the most perfect virtue, and then identifies it with exercising perfect virtue? I take up these questions in the next section.

4.17. IMPERFECT VIRTUE

Which are the imperfect virtues of the rational soul? On my interpretation they are the virtues of reason that are desirable only on condition that they lead to some further virtue. I suggest that Aristotle places two kinds of excellence in this category: the good qualities of children, and the skills of craftsmen. Let us consider these in turn.

In *NE* VI.13, Aristotle makes a distinction between natural and full (*kuria*) virtue: there is a way in which we have such qualities as justice, temperance, and courage as soon as we are born, but these first intimations of true virtue must be properly developed and must eventually be integrated with practical reason (1144b1–17). So, when a natural virtue is educated and operates in light of a justified conception of the good, then it becomes a full virtue. And that is something that only an adult can achieve. Children may be naturally inclined to good behavior, but they cannot fully understand how life should be lived. As Aristotle says in *Politics* I.13, the deliberative faculty of children is imperfect (*ateles*: 1260a14), and so when we attribute virtues to them, we use a different standard from the one that is appropriate for free male adults (a31–3).

Is it linguistically appropriate to refer to the justice of an adult as a perfect virtue, and the justice of a child as imperfect? The *Magna Moralia* shows that it is: "There are also virtues that arise in everyone by nature, like certain impulses in each person, lacking reason, towards courageous and just actions and to other such actions in accordance with each virtue. . . . When added to reason and choice, [these natural virtues] make perfect (*teleia*) virtue" (I.34 1197b38–1198a6). Since the kind of virtue that is integrated with reason is perfect, and the immature deliberative faculty of the child is called "imperfect," it would be natural to call the virtues of a child "imperfect." Their imperfection consists in their being the earlier stages of a more mature and desirable quality: natural justice is something that grows into full justice, if a person develops in the proper way.

Now, although Book I of the *NE* does not discuss the natural virtues of children, the function argument nonetheless makes a distinction between two aspects of the part of the soul that has reason: there is something in us that is obedient to reason, and this is different from the element that actually engages in thinking (I.7 1098a3–5). Aristotle returns to the distinction in I.13, and uses it to chart the course he will take throughout much of the *NE*: one part of the soul has reason fully (*kuriōs*: 1103a2), and the other has desires which obey reason to varying degrees, as children obey their fathers (a3). What we are to study, beginning with Book II, are virtues of both of these parts: virtues of thought, and ethical virtues (a3–10). And when we investigate the latter qualities, in Books II through V, we are reminded that they are skills that are put in the service of wise decision making.[40] In other words, the virtues Aristotle discusses are not the rudimentary beginnings of full virtue found in children. The *NE* is not a treatise on child-rearing, but a study of excellence in mature adults. Though a child's low-level virtues belong to the rational soul, they are of no more importance to Aristotle's discussion than the virtues of the body: they are not his topic, even though they have a necessary role to play in human life.

My suggestion, then, is that when Aristotle says that happiness consists in activity in accordance with perfect virtue, the latter term excludes the immature capacities of the rational soul that are not yet integrated with practical wisdom. No mere child, Aristotle tells us (I.9 1100a1–3), can be happy, for *eudaimonia* requires both perfect virtue and a certain length of life (a4–5). Children have neither, and when "perfect virtue" is understood in the way I propose, this is of course true.

We have seen that natural virtue is appropriately called "imperfect," and that in *NE* I Aristotle excludes natural or imperfect virtues from his purview. According to my reading, in calling these excellences "imperfect," he means that we desire them only on condition that they lead to further virtues that are desirable in themselves. The imperfect virtues are related to other states of the soul as wealth and instruments are related to the further goods that they promote. Now, can we take Aristotle to be saying this about the childhood tendencies that he calls natural virtues? Are they states that we want only on condition that they lead to further virtues? The answer is obviously yes. For if these tendencies are not combined with reason, they are harmful (VI.13 1144b9); presumably what Aristotle means here is not that they are harmful on all occasions, but that they can and will do harm no less than good. Someone who has a natural tendency towards generosity, or who likes to obey others, will injure both himself and others if he does not learn to think well about the proper use of these qualities. In this way, the natural virtues are precisely like instruments: since they can be used for good or evil, they are desirable not in themselves but only on condition that they lead to some further good. We call certain qualities of children virtues because they are the rudimentary stage of something that is desirable in itself. As Aristotle says, we would not want to lead our whole lives with the mind of a child, even if we could take maximal pleasure in childish things (X.3 1174a1–3). The protorationality of a child, like the pleasures of childhood, is de-

---

[40] See II.6 1107a1–2, III.7 1115b12, III.11 1119a20, IV.5 1125b35; cf. IX.8 1169a3–6.

sirable at an early stage of life, but if it were a permanent condition and led to nothing more mature, it would no longer be desirable.

I suggest that a different group of virtues can also fit comfortably into the category of imperfect excellences—namely, the skills exercised in craft activity. This kind of virtue is very much on Aristotle's mind when he writes I.7, for his search for the function of human beings is guided partly by the thought that craftsmen have functions and that each does his task well by acting in accordance with some appropriate virtue (1097b25–7, 1098a8–15). The virtues we have when we acquire these skills are not virtues of the body (like health, strength, and beauty), nor are they virtues of the subrational parts of the soul. In Book VI, Aristotle clearly houses them, along with theoretical and practical wisdom, in the part of the soul that reasons (VI.3 1139b14–17). And the virtues that enable supervisory craftsmen—such as architects and doctors—to do their jobs well clearly do include thinking skills. We should also notice that although Aristotle expects his readers to leave most crafts to others—he does not take himself to be talking to cooks, cobblers, and horse trainers—there is nonetheless one craft, at least, that every one of his readers needs: household management (*oikonomia*).[41] They must have or develop the virtues by which they can exercise proper management of their property (including their slaves) and family. If they cannot handle these material and personal goods, they will not have the leisure needed to engage in politics and philosophy.

Now, Aristotle holds that wealth, flutes, and all other tools are imperfect ends (I.7 1097a26–8); and I have taken this to mean these goods are desirable only on condition that they lead to something further. And surely he would say the same about the skills that enable one to produce these imperfect ends: if wealth is worth having only because it is used for some further purpose, then the skill that enables one to preserve wealth is also desirable only on condition that wealth is used to achieve its purpose. And so it would be entirely appropriate for Aristotle to say that the virtues acquired when we learn a craft are imperfect virtues of the rational soul. These imperfect virtues help us develop the perfect virtues, and similarly some of those perfect virtues help develop the one that is most perfect. Like goods in general, the virtues of the rational soul form a hierarchy.

Once we realize that natural virtues and craft skills are excellences of reason, we must admit that Aristotle does not want to equate happiness with the exercise of *every* virtue of this part of soul. Happiness does not consist partly in exercising natural virtue, and partly in exercising full virtue; nor does it consist partly in exercising the skills of the horse trainer

---

[41] Nearly half of *Pol.* I (8–13) is devoted to this topic.

or shipbuilder. It consists in using such virtues as theoretical wisdom, practical wisdom, and courage, and so on. Or, to put the point more precisely: perfect happiness is activity in accordance with theoretical wisdom; secondary happiness is activity in accordance with qualities that develop from the natural virtues of children, that is, ethical virtue combined with practical wisdom. And so Aristotle needs some way to signal the fact that certain virtues of the rational soul are not included in his account of what happiness is. And his distinction between perfect and imperfect ends gives him what he needs: he can say that the good consists only in exercising the perfect virtues. In fact, as we have seen, he wants to be even more exclusive: the highest good consists in activity in accordance with the most perfect virtue. The highest human end is not (a) all virtuous activity, or (b) all virtuous activity of the rational soul, or (c) all activity of the rational soul in accordance with perfect virtue. Looking for the pinnacle of the hierarchy of ends, Aristotle identifies it solely with (d) activity of the rational soul in accordance with the virtue that is best and most perfect. But taking this last exclusionary step allows him to move back and give (c) a special status: there are two degrees of happiness, and both forms of it consist in exercising a perfect virtue of the rational soul. That is why Book I equates happiness with both (c) and (d).

If my way of interpreting "perfect virtue" and "most perfect virtue" is right, then Aristotle could have expressed the conclusion of the function argument in the following way: "The human good consists in activity of the rational soul in accordance with perfect virtue, and if there is more than one perfect virtue, then in accordance with the most perfect virtue." Such a formulation would not mean a change of doctrine; it would merely put into a single sentence what Aristotle in fact expresses in different sentences. For in I.7 he equates happiness with exercising the most perfect virtue, and thereafter equates it with exercising perfect virtue; and there is no reason for him not to have said, at the end of the function argument, that it consists in both.[42]

Surely Aristotle might have spelled out his meaning more fully. The distinction between perfect and secondary happiness need not have been postponed until Book X; and the shift from "most perfect" to "perfect" might have been explained. Nonetheless, he tells us what he means by

[42] How are we to explain the fact that at I.9 1100a4, Aristotle says: "For *as we have said* one must have both perfect virtue and a complete life"? The reference here can only be to 1098a17–18; but that earlier passage uses the superlative "most perfect." Ackrill, "Aristotle on *Eudaimonia*," p. 28, emphasizes "as we have said," in order to support the claim that the earlier passage is referring to the most inclusive virtue. But the fact that 1100a4 alludes to 1098a17–18 does not necessarily support this interpretation. The most perfect virtue is of course a perfect virtue. And so even though 1098a17–18 picks out one virtue as being most perfect, it *has* said that "one must have . . . perfect virtue."

degrees of perfection, and he does eventually make it clear that the philosophical and political lives are both happy, though one is superior to the other. Furthermore, he has a good reason for waiting before deciding which virtue is most perfect: we will be in a better position to make this decision after we have examined the competing virtues of the political and philosophical lives. So, although Aristotle's account of happiness in Book I is sometimes confusing, it is not beyond comprehension.[43]

4.18. Confirming the Function Argument

I would now like to consider what Book I says about happiness after the presentation of the function argument in chapter 7. In the remainder of this book, we are not told what the best and most perfect virtue is, and we hear nothing of the life devoted to contemplation. But anyone who reads X.7–8 will see that these topics are not dropped; here, in these late chapters, we learn that theoretical virtue is best, and that the life of the philosopher is therefore happiest. Instead of attending to these matters immediately, Aristotle devotes the rest of Book I to the virtues and activities that constitute the end of the life that turns out to be second-best. He is treating the function argument as the basis for a defense of the moral life and of the intellectual life, and instead of trying to decide between these alternatives, his next move is to solidify the results he has already achieved. Having shown, by means of the function argument, why we should equate happiness with activity in accordance with the most perfect (that is, theoretical) virtue and with activity in accordance with perfect (that is, practical) virtue, he takes the latter result first, and expands on it in the remainder of Book I. He does not think he needs to tell us that the virtues he goes on to discuss are not the best; that is something we shall eventually learn. Since he takes the political life to be supported by the function argument, he thinks he can confirm the results achieved in that argument by showing how reasonable it is to believe that happiness is an

[43] My interpretation has not taken account of *EE* II.1 1219a38–9, where Aristotle identifies happiness with "complete" (*teleia*) virtue. The context clearly indicates that he is talking about the whole of virtue, and not any one part of it, however superlative. See 1219a37, 1220a2–4. Ackrill, "Aristotle on *Eudaimonia*," p. 27, appeals to this passage to support his inclusivist reading of "the most perfect virtue" in *NE* I.7. But surely it is possible that the *NE* has its reasons for rejecting the formulation used in the *EE*. The most important evidence for what Aristotle means by "perfect" and "most perfect" in *NE* I is Aristotle's own explanation of these terms in I.7; we should not assume that this work must be giving precisely the same account of happiness as the one found in the *EE*. If my reading of "perfect virtue" in *NE* I is correct, then we can see a defect in the *EE* formulation: certain virtuous activities of the rational soul are *not* components of happiness.

activity in accordance with such virtues as justice, generosity, and courage.[44]

Now, several points Aristotle makes in I.8–11 support one of my
claims: he does not equate happiness with a composite of all the goods
that are desirable for themselves; rather, he identifies it with just one kind
of good—virtuous activity. For example, to support his conception of
happiness, he appeals to the fact that when goods are sorted into three
categories—external goods, goods of the body, and goods of the soul—
the best goods have long been placed by respectable authorities into the
latter category (1098b12–18). Since Aristotle is saying that the end of human life consists in certain activities of the soul and not in external or
bodily goods (b18–20), his conception of happiness accords with a ven-
erable opinion about which goods are best. Clearly, in this passage, he is
not taking happiness to be a composite that includes both virtuous activity and (for example) honor, even though honor is desirable for itself.
Rather, the end—happiness—simply is virtuous activity; that is—to take
into account X.7–8—perfect happiness is one kind of virtuous activity
and secondary happiness another kind of virtuous activity.

Several lines later (I.8 1098b30–1099a7), Aristotle emphasizes the difference between his own view and the thesis that happiness consists in
virtue. Returning to his earlier point that one can have virtue and still be
inactive throughout one's life (I.5 1095b32–1096a1), he argues that happiness must consist not in the possession of virtue, but in its actualization
and use. Just as it is performance and not mere strength that wins an athlete a prize at the Olympic games, so the prize we seek—happiness—is
not the good condition of our souls but the activities we engage in when
we exercise its perfect virtues (cf. I.9 1099b16–17). So, we should not
attribute to Aristotle the belief that happiness is a composite of two kinds
of goods of the soul—the virtues, and virtuous activities. Rather, his view
is that the former are for the sake of the latter, and that happiness consists
entirely in virtuous activity.

In I.9, Aristotle turns to the traditional problem of how happiness is
acquired: is it by learning, habituation, divine allotment, or mere chance?
That, of course, depends on what happiness is; but it is unlikely, he
thinks, that the highest good of human life should turn out to be a matter
of sheer luck (1099b20–25). And he then points out that his own account

---

[44] See I.8 1098b9–12: if the account of the human good reached in the function argument
is correct, then it will "harmonize" with what is said about happiness. The additional considerations to which Aristotle appeals in I.8–12 are of many different sorts; but clearly one
point he makes in favor of his account is that it provides a place for the external goods in a
happy life, even though it makes these goods subordinate to virtuous activity (1099a31–b8).
Those who equate happiness with external goods are not entirely wrong, since such goods
do support happiness. See 1098b27–9, and cf. *Met.* II.1 993a30–b19.

of happiness avoids this unpalatable conclusion: "What we are seeking is also made clear by our account. For it has been said to be a certain kind of activity of the soul in accordance with virtue. And of the remaining goods, some must necessarily belong, whereas others are by their nature cooperative and useful in an instrumental way" (b25–8). This does not mean that happiness consists in a composite of virtuous activity *and* the remaining goods; it means, rather, that happiness is virtuous activity, and that the remaining goods are either necessary or useful for this purpose.[45] So Aristotle is saying here that every other good in human life has a causal role to play in the promotion of virtuous activity. Though anyone living happily will have a variety of purposes, these ends must be arranged in a hierarchy, with subordinate goods supporting the one highest goal, which consists in virtuous activity. That activity is not merely the best of human ends, but the one for the sake of which all others should be pursued. And so it turns out that, on Aristotle's theory, happiness itself cannot be acquired through sheer good fortune. Though fortune may give us some of the prerequisites and useful tools of a happy life, it does not give us happiness itself, since it takes great individual effort over a long period of time to develop the virtues whose exercise constitutes our ultimate end.

4.19. Two Kinds of Resources

Although every other good promotes virtuous activity in some way, they do not all contribute in the same way. As we have just seen, some are necessary, while others are "by their nature cooperative and useful in an instrumental way" (I.9 1099b27–8). And in I.8, a further distinction is made among the various resources of a good life. After emphasizing that he identifies happiness with the best activities, or with one of them—the

---

[45] Contrast Irwin, "Permanent Happiness: Aristotle and Solon," p. 95. When Aristotle says of certain goods other than virtuous activity that they "must necessarily belong," Irwin takes this to mean that they contribute to happiness apart from their causal connection with virtuous activity. I see no textual basis for this. Aristotle tells us in this very passage that happiness is virtuous activity, and so when he goes on to say that certain other goods "necessarily belong" to a virtuous person, he must mean that they are resources without which virtuous activity is impossible. This distinction between necessary and nonnecessary resources for virtuous activity is also made at 1099a32–3: "it is [a] impossible or [b] not easy to do fine things if one is unequipped." I discuss this passage more fully in the next section. Note that Irwin's interpretation of this passage is influenced by his inclusivist reading of Aristotle's claim that happiness is self-sufficient and the most choiceworthy good in a special way (I.7 1097b14–20). He takes this to mean that happiness includes external goods (pp. 93–4); if this were so, then external goods would contribute to our well-being both because they facilitate virtuous activity and because they are themselves components of happiness.

best (1099a24–31)[46]—Aristotle insists that other kinds of goods will also have a role to play in a happy life:

> Nonetheless it is clear that in addition it also needs the external goods, as we have said. For it is [a] impossible or [b] not easy to do fine things if one is unequipped. For, to begin with, [c] many things are done by means of instruments, as it were—by means of friends, wealth, and political power. Furthermore, [d] the lack of certain things, such as good birth, good children, and beauty, mars our blessedness. For someone is not very fit to be happy (*eudaimonikos*) if he is extremely ugly in appearance, ill-born, solitary, or childless, and presumably he is still less so if he has extremely bad children or friends, or if being good, they die. (1099a31–b6)

I take him to be making two different distinctions: first between (a) and (b), and then between (c) and (d). In some cases, it is impossible to engage in virtuous activity if one lacks the external equipment; in other cases, it is possible but not easy. This is the distinction between (a) and (b), and it seems to correspond to the distinction in I.9 between goods that are necessary and those that are not necessary but are nonetheless "cooperative and useful." If one lacks a good in the latter category, one may still be able to undertake fine actions, but one will do so only with great difficulty. Presumably, in this case, one is unlikely to engage in virtuous activity on a regular basis over a long period of time.

What of the distinction between (c) and (d)? Since (c) refers to goods that are used like instruments, it might be suggested that (d), by contrast, refers to goods that are components of happiness because they are desirable in themselves.[47] In that case, Aristotle would be saying that good birth, good children, and beauty contribute to happiness not because of their causal connection with some further good, but simply because they are good in themselves and happiness includes all such goods. But we have thus far found no basis for understanding happiness in this way. Furthermore, the distinction between (c) and (d) is intended to flesh out Aristotle's claim that "it is impossible or not easy to do fine things if one is unequipped." The point he is making, then, is that the lack of such goods as good birth, good children, and beauty puts one into a worse position "to do fine things," that is, to act virtuously. Whether the goods in question are desirable in themselves or not is irrelevant, and Aristotle says nothing here about this issue. Our blessedness is marred by defects in our social standing, family, and appearance because such disadvantages leave us less equipped than we would like to be as performers of fine actions. So Aristotle is referring to the causal role of these goods.

---

[46] This point was discussed in 4.15.

[47] This is Irwin's interpretation in "Permanent Happiness: Aristotle and Solon," p. 95.

How then are we to understand the distinction between (c) and (d)? Aristotle's idea, I suggest, is that even when a good is not used *like an instrument* for the promotion of virtuous activity, it may still be counted as part of one's equipment for such activity, because it puts one into an *advantageous position* for performing fine acts. Consider the political leader who has all the right equipment: he has friends, wealth, and power; and in addition he comes from an aristocratic family, has good children, and is physically attractive. He uses the goods mentioned in (c): his friends promote his political projects, and he draws on his wealth and power to achieve fine ends. But the goods mentioned in (d) are advantages to him even though he does not actually use them as instruments for achieving political goals. The general public will take more notice of him, and pay more attention to what he says, because he has high social standing, successful children, and good looks. When he speaks, he does not use his appearance as an instrument; but even so, the way he looks creates a setting in which his words have greater effect. Good birth and good children enhance one's influence in the same way, even if one never actually calls upon one's parents or children to provide political support.[48] By contrast, those who want to devote themselves to a lifetime of fine actions will be greatly disadvantaged by ugliness, low social standing, childlessness, or disreputable friends. The less one shines in the eyes of others because of one's low stock of external goods, the harder it will be to achieve positions of prominence, and the fewer opportunities one will have to do fine things.

4.20. THE DEATH OF FRIENDS

I would now like to call attention to the last few words of the passage discussed in the previous section, for they contain an apparent anomaly. Aristotle is pointing out that the lack of certain goods "mars our blessedness," even though they are not used as instruments, and he mentions birth, good children, and beauty as examples. He then continues: "For someone is not very fit to be happy (*eudaimonikos*) if he is extremely ugly in appearance, ill-born, solitary, or childless, and presumably he is still

[48] Contrast the explanation given by Cooper in "Aristotle on the Goods of Fortune," p. 183: "One central context for the exercise of the virtues is in the raising of children and the subsequent common life one spends with them, once adult, in the morally productive common pursuit of morally significant ends." The friendship between parent and child is a relationship between unequals (VIII.7 1158b11–13, VIII.11 1161a10–21), and such friendships are inferior to those that exist among equals (VIII.3 1156b7–8, VIII.5 1157b34–6). One's most valued associates in virtuous activity are those of equal virtue, and children (even when they have matured into young adults) have less experience than those who are at the height of their powers. It is therefore not plausible to take Aristotle to be saying that one should have children in order to create a "central context for the exercise of the virtues."

less so if he has extremely bad children or friends, *or if being good, they die*"
(1099b3–6). From the point of view of someone whose end is virtuous
activity, having extremely bad children and friends is a greater disadvantage than being solitary and childless. And we can understand why Aristotle believes this: he is thinking about the way social attitudes affect one's
opportunities for virtuous action, and he is saying that one faces more
opprobrium if one has bad friends and children than if one has none at all.
The childless person lacks the approval bestowed on those with children,
but at least he is not disgraced by what his children do. Thus far, there is
nothing mysterious in what Aristotle says. But when we come to the
words I have emphasized, we are faced with a puzzle: Aristotle is also
saying that it is a greater disadvantage to have good friends or children
who die than to be solitary and childless. Why should he think this?
Surely there is no shame incurred by those who lose friends and children
to death?

I suggest that when Aristotle mentions the death of friends and children, he is thinking of the pain we feel during a period of mourning, and
he is assuming that during this period it becomes more difficult, if not
impossible, to undertake virtuous activities. He holds that pain destroys
activity (X.5 1175b22–4), and says, in his discussion of great misfortunes,
that they "bring pain and impede many activities" (I.10 1100b29–30). If
this is the reasoning that lies behind the above statement, then it makes
perfect sense: to lack children and friends is bad enough, since some of
the equipment one needs for virtuous activity is absent; but it is even
worse to lose good children and friends through death. Both the childless
person and the person whose children have died are lacking the same kind
of good, but it would be absurd to say that one lack is no worse than the
other. For bereaved parents and friends are not only lacking a good they
once had, but are also incapacitated, to some degree, by the pain they feel
at the loss they have incurred.[49]

It should be noticed that on Aristotle's account the death of friends is a
double loss. First, one's resources for engaging in virtuous activity are
diminished; one can no longer use those friends as instruments for the
accomplishment of one's purposes. Second, during the time one mourns
for them, one is in pain, and this interferes in a different way with one's
virtuous activity. One does not merely lack instruments to serve one's
virtuous purposes; one's psychological state actually interferes with one's
willingness or ability to engage in fine action.

---

[49] Of course, since happiness can be recovered after it is lost (I.10 1101a11–13), Aristotle
is not saying that the person whose friends or children have died will always be worse off
than an equally virtuous person who is solitary or childless. Rather, his claim is that for a
time the bereaved person suffers not only from a lack, but from an impediment as well.

None of this should be taken to mean that the only reason we should not want our friends or children to die is that they provide us with resources for virtuous action. For Aristotle is at this point talking only about the reasons why such tragedies interfere with our own happiness. He can perfectly well say that we are also concerned about these people for their sake: they are other selves, and so we have an interest in their well-being comparable in depth to our self-love. It is of course this attitude that grounds the great pain we would feel were they to die. We experience their loss of life almost as though it were our own, because we want them to live and be happy almost as much as we want this for ourselves. When we consider our own happiness, we view them as resources for the achievement of fine acts; but since we are also concerned with their happiness, we do not view them merely as resources.

4.21. ADORNMENT AND PAIN

Though Aristotle disagrees with those who identify happiness with good fortune (I.8 1099b8), he does not go to the opposite extreme and deny chance any causal role in a happy life. The good in which happiness consists—activity of the rational soul in accordance with perfect virtue—is acquired through individual effort and not good fortune. But in order to sustain such regular activity over the course of a lifetime, we need many kinds of resources; and fortune is one factor that increases or decreases our supply of these subordinate goods. Unforeseeable strokes of misfortune may take away our wealth, friends, good repute, health, and so on; when such losses are large and frequent, our level of virtuous activity will diminish, and may eventually reach the point at which no one could reasonably say that we are living well. That does not show that happiness actually *consists in* such goods as wealth, health, friends, and honor. Rather, Aristotle is saying that happiness—that is, virtuous activity—*depends on* these goods. A happy life for a human being will contain many different types of good; yet the ultimate end of such a life is not a composite, but consists solely in one form or another of virtuous activity.

In I.10, Aristotle gives the following account of fortune's role in a happy life:

> Many things happen through fortune, differing in largeness or smallness; among good fortunes and the opposite class there are small things, and these obviously do not affect the scales of life. But when many great things turn out well, they will make life more blessed, for by their nature they help add adornment, and one's use of them turns out to be fine and excellent. But if they turn out the opposite way, they reduce and destroy blessedness, for they bring pain and impede many activities. (1100b22–30)

Some unfortunate events are so insignificant that they bring no decrease in our level of happiness; others are large enough to make us less happy than we once were; and when misfortune reaches major proportions, it can deprive us of happiness. It would be wrongheaded to ask Aristotle to give us a criterion for assessing the magnitude of events so that we can say precisely when a person is less happy and when he is not happy at all. Precision about these matters is impossible. The important point is that happiness increases or decreases according to the level of one's virtuous activity. For example, if we come across some money lying on the ground, that may be good fortune, but if the sum is trivial, our find may not allow any increase in the level of our virtuous activity. A large windfall, however, would enable us to undertake some magnificent act that would otherwise have been impossible. At the other extreme, when losses are so great that our virtuous activity severely diminishes, then we can no longer be considered happy. So Aristotle can accommodate the common belief that the victim of great misfortune is not happy; since the topmost end (whether it consists in practical or theoretical activity) depends on the support of many subordinate goods, no human life is invulnerable to misfortune.

It might be claimed, however, that my interpretation overlooks an important feature of the passage just cited: Aristotle seems to be giving two reasons why good or bad fortune affects happiness, and only one of those reasons refers to virtuous activity. He says that important fortunate events increase happiness because (a) "by their nature they help add adornment" and (b) "one's use of them turns out to be fine and excellent" (1100b26–8); similarly, great misfortunes diminish and undermine happiness because (a) "they bring pain" and (b) they "impede many activities" (b29–30). In both cases, (b) refers to the way good or bad fortune increases or diminishes virtuous activity. But Aristotle's appeal to (a) might be taken to undermine my interpretation. Perhaps he means that great good fortune increases happiness *whether or not* one uses it well: a higher level of external goods "helps add adornment," and that by itself brings an increase in happiness. Similarly, he might be saying that because great misfortunes are painful they deprive us of happiness *whether or not* they impede virtuous activity. And if we read our passage in this way, then we might also take him to be assuming that other goods besides virtuous activity are components of happiness. The loss of friends would in itself be a loss of happiness because having friends is one component of our ultimate end.[50]

But we have already seen a great deal of evidence against this reading.

[50] This is how Irwin reads our passage. See "Permanent Happiness: Aristotle and Solon," pp. 93–5.

For example, Aristotle says that the end of human life is a good of the soul and not an external good (I.8 1098b12–20); happiness consists in virtuous activity alone, and the remaining goods bear some causal relation to this highest good (I.9 1099b25–8). Friends are external goods (IX.9 1169b9–10), and so the loss of a friend is not *in itself* a decrease in happiness. Such misfortunes diminish and destroy happiness indirectly, because they impede virtuous activity. Furthermore, nothing in the passage under discussion requires us to give up this way of reading Aristotle. For he does not say that the factors mentioned in (a) increase or diminish happiness *whether or not* they promote or interfere with virtuous activity. We can take his point to be that when great good fortunes occur to a virtuous person, two things happen: (a) his life is further adorned, and (b) this causes further virtuous activity. These are not two independent results, both of which constitute an increase in happiness. Rather, Aristotle is saying that when major good fortunes befall an excellent person, they make him shine all the more in the eyes of others, and his increased prominence and attractiveness give him greater opportunities for achieving great ends. So, good fortune leads to (a), which causes (b); the latter is what constitutes the increase in happiness, and the former is the cause of that increase. Similarly, when major misfortunes diminish and destroy happiness by (a) bringing pain and (b) impeding many activities, the loss of happiness is constituted by (b) and caused by (a).[51]

---

[51] Though Aristotle explicitly says that one cannot be blessed if one is struck by the misfortunes of Priam (I.10 1101a7–8; cf. I.9 1100a5–9), this should not be taken to mean that the pain Priam suffered, or his loss of external goods, constituted his loss of happiness. Since happiness is a certain kind of activity (1098a16–17, 1098b30–1099a3, 1099a29–31, 1100a14, 1153b10–11, 1176a33–b2, 1177a9–12), the diminution and loss of happiness is constituted by the diminution of that activity over a significant period of time. Priam, having lost his family and city, could not regularly engage in ethically virtuous activity during the final period of his life; political activity was of course out of the question. And the diminished level of activity caused by this loss of external goods and suffering constituted his lack of happiness. (The fact that he lost his happiness hardly implies that he was not happy at an earlier stage of his life. Aristotle can say that, on balance, his life was more desirable than that of a less virtuous person who suffered no serious misfortunes.) It should not be thought that pain by itself is incompatible with *eudaimonia*: the courageous soldier being struck by the blows of an enemy does not lose his happiness while the pain lasts, for this suffering does not necessarily impede his virtuous activity over a significant period of time. The victim on the rack does lack happiness (VII.13 1153b19–21), but this is not simply because he is in pain. Rather, Aristotle is assuming that pain induced by instruments of torture is causally connected to the deprivation of other goods needed for happiness (b17–19). Slaves were sometimes tortured to elicit testimony at trials; see Burnet, *The Ethics of Aristotle*, pp. 337–8; MacDowell, *The Law in Classical Athens*, pp. 245–7. Plato, at *Gorgias* 473b–c, lists the forms of torture that might be applied to someone accused of great injustice. Obviously, slaves and victims of punishment lack much of the equipment needed for happiness; the pain they suffer stems from their low standing in the community, and someone who experiences pain in this situation cannot be happy.

Notice that these two products of fortune—adornment and pain—have entered into my interpretation already. As I argued in the preceding section, Aristotle takes good birth, good children, and beauty to promote fine action because these attributes increase one's social influence; they add adornment to one's life and in so doing provide resources for virtuous activity. Furthermore, when he claims that the death of good friends is an even greater impediment to fine action than solitude, he is thinking of the pain that occurs when we mourn these losses. In this passage (I.8 1099a31–b6), and throughout the remainder of Book I, he equates happiness with virtuous activity, and treats other goods not as components of the ultimate end but as the equipment one needs to attain it. His discussion of fortune and his reference to the role of adornment and pain in human life do not give us any reason to read him differently.

4.22. AVOIDING MISERY

Being a good person is no guarantee that one will live well, since happiness consists in virtuous activity over a significant period of time, and this requires many resources. Nonetheless, a person of good character can take comfort in the following thought: "If activities are in control of life, as we have said, then no one who is blessed could become miserable. For he will never do things that are hateful and base" (I.10 1100b33–5). To be miserable (*athlios*) is to be in the opposite condition of the person who is *eudaimon*, and these two poles must not be mistaken for moods or feelings. Aristotle is not saying that a virtuous person will never be distressed by what happens to him or others; on the contrary, he calls attention to this possibility, as we have seen (I.10 1100b29; cf. b32). What he means is that no one who has and exercises the ethical virtues will sink to a condition that is the opposite of happiness. Some stage of his life may fail to be a good one, but even during that stage he will never be in the worst condition a human being can be in.

We should not be surprised to find Aristotle saying this, for it is a direct consequence of his theory, as we have been interpreting it. Happiness consists in just one type of good—virtuous activity—and so misery, the opposite of happiness, must consist in the opposite condition: the miserable person is someone who lacks any perfect virtue (ethical or intellectual) and who instead has and exercises the vices of character. Aristotle portrays the unhappy person as someone who typically loves such goods as physical pleasure, amusements, wealth, and power, and who treats others unjustly in his pursuit of these goods.[52] Unhappiness is activity in

[52] This is the picture that emerges from such passages as IX.4 1166b6–29, IX.8 1168b13–23, and X.6 1176b10–24.

accordance with the vices that one acquires when one takes these goods to be the best there are. So, in saying that the good person never becomes miserable, Aristotle is saying that he will never engage in that activity. "He will never do things that are hateful and base."

Suppose happiness consisted in a variety of goods, and not just in virtuous activity. Then misery, the opposite of happiness, would consist in the opposites of those goods. For example, if happiness consisted in a balance of virtuous activity, physical pleasure, power, and wealth, then a completely unhappy person would be impoverished, powerless, full of vice and pain, and devoid of pleasure. Now, those whose strongest desires are for amusements or power or wealth stand a decent chance of getting some of these goods to some degree. At any rate, Aristotle would have to admit that so long as one has some of the other goods (besides virtuous activity) in which happiness consists, one will, like the virtuous person who has suffered great misfortune, fall between the two extremes of happiness and misery.

That would raise a serious problem: When we compare a virtuous person suffering great misfortunes with a base person who enjoys many pleasures and honors, can we say that one of them is better off than the other? Which would it be? Aristotle could assign more weight to virtue than to external goods, and then, on the basis of this assignment, assert that the unfortunate good person is always better off than the evil person who attains some of the components of happiness. But that would be an *ad hoc* solution. What Aristotle does instead is to assign all goods other than virtuous activity and its opposite no direct weight at all in determining how close a person is to happiness or misery. For happiness consists solely in contemplation or moral activity; if one lacks the relevant virtues and instead does what is hateful and base, then one sinks to the lowest human condition, even if one acquires power and spends one's time amusing oneself. Since the goods that the evil person can have are not components of happiness, his success in acquiring them does not bring him a good life, and does not even put him in a condition between misery and happiness. He is worse off than a good person who has fallen into misfortune; so the virtuous but unfortunate individual never has reason to think that he might as well have been evil.

Of course, since we have not yet considered the function argument of I.7, we have not seen how Aristotle arrives at this reassuring conclusion. But if he can show that happiness consists in virtuous activity (theoretical or practical), and that other goods are resources for but not constituents of the ultimate end, then he is entitled to his conclusion. The claim that the good person will never become miserable is not a gratuitous assertion, a wishful thought that has no connection with any argument Aristotle has given. It rests on an attempt to show that happiness consists in just one type of good. If we mistakenly take him to be saying that, on the contrary, happiness is a composite of all intrinsic goods, then we will fail to understand his defense of the ethically virtuous life. We will not see why he thinks that when a person of outstanding character suffers grave misfortunes, he is still better off than the evil person who gets his way.

4.23. The Controlling Good

In the passage cited at the beginning of the previous section, Aristotle says: "If activities are in control of life, as we have said, then no one who is blessed could become miserable" (I.10 1100b33–4). We have discussed the consequent of this conditional, and now I would like to consider its antecedent. What does Aristotle mean when he says that "activities are in control of life"? He refers to an earlier passage, in which he says: "Human life needs these things [good fortune] in addition, but activities in accordance with virtue are in control of happiness, while opposite [activities are in control of its] opposite" (b9–11). But this does not help much, for we still want to know what he is trying to get at when he speaks of control (*kurios*). When he says that virtuous activities control happiness, he cannot mean simply that they are necessary conditions of happiness. For good fortune is necessary as well: *eudaimonia* is lost if one suffers the misfortunes of Priam. But even though other types of goods are *needed* for happiness, virtuous activities alone *control* it. What does that mean?

The term *kurios* suggests a position of authority and leadership, and so for one type of good to be *kurios* over one's life is for it to be the supreme guide one looks to as one leads one's life. I suggest, therefore, that Aristotle uses this term because he has a hierarchical conception of the various goods of human existence: all subordinate goods are to be regulated by the one supreme good that is their ultimate end. Although virtuous activities and external goods (friends, honor, wealth, and so on) are both necessary ingredients of any well-lived life, virtuous activity alone controls our lives and our happiness because our ultimate end consists in that type of good alone. We should recall that Aristotle calls politics the most controlling—the most *kurios*—discipline (I.2 1094a26–7), because it decides which branches of knowledge are needed and the extent to which they should be studied (1094a28–b2). By extension, the type of good that it establishes as the ultimate end is the controlling good. And so, when he says that virtuous activity is what controls life and happiness, he is not introducing a new and mysterious idea. Having initiated a search for an ultimate end, and having found it, he naturally calls the good that is that end the controlling good.

Of course, in Book I, he does not say which virtuous activity is the one that is most in control—for he leaves aside the question of which is most perfect. Eventually, he will adopt a theory in which contemplation is the controlling good of the perfectly happy life, and ethically virtuous activity is the controlling good of the political life. This is why he says, at the beginning of X.7, that the faculty by means of which we contemplate is what "seems by its nature to rule and guide" (1177a14–15). This faculty does not actually give commands or deliberate about how we should act; it is practical reason that does that. Nonetheless, it makes perfect sense for Aristotle to say that theoretical reason is the natural ruler of one's soul. The exercise of this capacity is the good that has authority or control over all other goods, since it is the ultimate end of the best life. And Aristotle alludes to theoretical wisdom's authoritative position in the human psyche at the end of Book VI. Speaking of practical wisdom, he says: "It does not have control (*kuria*) over theoretical wisdom or over the better part [of the soul], just as medicine does not [have control over] health. For it does not make use of it, but sees to it that it comes into being. So it gives commands for the sake of it, but not to it" (VI.13 1145a6–9). I take him to be thinking here of the proper relation among goods in the best life. In such a life, exercising theoretical wisdom is the ultimate end, and practical wisdom subordinates itself to this goal—just as the practice of medicine serves the end of health. Though practical wisdom plays the role of command-giver, it is not really the controlling faculty, since it looks to something other than its own exercise in order to make its decisions.

It is possible, however, to read a sinister meaning into Aristotle's statement: we might take him to be saying that those who have theoretical wisdom should not be responsive to the commands of those who lack it. In other words, rather than taking him to be talking about the proper organization of goods and faculties in a single life and individual, we could take him to be discussing the proper relation among people. He would be claiming that nonphilosophers cannot legitimately claim control over philosophers, since the latter devote themselves to exercising the highest human faculty. On this interpretation, Aristotle is saying that philosophers should simply carry on with their theoretical activity, come what may for other members of the community. Since there is no better activity than contemplation, there can be no reason to stop contemplating in order to help one's family or community.

But surely this reads more into our statement than is there, and needlessly destroys the unity of Aristotle's thought. He is serious in his advocacy of the ethical virtues, and does not mean to deny that these traits of character should be cultivated or exercised by philosophers. And he cannot believe that a philosopher who ignores his parents or community in order to maximize his own theoretical activity is treating them justly.

The *NE* should not be read as a call to familial irresponsibility or political subversion, and there is no good textual basis for doing so. As we have seen in Chapter 2, it is open to Aristotle to say that in certain circumstances the good of others takes precedence over one's own good. And so even though contemplation is the best activity one can engage in, its great worth does not provide a reason for ignoring the reasonable requests and commands of others. The best life is one in which theoretical wisdom is one's ruler and guide, but that does not mean that it is the only kind of ruler one should acknowledge. Since it is not necessarily right to do what is best for oneself, one should sometimes be ruled not by the best part of one's own soul, but by the commands of leaders—not just any leaders, but those who exercise political wisdom and act for the good of the whole community.

4.24. SUFFICIENT EQUIPMENT

I want to turn now to a passage in which Aristotle brings together a number of different elements in his discussion of happiness: (a) perfect virtuous activity, (b) external goods, and (c) a long stretch of time. He asks: "What then prevents us from saying that a happy person is someone who is active in accordance with perfect virtue, and who is sufficiently equipped with external goods, not for some chance period of time, but for a complete life?" (I.10 1101a14–16). The only thing that might prevent us, he says, is a worry about how this person will fare in the future: "Or should we add that he will continue to live thus and will die in a way that accords with our account?" (a16–17). But this worry need not concern us now. For clearly Aristotle sees no need to make any alteration in his wording, and is merely asking whether a further clause should be added. He sees no objection to characterizing the happy person in at least these terms: he is someone who is, for the whole of his life, active in accordance with perfect virtue, and who is sufficiently equipped with external goods.

If one misreads this remark, and ignores the way Aristotle has developed his arguments in Book I, one might take him to be saying here that happiness is a composite of many goods, including both virtuous activity and external goods. One might treat the function argument as picking out only one (albeit the most important) component of happiness; the remaining material in Book I would thus be a discussion of the various other components. And the formula embodied in the above passage could in this way be read as the most accurate and fullest statement of what happiness is. Happiness, it turns out, is not just virtuous activity—not even if lasts for a lifetime; it also includes a sufficient amount of all the other goods.[53]

It should be noted, however, that in the passage cited Aristotle merely says that a happy person must be sufficiently equipped with external goods. This means not that these goods are components of happiness, but merely that one must have them in order to be happy. The external goods are mentioned in Aristotle's account of what a happy person *needs*; we cannot infer from this that they are part of what happiness *is*. And we have seen a great deal of evidence to support the view that virtuous activity alone is equated with happiness. In I.2, Aristotle identifies the good with the end for the sake of which all other ends are desired; and, starting with the function argument, we are told that the good is perfect virtuous activity of the rational soul. When Aristotle tries to lend further support to this conclusion, he makes it clear that the end consists just in goods of the soul, and not in external goods (I.8 1098b18–20); the other goods found in a happy life are brought into his discussion not because they are good in themselves, but because they contribute to virtuous activity (I.8 1099a31–b6, I.9 1099b25–8). Since the ultimate end must be that for the sake of which all other goods are desirable, Aristotle wants to point out that in fact these external goods—friends, wealth, power, and so on— have the requisite causal relation to virtuous activity. No text in Book I says that happiness is inclusive of all intrinsic goods; the widespread assumption that this is Aristotle's view is not based on any such direct evidence, but is a misreading of a passage we will soon discuss. All of the other passages in Book I point the other way: far from being an all-inclusive composite, happiness consists in nothing but virtuous activity (either theoretical or practical).

I want to emphasize one further point: Aristotle does not merely say that to be happy one must have external goods; he says that one must

---

[53] Thus Cooper, "Aristotle on the Goods of Fortune." After citing 1101a14–16, he says, p. 174, that "the requirement of equipment with sufficient external goods is given an explicit place in the 'definition' [of happiness] itself." From this point on, Cooper speaks of external goods as "actual constituents of *eudaimonia*." Notice that this commits him to the view that, according to Aristotle, *every* type of good that one should have—even those that are not desired for themselves—is an "actual constituent" of happiness. For it is obvious that merely instrumental goods are among the ones we need if we are to have sufficient external resources for virtuous activity. In "Contemplation and Happiness: A Reconsideration," p. 199, Cooper cites I.7 1097b16–20 (a passage to be discussed in Chapter 5), and takes it to be saying that happiness "somehow already contain[s] whatever good you might think to supplement it with by adding to it." But if happiness contains *every* good one should have, including those that are desirable only on condition that they promote further goods, then it is hard to see how it can be that for the sake of which all *other* goods are pursued. Furthermore, if happiness has many purely instrumental goods among its constituents, then it no longer unequivocally counts as a good that is desirable in itself.

have a *sufficient* amount of these goods. But what makes a certain amount sufficient? Surely, if my reading of Book I is right, then Aristotle's answer is that we must have as many external goods as are needed to promote virtuous activity. If we ask, "Taking any external good in isolation from all other goods, what is the right amount (or the right range) to have?" Aristotle will reply that this question cannot be answered. To determine how many external goods we need, we must ask what we need them *for*, and so if we abstract from the use to which an external good is put and simply consider it in isolation, there is no saying how much of it would be worth having. But once we make reference to the activity for which we are equipping ourselves, then we have a workable standard: if more friends, for example, would increase the level of our virtuous activity, then we do not yet have enough friends; but of course we should not have so many that we impede our ability to engage in virtuous activity. Aristotle's search for an ultimate end is, from the start, an attempt to find a standard that will tell us "to what extent" (I.2 1094b1) subordinate ends should be pursued, and his reference to "sufficient equipment" in X.7 (1177a30) should remind us that he has not forgotten questions of quantity. Later, in Chapter 6, we will see how his doctrine of the mean is connected with this search for a quantitative measure.

CHAPTER FIVE

Inclusivism

5.1. INTRODUCTION

In this chapter, I consider several passages that apparently commit Aristotle to the view that happiness is a composite of many different types of good, and not merely virtuous activity. The principal text to be examined is one I have already cited several times:

> The self-sufficient we posit as that which when taken by itself makes life choiceworthy and in need of nothing. Such we think happiness to be. Furthermore, it is the most choiceworthy of all, without being counted in addition—being counted in addition it is obviously more choiceworthy [when taken] with the least of goods. For what is added on is an increase of goods, and of goods the greater is always more choiceworthy. (1097b14–20)

According to Ackrill and many others, Aristotle is saying here that happiness should not be identified with any single good such as ethical activity, or contemplation, or honor, or pleasure.[1] For any such good is just one among many, and no matter how desirable it may be, it is always less desirable than the combination of that good and some other. Contemplation, for example, is less desirable than the composite that consists in contemplation plus physical pleasure—assuming that both of them are good in themselves. And so the best good is the largest composite. Happiness, in other words, is inclusive of all the goods (or all the compossible goods) that are desirable in themselves.[2] That is why Aristotle says that it is self-sufficient: it makes life "choiceworthy and in need of nothing" because someone who has everything needs nothing. Accordingly, happiness is the most desirable good in a special way: it cannot be supple-

---

[1] Ackrill, "Aristotle on *Eudaimonia*." Others who adopt this reading include Hardie, "The Final Good in Aristotle's *Ethics*," p. 300 (see too *Aristotle's Ethical Theory*, pp. 22–3); Cooper, *RHGA*, p. 99; Nussbaum, *The Fragility of Goodness*, p. 297; Irwin's translation of the *NE*, s.v. "happiness," pp. 407–408; Gauthier and Jolif, *L'Éthique à Nicomaque*, notes to 1097b16–20, vol. 1, p. 53; Burnet, *The Ethics of Aristotle*, p. 33; Keyt, "Intellectualism in Aristotle," pp. 365–6; Urmson, *Aristotle's Ethics*, p. 15.

[2] At one point, Ackrill writes that "*[e]udaimonia* is the most desirable sort of life, the life that contains all intrinsically worthwhile activities" ("Aristotle on *Eudaimonia*," p. 21). But we should bear in mind that this is not the main issue. Even if a happy life "contains all intrinsically worthwhile activities," it does not follow that happiness itself is a composite of all such activities. Happiness can be just one type of good (virtuous activity), even if a happy life needs many other intrinsic goods in addition.

mented by ("counted in addition" to) other goods to make a more desirable whole, because it already is an all-inclusive composite.[3]

This way of reading our passage is unacceptable if the arguments of the preceding chapters are sound. According to the interpretation I have been defending, Aristotle equates happiness with perfect virtuous activity of the rational soul, and with that good alone. More precisely, perfect happiness consists in excellent theoretical activity, and secondary happiness consists in excellent practical activity. The two lives devoted to these two ends contain many other intrinsic goods besides virtuous activity, but none of these subordinate ends is itself a component of happiness. Human goals are thus arranged in a hierarchy, and happiness is identified not with the whole of that hierarchy but with its pinnacle.

Now, it would be incredible if Aristotle contradicted himself within I.7: he cannot be saying in the above passage that happiness is all-inclusive, and then go on to say in the function argument, and thereafter, that it is just one type of intrinsic good. Since I think he clearly does equate the good with virtuous activity alone, I infer that the commonly accepted reading of the above passage must be mistaken. Accordingly, in this chapter, I offer an alternative reading that brings it into line with the rest of the *NE*. I will try to show that the orthodox interpretation creates all sorts of difficulties for Aristotle that he can easily avoid if the above passage is read in the way I suggest. And I will argue that other passages that seem to support Ackrill's interpretation do not do so.

Someone might ask: "What is the *practical* difference between these two rival interpretations? You say that, according to Aristotle, happiness consists in virtuous activity alone. By contrast, others take him to believe that other goods besides this are components of happiness. But aren't you simply arguing about how Aristotle uses the word *eudaimonia*? Both sides to the dispute agree that a happy life will include many different types of intrinsically desirable goods. A happy person must engage in virtuous activity, have friends, enjoy pleasure, receive honor, and so on. What difference does it make whether Aristotle singles out one of these goods and identifies it with happiness, or uses the term *eudaimonia* to name the whole composite? In either case, we know what kind of life he is advocating."

My reply is that we are not just arguing about how Aristotle uses a certain word; the more important question is what he takes the best kind of human life to be. Whatever happiness turns out to be—whether it is a single kind of good or an all-inclusive composite—Aristotle holds that

[3] None of the authors cited in note 1 above says precisely which goods are components of happiness. This may seem a minor omission, but I will argue in 5.12 that there is a serious difficulty here.

the more happiness a life has, the better a life it is. For him, this is a tautology. And this does not mean that, if other things are equal, more happiness is better than less; rather, if one person has more happiness than another, then that by itself settles the issue of which person has the better life. And so, if some one kind of good is identified with happiness, then Aristotle is saying that if A has more of that one good than B, A thereby has the better life, even if B has more of certain other goods. If A contemplates more than B, for example, then A has a better life, even if B has more physical pleasure. By contrast, if happiness consists in a composite of many different types of goods, then these straightforward comparisons cannot be made. The best life will not be the one that has the greatest possible amount of some single good; instead, the best life will be the one that has the appropriate amount of each component of happiness. Too great an increase in certain goods—even the best of them—will be undesirable because it will require too great a decrease in other goods. Someone may be engaging in too much philosophical activity for his own good simply because that activity leaves too little time for the enjoyment of various physical pleasures.

Obviously, if my reading of X.7–8 is correct, then Aristotle does endorse a simple formula: those who have more contemplation thereby have more happiness, for contemplation *is* perfect happiness. Ackrill's reading of the above passage thus brings it into conflict with Aristotle's advocacy of the philosophical life. This is not a claim Ackrill would dispute, since he sees no way to reconcile the treatment of happiness in Book I with the treatment of happiness in Book X.[4] But if the arguments advanced in Chapter 4 are correct, then the price he must pay for his interpretation is higher than he realizes: his reading of the above passage brings it into conflict not only with Book X, but with the rest of Book I.

5.2. The *Reductio*

The passage we are considering can be divided into two components:

(a) The self-sufficient we posit as that which when taken by itself makes life choiceworthy and in need of nothing. Such we think happiness to be. (1097b14–16)
(b) Furthermore, it is the most choiceworthy of all, without being counted in addition—being counted in addition it is obviously more choiceworthy [when taken] with the least of goods. For what is added on is an increase of goods, and of goods the greater is always more choiceworthy. (1097b16–20)

---

[4] Ackrill, "Aristotle on *Eudaimonia*," p. 33: "Aristotle's theology and anthropology make it inevitable that his answer to the question about *eudaimonia* should be broken-backed."

We can call (a) the "self-sufficiency" passage and (b) the "most-choice-worthy" passage. I will propose a reading of (b) first, and then turn to (a).

Although I will criticize Ackrill's interpretation, I should point out that I am in partial agreement with him. Like him, I take (b) to be putting forward an argument in the form of a *reductio ad absurdum*. The conclusion to be reached is that happiness is "most choiceworthy of all," but only when this phrase is construed in a special way. To show this, Aristotle assumes the contrary: for the moment, let happiness be "most choice-worthy of all" in a weaker way, and see what follows from this assumption. On this weak reading, happiness is compared on a one-to-one basis with every other good, and in each case it is seen to be the more desirable of the two. So conceived, it is just one good among many—albeit the best of them. It is "most desirable, being counted in addition" to other goods, in the sense that its primacy *merely* amounts to its being better than any other good in an enumeration of them all.

Aristotle's response to this way of looking at happiness is to point out that it turns it into a good that can be improved upon: if happiness is merely one good among many, then even though it is the best of them, it would be better to have it plus something else than to have it alone. For more goods are better than fewer. According to this misconception of happiness, a person who is happy is not as well off as someone who has happiness and some further good. Our highest aim, according to this confused way of thinking, would not be happiness alone, but happiness plus all the other intrinsic goods. And that simply is not what anyone in his right mind wants to say about happiness. We take that good to be most desirable in a special way: it is not just *a* good, however valuable; rather it is the sort of good that cannot be improved upon by being counted in addition to other goods. If we say that someone has as much happiness as he can have, then we cannot go on to impugn his life by saying that although he may excel in that one respect, he might be doing even better if he had certain other goods in addition to happiness. Once you have the greatest amount of happiness, that settles the matter: there are no other goods you could have that would make your life even better.

Now, Ackrill and many others infer from this way of reading Aristotle's argument that he is identifying happiness not with any one good such as contemplation but with the composite of all intrinsic goods. But I see no evidence that Aristotle takes this further step, and I do not think that the above *reductio* commits him to it. Instead, I take him to be saying that virtuous activity of the rational soul has the very property that is attributed to happiness in this passage: if one has the greatest possible amount of this activity, one thereby has a life that cannot be improved upon. The addition of some other kind of good to virtuous activity does not yield a sum that is more desirable than virtuous activity alone; it does not produce more happiness, because happiness consists in virtuous activity alone. And supplementing happiness with something other than happiness does not bring more happiness.

I agree, then, that this passage puts constraints on any adequate conception of happiness: the good or goods with which happiness is identified must not be subject to improvement through combination with others. But I do not find Aristotle saying that this condition of adequacy can be met only by identifying happiness with the composite of all intrinsic goods. As we have seen, there is a great deal of evidence that he equates it with virtuous activity alone.

There is a rival reading, endorsed by Anthony Kenny, according to which the most-choiceworthy passage does not take the form of a *reductio*.[5] On the contrary, Kenny takes Aristotle to be insisting that happiness is most choiceworthy only in the limited sense that when it is compared with any other single good, it can be seen to be more desirable. But when we add other goods to happiness, the resulting bundle is better. Accordingly, Kenny takes Aristotle to be putting this constraint on the search for happiness: it must be the single most desirable good there is. So conceived, the good turns out to be contemplation, for virtuous activities are the best goods and contemplation is the single highest virtuous activity. But on Kenny's reading, Aristotle would gladly admit that this one end plus any other is better than contemplation alone: its improvability does not disqualify it from being happiness, because it is understood from the start that happiness is made more desirable by the addition of any further good.

Kenny's interpretation is as unacceptable as it is unorthodox. For if Aristotle is saying that we can achieve a good that is more desirable than happiness, then he must also deny that all of our actions should be undertaken for the sake of happiness. His position should be this: some actions should be performed for the sake of happiness, and others for the sake of those other goods that increase the desirability of happiness when they are added to it. And this is of course inconsistent with what Aristotle says. Happiness is the good (I.4 1095a14–20), and the good is that for the sake of which we do all that we do (I.2 1094a18–22). Accordingly, we cannot take the most-choiceworthy passage to be saying that happiness can be improved upon by being combined with other goods. Rather, the common interpretation must be correct: Aristotle is saying that happiness

[5] Kenny, "Happiness," p. 51. See too Kenny, *The Aristotelian Ethics*, pp. 204–205; Clark, *Aristotle's Man*, pp. 153–5. This reading can be found in some of the ancient commentaries, including those of Eustratius, Albertus Magnus, and Aquinas. See Gauthier and Jolif, *L'Éthique à Nicomaque*, notes to 1097b16–20; Kenny, *The Aristotelian Ethics*, pp. 204–205 n. 2.

is the most choiceworthy good in the special sense that it cannot be improved upon through combination with other goods. For if it could be improved upon, then it would become more choiceworthy when even the least of goods is added onto it. And that is absurd.

5.3. The Concept of Eudaimonia

Neither the self-sufficiency nor the most-choiceworthy passage tells us which good or goods happiness consists in. In this sense, we might say that they do not themselves present a definite *conception* of happiness; instead, they seem to be making remarks about the very *concept* of happiness.[6] Whichever good or goods happiness consists in, it should be recognized as a certain type of good: it makes life choiceworthy and in need of nothing; and it is most choiceworthy, without being counted in addition. Ackrill would of course agree with this way of looking at our passages. He takes Aristotle to be saying that the concept of happiness is the concept of an all-inclusive composite good; which goods it includes is a further question, not answered by our passages.

Ackrill lays great stress on this "conceptual" aspect of Aristotle's discussion:

> It is impossible to exaggerate the importance of this emphatic part of chapter 7 in connection with Aristotle's elucidation of the concept of *eudaimonia*. He is not running over rival popular views about what is desirable, nor is he yet working out his own account of the best life. He is explaining the logical force of the word *eudaimonia*. . . . The first point is that *eudaimonia* is inclusive of all intrinsic goods; and if that is so by definition, it is unintelligible to suggest that *eudaimonia* might be improved by addition.[7]

Although I agree that in I.7 Aristotle elucidates "the concept of *eudaimonia*" before presenting his own conception, I cannot accept the further point that it is true by definition that "*eudaimonia* is inclusive of all intrinsic goods." For if that were so, then how could Aristotle hold up the gods as paradigms of happiness? As we have seen, in X.8 he takes his audience to agree with him that the gods have the greatest amount of happiness (1178b8–9), and he then goes on to argue that their only activity is contemplation: they engage in no ethical activities, win no victories, enjoy no physical pleasures, and so on. And so, even though a great many intrinsic goods are absent from their lives, they are not only happy but supremely happy; for their lives contain all the contemplation a life can possibly have. Now, if it were a conceptual truth that happiness includes

---

[6] This terminology is borrowed from Rawls, *A Theory of Justice*, pp. 5–6.
[7] Ackrill, "Aristotle on *Eudaimonia*," pp. 21–2.

all intrinsic goods, then it should also be a conceptual truth that the happiest kind of life is one that contains all these goods. But Aristotle himself argues against this thesis. He counts as false a proposition that Ackrill takes him to accept as a matter of definition.

It might be thought that Ackrill's reading can be easily repaired: we can take the self-sufficiency and most-choiceworthy passages to be elucidating the concept of *human eudaimonia*, and say that *divine eudaimonia* is a different concept and follows a different logic. But I see no reason for thinking that Aristotle took this position. He wants to compare the happiness of gods and human beings; for they have more of it than we do. And such comparisons make no sense if we are not saying the same thing about gods and human beings when we call them both happy. He must be appealing to a single standard of comparison when he judges our lives inferior to divine life, and this requires a single concept of happiness. So, what the self-sufficiency and most-choiceworthy passages are saying about happiness must apply equally to the happiness of gods and human beings.[8]

Perhaps a different strategy is available to Ackrill's defenders: they might say that those who are happy (whether they are divine or human) must have all the intrinsic goods they are capable of having. The gods are happiest because they are capable of only one good, and they have it all the time; we are less happy because although we are capable of many goods, our possession of them is interrupted and limited. But again, I know of no textual support for this reading. And in any case, if Aristotle did look at happiness in this way, then how could he avoid the conclusion that slaves can be happy so long as they fully develop and exercise the limited capacities they have? He wants to say that they cannot flourish because they are incapable of exercising reason in accordance with the perfect virtues; even if they do the best they can, that is still not good enough. So he does not apply different standards to different types of beings; happiness is not doing the best one can for a creature of one's kind. Instead, he has an absolute standard that applies to all living beings, and those who lack the capacity for possessing certain goods simply cannot be happy. Now, if Ackrill were right about Aristotle's concept of

---

[8] As we will see in 5.11, Aristotle's definition of self-sufficiency at 1097b14–15 is applicable to the contemplative activity of gods and human beings: this one good by itself makes both divine and human life choiceworthy and in need of nothing. His preliminary remark about self-sufficiency at 1097b8–9 ("We mean by self-sufficient [what suffices] not for someone by himself, living a solitary life . . .") warns us not to assume that the self-sufficient good could be achieved by *human beings* who lived in isolation from one another. But we should not take this warning as a denial that divine happiness is a self-sufficient good in the sense defined at 1097b14–15, or that the gods achieve self-sufficiency. On divine self-sufficiency, see *De Caelo* I.9 279a18–22, *Met.* XIV.4 1091b15–19. For further discussion of Aristotle's preliminary remark at 1097b8–9, see notes 24 and 28 below.

happiness, then the *NE* should say that the closer one can come to possessing all the goods, the happier one is. And once this standard is used, then the unmoved movers have a great many handicaps: they cannot enjoy physical pleasure, they cannot have friends, and so on. Rather than confidently hold them up as paradigms of happiness, Aristotle would have to admit that theirs is a mixed lot: they have a great deal of the best good, but nothing else.

At this point in the argument, defenders of Ackrill might concede that their interpretation cannot be reconciled with what Aristotle says in X.7–8. But, they would say, these later chapters are an aberration: what Aristotle says here is undermined by his elucidation of the concept of happiness in Book I. He *ought* to admit either that the gods are handicapped or that comparative judgments about different kinds of beings cannot be made; his theology gets in the way of his practical philosophy, and prevents him from acknowledging the consequences of the conceptual point made in I.7.

But we have as yet found no good reason for thinking that X.7–8 is radically at odds with the rest of the *NE*. And in any case, Ackrill's reading of the self-sufficiency and most-choiceworthy passages is inconsistent with the identification of happiness with virtuous activity alone in Book I. Furthermore, it is a mistake to think that *NE* X.7–8 is the only text in which Aristotle draws conclusions about human life by looking to the way the gods live. In *Politics* VII.1, he says: "Let it be agreed among us that to each there belongs as much happiness as there belongs virtue and wisdom (*phronēsis*) and action in accordance with these. As evidence, we use god, who is happy and blessed not because of external goods but because of himself and a certain quality he has in his nature . . ." (1323b21–6). I take this to mean that god's lack of external goods is no loss of happiness, and that accordingly we should not measure human happiness by the number and kinds of external goods a person has. Happiness increases or diminishes when certain goods of the soul increase or diminish, and the level of external goods has at most an indirect effect on how happy we are. This position is quite close to the thesis of the *NE* that happiness consists in virtuous activity alone; and, like the *Politics*, the *NE* sees no reason why we should not look to the gods to help determine what happiness is. So the argument from divinity in X.7–8 does not reflect an antipolitical phase in Aristotle's thinking; even when he is most concerned with the training of politicians, he draws conclusions about human well-being by reflecting on divine happiness.

5.4. The Pinnacle

The most-choiceworthy passage cannot be understood in isolation from its context, and so it will be read differently by those who propose rival interpretations of *NE* I and X.7–8. This explains why my reading of it differs from Ackrill's. Unlike him, I take the early portions of Book I to be saying that the good, that is, happiness, is whatever lies at the top of a hierarchy of ends connected by the for-the-sake-of relation. It is the pinnacle of that hierarchy, not the combination of that pinnacle and any subordinate goods, even if those subordinate goods are desirable in themselves. It does not include honor, or pleasure, or virtue, for although these are perfect ends, they are desirable for the sake of something further. Happiness is that further thing—or those further things—for the sake of which we desire these subordinate ends. And as I have argued, Aristotle clearly recognizes the possibility that happiness might consist in a composite of ends. Recall the statement he makes in I.7: "And so, if there is some end of all actions, this would be the good achievable by action; but if there are many [it would be] these" (I.7 1097a22–4). In other words, happiness might be A:

$$A$$

$$M \quad N \quad O \quad \ldots$$

$$X \quad Y \quad Z \quad \ldots$$

or it might be the composite of A and however many other goods there are in the top row:

$$A \quad B \quad C \quad \ldots$$

$$M \quad N \quad O \quad \ldots$$

$$X \quad Y \quad Z \quad \ldots$$

This second possibility is eventually rejected, since the best life has just one ultimate end. But it is still alive when Aristotle points out the special way in which happiness is the most choiceworthy of goods.

This point about happiness applies to either schema. Take the first possibility: A alone is the ultimate end. Since all other goods are desirable for its sake, it follows that it is more desirable than any of the others (I.1 1094a14–16). But it would be a mistake to think that this is its only or most significant way of being most choiceworthy. It is not just a good that is better than every other; it is happiness, and so it cannot be made more choiceworthy by being counted in addition. That is, the complex of goods that consists in A plus something else is not better than A taken by itself. Happiness plus something that is not happiness is not more desirable than happiness alone.

But what if the second schema holds instead? Suppose each of the goods in the top row is more desirable than any good in a lower row; and suppose one of the goods in the top row (let it be A) is more desirable than any other single good in that row. According to Aristotle's point about the special choiceworthiness of happiness, it would be a conceptual mistake to identify happiness with A, even though it is more desirable than every other good taken singly. With what should happiness be identified, in this case? The passage just cited (1097a22–4) tells us that it would be the goods that jointly constitute the highest row of the hierarchy. It would not be the combination of all goods (or all intrinsic goods) in the hierarchy, for happiness is something that lies at the top. So if the second schema holds, happiness consists in the combination of A, B, C, and whatever else is desirable for itself and for the sake of nothing further. And this composite good is most choiceworthy in a special way: being happiness itself, it cannot be made more desirable by being combined with other goods that are desirable for the sake of one or more of its components.

I do not take this way of reading the most-choiceworthy passage to be immediately obvious; it cannot be made plausible unless my interpretation of many other passages in Books I and X can also be defended. What I hope to show is that the most-choiceworthy passage does not create a problem for my interpretation: once it is agreed that Aristotle proposes a hierarchy of ends and locates happiness at the top of that hierarchy, then the most-choiceworthy passage can be read accordingly. In order to understand it, we do not need to attribute to Aristotle the view that happiness is inclusive of all intrinsic goods. The most-choiceworthy passage does not in itself reject or accept that all-inclusive conception of happiness. For the conceptual point Aristotle is making here about happiness is compatible with the possibility that the second schema holds, and that all the intrinsic goods are located in the top row. In that case, happiness *would* be a composite of all goods desired for themselves. The more important point, however, is that the most-choiceworthy passage does not in itself commit Aristotle to this all-inclusive conception of happiness. It only commits him to saying that, whatever happiness turns out to be, it must be something that cannot become more desirable by being supplemented with further goods.

I have already pointed out one advantage of my interpretation: it shows that there is no conflict between the most-choiceworthy passage and Aristotle's thesis that happiness consists solely in virtuous activity. Another advantage should be noticed: since I do not take Aristotle to be making the conceptual point that happiness consists in all intrinsic goods, his theology can be seen to be perfectly compatible with his practical philosophy. He can say that the gods are perfectly happy even though there are many goods that are missing from their lives. For it is a misunderstanding of the concept of happiness to think that the absence of goods from a life is in itself a deficiency. Everything depends on what is missing: someone who has the good that perfect happiness consists in, and needs nothing further in order to sustain that good over time, would not improve his condition by acquiring the missing goods. For the concept of happiness is the concept of a good that is most choiceworthy in a special way: it cannot be improved by being supplemented with subordinate goods.

5.5. THE LEAST OF GOODS

I want next to call attention to a further feature of the most-choiceworthy passage. But before I do so, let us review some familiar ground. Recall Aristotle's words: "Furthermore, it is the most choiceworthy of all, without being counted in addition—being counted in addition it is obviously more choiceworthy [when taken] with the least of goods. For what is added on is an increase of goods, and of goods the greater is always more choiceworthy" (1097b16–20). Ackrill and I share the view that this argument takes the form of a *reductio*. The material following the dash completes a proposition Aristotle wants to reject: "[Happiness] is the most choiceworthy of all . . . being counted in addition." According to this hypothesis, happiness is just one good among many, albeit the best: it is to be included in an enumeration of the goods, and is better than every other when they are compared one by one. Aristotle rejects this because of its absurd consequence: "It is obviously more choiceworthy [when taken] with the least of goods." According to this consequence of the hypothesis, happiness is not as desirable as happiness taken together with even the least of goods. And that, Aristotle thinks, is absurd. Thus far, Ackrill and I are in agreement. We differ because he thinks that the only way to avoid the absurd consequence that happiness can be improved upon is to equate it with all intrinsic goods. And that is a further step that I do not think Aristotle takes.

The feature of the argument that I would now like to stress is this: Aristotle does not simply say that, according to the false hypothesis, happiness can be improved upon by being combined with *some* further good; he says that it can be made more choiceworthy by being supplemented with the *least* of goods. Presumably he thinks that the force of his argument is all the greater because the false hypothesis makes happiness improvable by even the least of goods. But precisely how does Aristotle think that the smallness of the added good increases the power of his argument? My answer to that question differs from Ackrill's; and this difference reflects a disagreement about the kind of life Aristotle advocates in Book I.

On my reading, Aristotle is saying that the smaller the good added to happiness, the more ridiculous it is to think that adding that good in-

creases the desirability of someone's life. It is of course always a confusion
to think that a person's life can be made better by adding to it some good
other than happiness, but the smaller the good the more blatant the confusion. Suppose, for example, someone says: "He possessed the good or
goods that happiness consists in, but even so he was missing one small
good: he never enjoyed the taste of a tangerine. So, happy as he was, he
would have had an even more desirable life had he had that sensation."
Aristotle's response to this statement would be that there is no way to
improve upon happiness except by having more of the good or goods that
happiness consists in. If the amount of happiness remains the same, the
absence of any other good does not make a life any less desirable. And
the smaller the good that is missing, the more obvious it is that its absence
makes no difference. Now, someone who thinks that happiness can be
improved upon by being combined with other goods cannot avoid the
conclusion that it can be improved upon by being combined with the least
of goods. And that makes the confusion all the more evident. For the
smaller a good is, the more implausible it is to say that its absence detracts
from the desirability of someone's life.

For Ackrill, however, the force of Aristotle's reference to "the least of
goods" derives from utterly different considerations. He takes Aristotle
to be saying that happiness cannot be identified with any single noncomposite good, no matter how choiceworthy it is. For there will be many
other goods besides this one, and even the least of them would add to the
desirability of that single noncomposite good. In effect, then, Ackrill
takes Aristotle to be saying: "See how easy it is to improve on any one
good—even the best of them! All we have to do is add another good to
it. And it doesn't matter how small that additional good is; it will still
constitute an improvement." The absurdity of identifying happiness with
a noncomposite good is made more striking by the fact that even the
smallest good will improve it.

This difference between our interpretations reflects the point made earlier (5.1) that we are not merely disagreeing about how Aristotle uses the
word *eudaimonia*. What is at issue is the kind of life the *NE* advocates.
Ackrill's reading commits Aristotle to the view that even the least of intrinsic goods deserves some place in our lives; happiness includes these
small goods, and so if any of them are absent, we are thereby less well
off. Even if a small good makes no contribution to virtuous activity, its
intrinsic desirability gives us a sufficient reason to make a place for it in
our lives. By contrast, as I read the *NE*, Aristotle is saying that happiness
increases or diminishes only to the extent that the level of our virtuous
activity is raised or lowered; for that is all that happiness consists in.
Other goods normally affect us in important ways, for human beings
cannot engage in virtuous activity for long unless they are sufficiently

equipped with external goods. But increases and decreases in these external goods do not in themselves constitute an increase or decrease in well-being. And there is no reason to regret the absence from our lives of goods we do not need for virtuous activity.

While we are on the topic of small goods, I should recall a passage discussed earlier (4.21): "Many things happen through fortune, differing in largeness or smallness; among good fortunes and the opposite class there are small things, and these obviously do not affect the scales of life. But when many great things turn out well, they will make life more blessed . . ." (I.10 1100b22–6). Minor good fortune does not make life more blessed—but this is something Aristotle should not say if Ackrill were correct. For suppose a small turn of luck brings us a minor good that is desirable for itself. On his interpretation, Aristotle should say that it brings us a small increase in happiness. That he does not say this is easily explained: what makes a stroke of luck minor is the fact that it brings no increase in the level of virtuous activity. And this interpretation is confirmed by the way the passage continues: "But when many great things turn out well, they will make life more blessed, for by their nature they help add adornment, and one's use of them turns out to be fine and excellent" (b25–8). Strokes of good luck do not increase happiness unless one uses them in the right way. And it is no surprise that Aristotle adopts this view. Since happiness consists solely in virtuous activity, no increase in external goods can make us better off unless it raises the level of such activity.

5.6. PLATO AGAINST EUDOXUS

I have not yet paid much attention to a premise Aristotle uses in the most-choiceworthy passage: he assumes that "of goods the greater is always more choiceworthy" (1097b19–20). And it might be thought that these words cannot be reconciled with the reading that I propose. For doesn't this "more-is-better" principle by itself commit Aristotle to saying that happiness is a composite of however many intrinsic goods there are? According to this way of thinking, happiness cannot be equated with contemplation (for example) if there are other intrinsic goods besides this activity; for when even the least of those other goods is added to contemplation, the conjunction is better than contemplation alone. Accordingly, the best possible good must be the largest possible composite of intrinsic goods.

In order to evaluate this argument against my reading, we must be careful to distinguish *the* good from something that is just *a* good. As many agree, Aristotle thinks that the former cannot be improved upon, whereas the latter can. The good for human beings is happiness, and happiness cannot be made more desirable by being combined with something else: this is precisely what the most-choiceworthy passage is telling us. By contrast, if something is merely *a* good, then it can be improved upon; that, I take it, is what Aristotle is getting at when he says, "of goods the greater is always more choiceworthy." This principle cannot be taken to mean that the good can be made better by being combined with some other good.

Once these points are accepted, it should become clear that the argument just given against my interpretation is question-begging. For that argument assumes that contemplation is merely *a* good, whereas I take Aristotle to be saying that contemplation—or, more generally, virtuous activity—is *the* good. Since happiness consists in this activity alone, no better good can be named: when something other than happiness is added to happiness, the addition makes no improvement. Since the good is whatever lies at the top of the hierarchy of ends—whether the top is simple or complex—goods occupying lower rows cannot be added to the pinnacle to form a superior composite.

We should at this point consider a text in X.2 that is sometimes cited in support of the orthodox reading of the most-choiceworthy passage.[9] In it, Aristotle records an argument used by Eudoxus to support the thesis that pleasure is the good. The argument is: "When it is added to any of the goods—for example, to just action or temperance—[pleasure] makes it more choiceworthy; but it is by itself that the good is increased" (1172b23–5). To this Aristotle immediately replies:

> This argument, at any rate, seems to show that it [pleasure] is among the goods, and no more a good than any other; for every good is more choiceworthy with another good than it is by itself. In fact, it is with precisely this sort of argument that Plato makes a destructive case that pleasure is not the good; for the pleasant life is more choiceworthy with wisdom than without, and if the mixture is better, pleasure is not the good; for the good does not become more choiceworthy by the addition of anything to it. It is obvious, then, that nothing else either would be the good if it comes to be more choiceworthy with [the addition of] any of the things that are good in themselves. What then is of this quality, and is something we partake of? For we are searching for what has this quality. (1172b26–35)

Here the different additive properties of *the* good and something that is merely *a* good are clearly distinguished. Pleasure is indeed a good, for when it is added to something that is desirable in itself but is not *the* good, the result is better. But pleasure is not *the* good, because it too can be

---

[9] Of those cited in note 1 above, see Burnet, Gauthier and Jolif, Keyt.

improved upon in this way. The good is something that does not have this improvability.

In other words, if A is just a good (not the good) and B is just a good (not the good), then A + B is more desirable than either A or B alone (assuming that both are good in themselves). But this fails to hold if either A or B is the good. Aristotle does not say here that the only way to find this unimprovable good is to combine all intrinsic goods into a composite. So this passage no more commits him to an all-inclusive conception of happiness than does the most-choiceworthy passage of I.7. Furthermore, if he were already committed to an all-inclusive conception, it would be odd for him to say that his search for the good is not yet complete. By contrast, if he identifies the good with the topmost end in the hierarchy, then it is quite true that he has not yet determined what occupies this position. He has identified happiness with activity in accordance with the most perfect virtue, but we have not yet been shown what that most perfect virtue is.

But, it might be asked, doesn't Aristotle's acceptance of Plato's argument indicate that he must reject any attempt to equate the good with contemplation? After all, in the dialogue to which Aristotle here appeals, Plato argues both that the good is not pleasure *and* that it is not some intellectual activity. In the *Philebus*, he asks us to imagine a life that contains pleasures but is totally lacking in intelligence, memory, knowledge, and true belief (21a–c); that, he says, can surely be improved upon. Similarly, we are asked to imagine a life that contains understanding, intelligence, knowledge, memory, and so on, but is totally lacking in pleasure (21d–e); that too can of course be improved upon. Plato's conclusion is that the best life for a human being must contain a mixture of pleasure and understanding;[10] neither of these two types of good is *the* good (22a–c). Now, since Aristotle clearly accepts Plato's argument against pleasure, mustn't he accept the other half of the argument as well? Doesn't his use of the *Philebus* against Eudoxus show that he did accept that other half? If so, he cannot believe that the good consists solely in one type of good: it cannot be contemplation alone, but must instead be a mixture of goods.

But it is perfectly possible for Aristotle to approve of Plato's argument against pleasure even though he does not think the same argument will work against theoretical activity. His position, as I understand it, is as follows: Plato is right to say that a mixed life—one that contains wisdom as well as pleasure—is better for a human being than either (a) a life that contains pleasure but no wisdom (or any other cognitive activity) or (b)

---

[10] Note that *Philebus* 33b6–9 (cf. 22c1–6) expresses doubts about whether the gods experience pleasure. The life that mixes pleasure and understanding is best for human, but not necessarily for divine, beings. Aristotle disagrees, as we will soon see.

a life that contains wisdom but no pleasure. Furthermore, he is right to reject the claim that pleasure is the good; for pleasure in whatever amount is always less choiceworthy than that amount of pleasure supplemented by some other intrinsic good. But none of this shows that we cannot find some single good (namely, contemplation) that can be equated with *the* good. For the good can consist in just one end even though the best life contains both that good and pleasure.

Notice that, according to Aristotle, even the unmoved mover has a mixed life, that is, a life that combines different types of good: the god not only contemplates, but takes pleasure in that unceasing activity.[11] And of course the lives of human beings contain a far more diverse mixture of goods. But the fact that good lives must be mixtures does not show that the ultimate end of any such life must itself be a mixture. Pleasure must play a role in any good life—even that of a god—because pleasure and worthwhile activity are necessarily connected: taking pleasure in an activity perfects it and increases the degree to which one engages in it (X.5 1175a30–36). And so, when pleasure is totally absent from a life (whether divine or human), the level of virtuous activity will be quite low. The absence of pleasures is regrettable not just because they are desirable in themselves, but because of the contribution they make to excellent activity. By contrast, Aristotle can give a different analysis of what is wrong with a life that contains pleasures but has no excellent activity of the reasoning part of the soul: such a life is defective not because the pleasures are not great enough, but because it fails to attain its ultimate end.

So read, Aristotle is saying that there is a certain asymmetry between pleasure and excellent intellectual activity, even though it is better to have both of these goods than to have either by itself. Pleasure becomes more choiceworthy with the addition of thought not because the amount of pleasure thereby rises, but precisely because that other good has been added. By contrast, exercising reason in an excellent way is a good that cannot be improved upon, so long as there is as much of it as is possible. Those who have as much of that good as is possible thereby have something that cannot be made more desirable by being combined with other goods. They necessarily lead mixed lives, since that amount of excellent thinking must be accompanied by pleasure. But the ultimate end for which they live is simply excellent thinking, and not a combination of that good and pleasure.

In any case, it would be a mistake to take Aristotle to have learned a certain lesson from the *Philebus* simply because we think it is the lesson he ought to have learned. Perhaps his reading of Plato should have taught

[11] See *NE* VII.14 1154b26, *Met.* XII.7 1072b24.

him that the good is not some intellectual activity; even so, we must rely principally on *NE* I and X.6–8 if we want to know what he does take the good to be. And what we find is abundant evidence that he equates happiness with virtuous activity; that is the one ultimate end of the best lives, even though all such lives necessarily contain pleasure as well. There is no evidence against this interpretation to be found in his approval of Plato's argument against Eudoxus.

5.7. *Topics* III.2

What is the best possible good for a human being? Ackrill takes Aristotle to be saying that it is a mistake to answer this question by naming any single noncomposite good (such as contemplation), no matter how desirable that good is. For there are many intrinsic goods, and the aggregate of them all is better than any single one or any smaller group. According to this way of thinking, if A and B are desirable in themselves, then A + B is a better good than either alone, regardless of what the relation between them is. Even if B is desirable in part for the sake of A, the sum is more choiceworthy than either component.

One weakness of Ackrill's interpretation is that it overlooks a passage from the *Topics* in which Aristotle records an objection to this unrestricted principle of aggregation. He says:

> A larger number of goods [is more choiceworthy] than a smaller, either without qualification, or when some are included in the others, the smaller number in the larger. [There is an] objection if one is for the sake of the other; for the two are not more choiceworthy than the one. For example, becoming healthy and health [are not more choiceworthy] than health, since we choose to become healthy for the sake of health. (III.2 117a16–21)[12]

The first sentence distinguishes between two more-is-better principles: the first unrestrictedly holds that having n goods is less choiceworthy than having $n + m$; the second says that this is true only when the larger bundle has (a) the very same goods as the first, and (b) more. It is clear that in the *NE* Aristotle employs only this more restricted principle. For in the most-choiceworthy passage of I.7 he says, "what is added on is an increase in goods" (1097b18–19), suggesting that the larger bundle has grown from the smaller through the addition of another good, however small.

But the second sentence records an objection to even this more cautious principle of aggregation. The objection is that when B is for the sake of

[12] This passage is cited by Keyt, "Intellectualism in Aristotle," pp. 365–6, in support of the orthodox reading of the most-choiceworthy passage.

A, then A + B is not more choiceworthy than A. Now, it may be tempting, in light of Aristotle's example, to take him to be saying that the principle of aggregation fails when B is not good in itself, but desirable only
for the sake of A. For it is plausible to take becoming healthy as a mere
means to health. But nothing in the text justifies such a restricted reading.
Aristotle's words clearly indicate that the objection applies more generally: whenever B is desirable for the sake of A, it may be denied that the
sum is more desirable than A.

To see the force of this objection, imagine that one party in a dialectical
debate proposes that virtuous activity is the most desirable good, and the
other party responds by saying that virtuous activity is not as desirable as
the combination of virtuous activity, virtue, and life,[13] for this is a larger
number of goods, and more goods are always better than fewer. The
proper move for the first party to make is to say that the principle of
aggregation must be restricted to cases in which the added goods in the
larger bundle are not desirable for the sake of the goods in the smaller
bundle. For, if someone has A, then he already has whatever other goods
are needed in order to possess A. To use Aristotle's example: if he is
healthy, then he has already become healthy; the latter is not a good he
lacks, and so it is not a good the addition of which would improve his
situation. And this has nothing to do with the question whether becoming healthy is desirable in itself. If someone exercises the virtues, then he
must be alive and he must have the virtues; having all three goods is not
an improvement over having the one for the sake of which the others are
desirable.

Now, Aristotle does not say, in the *Topics*, whether this is a good or a
bad objection. And in the *NE*, as we have seen, he invokes a principle of
aggregation when he argues that happiness is most choiceworthy in a
special way. One possible interpretation, therefore, is that he sees no
merit in the objection: he records it, but decides to reject it when he develops his own ethical theory. It should be obvious, however, that if my
reading of *NE* I is correct, then Aristotle does see some merit in the objection. For he identifies happiness with whatever lies at the top of the
hierarchy of ends, and insists that this pinnacle cannot be improved upon
by being combined with other goods. The ultimate end plus subordinate
ends is not more desirable than the ultimate end alone, and in adhering to
this thesis, Aristotle places a restriction on the use of aggregation to produce more desirable goods. He agrees that if A is a good (but not the
good) and B is a good (but not the good), then A + B is more choice-

---

[13] Both life and virtue are desirable in themselves: see *NE* IX.9 1170a19–21, *Rhet.* I.6
1362b26–7 (on life); and *NE* I.7 1097b2, VI.12 1144a1–3 (on virtue).

worthy than either by itself. But if A is *the* good, and B is desirable for the sake of A, then it is no longer true that A + B is better than A.

In effect, then, Aristotle uses the more-is-better principle in a way that is not vulnerable to the objection recorded in the *Topics*. It is not a device by means of which he constructs his own conception of happiness, as Ackrill thinks. Rather, it is merely a premise in an argument that warns against misconceiving the way in which happiness is the most choice-worthy good. This conceptual error would occur if we overlooked the place of happiness in the hierarchy of ends, and merely thought of it as the best of goods when compared one by one with every other. When this error is made, then the more-is-better principle applies to happiness no less than to other goods: happiness plus any other good will yield a more choiceworthy sum, because we are forgetting that the supplement-ing good is desirable for the sake of happiness. It is quite true, Aristotle agrees, that two goods are better than one—so long as the added good is not for the sake of the first. Ignoring this restriction obliterates the dis-tinction between *the* good and *a* good, and leads to the absurd result that happiness can be improved upon.

Perhaps no one in Aristotle's audience would make so gross an error as to overlook the fact that happiness is the good for the sake of which all others are desired. But the error might be more tempting for someone who thinks that there is no one ultimate end. His picture might be as follows:

$$A \quad B \quad C \quad \ldots$$
$$M \quad N \quad O \quad \ldots$$
$$X \quad Y \quad Z \quad \ldots$$

Suppose that (1) each good in the top row is desirable in itself and not desirable for the sake of anything else; (2) each good in that row is such that every good in lower rows is desirable for its sake (directly or indi-rectly); and (3) A is the most desirable good in the top row (and therefore in any row). Aristotle has said nothing to exclude such a possibility, and as we saw earlier he explicitly mentions it in I.7 (1097a22–4). Now, if A is the most choiceworthy good, and if every other good (save B, C, . . .) is desirable for the sake of A, then someone might think that there is good reason to equate happiness with A. True, there are a few goods that are not desirable for its sake. But on the other hand, it is the most desirable good, and so it is a better candidate for happiness than B, C, and so on. Aristotle's response to this line of thought is to point out that if we iden-tify happiness with A, then we have to admit—absurdly—that happiness can be improved upon. For there can be no legitimate objection to applying the more-is-better principle to the top row of goods: none is desirable for the sake of any other, and so A + B + C is more choiceworthy than A alone. So, if it should turn out that the pinnacle of the hierarchy consists in a row of goods, then happiness must be identified with that whole row, and not with the most desirable single good in it.

5.8. *RHETORIC* I.7

We should note that Aristotle also affirms a more-is-better principle in *Rhetoric* I.7:

> Since we call good that which is choiceworthy for its own sake and not for the sake of something else, and that at which all things aim, and that which one who has understanding and wisdom would choose, and that which is productive or protective, or that which such [goods] accompany, . . . and an end is what the other things are for the sake of, and a good for an individual is what has these [properties] in relation to him, it is necessary that more is a greater good than one or than less, if the one or the less are counted in addition. For it is an increase, and what is contained is increased. (1363b12–21)[14]

Here Aristotle is affirming the weaker of the two aggregative principles mentioned in the *Topics*: one set of goods is more desirable than a second if the first contains everything in the second and more. And he does not merely state this principle, but gives it an inductive defense: he enumerates the ways in which things are called good, and holds that in each case it is better to have more rather than less. The general principle holds because each of its instances holds: for example, it is better to have more intrinsic goods, better to have more of that at which all things aim, better to have more productive and protective goods, and so on.[15]

There is nothing here, I think, to upset the conclusions we have reached thus far. Aristotle is saying that however many instrumental goods it is desirable to have, it is better to have a larger number of them than a smaller. For example, a craftsman who has only some of the tools of his trade would be better off if he had all of them. Similarly, to lead one's life well, certain resources are needed, and having more of them is preferable to having fewer. Furthermore, if there are two goals at which all things aim, then it is better to have both of them than to have just one. The more-is-better principle does not in itself tell us how many ends or means there are; it merely says that once this question is settled, then it is better

[14] This too is cited by Keyt, "Intellectualism in Aristotle," p. 365–6, in support of the orthodox reading.

[15] I am relying on the fact that the more-is-better principle is introduced by a clause beginning "Since . . ." That clause must in some way support the principle, and I do not see how this can be the case unless we are being asked to generalize from many instances.

to have more rather than less. Accordingly, if it can be shown that there is just one ultimate end, the more-is-better principle will not be overthrown. For that principle merely tells us that however many goods occupy the top row of the hierarchy of ends, it is better to have all of them than to have some smaller number.

The more-is-better principle, in other words, plays a secondary role in Aristotle's thinking. The main question is what our end or ends should be; after that, we must determine how to equip ourselves to achieve that end or those ends. The principle that more is better then comes into play, and its counsel is obvious and unexciting. It does not tell us to lead our lives by simply constructing a list of goods and going after them all. We must instead decide which goods are for the sake of which others, and to answer this question we must determine what the ultimate end is. If that ultimate end is a composite, then we will want to have as many of its components as possible. But the more-is-better principle cannot by itself tell us whether the ultimate end is a single good or many.

5.9. *MAGNA MORALIA* I.2

The *Magna Moralia* also contains an observation that seems to have some connection with the most-choiceworthy passage of *NE* I.7:

> Next, how must one look for what is best? Is it to be done in such a way that it too is counted in addition? That is absurd. For what is best is a perfect end, and the perfect end, to speak without qualification, would seem to be nothing other than happiness; and we put together happiness out of many goods. And so if, in looking for what is best, you count it too in addition, it will be better than itself. For it is the best thing. For example, consider healthful things and health, and look for what is best of all of them. The best is health; but if this is best of all, it is best in comparison with itself, and an absurdity results. So presumably it is not in this way that one must look for what is best. (I.2 1184a14–25)[16]

Here, as in the *NE*, we are being warned against a confused way of thinking about the best of goods; somehow this confusion involves "counting in addition" (*synarithmoumenou*)—the same verb that occurs in the most-choiceworthy passage. Furthermore, we are told here that happiness is a

[16] Cooper, *RHGA*, p. 122, says of a closely related text in the *MM* (1184a34–8): "This passage . . . is . . . the key to the obscure remark in the *Nicomachean Ethics* (1097b16–17) . . . that *eudaimonia* is most choiceworthy of all things. . . . The point being made in both passages is the same: in *eudaimonia* one attains a number of good objects, which together meet all one's needs and desires. This is plainly to treat *eudaimonia* as what I have been calling an 'inclusive end.' " The *MM* is here used to show that in *NE* I Aristotle rules out the possibility that happiness consists in just one type of good. See too Urmson, *Aristotle's Ethics*, pp. 13–14.

composite of many goods. Putting these points together, it might be thought that this *MM* passage supports an all-inclusive reading of happiness in the *NE*; in other words, Aristotle is saying in I.7 that "we put together happiness out of many goods"—including the least of them.

Closer inspection, however, shows that the argument of the *MM* passage differs from the one Ackrill attributes to its parallel in the *NE*. Recall that, according to Ackrill, the most-choiceworthy passage is meant to show that happiness is a composite of goods. It allegedly reaches that conclusion through reflection on the fact that happiness is choiceworthy in a special way: it cannot be improved upon by being combined with other goods. By contrast, the above passage makes no attempt to show that happiness is a composite; it simply assumes that this is so. Then, on the basis of this assumption, it calls our attention to a mistake that must be avoided: in saying that happiness (that is, a certain composite of many goods) is the best of all goods, we must not include among the goods with which happiness is being favorably compared the very ones of which it is composed. For then we would be saying that happiness is better than itself. We are asked to consider, as an analogy, health and the healthy things that produce it: to say that health is best of *all* would be wrong if in enumerating the goods referred to by "all" we counted health itself. This argument does not and could not show by itself that health is a composite of many goods; rather it illustrates the idea that when we call something best, it should not show up among the goods with which it is being compared. The point is a trivial one, but when it is applied to goods that are composites, it becomes slightly more interesting: if the best of goods is happiness, and happiness is A + B + C . . . , then the supremacy of happiness cannot be taken to mean that it is better than A + B + C . . .

Ackrill takes the most-choiceworthy passage to be arguing not only that happiness is a composite of many goods, but that even the least of goods must be included in that composite. If *any* intrinsic good, no matter how small, can be included within happiness, then it should be. But notice that the *MM* does not say this: it says that "we put happiness together out of many goods," but does not argue or even claim that *all* goods (or all compossible goods), including the least of them, are part of this combination. Now, when we look at the remainder of the *MM*, we find that it equates happiness not with a combination of virtuous activity, physical pleasure, honor, friendship, and so on, but simply with the first of these goods: "Being happy and happiness consists in living well, and living well consists in living in accordance with the virtues" (I.4 1184b28–30).[17] This is perfectly consistent with the earlier statement that happiness is composed of many goods: what Aristotle means is that activity in ac-

---

[17] See too 1185a25–6: "happiness is the activity of complete virtue."

cordance with justice is one good of which happiness is composed, activity in accordance with generosity another, and so on. Happiness has as many parts as there are virtuous activities, and it is these parts that the *MM* is alluding to when it equates happiness with a large composite.[18] Nothing in this work suggests that the composite is larger than that, and extends to even the least of intrinsic goods. In fact, with the apparent exception of one text that we shall consider below, no passage in Aristotle's writings equates happiness with a composite that includes external goods as well as goods of the soul. His view is that happiness is virtuous activity, and nothing else.

Now, what significance should we attach to the fact that outside the *NE*, Aristotle equates happiness not with the exercise of some one virtue, but with the exercise of them all?[19] Is he advocating a different sort of life from the one I take him to be supporting in the *NE*? In order to defend an answer to this question, I would have to undertake a thorough investigation of all of Aristotle's practical treatises; and my aim here is simply to understand his conception of happiness in the *NE*. I submit, however, that we are not entitled to draw far-reaching conclusions from the fact that outside the *NE* Aristotle equates happiness with activity in accordance with *all* the virtues: this does not necessarily show that in those other works his conception of the best life for a human being differs from the one presented in the *NE*. For Aristotle can perfectly well say, even in the *NE* itself, that happiness does not consist solely in exercising one virtue. True, activity in accordance with theoretical wisdom is perfect happiness; but there is a secondary happiness too, and it consists in exercising the other perfect virtues. So if someone says that happiness consists only in contemplation, and means by this that contemplation is all there is to happiness—no one but the pure thinker can be happy—then Aristotle will strongly disagree. Similarly, he would protest against anyone who claimed that happiness consists in exercising all the virtues except for theoretical wisdom—if that claim means that exercising theoretical wisdom as well would make one no happier. So, if we construe the statement "happiness consists in exercising all the virtues" in the way I am suggesting, then the *NE* will agree.[20] And therefore, the mere fact that we find

[18] Contrast Cooper, *RHGA*, p. 122. He takes the *MM* to be saying that the components of happiness are the ones mentioned in *Rhet.* I.5 1360b14–23: good birth, friends, wealth, and so on. See too Urmson, *Aristotle's Ethics*, p. 118. I see no reason to attribute such an expansive list of components to the *MM*, and as we will see later in this section, even the *Rhetoric* does not commit Aristotle to the view that these goods are parts of happiness.

[19] See especially *EE* II.1 1219a34–9.

[20] I take this agreement to be expressed at *NE* VI.12 1144a1–6: theoretical wisdom "produces" happiness in the sense that, being a part of virtue, it "makes" the person who has it happy. The implication here is that other parts of virtue can also make a person happy. And this is consistent with my interpretation: just as contemplation is the ultimate end of the

this statement or its equivalents in other works does not show that these other treatises advocate a different way of life from the one defended in the *NE*. In fact, it is obvious and uncontroversial that both the *MM* and the *EE* take the best life to be philosophical;[21] and there is no evidence that the kind of philosophical life they defend is different from the one being discussed in *NE* X.7–8.

We should notice that in a certain way it is misleading and therefore objectionable to say that happiness consists in exercising every virtue, or every perfect virtue of the rational soul: it might seem to follow from such a statement that the unmoved mover is deficient, insofar as it exercises just one virtue. This implication is entirely avoided if one says that perfect happiness consists in exercising the most perfect virtue, and secondary happiness consists in exercising the other perfect virtues. This formulation makes it clear that the gods are perfectly happy even though they engage in no social activities; and it still allows Aristotle to hold that contemplation is not all there is to happiness.

I mentioned earlier an apparent exception to the assertion that Aristotle nowhere equates happiness with a composite of *all* intrinsic goods. The passage I have in mind occurs in the *Rhetoric*:

> Let happiness be good action together with virtue, or a self-sufficient life, or the most pleasant life that has security, or an abundance of possessions and bodily things together with the power to protect them and put them into action. For one or more of these things is pretty much what all agree happiness is. Now, if that is the sort of thing happiness is, it is necessary for its parts to be good birth, many friends, useful friends, wealth, good children, many children, a good old age; furthermore, the virtues of the body (for example, health, beauty, strength, size, competitive power), reputation, honor, good luck, virtue . . . (I.5 1360b14–23)[22]

Clearly, the parts of happiness include a great deal more than the various types of virtuous activities. But it should be equally obvious that this

---

philosophical life and makes one perfectly happy, so excellent practical activity is the ultimate end of the political life and makes one happy to a secondary degree. Contrast Cooper, *RHGA*, p. 112: he says that in this passage "Aristotle makes the ultimate end something complex, consisting of more than one type of activity." In n. 23 he adds: "it is clear that Aristotle here makes *eudaimonia* consist of the exercise of moral *and* intellectual excellences, and not the intellectual alone" (his emphasis). Nussbaum, *The Fragility of Goodness*, p. 375, reads this passage in the same way, and points out that, so interpreted, it is incompatible with X.7–8.

[21] *EE* VIII.3 1249a21–b25, *MM* I.34 1198b7–20. Aristotle's defense of the philosophical life in the *Protrepticus* is preserved in fragments. See Düring, *Aristotle's Protrepticus: An Attempt at Reconstruction*.

[22] This is the passage taken by Cooper to fill out the notion of the *MM* that happiness is a composite of many goods. See note 18 above.

diverse list is based upon the disjunctive analysis of happiness that has preceded it. Aristotle has not committed himself to *all* of the possibilities mentioned in this passage: he does not himself say that happiness is *both* "good action together with virtue" *and* "abundance of possessions and bodily things" and so on. He has merely listed a number of different alternatives, and it does not matter, for the purposes of his present discussion, which of them (or which group) is most defensible. So, the many external and bodily goods that are here said to be parts of happiness are not accepted as parts by everyone. If happiness is "good action together with virtue" *rather than* "abundance of possessions," then good birth, friends, children, and so on are not parts of happiness: they will have an important role to play in a happy life, but they will not be the goods in which happiness actually consists. And this is precisely the position that Aristotle himself adopts in all of his other practical works: the only types of goods with which happiness is identified are goods of the soul, that is, virtuous activities. This passage from the *Rhetoric* therefore provides no evidence against my reading of the most-choiceworthy passage or its distant parallel in the *MM*. In neither of these texts is Aristotle equating happiness with a composite of virtuous activities and other types of goods.

5.10. Variety

Aristotle says in I.7 that "of goods the greater is always more choiceworthy" (1097b19–20), and I have been trying to show that he is not thereby committed to an all-inclusive conception of happiness. He is not using the more-is-better principle to show that all intrinsic goods must be placed at the top of the hierarchy of ends. It plays a more limited role, by helping us see the special way in which happiness is the most choiceworthy good. And it thereby puts a constraint on conceptions of happiness: if you take happiness to be A, and if it can be shown that those who have A + B lead better lives—not because they thereby have more A, but simply because B has been added—then your candidate has been defeated. But Aristotle does not think his own candidate is vulnerable to this objection: contemplation—and, more generally, activity of the soul in accordance with perfect virtue—cannot be improved upon. When we add some other kind of good to such activity, we do not name a more choiceworthy whole, because every other kind of good is desirable for the sake of virtuous activity. When B is desirable for the sake of A, A + B is not more choiceworthy than A alone.

How else might the more-is-better principle be interpreted? One radically different alternative would be this: Aristotle thinks that the best life is the one that has the greatest amount of variety, and the more-is-better principle tells us to squeeze into our lives as many different types of good as possible. Once we have a certain type of good, we should not keep trying to have more and more of that same type; we should be content with fewer tokens of a type in order to leave time and energy for a greater number of types. Accordingly, the best human life will not be one that has the fullest amount of contemplation. Instead, we should cut short our philosophical activity in order to make room for the many other types of goods that life has to offer, including not only ethical activities but physical pleasures and any other activities that are good in themselves. Even the least of goods should be included in one's life, and more important activities should be curtailed to make room for it.

Obviously, this reading brings the most-choiceworthy passage into conflict with X.7–8, as I interpret those chapters. For I take Aristotle to be saying there that a decline in the level of contemplation is in itself a decline in the level of happiness; it cannot be compensated by any increase in the variety of other goods. And in any case such a reading cannot be reconciled with many statements found outside X.7–8 that equate happiness with just one type of good, namely, virtuous activity. If that is what happiness is, then a greater variety of other types of goods cannot constitute an increase in happiness.

We should also recognize that Aristotle explicitly rejects the policy of seeking greater variety. At the end of the discussion of pleasure in Book VII, he laments the fact that we are unable to enjoy just one activity, and characterizes our need for change as a defect that should be kept to a minimum:

> The same thing is not always pleasant, because our nature is not simple; rather, something further is present, and so we are perishable. As a result, if one thing acts, this is contrary to the nature of the other, but when they are equally balanced, what is done seems neither painful nor pleasant. If the nature of something should be simple, the same action will always be most pleasant. That is why the god always enjoys a single and simple pleasure. For there is activity not only of motion but also of motionlessness, and there is more pleasure in rest than in motion. Change in all things is sweet, according to the poet, because of a certain baseness; for just as the person who changes easily is base, so too is the nature that needs change. For it is not simple or decent. (VII.14 1154b20–31)

Human beings lack a simple nature—that is why we eventually perish, and that is why we cannot go on enjoying the same activity without needing a change. When we satisfy one element in our nature, we feel pleasure, but the presence of an opposing element within us eventually brings the pleasure to an end. And although this is an unavoidable feature of human nature, it is present in some more than others: the vicious are less stable in their enjoyments, and more quickly tire of their present activities. Obviously, the attitude Aristotle expresses in this passage is inconsistent with one reading of the more-is-better principle: he cannot be saying, in I.7, that we should seek variety by squeezing as many different types of intrinsic goods into our lives as we can. For in that case he would be telling us that however valuable an activity is, we should never go on enjoying it longer than we have to: such unnecessary prolongations would leave us with less time for less desirable kinds of goods. Whatever the more-is-better principle means, it cannot be saying that. On the contrary, Aristotle believes that the more we devote ourselves to some single most enjoyable activity, the more godlike we become.

Suppose we agree, then, that the more-is-better principle does not call for ever greater variety. An alternative suggestion would be this: Aristotle is saying that having a certain quantity of A and a certain quantity of B is better than merely having that same quantity of A. In other words, if two lives have the same amount of every other good but one has some further intrinsic good (however small) in addition, then we should judge the fuller life to be happier. So read, the more-is-better principle does not call for the curtailment of superior goods in order to make room for greater variety. And in this way I.7 can be brought into line with the thesis of X.7–8 that the more contemplation a life has the better a life it is, and with the thesis of VII.14 that the more we seek variety the greater a defect we express.

Even so, there is solid textual evidence against this reading. For Aristotle equates happiness with virtuous activity and no other kind of good; and he holds that happiness cannot be improved upon by being combined with other goods. As a result, he must say that if two lives have the same amount of virtuous activity, then they are equally happy, even if one has some further intrinsic good that the other lacks.[23]

---

[23] What if two lives have the same amount of contemplative activity, but one has more ethical activity than the other? For example, suppose A and B spend equal amounts of time on philosophy, but then B dies and A switches to a political career. Nothing prevents Aristotle from saying that A's life is more desirable, for it has as much perfect happiness as B's, and more secondary happiness. Similarly, he can say that if A needs less sleep than B, and therefore engages in more ethical activity than B, then A's life is happier, even if they contemplate to an equal degree. In these cases, A more fully approximates the unmoved mover than B, for contemplation is not the only human activity that bears some resemblance to divine thought. They have equal amounts of the human good that is most similar to the divine good, but one has a higher degree of the next-best approximation. Aristotle holds that one cannot do better for oneself than to have as much perfect happiness as one is capable of; and he holds that a limitless quantity of the highest good is something that cannot be improved upon. But this allows him to say that a limited quantity of this good can be improved upon by having that same limited quantity plus an approximation of that highest good. The good can be improved upon by having more of the same, or by having as much

I see no textual basis, therefore, for assigning the more-is-better principle a larger role than the one I have given it. Aristotle seeks to establish a hierarchy among ends, but he does not appeal to this principle to determine how many goods should go at the top; rather, he uses it to make a conceptual point that is compatible with either the view that happiness is some one end or the view that it is a compound of diverse ends. Whether it is one or many, it is most choiceworthy in a special way, and the more-is-better principle is invoked to show that it is absurd to think otherwise. I am not claiming, of course, that Aristotle *rejects* this principle—that is, that he takes it to be acceptable only as the consequence of a hypothesis (happiness is most choiceworthy in a mundane way) that turns out to be false. He agrees that however many goods are at the top of the hierarchy, more are better than fewer; and similarly, it is better to have more of the resources needed for happiness than to have fewer. This aggregative principle tells us how to live, but only when it is conjoined with a theory that determines what is desirable for the sake of what. It is wildly implausible to suggest that for Aristotle living well is simply a matter of making a list of intrinsic goods (down to the most trivial) and then going after them all, without establishing any order among them. What we should do, instead, is to understand the ultimate end, and pursue subordinate goods to the extent that they help us achieve that end as fully as possible. The more-is-better principle helps us clarify what is at issue in our search for the ultimate end. It explains why even the most choiceworthy candidate should be rejected if it is most choiceworthy in too weak a way; and (in X.2) it helps us see that pleasure is not the good. But once we recognize that happiness is virtuous activity, this principle diminishes in significance. It is better to have more of the goods that are in the top row than fewer, but this is trivial when we have learned that there is just one type of good in the top row. And once we see how the various subordinate ends—friendship, honor, wealth, and so on—contribute to virtuous activity, it becomes obvious that it is better to have as many of these goods as possible.

5.11. SELF-SUFFICIENCY AGAIN

I turn now to the lines that immediately precede the most-choiceworthy passage: "The self-sufficient we posit as that which when taken by itself makes life choiceworthy and in need of nothing. Such we think happiness

---

of the same together with an approximation. But it cannot be improved upon by the addition of some good other than virtuous activity.

to be" (I.7 1097b14–16).[24] Ackrill takes this to show that happiness is inclusive of all intrinsic goods. It makes life "in need of nothing" precisely because it is such a composite; once you have everything that is desirable in itself, there is nothing missing from your life that is worth having, and so you are in need of nothing. But I will argue that Aristotle's words are open to a different interpretation: his definition of self-sufficiency, on my reading, allows for the possibility that happiness consists in just one type of good. Since that is the conception of happiness he then goes on to defend—happiness consists solely in virtuous activity—Ackrill's reading of the self-sufficiency passage must be rejected.

We should remember that Aristotle appeals to self-sufficiency when he returns to the topic of happiness in Book X. In X.6, he recapitulates some of the main points of Book I, and points out that "happiness is not in need of anything, but is self-sufficient" (1176b5–6). And this concept plays an important role in his defense of the philosophical life, for he argues that "the self-sufficiency that has been mentioned is greatest in the case of theoretical [activity]" (1177a27–8). This suggests that there is a continuity in his treatment of this concept: the self-sufficiency of contemplation must have something to do with the way in which the self-sufficiency of happiness is defined in Book I. But Ackrill's interpretation does not explain what this connection is. For in X.7 contemplation is said to be most self-sufficient because this activity is less dependent than any other on external equipment (1177a30–b1). Of course, every human being needs certain goods simply in order to stay alive, and in this respect the philosopher is no different from the politician or anyone else (1177a28–9,

[24] This definition of self-sufficiency is preceded by the following: (a) Aristotle defends the point that happiness is the most perfect end (1097a34–b6); (b) he says that "the same thing appears to result from self-sufficiency; for the perfect good seems to be self-sufficient" (1097b6–8); and (c) he warns against a mistaken conception of self-sufficiency: "We mean by self-sufficient [what suffices] not for someone by himself, living a solitary life, but rather also for parents, children, a wife, and in general friends and citizens, since by nature human beings are political. But some limit must be set to these; for if one stretches this out to ancestors and descendants and friends of friends, it will go on indefinitely. But this must be investigated later" (b8–14). The point being made in (c) is that although happiness is a self-sufficient good, it should not be inferred that a happy human being is someone who has no relations with others, or whose well-being is unaffected by theirs. This does not mean that happiness must consist partly in friendship, or that their good is a component of mine; but it does mean that human beings cannot attain happiness in the absence of friends and other close relations. The self-sufficient good is sufficient for me and others, rather than for me living alone, in the sense that the human life made most desirable by the self-sufficient good is one lived with those others. (The problem of extending the number of relations without limit is addressed in I.11. Aristotle's claim is that after one dies, the happiness of the life one had is not affected by the fortunes of others. See 2.19.) But what is the point being made in (b)? I take Aristotle to be saying that we can infer from the self-sufficiency of happiness that it is topmost in the hierarchy of ends. For further discussion, see note 26 below.

1178b33–5). But if one enters the political realm, one will want to undertake major projects of great distinction, and in order to succeed, one will need large quantities of such external goods as friends, power, and wealth (X.8 1178a34–b3). By contrast, although the philosopher chooses to live with others (1178b5–7), and must attend to his physical needs (b33–5), he does not require large quantities of external and physical goods (1178a23–5, 1179a1–13), and can even contemplate in the absence of others (X.7 1177a32–b1). He is the most self-sufficient person, and this point of superiority reflects the fact that contemplation is the most self-sufficient good. But it is quite unclear what this argument has to do with self-sufficiency as Ackrill interprets it. For him, the self-sufficiency of a good is a matter of its being inclusive of all other intrinsic goods. And it is nonsense to say that contemplation includes all other goods, or that it is more inclusive than ethical activity.[25]

Let us return to our passage and take a closer look at Aristotle's words: "The self-sufficient we posit as that which when taken by itself makes life choiceworthy and in need of nothing. Such we think happiness to be" (I.7 1097b14–16). Two questions should be asked: First, what is it for a life to be "choiceworthy and in need of nothing"? Second, what is it for happiness, taken by itself (*monoumenon*), to make (*poiei*) a life have this property?

I suggest that if a life is choiceworthy and in need of nothing, then it is not merely a desirable life, but a life so desirable that it lacks nothing that could make it more so. For example, if a person has no friends, and the addition of this good would improve his life, then his life lacks or needs something. This is precisely what Aristotle says about the virtuous person in his treatment of friendship: "whatever is choiceworthy for him, this must belong to him, or he will be in need of it" (IX.9 1170b17–18). A life that is in need of nothing would therefore be one that had every type of good that is desirable for the person living it. But we should not

---

[25] It might be suggested that although the most self-sufficient good is the largest composite, contemplation is nonetheless the most self-sufficient among single goods, because when it is compared with each of the other single goods, it is the one that comes closest to making life choiceworthy and in need of nothing. In other words, a life that simply has contemplation (supported by the bare necessities of life) is more desirable than a life that simply has ethical activity (supported by the bare necessities). Notice that, according to this suggestion, the composite of contemplation and ethical activity would have to be more self-sufficient than either good taken by itself. (The most inclusive good is most self-sufficient, and so the more inclusive of two goods is the more self-sufficient.) But Aristotle's treatment of self-sufficiency in X.7 makes it clear that the composite of contemplation and ethical activity is *less* self-sufficient than contemplation alone. To have the composite, one needs other people; but we can contemplate even when we are by ourselves. I think it unlikely that Aristotle has two tests for self-sufficiency—one applying to composites (the larger the better), the other applying to noncomposites (the less support they need, the better).

infer from this fact alone that happiness itself is inclusive of all goods, or of all intrinsic goods. For we must not run together (a) the question of what a happy life or person must have and (b) the question of what happiness is. The fact that the answer to (a) will refer to all the goods it is desirable for a person to have does not commit Aristotle to giving an equally expansive answer to (b).

So, a life is "choiceworthy and in need of nothing" if it is maximally desirable. But what does it mean to say that happiness, taken by itself, makes a life have this property? It would be a mistake to say that Aristotle is asking us to perform this thought experiment:

> Consider just those goods in which happiness consists, and imagine that a person is missing all other goods. What would be the effect of that absence? Would this person still have a life that is maximally desirable? If so, then whatever happiness consists in—whether it is simple or complex—is what makes his life maximally desirable. Just as the sugar in our coffee makes it sweet (for even in the absence of the cream it is just as sweet), so happiness is whatever makes our lives happy even when the other goods are absent.

There is an obvious problem with this suggestion: if someone needs certain resources in order to stay alive or to live well, then the absence of those means would have disastrous consequences. To take the most obvious case: we cannot live without food, drink, shelter, and so on; and *a fortiori* we cannot have a maximally desirable life if these goods are absent. So, whatever Aristotle means when he says that happiness, taken *by itself*, makes a life maximally desirable, he cannot mean that lives need no support from other goods.

What he must mean is that the choiceworthiness of the best life is solely a function of the choiceworthiness of its ultimate end. So, when a life is maximally desirable—when it is "choiceworthy and in need of nothing"—that is because it has attained the greatest possible amount of the highest possible ultimate end, which of course is happiness. Other goods that are needed by someone leading a maximally desirable life have an important causal role to play, since they sustain the ultimate end; and therefore their absence will indirectly diminish a life's desirability, or destroy life altogether. But the fact that they play that causal role does not mean that the goodness of that life is a sum arrived at by adding the worth of these subordinate goods to the value of the ultimate end they promote. Only the topmost good in a hierarchy gives the best life the degree of desirability that it has, and so when the fullest amount of happiness is attained, that supreme good by itself makes a life maximally desirable.[26]

[26] The fact that happiness confers maximal desirability on a life is connected with the fact that it is the highest end in the hierarchy. If a life has any good B other than the one, A, in

Now, if this way of reading the self-sufficiency passage is correct, then Aristotle's definition of this concept certainly *allows* him to say that happiness is inclusive of all intrinsic goods. That is, he could say that although a maximally desirable life must contain contemplation, and virtuous activity in general, these goods do not by themselves account for that life's maximal desirability. A life that contained just these goods would be less desirable than one that contained them and even the least of other goods. But, although inclusivism is compatible with his definition of self-sufficiency, that definition does not by itself commit him to inclusivism. He can say that happiness consists in just one type of good—virtuous activity—if he believes that this alone confers maximal desirability on a life. And, according to my interpretation, this is precisely what he is saying. Happiness consists in this good alone, and so virtuous activity cannot be improved upon by being combined with other goods. Ackrill's interpretation of self-sufficiency simply assumes that when a life is maximally desirable, every intrinsic good, however small, is partly responsible for that fact. But nothing in the self-sufficiency passage itself supports such an assumption.

If my interpretation of Book I is correct—if happiness consists in virtuous activity alone—then Ackrill's reading of the self-sufficiency passage cannot be correct. And in any case, his understanding of self-sufficiency already has a drawback, in that it gives no explanation of why Aristotle connects the self-sufficiency of contemplation with the concept of self-sufficiency defined in I.7. If self-sufficiency is a matter of containing all the intrinsic goods, then contemplation cannot be self-sufficient, let alone most self-sufficient. Having rejected Ackrill's interpretation, let us try to see how self-sufficiency in I.7 and X.7–8 are related.

Self-sufficiency is an appropriate form of independence from other things. A self-sufficient political community, for example, is not dependent for its well-being on other such communities; and this is as it should be.[27] Similarly, a mark of the great value of happiness is its self-sufficiency, and this too is a certain kind of independence. Aristotle's definition of self-sufficiency brings out that independence in two different ways: *by itself* it makes life desirable and *in need of nothing*. First, it does not need to join forces with other goods to produce this effect; it does

---

which happiness consists, then that further good is desirable for the sake of happiness; therefore the aggregate of B and the maximal amount of A is not more desirable than the maximal amount of A by itself. This is why Aristotle says (1097b6–8) that the position of happiness in the hierarchy follows from its self-sufficiency. (See note 24 above.) Happiness "taken by itself makes life choiceworthy and in need of nothing" by being the ultimate end for which all other goods are pursued. It "makes" life maximally desirable not by supplying the material resources of a good life, but by providing it with its highest end.

[27] See *Pol.* I.2 1252b27–30, IV.4 1291a8–10, VII.4 1326b2–3.

this all by itself. Second, the effect it has on lives is to make them in need of nothing. Now, when we asked how the phrase "choiceworthy and in need of nothing" is to be understood, we found that the second component intensifies the first: happiness makes life maximally choiceworthy. And this way of reading the self-sufficiency passage is supported by the most-choiceworthy passage that immediately follows it. Clearly, Aristotle thinks it insufficient to say of happiness merely that it makes life *choiceworthy*; rather it makes life *most* choiceworthy, that is, in need of nothing.

But in light of what Aristotle says in X.6–8, it emerges that "in need of nothing" is being put to a further use. A good can make someone in need of nothing by giving him a certain kind of independence from other goods: the philosopher needs no tools or equipment to engage in an act of contemplation, and he can even contemplate in the absence of other people. Of course, Aristotle is under no illusion that the philosopher can do without food, health, and other resources. His point is that if we abstract from these common necessities, and ask which virtuous activity creates the least dependence on further equipment, the superiority of contemplation will be apparent. Happiness is a self-sufficient good because once you have it you need nothing further, and one way in which a good can leave you with further needs is by requiring additional resources beyond the ones that are necessary for life itself. Just as I.7 does not take the self-sufficiency of happiness to mean that it can exist in complete isolation from other goods, so X.7–8 treats the self-sufficiency of contemplation as a fact that is compatible with the need for biological resources. The most self-sufficient good is the one that creates the least need for additional equipment.[28]

---

[28] What Aristotle says about self-sufficiency in X.7–8 is a new development, for which his definition in I.7 has not adequately prepared us. Or, to put the same point more charitably, he has only given a partial explanation of the concept in I.7, and fills in the picture later. I am not denying that what he says about self-sufficiency in X.7–8 is to some extent a surprise. Even so, my interpretation allows us to see this late development as consistent with his earlier definition. We can see why he thinks that he is talking about a single concept. The situation would be quite different if we took the self-sufficiency of happiness to be a matter of its inclusiveness. Notice that if Aristotle's prefatory comments about self-sufficiency in I.7 (1097b8–11) are misconstrued, then his treatments of this concept in I.7 and X.7 are inconsistent. He says: "We mean by self-sufficient [what suffices] not for someone by himself, living a solitary life, but rather also for parents, children, a wife, and in general friends and citizens, since by nature human beings are political." This should not be taken to mean that self-sufficiency has nothing to do with how much one needs other people. For Aristotle does want to say that a person who needs more friends (and more external equipment in general) is less self-sufficient than someone who needs fewer friends (and fewer other goods); and god, of course, is the most self-sufficient being. What he is warning against is the false assumption that if we possess the good that is self-sufficient (that is, happiness), then we will have *no* need of others, and will lead a solitary life. This is the

We should bear in mind, of course, that Aristotle is not advocating a life in which we have no friends. The fact that we can contemplate even in their absence is not meant to support a proposal that we do so. His point is that a philosopher is less vulnerable than a politician to misfortune, and has more to salvage even if misfortune should strike. The fact that an act of contemplation requires no tools does not mean that happiness needs no further equipment, for happiness does not consist in a single act of contemplation; to live well, we must regularly engage in philosophical activity over a long period of time, and in order to do so we must be properly equipped with a certain level of wealth, friends, and so on. But since contemplative acts do not intrinsically involve wealth or power or friends, the level of equipment needed over the long run for the philosophical life is lower than the level required for the political life.[29]

When we look at self-sufficiency in the way I suggest, we can connect Aristotle's brief explanation of this concept in I.7 with the way in which he defends the philosophical life. A good can be self-sufficient without being an all-inclusive composite, so contemplation is not automatically disqualified. A self-sufficient good is one that makes a life maximally desirable (as I.7 says) and creates a minimal degree of dependency on external equipment (as X.7 adds). And Aristotle thinks contemplation meets both of these conditions.

5.12. Two Kinds of Intrinsic Goodness

This completes my attempt to offer an alternative to Ackrill's reading of the most-choiceworthy and self-sufficiency passages. I would now like to raise an obvious question about what his interpretation amounts to: if happiness consists in all the intrinsic goods, then precisely which goods are these? Ackrill himself provides no answer, nor do those who have accepted his reading. Of course, they hold that the main constituents are ethical and philosophical activities. And it is also clear that for Aristotle honor, pleasure, and friendship are desirable in themselves. But is this a complete list? How are we to tell whether a certain activity is something that Aristotle would take to be choiceworthy in itself? For example, does he think that writing poetry is desirable in itself? What about playing a

---

mistake made by the antifriend faction mentioned in IX.9 (1169b4–8). If there were someone who could achieve the good without friends (or other external equipment), then that person would be more self-sufficient than the rest of us. But it does not follow that we should try to achieve the good without friends. (Similarly, if someone could achieve the good without having to eat or drink, that person would be more self-sufficient than normal human beings. This implies that the smaller one's physical needs the better, but it would be crazy to infer that we should eat and drink less than we need to.)

[29] This paragraph summarizes ideas presented more fully in 3.6.

musical instrument, or singing in a dramatic chorus, or riding horses, or hunting? How does he think these questions are to be answered? (He cannot reply that these goods are too small to be included within happiness, for inclusivism takes the most-choiceworthy passage to mean that even the least of goods is to be included. And in any case, it would be fallacious to reason that since happiness is of great value, each of its parts must also be of great value.) If Aristotle's readers are given no help in this area, then they will have no way of telling whether they have all the intrinsic goods. To a certain extent, they won't know how they should lead their lives.

I will try to show that Aristotle has a broader and a narrower way of talking about intrinsic goods. In the broader sense, any craft activity—writing poetry, playing the lyre, baking cakes, building houses—is desirable in itself. And inclusivism is forced to the conclusion that happiness consists in all these goods, no less than in moral and philosophical activity. As a result, inclusivism commits Aristotle to a crazy doctrine: it would be madness to lead one's life by trying to engage in as many craft activities as possible.

Let us begin by recalling a point that Aristotle makes in I.5: wealth is distinguished from such goods as pleasure, honor, and virtue because they are loved for themselves, whereas it is not (1096a5–9). Similarly, he says in I.7 that honor, pleasure, and virtue are chosen both for themselves and for the sake of something else; the former property is what distinguishes them from wealth and other instruments (1097a25–b5). But, surprisingly, in VII.4 wealth is said to be choiceworthy in itself. There Aristotle distinguishes between two types of goods that produce pleasure—those that are necessary and those that are choiceworthy in themselves—and in the latter category he places victory, honor, and wealth (1147b23–31). He repeats the point a page later: wealth, profit, victory, and honor are by nature choiceworthy in themselves (1148a25–6, with b3). And in the *Rhetoric* he presents a list of goods, among which we find the following: "Justice, courage, temperance . . . and other such states; for they are virtues of the soul. Health, beauty, and such things; for they are virtues of the body, and are productive of many things. . . . Wealth; for it is a virtue of possession and productive of many things. A friend, and friendship; for a friend is both choiceworthy in himself and productive of many things . . ." (I.6 1362b12–20). This suggests that wealth is choiceworthy in itself; for Aristotle says that there is a reason for taking it to be good apart from the fact that it is useful ("productive of many things"): it is the virtue of possession. I take this to mean that to be wealthy is to be good at safeguarding one's assets. And Aristotle holds that any excellence is both choiceworthy in itself and productive of good results (*NE* VI.12 1144a1–3). The point, then, is that we see something good about the ability to manage sizable possessions, apart from the great usefulness such a skill has.[30]

But how can Aristotle say that wealth is choiceworthy in itself if he holds in *NE* I.7 that we desire it only for the sake of something else? I suggest that two different but compatible claims are being made: (a) In I.7, his point is that we would not choose wealth—that is, we would not pursue this end—unless we thought that being wealthy would bring us further goods. If wealth were somehow deprived of its usefulness and brought us no further good, we would not have sufficient reason to choose it. (b) But this does not mean that when we choose it, our only reason for doing so is its usefulness. It has a goodness apart from its usefulness as a means: there is more to be said in favor of having wealth than its role in bringing us other goods. But that intrinsic goodness would not by itself be enough to make us seek wealth were nothing further to come of it.

Another example may help to bring out the distinction more clearly. The process of baking a cake may be thought by some to be desirable in itself, apart from its usefulness as a way of bringing a cake into existence. Baking exercises certain skills, and is in itself a pleasant activity. But someone who has this attitude is by no means committed to saying that baking a cake is something that would be worth doing even if it never gave rise to any results—that is, even if it never produced a cake. There is something good about the activity, considered by itself, and so when we choose to engage in it, we do so both for its results and for itself. Still, we could also say that baking cakes is not an activity that is worth choosing just for itself, apart from its results. Our choice depends on the expected results, even though, when we make that choice in expectation of those results, the intrinsic value of the activity too may be taken into account.

So, we need not conclude that Aristotle is contradicting himself in the various things he says about wealth. He could mean that no one would seek it if it had no use, but that when it is sought, its use is not the only reason for thinking it good. Its instrumental role is a necessary condition of its being worth choosing, and so its intrinsic goodness does not suffice to make it worth choosing for itself.

But once it is recognized that, according to Aristotle, wealth is (in one way) good in itself, then many other items must be put in this same category. Consider any craft activity: in producing a building, or a poem, or a pair of shoes, one skillfully exercises one's reason, and there is some-

[30] Note too that in Plato's *Gorgias* wealth is not put in the same category as such neutral items as sitting, walking, running, sailing, sticks, and stones. See 467e4–468a2. The latter are neither good nor bad; but wealth—like health and wisdom—is counted as a good. This passage (467c–468d) does not say that wealth is good *in itself*, but at the same time it suggests that this good cannot be treated unequivocally as a mere means.

thing good about doing this apart from the fact that it brings into existence a valuable product. As the example of baking illustrates, the intrinsic goodness of any craft activity is not sufficient by itself to make such activity worth undertaking, apart from the results; yet such uses of reason are good not just because of what they produce but also because they are skillful uses of reason. It should be noticed that in *NE* I.6 Aristotle speaks of looking (*horan*) as an activity that is good in itself (1096b16–19); and he elaborates on this point in the opening lines of the *Metaphysics*: "All men by nature want to know," as is shown by our delight in sensing—especially in sight—apart from any use this has (I.1 980a21–7). Aristotle then discusses cognitive faculties that are superior to perception, and credits craftsmen with having achieved a low-level form of wisdom: though they may accomplish no more than those who have experience, they have an understanding of causes, which they can convey to others (981a12–b10). Since perception has an intrinsic goodness, apart from its use, simply because it makes us acquainted (*gnorizein*) with things and "reveals many differences" (980a26–7), the exercise of the crafts must have an even higher degree of intrinsic goodness. Of course, this does not mean that anyone would be right to engage in craft activity even if it brought forth no results. It means only that the results are not the only thing that makes such activity worth choosing.

What about the ends at which craftsmen aim—such products as houses, bridles, and poems? Are they too choiceworthy in themselves, broadly speaking? Aristotle must say that they are, because he accepts two principles: (a) a craftsman's activity is a lesser good than the object at which it is directed (*NE* I.1 1094a5–6); (b) whatever is choiceworthy in itself is a greater good than whatever is not (*Rhet.* I.7 1364a1–2). Notice too that in the *EE* he says, "Among all goods, those are ends that are choiceworthy for their own sake" (VIII.3 1248b18–19). Since each craft aims at an end, and ends are (broadly speaking) choiceworthy in themselves, it follows that houses, bridles, poems, and so on are desirable for their own sake. Of course, none of these products are worth choosing regardless of whether they bring us further goods: no one would choose to have a house if it provided no shelter or warmth. But Aristotle thinks there is something worthwhile about the products of crafts beyond the fact that they bring us further goods: they have an internal order that we rightly find attractive, and although this good feature is connected with their ability to produce good results, it is nonetheless an additional feature. For example, the tragedy produced by a skilled author will be made of beautifully arranged parts (*Poetics* 7, especially 1450b34–7), and this internal order is one of the features that makes it a good play; its goodness does not consist simply in its effect on the audience (the recognition of truths, the release of certain emotions). And Aristotle makes the same point about the well-made objects produced by other skilled craftsmen: they too exhibit a proper blend of elements, so that nothing can be added or taken away without destroying their excellent condition (*NE* II.6 1106b9–14). We should also note that the virtues of the body—health, beauty, strength, and so on—are good in themselves (*Rhet.* I.6 1362b14–15, I.7 1364a1, 4–5), and their goodness is said to be dependent on the fact that they are states of balance (*Physics* VII.3 246b3–8, *EE* I.8 1218a21–4). Life too is good in itself (*Rhet.* I.6 1362b26–7, *NE* IX.9 1170a19–20), since it is a kind of balance of physical conditions (see, for example, *De An.* III.13 435b13–16, *De Juv.* 4 469b6–20). As Aristotle says, "it is the nature of the good to be determinate" (*NE* IX.9 1170a20–21: *hōrismenon*).

Speaking broadly, then, a great many things are choiceworthy in themselves; that is, there is something good in them in addition to the fact that they promote further goods, and this internal goodness provides one reason for choosing them. When we choose a shield or a bridle or a house, we do so partly because of the further goods these objects bring us, but our belief that these objects are good is also based on our perception of a certain proportion in the relation between their parts. In this weak sense, they—like the reasoning activities that produced them—are good in themselves.

Of course, no one would take Aristotle to be saying that happiness consists in having all of *these* intrinsic goods, or in as many as we can acquire. It would be crazy to try to master every trade—to become a builder, a bridlemaker, a cook, a tragedian—and to acquire every type of well-crafted product—axes, lyres, ships, and so on. So, those who defend Ackrill's reading of Book I must say that happiness consists in all intrinsic goods *narrowly speaking*. Something is choiceworthy in itself, narrowly speaking, if we would rightly choose it whether it leads to further results or not. And of course, we would not choose to engage in craft activity if nothing resulted from it. No one would try to bake a cake if he thought no cake would ever result, and similarly, however good an ax may be, no one would make or buy it merely in order to have a well-crafted ax.

But it would be arbitrary for inclusivists to restrict happiness to intrinsic goods in this narrow sense. For what reason can they give for not engaging in as many different types of craft activity as possible? They must acknowledge that there is, according to Aristotle, something good about such activity apart from its results: it is excellent activity of the reasoning part of the soul. Seeing is desirable in itself because it is a low-level form of knowledge, and since craft activity is a higher form of cognition, it is, in itself, even more choiceworthy. Inclusivists tell us that happiness consists in having as many different types of intrinsic goods as we can, no matter how small those goods may be. So why not pursue as many craft activities as possible? Can they answer, "because these activities would not be choiceworthy if they produced no results"? Obviously not. It would be crazy to decide not to undertake a project simply on the grounds that it *would* not be worth doing *if* it led to nothing further. And in fact craft activities do normally lead to very good results. Since there is something to be said for these activities apart from their consequences, and even more to be said when these consequences are taken into account, the inclusivist can give no good reason why we should not become builders, bakers, bridlemakers, and so on.[31]

What Aristotle ought to be able to say is this: If one is already engaged in moral or intellectual activity on a regular basis, then there is no good reason for setting these activities aside and pursuing craft activity instead. For moral and intellectual activities are more desirable than craft activity, and it is a mistake to substitute a lesser good for a greater. True, any craft activity has something to be said for it, since it is an excellent activity of the rational soul. But it is a less desirable way of expressing one's reason than political or philosophical activity.

This, however, is not a argument that inclusivism can attribute to Aristotle. It takes him to be saying that happiness includes all the intrinsic goods, or all compossible intrinsic goods, no matter how small. And if this is what he believes, then he cannot exclude craft activity from happiness because it is not desirable enough.

5.13. ALL THE INTRINSIC GOODS

I have stressed above the importance of distinguishing two different claims that might be attributed to Aristotle:

(a) Happiness consists in all the intrinsic goods.
(b) A happy person possesses all the intrinsic goods.

Though I have tried to show why (a) should be rejected, it might nonetheless be suggested that Aristotle is in deep trouble because he accepts (b). For we have just seen that, broadly speaking, there are a great many intrinsic goods, and it would be insane to insist that a flourishing life must possess them all, or as many as possible. It might be suggested, on Aristotle's behalf, that a happy life must possess all the intrinsic goods *narrowly* speaking. That is a more manageable task. But we have seen in the

---

[31] By a different route, Irwin raises a similar problem in "Disunity in the Aristotelian Virtues." He asks whether Aristotle can demand practical wisdom of the good person without going further and demanding vast amounts of empirical information. That information would be available only to someone who had mastered many different crafts, and so the good person would have to become a jack-of-all-trades. See my "Comments on 'Disunity in the Aristotelian Virtues' " for one way in which Aristotle may be able to escape this difficulty.

preceding section that this appears to be an *ad hoc* maneuver: if baking exercises reasoning skills and is therefore good in itself, why should we avoid it merely because it is worth pursuing only on condition that it leads to something else?

A different way of rescuing Aristotle would be this: He can say that a happy person has all the intrinsic goods, so long as he is careful to individuate goods in a broad enough way. For example, he might count all tools as constituting a single type of good; and similarly he could say that all recreational activities form a single kind. In requiring that a happy person have all the goods, he need only mean that we must have at least one good from each type (properly individuated). So we must have some tools (such as slaves) but not every subtype (axes, mining equipment, lyres); and we must engage in recreational activity of some form, but not of every form. If goods are individuated in some such way, then a happy life will not be a mad pursuit of activities and possessions.[32]

One obvious problem with this suggestion is that it has no basis in the text. Aristotle is simply not concerned with the question of how to individuate goods. A further problem is that the project of individuating goods seems hopelessly arbitrary: how are we to determine whether goods constitute a single type or merely a subtype? For example, do excellent practical thinking and excellent theoretical thinking form a single type, so that if we engage in the former activity, there is no point in undertaking the latter too? Aristotle would of course reject that suggestion, but he would be in a weak position if he merely said that theoretical activity is a different type of reasoning from practical reasoning, and so we must engage in both. The reasoning of a craftsman is different from that of a politician, and the reasoning of one type of craftsman is different from that of another. To think that we can save Aristotle by making discriminations among types of goods is a delusion.[33]

---

[32] This corresponds to a suggestion made by Irwin, "Permanent Happiness: Aristotle and Solon," p. 99: "Aristotle probably believes that the complete good is composed of a sufficient number of tokens of some determinate types of each of the determinable types of good. . . . It may not matter which determinate type of activity I prefer, as long as I include the right number of tokens of the right determinable types."

[33] Similarly, Irwin says, ibid.: "These distinctions certainly raise difficulties of application. How are we to choose the right level of generality to identify the appropriate determinable types?" But he goes on to say that Aristotle cannot avoid such questions. "He must face them in any case once he defines happiness as a realization of human capacities in a complete life. If we count capacities perversely, the fulfillment of my capacities will be too difficult (if they are too specific) or too easy (if they are too generic)." I disagree, since I think that Aristotle does not define happiness as a realization of *all* human capacities. It is the realization of our capacity to engage in reasoning in accordance with perfect virtue. If, like Irwin, I took Aristotle to equate happiness with the realization of all human capacities, I would conclude that his conception of happiness is hopelessly flawed. In the absence of a theory of human well-being, I do not see how we could find the one right way to individuate

What I suggest is that we make a distinction between these two claims:

(b) A happy person possesses all the intrinsic goods.
(c) A happy person possesses all the intrinsic goods he needs.

It is (c) rather than (b) that we should attribute to Aristotle. Or, to put the point more generally, we should take him to be saying:

(d) A happy person possesses all the goods he needs.

Obviously, this will save him from the problem we have been discussing. He can say that certain goods (such as axes and baking) are simply not needed for a happy life, and he can back this up by appealing to his conception of what happiness is. The good consists in perfect virtuous activity practiced over the course of a lifetime, and human beings need other goods (tools, recreation, and so on) to the extent that these subordinate ends provide the resources for a happy life. We do not need to become bakers, because such activity would only take time away from the pursuits that constitute human well-being. We need not show that baking is an activity of the same type as ethical or philosophical activity in order to conclude that once we have the latter we can omit the former.

So, if we attribute (c) and (d) to Aristotle, rather than (b), we enable him to avoid an intractable problem. And in any case, once the distinction between these statements is made, it seems crazy to take him to accept (b) rather than its alternatives. Why would he reject (c) and insist on something stronger, namely, (b)? What sense would it make to say that a happy person should have *all* the goods, and not just the ones he needs? If we must have the additional goods in order to be happy, then why are they classified as goods we do not need?

I suggest that the only position that we can sensibly attribute to Aristotle is the one presented in (c) and (d). Now, against this suggestion, it might be argued that our hands are tied, since the text clearly indicates that it is (b), rather than (c) and (d), that Aristotle accepts. But what passage would force us to this conclusion? It might be thought that we can find such a text at the beginning of IX.9, where Aristotle raises the question whether a happy person needs friends, and considers the following argument for a negative reply: "They say that those who are blessed and self-sufficient have no need of friends. For the goods belong to them; so, being self-sufficient, they need nothing further. But a friend, being another self, provides the things one cannot get on one's own. Hence the saying: 'when the god gives well, why does one need friends?' " (1169b4–8). He immediately responds: "But it seems absurd to distribute all the

_____

human capacities. But Irwin is more sanguine: "further inquiry is needed to see if Aristotle can satisfy us on these questions" (p. 100).

goods to the happy person and not to give him friends, who seem to be the greatest of external goods" (b8–10). And this makes it look as though Aristotle himself wants "to distribute all the goods to the happy person." He does not say merely that flourishing individuals have all the goods they need, but, more strongly, that we should "distribute all the goods" to them, including friends.

But surely the context allows us to say that Aristotle is speaking elliptically here; he means to say, in other words, that we should not absurdly distribute to the happy person all the goods *he needs*, and yet fail to give him friends. For the opening sentence (1169b3–4) of this chapter raises the question whether the happy person *needs* friends, and Aristotle's positive reply throughout the rest of the chapter is an attempt to show that since happiness consists in virtuous activity, a happy person does *need* friends.[34] His argument does not take the form: "To be happy one must have all the intrinsic goods. Friends are intrinsic goods. So, to be happy one must have friends." Rather, his several arguments point to the various reasons why an ethically virtuous person needs to observe or join together with like-minded companions. So the context clearly allows us to take his principal assumption to be (c) or (d), rather than (b).[35]

Our conclusion is one that is simply stated in the self-sufficiency passage: happiness is a good so desirable that, when one has it, one leads a life that is choiceworthy and in need of nothing (I.7 1097b14–15). A perfectly happy person, therefore, will have all the goods he needs—not all the goods there are. And what a person needs is determined by a theory of what happiness consists in: perfect happiness consists in contemplation, moral activity being a close approximation to this, and our further needs are for the resources that support these pursuits. Aristotle does not construct a theory of happiness by making a list of all intrinsic goods and equating the good with that messy aggregate. Such a project would require a principle of individuation (how fine should our distinctions among goods be?) and would have to be supplemented by some ordering among goods (which are most worthwhile?). Instead, he notices (in I.1) that goods are hierarchically ordered, and asks (in I.2) what is located at the top of that hierarchy. Once he determines what happiness is, he has answered his question about which goods are most worthwhile, and has bypassed the problem of individuation.

[34] See 1169b13–16, 1169b22–8, 1170a2, 1170b17–18.

[35] Note too Aristotle's remark in VIII.10: "One is not a king if one is not self-sufficient and does not excel in all the goods. Such a person is in need of nothing further; therefore he would not look for benefits for himself, but rather for those who are ruled" (1160b3–6). The context supports taking "all the goods" to mean "all the goods he needs." In IV.3, Aristotle says that since the magnanimous person is self-sufficient, he has fine and unproductive possessions, rather than productive and advantageous ones (1125a11–12).

5.14. SAVING THE APPEARANCES

I said in 3.3 that Aristotle's moral philosophy will be misunderstood if we bring to it a certain preconception of intrinsic value. An intrinsic good, according to this preconception, is something that must receive more weight in decision making than merely instrumental values. But, if my reading of the *NE* is correct, Aristotle uses this notion in a different way. He is looking for a good that occupies the topmost position in the hierarchy of ends, and any such good must pass a certain test: it must be something that is desired for itself (I.2 1094a19). That is, it must be something we would choose and pursue whether or not it helps bring about further goods (I.6 1096b18–19, I.7 1097b2–5). This test by itself eliminates wealth and the equipment (buildings, tools, instruments) produced by the crafts; but it does not eliminate such ends as honor, pleasure, and virtue, for we would want them even if they did not result in anything further. Even so, Aristotle claims, we do not take these to be the most perfect ends: they are desirable for the sake of further goods, and it is among those further goods that we must look to find the most perfect end. And once we find that most perfect end, we have a way of telling how much we need the lesser goods. The nonperfect and less perfect ends are seen to be the resources we need for achieving the best possible life. Whether these resources are good in themselves or not, we should try to have as many of them as we need in order to achieve the ultimate end; larger quantities are superfluous at best, impediments at worst.

I have also tried to show that Aristotle has a second way of thinking about intrinsic goods: he counts anything that is balanced and harmonious as being good in itself, and this leads to the conclusion that any virtue, however lowly, or any product of skill, is desirable in itself. But this broad conception of intrinsic goods plays no important role in his ethical theory. The crucial question for him is whether a good would be desirable even if it led to nothing else; and most of the goods that are desirable in themselves, broadly speaking, fail this test.

However, a problem for my interpretation may still be raised. I have said that the degree to which a subordinate intrinsic good should be pursued is the degree to which it promotes the ultimate end. But, it may be objected, this commits Aristotle to saying that if some subordinate good were to make *no* contribution whatsoever to happiness, then we should not choose or pursue it. How can that be if, by hypothesis, the subordinate good in question is choiceworthy in itself? For example, when Aristotle says that we choose honor, pleasure, and virtue for themselves, he means that we would choose them whether they lead to anything else or not. And presumably he approves of this attitude. But on my reading, he must say that we would be *wrong* to choose them if they did nothing to promote virtuous activity.[36]

In order to reply to this objection, I must say more about the way Aristotle defends his conception of happiness. He begins by taking it for granted that many different types of things are good: "every craft and inquiry, and similarly every action and choice, seems to aim at some good" (I.1 1094a1–2). We soon see that some of these goods are subordinate to others, and we are launched upon a search for something—*the* good—for the sake of which all of these lesser ends are pursued. Now, this puts an important constraint on any successful candidate for the good: it must be something that is promoted, in some way or other, by all the other human activities that we initially assumed to be good. And Aristotle is eager to show that his own candidate for happiness—activity of the soul in accordance with perfect virtue—passes this test. For after he arrives at this conception of happiness by means of the function argument, he seeks to confirm it in part by pointing out that other goods do provide the resources we need for engaging in ethical activity. Such goods as wealth, power, friends, beauty, and good birth all contribute in some way to virtuous activity (I.8 1099a31–b6); and although he claims in X.7–8 that we need some of these resources to a lesser degree if we lead a philosophical life, he continues to believe that the subordinate goods have some role to play in sustaining theoretical activity. The philosopher lives with others and exercises the ethical virtues, and so he needs the moderate resources that will sustain such a life. So, either of the two ultimate ends—practical or theoretical—provides us with a way of organizing the goods that we initially took for granted when we started our investigation of happiness. If these ends failed to meet this condition, then we would have strong reason to doubt that we had really discovered what happiness is. For how can something be the good if its acceptance as our ultimate end requires us to deny the goodness of many things that are widely assumed to be desirable? In our search for happiness, as in any other investigation, we must start with what appears to be the case, and preserve as many of the common opinions (*endoxa*) as we can (VII.1 1145b2–7).[37]

With this in mind, let us return to the objection expressed above. On my reading, a subordinate end should be pursued only to the extent that it promotes happiness, even if that subordinate end is desirable in itself. But, the objection runs, this means that if that intrinsic good contributed nothing to happiness, then it would not be worth pursuing. And this is incompatible with calling it a good that is desirable in itself.

[36] I am grateful to Jennifer Whiting for raising this problem.

[37] For further discussion of Aristotle's philosophical procedure, see Barnes, "Aristotle and the Methods of Ethics," pp. 498–502; Irwin, "Aristotle's Methods of Ethics."

But as we have just seen, Aristotle's methodology ensures that nearly all the goods we initially assume to be desirable in themselves *will* have some role to play in a happy life. They must either be happiness itself or be desirable for the sake of happiness; and if a small number of them fit nowhere in this hierarchical scheme, then we must conclude that they only *appeared* to be good, but were not really so. And so we cannot say, of the whole group of goods that turn out to be subordinate to happiness, that we would be wrong to pursue them if they did not contribute to the good we take to be the ultimate end. For if they did not contribute to that good, it would not be the ultimate end. On the other hand, there is nothing wrong with saying, of certain goods that we initially assumed to be desirable in themselves, that we would be wrong to pursue them if they made no contribution to the good we take to be the ultimate end. For if they were to make no such contribution, they would not be goods. When we classify something as choiceworthy in itself, prior to an investigation of happiness, we are not thereby assured that our assumption can be vindicated; we can be sure, however, that a great many of these initial appearances will prove correct. For theory proceeds by vindicating as many of these appearances as possible.

Of course, if one has not been trained in the proper way, one may come to ethical theory with too small a stock of justifiable assumptions (I.4 1095b4–6). One might wrongly take pleasure in certain activities, and reject Aristotle's conception of the ultimate end because one's pleasures are allowed no place, or too small a place, in any life organized around virtuous activity. Aristotle does not think he can bring everyone to accept his conception of happiness, but he does not propose universal effectiveness as a proper aim for ethical theory. So long as his audience has a sufficient stock of true assumptions about which things are good, he believes that he can present arguments in favor of organizing those goods into a certain pattern. In order to recognize that pattern, we must distinguish between goods we desire for themselves and those we do not; for the highest good must be drawn from the first of these categories. And once we find what we are looking for, and assure ourselves that this ultimate end allows us to vindicate most, if not all, of our original assumptions, then we pursue subordinate goods to the extent that they contribute to happiness. There is no reason to assume a priori that intrinsic goods must play a more important role in Aristotle's theory than this.

CHAPTER SIX

Function, Virtue, and Mean

6.1. LOOKING FOR PECULIARITY

In this chapter I discuss the "function argument" of I.7 and its connection with the rest of the *NE*. In this passage Aristotle suggests that the human good consists in fulfilling our special function (*ergon*),[1] and equates this with "activity of soul in accordance with virtue, and if there are more than one virtue, in accordance with the best and most perfect" (1098a16–18). I think that the argument by which he arrives at this conclusion is the foundation for his defense of both the philosophical and the political lives. But precisely what is that argument? How do the considerations put forward in this passage provide reasons for leading either of these lives? That is the question I will try to answer here.

My treatment of the function argument will take us beyond Book I of the *NE* to a discussion of the ethical virtues and the doctrine of the mean. For I believe that the function argument is only one part of Aristotle's defense of the two lives, and that it cannot be properly evaluated unless we consider it in this larger context. There is a single complex argument that stretches over the whole of the *NE*, and to see what it is we must take into account the connection between the function argument and Aristotle's conception of the ethical virtues. As we will see, his thesis that the ethical virtues are intermediate states plays a crucial role in that argument.[2]

Aristotle begins with the idea that since the good in specialized spheres (for example, the good of a flutist or of a sculptor) consists in fulfilling a

---

[1] "Task" is the translation advocated by Adkins in "The Connection between Aristotle's *Ethics* and *Politics*," pp. 34–7.

[2] For critical discussion of the function argument, see Glassen, "A Fallacy in Aristotle's Argument about the Good"; Suits, "Aristotle on the Function of Man: Fallacies, Heresies, and Other Entertainments"; Siegler, "Reason, Happiness, and Goodness"; Wilkes, "The Good Man and the Good for Man in Aristotle's Ethics" (hereafter: "The Good Man"). I do not think these treatments give enough attention to the way the function argument fits into the larger context of the *NE*. More sympathetic discussion can be found in Clark, *Aristotle's Man*, pp. 14–27; Nussbaum, *Aristotle's De Motu Animalium*, pp. 100–106; and Korsgaard, "Aristotle on Function and Virtue"; but my interpretation of the function argument, and its role in Aristotle's theory, differs from theirs. I do not claim that when the function argument is supplemented by all of the further material found in the *NE*, the result is a convincing argument for Aristotle's conclusion that the best life is one devoted to the ultimate end of activity of the rational soul in accordance with perfect virtue. In 6.10, I say why I think this conclusion should be resisted.

certain function, the same should hold true of human beings in general: if we have a function, then our good consists in doing whatever it is our function to do (1097b24–8). And he proceeds to argue, again by analogy, that we do have a function: Can it be that there is a function for every craftsman, but none for human beings? Can each of our organs have a function, while we, as human beings, have none (b28–33)? The question then becomes what our function is, and Aristotle tries to supply one by a process of elimination. Our function cannot simply be to live, since that is something we have in common with plants, and we are looking for what is *idion* (b34)—that is, what is peculiar—to human beings. So our good (that is, our ultimate end) cannot consist in keeping ourselves alive through nourishment and growth (1097b34–1098a1). For the same reason, it cannot consist in sensation: this is something we have in common with the horse, the ox, and every animal (1098a1–3). And then Aristotle comes to the beginning of his own answer: our function consists in a "certain active (*praktikē*)[3] life of the [part] having reason" (a3–4). He elaborates on this initial answer in ways that we will have to examine, but before we do so, a question must be raised about his claim that he is looking for what is peculiar (*idion*) to human beings.

As we have seen, Aristotle eventually wants to conclude that our function consists in "activity of soul in accordance with virtue, and if there are more than one virtue, in accordance with the best and most perfect" (1098a16–18). I side with those who see these last words as an allusion to theoretical wisdom, a reading I have defended in Chapter 4 (see especially 4.14–15). So, I take Aristotle to be saying that our function consists in contemplation (or more fully, that contemplation perfectly fulfills our function, and ethical activity fulfills our function to a secondary degree). But an objection to this reading can be raised, since Aristotle clearly takes the function of human beings to be something peculiar to us. The gods contemplate, and so when we engage in this activity, we do something that is shared by another kind of living thing. How then can Aristotle be saying that it is our function to contemplate?[4]

---

[3] I follow Stewart, *Notes on the Nicomachean Ethics of Aristotle*, vol. 1, p. 99, in taking *praktikē* at 1098a3 to be broad enough in meaning to include theoretical activity as well as practical activity in the narrow sense. See *Pol.* VII.3 1325b16–21 for this broad sense. This is the interpretation adopted in the commentaries of Burnet and Gauthier and Jolif. See too Hardie, *Aristotle's Ethical Theory*, p. 25. For a contrasting view, see Joachim, *Aristotle, The Nicomachean Ethics*, p. 50, notes on 1098a3; he takes Aristotle to be saying that contemplation is not part of the *human* function, since it is not an activity we engage in by virtue of being human. I discuss this view further in note 6 below. Joachim is followed by Irwin, "The Metaphysical and Psychological Basis of Aristotle's Ethics," p. 53 n. 21. The view of Joachim and Irwin is untenable if the best and most perfect virtue, alluded to at 1098a17–18, is theoretical wisdom.

[4] Ackrill notices the difficulty in "Aristotle on *Eudaimonia*": "In fact, practical reason, so far from being in any way less distinctive of man than theoretical, is really more so; for man

One way out of the difficulty would be to say that "the best and most perfect virtue" is not an allusion to theoretical wisdom, but refers instead to the composite of all the virtues of the soul. In that case, Aristotle would be saying that the human good, that is, the ultimate end of human life, consists in a composite of virtuous activities of the soul. It consists in exercising justice, courage, practical wisdom, and so on. We have seen in Chapter 4 reasons for resisting the suggestion that "the best and most perfect virtue" should be read in this inclusivist fashion. What we should notice now is that in any case this proposal does not give a satisfactory solution to our puzzle. Aristotle is looking for the ultimate end of human life, and he has argued that our good consists in some activity of the reasoning part of the soul, rather than in perception or any other activity shared with plants or animals. The fact that these activities are shared is his reason for thinking that they are not even part of our function. For he does not say that our good consists in eating, drinking, and perceiving as well as in exercising the part of the soul that has reason. Rather, it consists solely in the latter activity.[5] And so, having argued that perception (for example) is no part of our function, since it is shared, Aristotle seems to be committed to the view that contemplation too is no part of our function, since it too is shared. If we read "the best and most perfect" as a reference to *all* of the virtues of the reasoning part of the soul, we must take Aristotle to be saying that contemplation is one of the activities in which our function consists. But he is not entitled to say this, since he claims that perception, being a feature we share with other living things, is not part of our ultimate end.

Those who see disunity between Book I and X.7–8 might respond to this puzzle by simply adding it to their list of inconsistencies. They could say that in the function argument Aristotle intends to deny that contemplation is a component of the human good, but that he changes his mind when he writes his defense of the philosophical life. In the preceding chapters, however, we have learned how to maintain the unity between X.7–8 and the rest of the *NE*, and in any case we can see from Book I itself that contemplation is not being snubbed in the function argument. When we turn to I.13, we find Aristotle making a transition from the topic of happiness to the good in which he says it consists: "Since happiness is a certain activity of soul in accordance with perfect virtue, it is necessary to examine virtue" (1102a5–6). And we then learn more about

---

shares with Aristotle's god the activity of *theōria*" (p. 27). See too Wilkes, "The Good Man," pp. 345, 347. It is not clear why Ackrill does not infer that the best and most perfect virtue alluded to at 1098a17–18 is the composite of all psychic virtues *other than* theoretical wisdom.

[5] Contrast Irwin, "The Metaphysical and Psychological Basis of Aristotle's Ethics," p. 49. My reasons for rejecting his position are given in Chapter 4, note 32.

which virtues we are to study in the rest of this work. For example, we will not be studying the virtues of the part of the soul responsible for nutrition and growth (such as the qualities that enable us to eat well), since these excellences are "common and not human" (1102b3). The virtues that we will study are of course restricted to those that pertain to the reasoning part of the soul; these include (1103a1–10) the virtues of character (such as generosity and temperance) and the virtues of thought (such as theoretical and practical wisdom). Here Aristotle explicitly tells us (a5) that theoretical wisdom is included within his program of study, whereas the virtues pertaining to nourishment are to be ignored. We therefore cannot take Book I of the *NE* to be saying that since contemplation is something we share with the gods, it (like the virtues of the good eater) has no place in a study of human happiness.[6]

So we are still left with our puzzle: If the virtues we share with plants and animals are eliminated in the function argument,[7] why not the virtues we share with gods as well? How can contemplation be even a part of our function, let alone the one activity that perfectly fulfills it, if it is something that is common to gods and human beings? My suggestion is that

[6] One other solution to our difficulty should be mentioned: that of Joachim, *Aristotle, The Nicomachean Ethics*, p. 50, notes on 1098a3 (cf. p. 287). He takes the function of human beings to consist in excellent practical activity, since contemplation is an activity we engage in by virtue of some element in us that is not human (see X.7 1177b26–8). On this interpretation, Book I restricts itself to the question "What is the human (that is, the second-best) good?" and answers that it consists in ethical activity. Book X then moves on to the question "What is the best good we can achieve?" and identifies it with contemplation. Discovering the function of human beings is pertinent to the first but not the second question, since our function must be something that sets us apart from both gods and all other forms of life. But why should I.7 ask what the human function is if that question prevents us from considering anything we share with the gods? If the search for the human function is by definition restricted to uniquely human activities—that is, activities declared in X.7–8 to be second-best—then what place does this argument have in Book I, where Aristotle tells us that he is looking for the best good? In any case, I.13 takes up where the function argument leaves off (1102a5–6), and treats theoretical wisdom as one of the virtues that have been shown by that argument to require further investigation (1103a5). Joachim's treatment of this difficulty fails to take into account the possibility that Aristotle is using "human" (*anthrōpinon*) in a broader and a narrower sense. In I.13, he restricts himself to an inquiry into human virtues (1102b2–12), and this eliminates the skills of the good eater, but includes theoretical excellence. Elsewhere—for example, in X.7–8—he uses "human" more narrowly (see too VI.7 1141b3–8). Broadly speaking, a good or a virtue is human if it distinguishes us from lower forms of life; narrowly speaking, it is human if it distinguishes us from both higher and lower forms of life. Joachim's interpretation is more fully discussed in my paper "The Peculiar Function of Human Beings," pp. 469–471.

[7] They are eliminated in the function argument only in the sense that exercising these virtues is not a part of our ultimate end. Obviously, Aristotle believes that they have an important role to play in a good human life. The function argument only tells us what should be placed at the pinnacle of human ends. It does not deny that we need many other goods besides the ones that occupy that position.

we have been led into this puzzle because we attributed to Aristotle a statement that is not really there in his text. Recall the point at which "common" and "peculiar" (*koinon* and *idion*) enter his argument: having asked what the function of a human being is, he replies that it cannot consist simply in living (that is, in nourishment and growth), since this is common, and we are seeking what is peculiar (1097b33–4). We hastily assumed that this must mean: "any feature common *to all living beings* cannot be our function; we are seeking something that human beings and *no other living being* can do." But in fact Aristotle does not spell out his point so fully. He says that our function cannot consist in anything that we have in common with plants or other animals, but must consist in something peculiar. This could simply mean that we are looking for something that sets us apart from plants and animals—rather than something that sets us apart from *all* living things whatsoever, including the gods. In other words, the context indicates that Aristotle is thinking of the class that consists of humans, other animals, and plants; and he insists that our function must be something peculiar to us, that is, it must distinguish us from other members of this class. If we take him to be considering a broader class—one that includes gods as well—then we land him in a difficulty from which I see no escape. For in X.7–8 he holds up the gods as models to be imitated, and this is incompatible with the idea that our good must consist in something that no god can do. And when we read the function argument in a way that is sensitive to its context, we can easily avoid this difficulty. The point being made in that argument is that our good must consist in something that no plant or animal can do. There is no good textual reason, in I.7, for taking Aristotle to be making a more general point, namely, that our function must be absolutely unique to us. And if we think that Book I should be unified with X.7–8, then we have every reason to reject such an interpretation.[8]

It might be protested, however, that this way of saving Aristotle from difficulty is *ad hoc*. For why should he make this distinction between gods and animals, and seek something we share with the former but not the latter? In other words, it might seem that if Aristotle is going to locate our good in some activity that sets us apart from plants and other animals, then his underlying idea must be that the good for any species is what sets it apart from all other types of living beings. And if that is the basic premise he uses in this part of the function argument, then he is committed, whether he realizes it or not, to the conclusion that the hu-

---

[8] Note that at *Topics* I.5 102a18–28 Aristotle distinguishes absolute from relative peculiarity. My claim is that if we are sensitive to the context of his argument in I.7, and to the connection between that chapter and X.7–8, then we will treat peculiarity as a relative matter. This interpretation is more fully presented in my paper "The Peculiar Function of Human Beings." See especially pp. 474–7.

man good cannot consist in contemplation. But to this charge of arbitrariness there is an easy reply: the reason he looks for something that sets us apart from other animals and plants, but not something that sets us apart from gods, is that the former species are inferior to human beings, whereas the gods are superior. My suggestion, in other words, is that Aristotle is not relying on the assumption that merely being different is a goal worth striving for. Instead, he is taking it for granted that human life can be better than the lives of other animals and plants (at any rate when it is properly led, and conditions are favorable). The best we can achieve is something better than anything another animal or plant can do, and since we are seeking the highest good, we must eliminate anything that can also be done by these lower species. Gods are excluded from the comparison class of I.7 because of their superiority to human beings. So, there is nothing arbitrary about the way Aristotle proceeds in the function argument and in the continuation of that argument in X.7–8. He starts from the premise that human beings occupy an intermediate position in the hierarchy of living forms: our lives are not as good as those of gods, but they are (or at least can be) better than the lives of other animals and plants. He seeks a theory of the human good that not only accords with this assumption, but explains it: we want to know what it is that makes our lives occupy this intermediate position, and when we discover which good is at the top of the hierarchy of ends, we should have our answer. And Aristotle's own candidate does fulfill this expectation: no human being can contemplate as continuously as the gods, but the other species cannot contemplate at all; excellent practical reasoning allows us to approximate the condition of the gods, but this too is beyond the reach of other species.

Another objection to Aristotle's search for the peculiar is that a great many other activities are peculiar to us, aside from his own favored candidate (activity of the part of the soul that has reason). For example, Bernard Williams says:

> If one approached without preconceptions the question of finding characteristics which differentiate men from other animals, one could as well, on these principles, end up with a morality which exhorted men to spend as much time as possible in making fire; or developing peculiarly human physical characteristics; or having sexual intercourse without regard to season; or despoiling the environment and upsetting the balance of nature; or killing things for fun.[9]

These observations would undermine Aristotle's project only if he were saying that the peculiarity of an activity is a *sufficient* condition for making it the ultimate end of human life. But there is no reason to think he is

---

[9] Williams, *Morality: An Introduction to Ethics*, p. 64.

making that mistake. We should instead take him to be saying that peculiarity is one among several *necessary* features of our ultimate end. That is,
if an activity is something shared with other animals and plants, then it
cannot be our function. This is all Aristotle needs to say in order to reject
nutrition, growth, sensation, and other common features of living creatures. His argument has no need of the further (absurd) assumption that
anything we can do that no other animal can do is a plausible candidate
for the human good. For example, consider the fact that human beings
alone make bridles. That hardly suggests that this is the human function,
if we take our function to be something that serves as our ultimate end.
Bridles (and other crafted products) are made only on condition that they
will serve some further purpose, and the human good must be something
that we desire for its own sake. Any successful candidate for the human
function must be an ultimate end for whose sake many other subordinate
ends are worth pursuing; we should recall that after Aristotle completes
the function argument, he tries to confirm his conception of happiness by
showing that many other kinds of goods have a role to play in human life
if we take virtuous activity to be our final end. The various peculiar activities Williams mentions cannot be taken seriously as candidates for this
central role, and this by itself shows that they cannot be our function.[10]
The lesson to be learned, then, is that peculiarity is only *one* test Aristotle
uses to dispose of candidates for the good.[11]

[10] Recall that the appropriate method in ethics, as in other disciplines, is to preserve as
many *endoxa* ("common opinions") as possible. See Chapter 4, note 44. That is, so far as
possible, the many things assumed to be good when we began our inquiry should remain
good once that inquiry is completed. For example, Aristotle begins with the assumption
that all of the many crafts that have arisen in Greek cities serve some useful purpose: whatever happiness turns out to be, they presumably promote it, in some indirect way. A proper
conception of the human function (and therefore of the human good) would explain why
these many different crafts (including music, drama, and poetry) are needed, and it is not
clear that the activities mentioned by Williams (lighting fires, despoiling nature, and so on)
would require the support of a varied and complex range of crafts. Of course, the crafts are
not the only goods that ought to be preserved in any plausible account of the human good:
a place must be found for friendship, political activity, and purely intellectual interests as
well.

[11] For a different way of responding to Williams's criticism, see Hutchinson, *The Virtues
of Aristotle*, p. 62–3. He thinks that Aristotle is equating the human function not with some
one type of activity but rather with "a form of activity which, because it includes others,
characterizes human life as a whole." The *ergon* of human beings, according to Hutchinson's
reading, is "doing things with reasons" (p. 59), that is, "a kind of life comprised of activities
informed by reason" (p. 57). It is not clear to me that this is an effective reply to Williams:
if the human good consists in anything that distinguishes us from other animals, then why
should it not consist in some uniquely human activities done for no reason, such as the
satisfaction of bizarre whims? In any case, I reject Hutchinson's idea that in the function
argument Aristotle is equating human happiness with merely "doing things with reasons."
For then Aristotle would have to allow that any planned life is well lived: so long as we

Of course, it may be asked why there must be some one end for the sake of which all others are pursued. Why cannot our lives be well-lived if we devote ourselves to a heterogeneous mixture of ends? As I said earlier (4.7), I do not think that Aristotle fallaciously moves from the premise "every action aims at some good" to the conclusion "there is some one good at which all actions aim." He does give some weight to an argument from analogy: since craftsmen and bodily organs have functions, we should expect there to be a human function as well (1097b25–33). Presumably he would also say that since these lower functions consist in some one type of activity, rather than a heterogeneous multiplicity, we should expect the same of the human function. But it does not matter whether we are inclined to give those analogies less weight than he did, for the crucial part of the function argument is its attempt to support the conclusion that in fact one type of good—virtuous activity of the part of the soul that has reason—deserves to be situated by itself at the pinnacle of human endeavors. If he can convince us that human lives are best organized around this end (whether it is expressed philosophically or politically), then he has in effect shown that there is a human function, even though it is something (when expressed philosophically) we share with the gods. He would then be entitled to claim that the common function of gods and human beings is to contemplate, and that many human beings who cannot achieve this end are nonetheless able to approximate it through moral activity. If we grant him all the materials he needs to reach this conclusion—and I am not saying we should—then we will be in no position to protest that human beings don't have a function, or that, if they do, it must be absolutely unique to them, and unshared by the gods.[12]

---

rationally arrange our goals in some pattern, we are doing things with reasons, and so we are living well, regardless of what our goals are.

[12] I take the notion of a function to be partly specified by Plato's characterization in Book I of the *Republic* (352d–353b): the function of a thing of type A is something that can be done only by things of that type, or it is something at which things of that type excel, as compared with other types. Obviously, when we ask about functions, the question of how to individuate types is crucial, and in some cases it may be controversial. If practical philosophy is inflexibly tied to the assumption that human beings are of a different type from gods, then Aristotle cannot accept Plato's characterization and also claim that our function is to contemplate. But I take Aristotle to be rejecting this assumption. An alternative interpretation would say that Aristotle rejects Plato's characterization. This is the view I put forward in "The Peculiar Function of Human Beings," p. 478. But I now think that Aristotle needs Plato's characterization in order to give sufficient content to the notion of a function. For the function of A cannot consist simply in the ultimate end towards which A is or should be striving; for then there would be no movement of thought in I.7, when Aristotle suggests at 1097b22–5 that we might learn what happiness is by considering the human function. I now take that suggestion to mean that we should consider what can be done by members

6.2. From Reason to Virtue

Aristotle's assumption, as we have seen, is that the best good for a human being must be something that no other animal or plant can achieve. Our lives can be better than theirs, and this would not be so if our ultimate end consisted in a good they too possess. On these grounds, such activities as nourishment, growth, and sensation are eliminated, and Aristotle then moves to the activity that he thinks sets us above the other animals: "there remains a certain active life of the [part] having reason" (1098a3–4). He next distinguishes two parts of the soul that can be said to have reason: one by virtue of which we can be obedient to reason, and one by virtue of which we engage in thinking (a4–5). And he expands on what he meant when he said that our function consists in an *active* life of the part that has reason: one can be alive by virtue of having a certain capacity, or by virtue of actualizing that capacity in an activity, and our function consists in the latter (a5–7).[13] In other words, as Aristotle then says, "the function of a human being is an activity of soul in accordance with reason, or not without reason" (a7–8).

Why, at this point in the development of his argument, does Aristotle bother distinguishing two parts of the human soul—one that can obey reason, and one that thinks? I take him to be indicating that both of these parts of the soul must be studied if we are to give a full account of human happiness.[14] And what he goes on to say in I.13 confirms this, for he tells us there that there is a certain arational (*alogos*) element in the soul that nonetheless shares in reason (1102b13–14), and that the virtues of this element must be studied no less than those belonging to the part that has reason in the strict sense (1103a1–10). So the activities in which happiness consists include both those that involve thinking (such as contemplation and deliberation) and those in which the arational part of the soul obeys reason (such as expressing anger or fear in the proper way). That is why Aristotle says that "the function of a human being is an activity of soul in accordance with reason, *or not without reason*." When someone has mastered his emotions in the proper way, and made them obedient to reason, the expression of that mastery is one of the activities in which the human

---

of our type (a type that turns out to include gods) but not (or at least not well) by other types (that is, other animals and plants).

[13] Here Aristotle is thinking of the objection made in I.5 (1095b31–1096a2) to the thesis that the good consists in virtue. He calls attention to the way his own theory avoids this objection at I.8 1098b30–1099a7, where he makes two contrasts: (a) that between possessing a good and using it; (b) that between a state (*hexis*) and an activity or actualization of that state (*energeia*). Happiness belongs to those who exercise the virtues, that is, to those who act (*prattontes*: 1099a6) in a certain way, and not to those who merely possess the virtues.

[14] See Roche, "*Ergon* and *Eudaimonia* in *Nicomachean Ethics* I: Reconsidering the Intellectualist Interpretation."

good consists. If one is appropriately angry, for example, one is not engaged in a process of thinking, but nonetheless one's activity is "not without reason," since it expresses the proper integration of reason and emotion.

None of this need be taken to mean that the ultimate end of human life is a mixture of reasoning and proper emotional expression. Instead, if the arguments I have given are correct, then Aristotle's idea is that perfect happiness consists solely in philosophical activity, while secondary happiness consists in practical reasoning and the expression of that thinking in one's emotions and actions. The function argument is an attempt to defend both of these conceptions of our ultimate end, and Aristotle's reminder, within that argument, that we can have reason by being obedient to it reflects the fact that he will be advocating not only a life of pure thought, but also a second-best life devoted to excellent deliberation and the rational mastery of emotion.

Of course, Aristotle does not want to say that happiness consists in just any process of thought, or in just any way of exercising rational control over the emotions. These activities must be carried out in an excellent way if they are to be appropriate candidates for our ultimate end. And so he argues, in the next eight lines (1098a8–15), that "the human good [consists in] activity of soul in accordance with virtue" (a16–17). That is, to put the point more fully, happiness is activity of the reasoning part of the soul (or of the part that is not without reason) carried out in an excellent way. In order to build the virtues into his account of happiness, Aristotle appeals once again to an analogy with the crafts. He had said that in these specialized spheres the good and "the well" consists in performing a certain function (1097b24–8). But now he adds that "the well" is achieved only by an excellent craftsman (1098a12), and that something is done well if it is carried out in accordance with certain excellences (a15). If the function of a craftsman is to do A, then the function of a good craftsman is to do A well, that is, to do it in a skillful way; and the good in each specialized sphere does not consist merely in making a product or engaging in some activity, but in doing these things well. By analogy, if it can be shown that the ends of any well-lived life are hierarchically arranged (as are the subends of any craft: 1097a15–22), then it would stand to reason that the human good consists not simply in doing something but in doing it well—that is, in accordance with certain virtues. And so happiness must consist in activities of reason carried out in an excellent way.

Aristotle then adds the clause that we examined in 4.14–15: "and if there are more than one virtue, in accordance with the best and most perfect" (1098a17–18). But he leaves aside all the questions provoked by this mysterious addendum: Is there some one best virtue? What is it? Why is it better to have that one kind of virtuous activity as one's ultimate end than to live for the sake of a more complex goal? Rather than take up these questions immediately, he first examines the various virtues of the reasoning soul and of the part that listens to reason, and then, in X.7–8, presents his case for making one virtuous activity—contemplation—the sole ultimate end of our lives. We will consider in 6.9 his various arguments on behalf of the philosophical life. Though several of them have been discussed already in Chapters 1 and 3, it will be useful to bring all of them together in a single place.

What I would like to discuss now is the case Aristotle makes for the nontheoretical virtues—that is, such excellences as justice, generosity, courage, temperance, and practical wisdom. For I take him to be saying that activities in accordance with these less perfect virtues constitute a secondary kind of happiness. That is, a life can be well lived if it is devoted to the ultimate end of expressing these practical virtues and is adequately supplied with the resources needed to exercise them over a long period of time. In this sense, Aristotle holds that the moral virtues are good enough to stand on their own: even though they are good partly because they promote a higher end (contemplation), they deserve a prominent place in our lives whether or not they are used for this further purpose. And we can be precise about what that prominent place is: if we do not choose contemplation as our ultimate end, then we should take our highest goal to be activity in accordance with practical virtue.[15] Every other good should be pursued to the extent that it promotes such excellences as justice, courage, and generosity. So, Aristotle would say that if someone equates happiness with contemplation, but thinks that no other kind of activity is good enough to serve as the ultimate end of a well-lived life, then he has a serious misunderstanding of what happiness is: he sees what the best human life is, but fails to recognize how it can be approximated by engaging in moral activity. We must try to understand what kind of case the *NE* makes for this part of its theory.

6.3. The Defense of the Practical Virtues

Not a word is said in the function argument about the particular virtues that occupy so much of Aristotle's attention in later portions of the *NE*. He concludes that happiness consists in activity in accordance with virtue, but does not tell us what the virtues are. And this may strike us as an

[15] It would be a mistake simply to say that ethically virtuous activity is good in itself, and leave it at that. For Aristotle takes many different kinds of goods (such as honor, pleasure, and life) to be desirable in themselves. Putting virtuous activity in this category says nothing about whether its value is greater than theirs. And Aristotle does want to say that, with the exception of theoretical activity, activity in accordance with the practical virtues is more desirable than any other kind of good.

enormous defect. For even if we were to concede, at least for the sake of argument, that the human good consists in excellent activity of the part of the soul that has reason, we have not yet been given any grounds for thinking that such virtues as temperance, courage, and generosity are precisely the excellences that we need.[16] It looks as though Aristotle is doing too little work: he apparently thinks that he can get a defense of these particular qualities simply by advancing an abstract point about the conceptual connection between doing something *well* and doing it *in accordance with virtue*. But that point by itself will not get him very far, for it could be accepted even by a lover of physical pleasure (that is, someone who proposes this as our ultimate end). Such a hedonist could say, with Aristotle, that living well is living in accordance with virtue; he would differ from Aristotle by regarding the ability to maximize pleasure as a virtue.

I agree that the function argument does not by itself show that temperance (for example), as Aristotle conceives of it, is a virtue. But we would be impatient students of the *NE* if we expected it to present the whole of its argument at once. Instead of regarding the function argument as a complete but defective argument on behalf of the ethical virtues, we should treat it as the foundation for a defense that Aristotle continues to develop throughout the rest of his work. Obviously, the function argument cannot by itself show why temperance and other particular virtues are important; to do that, one must first have a proper understanding of these virtues. What we can legitimately demand of Aristotle is this: once he has finished his treatment of the practical virtues, he should be able to connect them with the conception of happiness put forward in the function argument, and in light of that connection, we should be able to see why happiness consists in exercising precisely those skills. To put the point more precisely, we should understand why the secondary form of happiness consists in these excellent activities.

In the remainder of this section I present a rough account of Aristotle's whole argument. In later sections I will add more detail and try to defend this way of reading him. The leading idea is that the *NE* treats the good person—that is, someone who has such virtues as justice, temperance, and courage—as an intellectual of sorts. The paradigm of an outstanding

---

[16] For this criticism, see Adkins, "The Connection between Aristotle's *Ethics* and *Politics*," p. 33: the conclusion of the function argument "has no moral content," and so "Thrasymachus could cheerfully accept it." See too Cooper, *RHGA*, p. 146: "What is disappointing about this argument . . . is that it is too abstract to be informative. . . . And even if one accepts, as Aristotle seems to do without argument, that justice, temperance, and so on, as conventionally conceived, plus theoretical wisdom and practical intelligence as he analyzes them, are the excellences in question, we still cannot derive from this argument any significant information as to how it is that these qualities contribute to a flourishing life."

person, in the practical realm, is the excellent political leader, and the most important qualities of such an individual are his skills as a thinker. To understand what Aristotle is talking about, we might think of the abilities that make someone an excellent judge: such individuals have a deep understanding of the law and of the diverse needs of the community, and use their considerable powers of intellect to reach wise decisions about particular cases. Aristotle's paradigm of a good person has all of these qualities, and in addition has the skills of an excellent legislator; such individuals excel not only in applying the law, but in making it as well. Now, Aristotle thinks that to be outstanding in these areas, one needs both intellectual and emotional resources. One must have a general understanding of the good and the ability to see what must be done in particular cases; and furthermore, one's emotions must be fully integrated with these judgments, so that anger, fear, appetite, and so on are made to serve reason. The chief virtue of the good person is an intellectual skill—practical wisdom—and the other, nonintellectual skills of such a person are those that best enable him to exercise that highest practical virtue. Temperance, courage, justice, and so on are precisely the features of the arational soul that we need in order to perfect ourselves as outstanding political leaders. And exercising such leadership over a considerable period of time is as close as one can come to perfect happiness, when one confines oneself to practical activity.

When we look at Aristotle in this way, we can understand why he thinks that the function argument provides a common foundation for the philosophical life and the life that exercises ethical virtues. For that argument attempts to show that happiness consists in "a certain active life of the [part] having reason" (1098a3–4), "activity in accordance with reason or not without reason" (a7–8), or "activity and actions with reason" (a13–14). In other words, the ultimate end of a well-lived human life must be some activity that actualizes our capacity to reason, and since we can reason about either theoretical or practical matters, there are two models of how one's ends should be organized: one's highest end can be to engage in theoretical reasoning, and to exercise the skills of an outstanding philosopher, or one's highest end can be to engage in practical reasoning, and to exercise the skills of the political deliberator (including the reason-supporting skills of the arational part of the soul). The function argument does not itself tell us which of these two is the better model. Nor does it say everything Aristotle needs to say in order to show that either of these two ends can by itself adequately fulfill the role of an ultimate end, by being the goal for the sake of which all lower ends are desired. The function argument is just one element in Aristotle's defense of the philosophical and political lives, and should not be expected to carry the entire burden of that defense. We will of course want to know how well the NE, taken as a whole, presents its case, but we should not expect to find Aristotle's complete argument within the confines of I.7.

When we read the function argument as part of Aristotle's defense of a life devoted to reasoning well (whether philosophically or practically), we can use it to explain several other passages discussed earlier. In 1.14, we noticed that in Aristotle's "argument from divinity," the gods are held up as paradigms of happiness, and that the well-being of all creatures is assessed in terms of their approximation to this divine model (see especially X.8 1178b22–8). Philosophers are the closest approximation, since they intermittently engage in the very same activity that the gods enjoy continuously; and lower animals are not happy at all, since they have no share in this intellectual activity. Now, since Aristotle thinks that those who lead a political life can be happy even though they are not theoreticians, he must see some similarity between their favored activities and the sole activity of the gods. And when we realize that the function argument presents a common defense of the philosophical and practical lives, we see what that similarity is: both philosophers and statesmen have the ultimate end of reasoning in an excellent way. A similarity between philosophers and statesmen also became apparent when we considered (3.9) several remarks Aristotle makes in his treatment of friendship: when the ethically virtuous person acts for his own good, he acts for the sake of the thinking part of his soul (IX.4 1166a16–17), and this part (*nous*) is the one he loves most of all (IX.8 1168b34–1169a3). When he joins together with his friends to participate in the activities they love most of all (IX.12 1172a1–3), they "share in discussion and thought" (IX.9 1170b11–12). The ethically virtuous person is here made to sound like a philosopher of sorts, and that is because he *is* a philosopher of sorts, according to Aristotle. He devotes himself to the activity of practical reasoning, just as a theoretician devotes himself to contemplation.

At the beginning of this section, I considered the suggestion that the function argument is so abstract that it could be endorsed even by someone who takes our ultimate end to be physical pleasure. In my opinion, that suggestion would be acceptable only if we were to misinterpret Aristotle's assertion that happiness consists in "activity in accordance with reason or not without reason" (1098a7–8). If that phrase simply means that the good consists either in activities that have been decided upon by reason or in activities that have not been rejected by reason, then Aristotle is indeed giving little or no content to his conception of happiness.[17] For

---

[17] I take this to be the view of Hutchinson. See note 11 above. A similar view can be found in McDowell, "The Role of *Eudaimonia* in Aristotle's Ethics." He holds that the function argument is not meant to identify happiness with Aristotle's own candidate for that role, but merely eliminates a "brutish life" devoted to the "*un*reflective gratification of appetite" (p. 366, emphasis added). If this were so, then Aristotle would have said nothing in

he would have said nothing about why reason should not choose physical pleasure as the ultimate end. Or, if this seems too simple a goal, then reason could choose some complex mixture consisting of physical pleasure, military victory, athletic prowess, and so on. So long as we decided, upon reflection, to engage in these activities, and performed them with excellence, we would be leading a happy life. But I take Aristotle to be saying something quite different. When he speaks in the function argument of "a certain active life of the [part] having reason" (a3–4), "activity in accordance with reason or not without reason" (a7–8), and "activity and actions with reason" (a13–14), he is saying that our ultimate end consists solely in activities of thought (theoretical or practical) or in activities in which our emotions reflect the mastery of reason. All of the goods rejected in I.5 (physical pleasure, honor, virtue, wealth) are to play a subordinate role in our lives, and so too are the others (friends, political power, and so on: I.8 1099b1–6) mentioned later. Since these subordinate goods are not what happiness consists in, they should be pursued only to the extent that they promote that further end.

So read, the function argument is doing a good deal of work for Aristotle. It does not leave the door open to many different types of life, but narrows down our options to those devoted to thinking and the mastery of thought over all other elements of human life. A life lived for the sake of physical virtues (health, strength) or external goods (power, honor) or any combination of them is ruled out. And so is any conception of the virtues which overemphasizes the importance of these goods and underemphasizes the value of excellent reasoning. Though Aristotle has not yet said, in Book I, what the perfect virtues of the soul are, he has committed himself to an intellectualist way of understanding them.[18] It cannot be a virtue, for example, to act out of untutored and unthinking compassion for others. Instead, the virtues must be skills of thought and emotion that enable one to live a life devoted to excellent reasoning as one's highest end. If we read Aristotle differently and take the function argument to admit all plans of life and all conceptions of the virtues, then we will not see why he proceeds as he does in the remainder of the NE. We will not understand why he takes the philosophical and political lives to be best, or why he analyzes the virtues as intermediate states.

Aristotle's theory of the good, as I interpret it, could not succeed if

---

I.7 to support either a political or a philosophical life, as opposed to one devoted to the *reflective* maximization of physical pleasure over the long run. But clearly he thinks, in I.13, that his conclusion in the function argument points to such virtues as temperance and generosity as the excellences whose exercise constitutes human happiness. He takes the function argument to have shown that a good human life cannot be one in which reason is used to promote the ultimate end of physical pleasure.

[18] Note the contrast with Cooper's reading, cited in note 16 above.

practical reasoning were by its nature confined to the question of how other types of goods can be attained. It might be said that when we reason about what to do, we always take some other type of good (theoretical reasoning, health, victory, the satisfaction of desire) as our goal, and use our reason to discover the best means to these ends, or to their harmonious coordination. If that were true, then all practical reasoning would be for the sake of something other than practical reasoning itself. But I see no merit in this suggestion. It is true that every act of deliberation is directed at some end other than the process of deliberation that is currently going on. That does not mean, however, that deliberation cannot be devoted to the question of how deliberative skills (one's own and those of others) are to be developed and sustained in the future. The excellent political leader, according to Aristotle's theory, takes excellent practical reasoning to be his highest activity, and the topic about which he reasons is the perpetuation of these skills in himself and others.[19] Of course, if good reasoning is to flourish in the political community, then many other resources must be present as well, and the politician must devote his attention to them. But when he deliberates about the community's health, defense, finances, and so on, his ultimate end is to foster the conditions in which his fellow citizens will continue to excel as practical reasoners. His practical reasoning ultimately concerns practical reasoning, and any paradox here is only apparent.

6.4. THE MEAN AND THE *HOROS*

To understand Aristotle's defense of the virtues of character—the skills that enable us to listen to reason (I.13 1102b25–1103a3)—we need to see how they are connected to the preeminent practical virtue, namely, *phronēsis* (practical wisdom). And to understand the proper place of this virtue of thought, we must see how Book VI of the *NE* saves Aristotle's earlier statements about the mean from emptiness.

He tells us in II.2 that his present project is undertaken for a practical

[19] The political leader may also deliberate about how to promote philosophical thinking. But I find no evidence in Aristotle that politicians *must* devote themselves to this end if they are to do their job well. A well-governed polis, guided by outstanding men of practical wisdom, may contain no citizens who have philosophical interests or abilities, and in this case these leaders will devote themselves entirely to the promotion of *practical* wisdom in the community. Even when some of the citizens are philosophers, they may not need the special attention of political leaders in order to flourish. The ideal polis, described in *Politics* VII–VIII, is not devoted to the promotion of philosophy. I take Aristotle to be assuming that in most circumstances—certainly in ideal circumstances—some people will develop an interest in theoretical matters, and there is no need for political leaders to devote special attention to this. In *Met.* I.1–2, he treats the rise of philosophical interests as a natural outgrowth of the delight we take in learning.

purpose: we do not want to contemplate truths about what virtue is, but to become good people (1103b26–8). And although precision in this subject is impossible, we must try to say whatever will be helpful (1103b34–1104a11). In this spirit, Aristotle then introduces the notion of a mean: such bodily virtues as strength and health are destroyed by deficiency and excess (too much or too little exercise, too much or too little eating), and the same holds true of such virtues of the soul as temperance and courage (1104a11–19). For example, to be courageous, we must not fear everything and avoid every danger, nor must we be without fear and accept every risk; to be temperate, we must not pursue every pleasure, nor must we go to the opposite extreme of pursuing none (a20–25). Aristotle returns to this theme in II.6, where he points out that the mean for one person in one situation will differ from the mean for someone else in a different situation (1106a26–b7). The idea is that there is not some one right amount of anger (for example)—a halfway point between the greatest possible anger and none. Rather, when we aim at the mean, we must aim at something that is *for us* neither too great nor too little: it must be the appropriate amount of anger, fear, or appetite at this time, in relation to this person, and so on (1106b18–24).

So, we are told that to be virtuous, we must aim in our actions and feelings at a mean between deficiency and excess. Just as a good craftsman tries to produce something from which nothing should be taken away, and to which nothing need be added, so we should strive for something equally appropriate to the situations in which we find ourselves (1106b8–16). Finding this intermediate point is difficult, because there are so many different ways to under- or overshoot one's target (b28–35). Hitting the mean in one's actions and feelings is a task that requires practical reason, and so, when Aristotle defines ethical virtue, he calls it a "state concerned with choice, being in a mean that is relative to us, as determined by reason—the reason by which the practically wise person would determine it" (1106b36–1107a2). We hear echoes of this formulation throughout Aristotle's discussion of the virtues—to exercise the virtues is to follow reason[20]—and his doctrine of the mean is the guiding idea behind his classification of virtues and vices. To possess an ethical virtue is to know how to hit the mean, and so there are two kinds of character defects: one may regularly do and feel either too much or too little. Every such virtue is therefore to be understood by comparing it with its corresponding vices.

Two questions should be raised about what Aristotle has said. First, whether or not his claims are *true*, we can ask whether they are at all *helpful*. As we saw, he prefaces his remarks about the mean with a re-

---

[20] See III.7 1115b12, III.11 1119a20, III.12 1119b10–15, IV.5 1125b35. "The right reason" is first brought into play at II.2 1103b31–3.

minder about the practical nature of his undertaking (1103b26–1104a11): though we cannot expect precision, we do want to say something of practical value. But it is not clear how the doctrine of the mean contributes to this project. How can it serve as a substantive guide to proper action and feeling? We are told to aim at what is intermediate between too much and too little (1106b28, 1107a5–6). But are we any better off with this piece of advice than we would be if we had simply been told to do what is right, or what is best, or what is virtuous? And if the doctrine of the mean does not help us to make decisions and to mold our feelings, then why has Aristotle introduced it? He is not asking us to contemplate this thesis simply because it is true (II.2 1103b26–9).

A second question concerns what the doctrine of the mean actually says. When Aristotle first introduces it, he does so by way of analogy and example: just as deficiency and excess are destructive of bodily virtues, so too they undermine the virtues of the soul; to be courageous or temperate, we must avoid the excesses of too much fear and too great an appetite, and the deficiencies of too little fear and too little appetite. But how are we to generalize from these examples? Surely Aristotle is not saying that we should have *every* feeling and undertake *every* sort of activity to some extent (but neither too much nor too little)? Consider horseback riding, for example. Is Aristotle saying that we exhibit a vice if we never engage in this activity, and have too little feeling for it? Would he say the same about hunting, playing dice, writing plays, and so on? Obviously, he needs some nonarbitrary way of saying which emotions should be felt and which actions undertaken.[21] Does he have the resources for doing this?

Let us set aside this second question for the moment and concentrate on the first, for by focusing on the apparent emptiness of the doctrine of the mean, we will be led to recognize the central role played by practical wisdom in Aristotle's defense of the ethical life. Once we have an answer to our first question—how does the doctrine of the mean help?—an answer to the second will easily follow.

The most important point to recognize, when we try to answer the first question, is that Aristotle himself complains about the unhelpfulness of the doctrine of the mean as it has been presented in Books II–V. At the beginning of VI.1 he says:

> In all the states mentioned, as well as others, there is a certain target to which the person who has reason looks as he tightens or relaxes; and there is a certain *horos* [limit, standard, boundary, definition] of the mean states. . . . To say this is true, but not precise. . . . If one had only this, one would be none the wiser.

---

[21] The problem is recognized in the notes to Irwin's translation. See p. 314, notes to 1107a9–27.

For example, [one would be none the wiser about] what sorts of things must be applied to the body if someone were to say: whatever medical science prescribes, and as the one who has this [science applies them]. Therefore, this also holds for the states of the soul: one must not only say this thing truly, but one must also determine what the right reason is and what is its *horos*. (1138b21–34)

Any satisfactory interpretation of this passage, and of Book VI in general, must say how that book strengthens the doctrine of the mean, so that it escapes the criticism Aristotle makes here. He knows that he has said nothing helpful in advising us to aim at what is intermediate, and to neither over- nor undershoot our target. And Book VI is supposed to remedy this defect. But how does it do so? What does the doctrine of the mean amount to when it is supplemented by the claims made in this book? Unfortunately, Aristotle does not spell out any answer to these questions. He goes on to discuss the various virtues of the reasoning part of the soul, but never returns to the doctrine of the mean, and so he never tells us how his discussion of those virtues solves the problem stated at the beginning of Book VI. Nor is it easy to find any statement in this book that would give us a more concrete standard for making decisions and for shaping our feelings. For example, Aristotle says that those who have practical wisdom are good at deliberating about living well in general (1140a25–8); they know both universals and particulars (1141b14–15); and they possess both the ethical virtues and cleverness (1144a23–b17). None of this helps us find the mean.[22]

I suggest that Book VI strengthens the doctrine of the mean and thereby provides a workable standard for decision making in the following way: Nearly the whole of this book (VI.3, VI.5–13) is devoted to the

---

[22] According to Ackrill, "Aristotle on *Eudaimonia*," the *NE* is not trying to answer the question raised in VI.1 by appealing to *theōria*, and yet "no alternative answer . . . seems to present itself" (p. 31). I take him to be saying that the *NE* simply gives no answer to the question of VI.1. This is also the view of Cooper, *RHGA*, pp. 101–115. Allan, *The Philosophy of Aristotle*, p. 136, says, "This part of the treatise, as it stands, does not bear the great weight which falls upon it in the argument." According to Rowe, *The Eudemian and Nicomachean Ethics*, pp. 109–113, Aristotle does give an answer to the question raised in VI.1, but it is an imprecise one: we need experience, and this will enable us to see what must be done in each case (VI.11 1143b13–14, VI.12 1144a30). Rowe agrees that Aristotle fails to meet the expectations he raises in VI.1, but is more forgiving than other scholars. The connection between *NE* VI.1 and *EE* VIII.3 is discussed by Kenny, *The Aristotelian Ethics*, pp. 181–3. For Sidgwick's complaint about the mean, see *Outlines of the History of Ethics*, p. 64. Perhaps his disappointment partly explains his later statement that "[o]n the whole, there is probably no treatise so masterly as Aristotle's *Ethics*, and containing so much close and valid thought, that yet leaves on the reader's mind so strong an impression of dispersive and incomplete work" (p. 70). I have learned a great deal about the mean from Peterson, "*Horos* (Limit) in Aristotle's *Nicomachean Ethics*."

study of two kinds of virtues: practical wisdom and theoretical wisdom. And Aristotle is saying that either of these should be the "target to which the person who has reason looks as he tightens or relaxes" (VI.1 1138b22–3). Once we supplement the account given in II–V of the ethical virtues with an understanding of these two virtues of thought, we will have a more precise idea of how much physical pleasure to pursue, how much money to give away, how much anger is appropriate on particular occasions, and so on. For activity in accordance with either of these two virtues is the ultimate end of any well-lived life. The right amount, in our actions and feelings, will be whatever amount best contributes to the fullest expression of these two rational skills.

So, no single statement or group of statements in Book VI gives us a workable standard for making decisions. Instead, we are to bring to this book the notion, spelled out in *NE* I, that virtuous activity of some sort is to serve as our ultimate end; and we are to take the material in VI as a further specification of what that ultimate end is. We have already been told, in I.2, that a conception of happiness will give us a target by means of which we can decide the extent to which subordinate pursuits should be undertaken (1094a22–b2). And in Book VI, Aristotle is coming to the most important part of that target: the skills he has discussed in II–V are the qualities of the arational part of the soul that we need because they serve the superior capacities of the part of the soul that actually thinks. If we know only as much as we are told in these earlier books, then we will be none the wiser. But we will see why we need these lower virtues, and be in a better position to hit the mean, once we study the reasoning skills that constitute the ultimate end of our lives. Once we make a choice between the two ultimate ends—excellent theoretical reasoning and excellent practical reasoning—our task will be complete, for we will have as much of a standard for decision making as philosophy can provide for us.

Why should we read Aristotle in this way? To begin with, it fits with and makes sense of everything he says, both within Book VI and beyond it. After complaining about the emptiness of the mean, he turns immediately to a discussion of the virtues housed in the thinking part of the soul (1138b35–1139a3). He divides this part into two subcomponents, one of which engages in scientific reasoning about necessary truths, the other of which deliberates (1139a3–15); and he says that we must determine what the best state of each part is, for that determines the virtue and proper function of each (a15–17). Evidently, he thinks that the study of these two highest virtues will strengthen the doctrine of the mean, and our interpretation of Books I and X enables us to see why this is so. He is looking for an ultimate end, and in I.7 he locates it in the part of the soul that has reason or is not without reason. In Book VI he carries forward his search by narrowing down his target to two kinds of activities:

one in accordance with practical wisdom (the highest state of the deliberating soul) and the other in accordance with theoretical wisdom (the
highest state of the theorizing soul). When we read Book VI in this way,
everything he says in it is relevant to the solution of the problem with
which it begins. For his entire discussion contributes in one way or another to understanding of the two highest virtues: when he is not discussing these states directly, he is contributing to our understanding of
them by contrasting them with other excellences of thought (such as the
crafts, discussed in VI.4, and cleverness, briefly considered at VI.12–13
1144a23–9).

Furthermore, if Aristotle is read in the way I suggest, then he really has
strengthened the doctrine of the mean, so that it loses its emptiness and
becomes a workable standard for decision making. To see this, consider
a sample virtue, temperance: how does Book VI contribute to our understanding of what we must do in order to exercise this virtue? In III.11–
12, temperance is described by way of a contrast with two corresponding
vices: at one extreme, there is a type of person whose enjoyment of physical pleasures is less than it should be (1119a5–11); at the other, there is a
type who goes to excess by seeking and enjoying physical pleasures more
than is appropriate (1118b15–1119a5). The temperate person lies between
these two types: he takes pleasure in only certain activities that involve
food, drink, or sex; his appetite is moderate; and if any pleasure would
undermine his health or is beyond his means, he does not pursue it
(1119a11–18).

In saying that we should avoid the two extremes, Aristotle does not
mean that any point falling between these limits is as good as any other.
And of course he rejects the notion that the arithmetic mean (whatever
that would be) is the appropriate target (II.6 1106a26–b7). If he were saying that we should pursue every physical pleasure that does not undermine our health or deplete our resources, then he would hardly say in
VI.1 that a more precise standard is needed. How then does Book VI help
us decide how to hit the mean when it comes to the pleasures of eating,
drinking, and sex? Consider someone who is deliberating about whether
to buy a sizable quantity of expensive wine. He asks: is the pleasure he
and others would get worth the financial cost and the amount of time it
would take to purchase the wine and drink it in the appropriate setting?
Aristotle is saying that one of the two correct ways to approach this issue
is to look at the consequences various alternatives would have for one's
activity as an excellent practical reasoner.[23] (The other way to approach

---

[23] Contrast Greenwood, *Aristotle Nicomachean Ethics Book Six*, pp. 82–3: "Actions are
good, according to Aristotle, in proportion as they lead to the [theoretical life] as the end.
For the man who does not consider this to be the end, and does not in any way aim at it as

the issue is to take contemplation as one's ultimate end.) To consider those consequences, one must have some conception of what good practical reasoning is, and so one of the tasks of Book VI is to propose such a conception. Once we have an idea of what is involved in reasoning well, we can go on to ask: would buying this wine contribute to my ultimate end, namely, to engage in the greatest possible amount of activity that exercises practical wisdom? Of course, this question cannot be answered unless one knows more details. If there is some special festival to which I am contributing, and if it facilitates good relations with others who regularly help me in my deliberations, then the expense may be justified. But if I, as a person who enjoys excellent deliberating most of all, have no need to spend that much money and to engage in those festivities, then I should decide to forgo this particular pleasure. To seek pleasure that makes no contribution to excellent reasoning is to want it more than it is worth.

It should be evident that even when the doctrine of the mean is combined in this way with a definite conception of one's ultimate end, practical reasoning still retains a certain imprecision. In many cases, it will be unclear whether a certain physical pleasure (or any other subordinate good) will be worth pursuing. So we can well understand why Aristotle emphasizes the imprecision inherent in his subject,[24] even though he introduces the doctrine of the mean as something that will help us lead our lives. But we can now understand why he finds that doctrine helpful once it is supplemented by the material in Book VI. We are far better able to make decisions and mold our emotional responses when we take some form of excellent reasoning to be our highest goal than we would be if we were merely told to avoid deficiency and excess. And Aristotle adds still more content to his theory when he tries to show that one of these forms of reasoning is a more fitting ultimate end than the other.

One further advantage of reading Aristotle in this way is that it provides him with a principled answer to the second question raised earlier in this section. Recall that, aside from the unhelpfulness of the mean, we were concerned about how the doctrine is even to be stated. It tells us to aim in our actions and emotions at the mean between deficiency and excess. And this proposal is conveyed by way of analogies and examples: fear and anger can be too great or too little; we can give away too much money or too little; honor can be loved too much or not enough; and so on. But how can the doctrine of the mean be stated in a way that does not raise obvious objections? Aristotle is not saying that everyone should

the end, what standard remains to make any action better or worse than any other? Aristotle evidently cannot make out that there is any standard."

[24] For references, see Chapter 1, note 16.

write an intermediate number of plays, or have a moderate love of horse-back riding. Which actions and feelings should be in a mean, and on what basis does Aristotle make this decision?

He cannot say that the doctrine applies only to those actions and feelings that no human being can possibly avoid. For there are people who lack the emotions that Aristotle thinks we should experience to some degree: some are totally without fear (III.7 1115b24–8), some derive no pleasure from their association with other people (IV.6 1126b11–16), and some fail to enjoy humor and other forms of relaxation (IV.8 1127b33–1128a9). All of these emotions are avoidable, but even so, Aristotle holds that they should be experienced to a moderate degree. So the doctrine of the mean obviously does not apply only to feelings that it is impossible to escape. And once we recognize the way his conception of happiness is connected with that doctrine, we can see why it applies to certain emotions and actions and not others. For example, it tells us to hit the mean when wealth and honor are at issue, because, in Aristotle's opinion, the successful pursuit of either ultimate end (contemplation or excellent practical reasoning) requires the right amount of these goods and a moderate desire for them. (What the right amount is will vary depending on which ultimate end one chooses.) Similarly, he thinks that we will be in a better position to lead a life of perfect or secondary happiness if we train our emotions so that we feel some anger, some fear, and some desire for physical pleasure—so long as the occasion is appropriate, and our emotion is not too strong. By contrast, he thinks that we need not write a certain number of plays (neither too few nor too many) or have a moderate love of horseback riding in order to live a good life—that is, a life devoted to the ultimate end of excellent reasoning. So the doctrine of the mean can be stated in a general way as follows: we should aim at the mean when we undertake those actions and experience those emotions that any human being needs in order to engage in excellent reasoning over the course of a lifetime.

I claimed in the previous section that Aristotle thinks of the good person as an intellectual of sorts, and I have tried, in the present section, to explain why I read him in this way. To have the ethical virtues—that is, such virtues as courage, temperance, and generosity—one must aim at a mean between excess and deficiency, and in order to do this, one must look to either of two intellectual standards. By showing, in the function argument, why the ultimate end of one's life should be excellence of the reasoning part of the soul, Aristotle is at once defending the philosophical and the political life. Both are devoted to excellent reasoning as an ultimate end, and so there is a strong similarity between them. If one of them is worth living, so is the other.

6.5. THE RIGHT REASON

A number of important questions about the doctrine of the mean, and about Aristotle's defense of the two lives, still remain. To begin with, let us see how the interpretation I have proposed helps us understand his many remarks about "the right reason." We are told in II.2 that one must act "in accordance with the right reason" (1103b31–2), and are promised a fuller account of what this is (b32–3). Virtue involves aiming at a mean, and the mean is "determined by reason—the reason by which the practically wise person would determine it" (II.6 1107a1–2). All of this is too vague, as Aristotle realizes, for as we have seen, he complains that the doctrine of the mean is empty unless it is supplemented by a specification of what the right reason is:

> Since we were saying earlier that one must choose the mean, and not excess or deficiency, and the mean is what the right reason says, let us define this. In all the states mentioned, as well as others, there is a certain target to which the person who has reason looks as he tightens or relaxes; and there is a certain *horos* [limit, standard, boundary, definition] of the mean states, which we say lie between excess and deficiency, being in accordance with the right reason. To say this is true, but not precise. (1138b18–26)

And the task of Book VI is to "determine what the right reason is and what is its *horos*" (b33–4).

I take Aristotle to be saying in Books II–V that a virtuous person must be able to give an account of why he undertakes virtuous activities. He cannot just happen to like temperance, justice, and so on for no particular reason, and the reason he gives to back up his actions must be of the right sort. But what is the right reason for having and actualizing these virtues? How does having the right reason help us find the mean? And what is the *horos* of this right reason?

I believe that all of these questions receive intelligible answers in Book VI. The right reason for acting in accordance with any of the ethical virtues is that such actions enable us to cultivate, sustain, and exercise either of the two master virtues, namely, theoretical and practical wisdom. Once we see the connection between having the ethical virtues and these two virtues of thought, we have a *horos*—a definition—of the right reason; in other words, we can say in all cases what the right reason for action is, and we can understand why it is the right reason. And having this general account, we can make more precise estimations of where the mean lies, for we can adjust our actions and emotions in such a way that we are more able to engage in excellent reasoning over a long period of time.

To see more clearly what Aristotle is getting at in Book VI, let us ex-

amine several of the ethical virtues discussed in Books II–IV, and see how
that later book helps us understand the right reason lying behind each of
them. Consider temperance. Those who have this virtue choose certain
pleasures of taste and touch, but reject others (III.11). But what is the
right reason for choosing one pleasure and rejecting another? That is a
question best answered by someone who has practical wisdom (II.6
1107a1–2), but as Aristotle indicates in VI.1, this does not mean that
nothing further can be said about what the right reason is. The proper
reason for choosing certain pleasures and rejecting others is that the former facilitate and the latter impede our efforts to lead a life whose ultimate end is excellent reasoning. Only the person who uses this standard
chooses in the right way. For example, if someone thought that the ultimate end of human life is health, or some aggregate of health, longevity,
and physical fitness, he might make precisely the same choices among
pleasures as the person who has the right intellectual standard. Even so,
he would not count as a temperate person, according to Aristotle, since
real temperance cannot exist in the absence of practical wisdom (VI.13
1144b16–17), and this person's faulty conception of the ultimate end
shows that he lacks this intellectual virtue. He acts as the temperate person would, but not for the right reason, and so he is not a temperate
person.

A courageous person is not totally without fear (III.7 1115b7–13), but
he is not afraid of everything (1116a2–3). Following reason, he stands
firm in battle when this is what he must do, and he acts for the sake of an
appropriate goal (1115b17–20). But what is the right reason for undertaking courageous actions in defense of one's political community? Nothing
is said about this issue in Books II and III, but we know from what Aristotle says elsewhere that not any rationale for military action is acceptable. We make war in order to bring about peace (X.7 1177b5–6), and so
if someone thinks that the highest human activity is simply to express
valor in the face of death, then even if he controls his fear and acts as the
courageous person does, he does not have genuine courage. But Aristotle
would add that peace is not the ultimate end at which courageous people
should aim; surely we value peace because it allows us to undertake certain peacetime activities. And not just any such activity will serve as an
adequate justification for war. For example, if one fights so that one can
live a life of amusement and physical pleasure, then one fights for the
wrong reason, and one's battlefield valor is not real courage. What Aristotle is telling us, in Book VI, is that the right reason for defending the
polis must appeal to the intellectual activities (whether practical or theoretical) that are protected by that community. The truly courageous person is someone who wants to lead a political or a philosophical life, since

his ultimate end is to use reason well, and this is the right reason for mastering one's fear and withstanding enemies on the battlefield.

Though generosity and magnificence differ in scale, they both concern the proper use of wealth, and for our purposes they can be treated together. In either case, one must take the right amount of money from the right sources, and give the right amount to appropriate beneficiaries; and one must give and take for the sake of the right goal (IV.1 1120a23–6, b27–30). Aristotle's discussion of these virtues cries out for a criterion: How much is the appropriate amount of money to seek for oneself? When does one have more than one needs? To whom should one give? How much? For what reason? Significant help with these questions is provided by his discussion of the virtues of thought in Book VI. One has enough money for oneself when one has all one needs in order to lead either a political life (that is, one devoted to practical reasoning) or a philosophical life. And the best use one can make of one's money when one gives to others is to help them lead either of these two lives. Of course, this does not make financial decisions easy, for it is often difficult to decide how much one needs, even when one is clear about one's ends; and when one owes others good treatment because of the benefits one has received from them, it is hard to know how much financial hardship to endure for their sake. Even so, Book VI puts us in a better position to think about such problems, for it gives us a clearer picture of the two kinds of virtuous activities for whose sake wealth exists. It enables us to see what the right reason is for safeguarding our wealth and helping others.

Magnanimity and the virtue concerned with small honors can also be discussed together, for both are excellences possessed by those who desire honor neither more nor less than they should, and who seek honor in appropriate ways from proper sources (IV.4 1125b1–8). The magnanimous person, for example, thinks that the great honors he receives are deserved, but even so he is only moderately pleased by them (IV.3 1124a5–9). In Book VI, we have a more complete picture of what this virtue involves, for we are given a description of the two kinds of virtues that deserve the greatest honor. It is from people who have theoretical or practical wisdom that we should seek honor, and we should take such honors to be deserved only if we agree that we possess these virtues. If one is pleased by and strives for honors that do not reflect one's excellence as a reasoner, or if one is eager to receive honor from those who are in no position to recognize such excellence, then one is treating that external good more seriously than it deserves. On the other hand, one should not become totally indifferent to the prospect of receiving honors from those who possess the virtues of thought, for such indifference will weaken one's desire to excel as a practical or theoretical reasoner. In order to develop the virtues that govern honor, one must discover what one is capable of accomplishing in the way of practical or theoretical reasoning, and one must undertake no more and no less than one is likely to achieve in either the political or the theoretical realm. Obviously, to attain such self-knowledge, and to choose appropriate sources of honor, one must have some idea of what practical and theoretical wisdom are, and Book VI provides some help by giving a general description of these virtues. And this book also clarifies the right reason for seeking honor: we should want certain honors because having such a desire spurs us on to practical or intellectual accomplishments. Those who seek honor simply because they like to shine in the eyes of others are seeking it for the wrong reason.

When one has the virtue of mildness, one has the amount of anger that is appropriate for one's circumstances (IV.5 1125b31–3); one is not led by one's feelings, but instead one reacts in a way prescribed by reason (b34–5). But what is the right reason for being angry, and how does Book VI help answer this question? Anger is a response to perceived injustice (V.8 1135b28–9), and one's conception of what counts as an injustice will be affected by one's notion of what one deserves (V.3 1131a24–9). If one is not angered by, and puts up with, the insulting treatment commonly meted out to slaves (IV.5 1126a6–8), then that reflects a belief that one deserves no better. And why is it that we do not deserve such treatment? What is it about us that sets us apart from slaves, and entitles us to the respectful treatment owed any free citizen? Aristotle's answer is that free citizens are able to engage in reasoning about political matters, and in some cases about theoretical matters as well. And so, although Book VI gives us no precise answers about how much anger we should show on particular occasions, it gives us a deeper understanding of the underlying reason that sometimes makes anger an appropriate response. And someone who does not understand the virtues described in Book VI, or who does not aim at their expression as an ultimate end, does not really have the virtue that governs anger. For example, if someone takes physical pleasure to be his ultimate end, then he does not have a good argument to back up the anger he displays at insults: since he chooses to lead a life that has an end no better than one other animals can achieve, why should he not be treated in ways that are more appropriate to animals than to free persons? The virtue of mildness, like any other Aristotelian virtue, must be backed up by an understanding of our ultimate end, and it is not enough if one's emotional reactions have a variation in strength that mimics the emotional range displayed by the genuinely virtuous person. Mildness is not simply a matter of matching the strength of one's anger to the magnitude of the insult perceived; it must be deepened by an understanding of why insults are inappropriate, just as genuine courage is deepened by an understanding of why one should go to war. And we can see why Aristotle thinks Book VI gives us this larger understanding.

6.6. MODERATION

The doctrine of the mean tells us that our actions and feelings should lie between two extremes: we can feel too much anger, fear, appetite, and so on, or too little; and we can pursue wealth (for example) either more or less than we should (II.6 1106b16–24). I have tried to show how Book VI saves this doctrine from emptiness, but it still contains an important ambiguity. Consider anger, for example: when Aristotle says that we can feel this emotion too much (b18–20), does he mean that on every occasion we should avoid the greatest point of intensity that this emotion can reach? Is there an extreme of anger that is always wrong, no matter what the provocation? Or is he instead merely saying that over a period of time one can feel this emotion too often? In that case, the greatest possible anger might sometimes be appropriate, and his point about avoiding excessive anger would be that this emotion should never be greater than suits the occasion. The same sort of ambiguity applies to other cases: for example, is Aristotle merely saying that we should not pursue physical pleasure too often, or does he also mean to say that there is an intensity of appetite that must always be avoided, regardless of circumstances?

On one reading, the doctrine of the mean is merely a doctrine of appropriateness: it tells us that the intensity of our feeling should be whatever the circumstances call for. On the other reading, the doctrine of the mean includes as well a call for moderation: when the occasion is appropriate, we should exhibit some degree of anger, fear, appetite, and so on, but we should never let these feelings be as intense as possible. (Similarly, we should have some desire for wealth and honor, but not as intense a desire as possible.) If Aristotle is calling for moderation, he can of course still insist that there is no one right amount of emotion that should be exhibited on all occasions that call for anger, fear, and so on. He can say that sometimes we should be very angry, and at other times only slightly angry. His claim would be that although the appropriate amount of anger varies, and is sometimes quite high, it is in a sense always a moderate (that is, intermediate) amount: whenever anger is called for, the appropriate amount is always greater than zero but less than the greatest amount that is possible.

When several passages are considered together, they make it clear that the doctrine of the mean is a call for moderation in this sense.[25] To begin

[25] Verbally, this brings me into conflict with Urmson, "Aristotle's Doctrine of the Mean," since he says that "the doctrine of moderation is no part of the doctrine of the mean" (p. 162). It might seem that the disagreement is only verbal, since he is taking the doctrine of moderation to be the view that usually when people say "none of that at any price," or "as much of that as possible," they are wrong, and a moderate amount is best (pp. 161–2). But there is real disagreement after all, since I do not attribute *this* doctrine of moderation to Aristotle. The vagueness of Urmson's formulation makes it difficult to determine

with, let us look at the way Aristotle characterizes the intemperate person in III.11. After distinguishing between appetites that are common to all people and those that are peculiar (*idion*), that is, not widely shared (1118b8–15), he says: "With regard to the peculiar pleasures, many go wrong, and in many ways. For when people are called lovers of such things, it is because they enjoy things they should not, or *more than most*, or not as they should; those who are intemperate go to excess in all these ways" (b21–5). By contrast, those who are temperate are repelled by the activities loved by intemperate people, and the pleasure they do take in certain other physical activities is not intense (*sphodra*: 1119a12–14); instead, they have a moderate (*metriōs*) desire for pleasures that are conducive to health, good condition, and so on (a16–18). So, even when it is appropriate for a virtuous person to enjoy physical activities, the strength of his desire for them, and the pleasure derived from them, is not as strong as it could be.

Similarly, the courageous person, even in the face of death, is as unperturbed (*anekplēktos*: III.7 1115b10–11) as a human being can be. Though he feels fear when this is unavoidable (b11–12), he is never in a panic, as people often are in life-threatening situations. So, although the amount of fear one should feel varies with circumstances (b9–10), there is a pitch of fright that should always be avoided. In the same way, when Aristotle says of the mild person—that is, the person whose anger lies in a mean—that he is "undisturbed" (*atarachos*: IV.5 1125b33–5), he does not mean that he is never angry, but rather that his feeling is not so intense that it undermines his ability to carry out a reasoned decision. In this sense, when anger is felt, it should—like physical pleasure and fear—always be moderate in strength. And Aristotle finds some place for moderation in his discussion of all the other virtues treated in Book IV. For example, he says that when we have the appropriate attitude towards honor, we will be only moderately pleased even when we receive great honors from excellent people (IV.3 1124a5–7). To get as excited as some people do about honor is as much of a mistake as total indifference.

Of course, Aristotle is hardly saying that *all* of our feelings should be moderate in strength. Though one can have too much anger, fear, or appetite for one's own good, one can hardly have too strong a desire for happiness for one's own good. And the same holds true of virtuous activity, since that is what happiness is. Aristotle's distinction between feelings that should be intense and those that should be moderate can be understood only in light of his hierarchy of ends. There cannot be too much of

whether Aristotle would assent to it or not. (What are people "usually" talking about when they say "none of that at any price"?) But my main complaint about Urmson's interpretation is that he has overlooked a counsel of moderation which can definitely be found in Aristotle, and which is part of the doctrine of the mean.

what lies at the top, and all other features of human life should be valued to the extent that they contribute to this highest activity.

It might be asked why Aristotle thinks our enjoyment of physical pleasures should be kept within a certain limit. So long as one is eating, or drinking, or having sex, why not get as much pleasure as one can? How can it possibly be a virtue to enjoy these activities less than one might? I think that his call for moderation, in this case as in all others, rests upon certain empirical assumptions. When fear and anger reach a certain level of intensity, they threaten and sometimes undermine our ability to carry out our reasoned decisions (see, for example, IV.5 1125b33–5); similarly, when our love of honor or desire for wealth is too strong, we may not do as well as we might in making decisions about how much to pursue these goods. It is clear that a similar assumption lies behind Aristotle's call for moderation in our enjoyment of physical pleasure. If one greatly enjoys a certain activity, one's desire for it will grow (III.12 1119b3–18), and it will eventually become difficult to make reasonable decisions about how often such physical pleasures should be pursued. Because the question of how much pleasure one needs has no precise answer, there is plenty of room for overestimating the extent to which such activities promote one's ultimate end. To guard against such distortions, it is best to keep one's desire for physical pleasures at a moderate level, and the consequence will be that when one does pursue them, one will not enjoy them as much as is humanly possible. The loss of pleasure, Aristotle thinks, is well worth the gain.

6.7. THE ETHICAL VIRTUES AGAIN

We can now return to the problem we raised in 6.3: why does Aristotle think that such qualities as temperance, courage, and mildness are virtues? Book I by itself does not explain why it is to the good of any human being to cultivate precisely these dispositions, but now that we have a fuller idea of what they involve, it should be clear how Aristotle's defense proceeds.[26]

The function argument attempts to show that our ultimate end should

---

[26] For a different way of interpreting Aristotle's defense of the ethical virtues, see Irwin, "Aristotle's Methods of Ethics," secs. 7–9. He takes Aristotle to be saying that the good consists in the full exercise of all our capacities, and so the vices are to be rejected because they severely limit the development of desires we could have. "Aristotle assumes that a virtuous man enjoys and values more activities rather than fewer" (p. 220). Irwin relies heavily on the principle that more goods are better than fewer (p. 212), and his discussion of the virtues makes no appeal to Aristotle's hierarchical arrangement of goods. If the interpretation given in Chapters 4 and 5 is correct, this misrepresents the weight Aristotle attaches to these two notions. The more-is-better principle plays a minor role in his thinking; the hierarchy of ends and virtues is central.

be an excellent activity of the part of the soul that has reason. Since it is an ultimate end, excellent reasoning should not serve any other type of end, but should instead be that for the sake of which all other goods (honor, wealth, pleasure, and so on) are pursued. Now, once we understand what temperance, courage, mildness, and so on are, and see the empirical assumptions that lie behind Aristotle's call for moderation, it becomes obvious why he thinks we need precisely these dispositions. Suppose one's ultimate end is excellent *practical* reasoning, and one seeks to exercise this virtue on a grand scale, in the political arena. It will suit one's purposes best if one has a temperate person's moderate desire for physical pleasure. Too little appetite endangers one's health, whereas too much disrupts one's reasoning. Similarly, one will need courage: the political community that safeguards one's activities must be defended against enemies, and if one can remain steady in one's post on the battlefield, one's chances of contributing to a successful defense are increased; on the other hand, some degree of fear is needed, since it alerts one to danger and quickens one's reactions. Moderation in anger, and in one's attitude toward wealth, honor, and other external goods that must be distributed in a just fashion, can be recommended by similar arguments. Once we see the pattern Aristotle's thought is following, it becomes easier to understand why he himself does not bother with the details. And his implicit defense of the ethical virtues does not alter if one takes excellent *theoretical* reasoning to be one's end (see 3.8). Moderation in one's emotions and in one's attitude toward external goods is desirable whether one aims at a political or a philosophical life.[27]

[27] On my reading Aristotle is not merely trying to defend the virtues on the grounds that they represent "the Common Sense Morality of Greece, reduced to consistency by careful comparison." The phrase is from Sidgwick, *The Methods of Ethics*, p. xix. Sidgwick also complains that defects in Aristotle's treatment of the ethical virtues "illustrate the fragmentariness and superficiality of treatment to which mere analysis of the common usage of ethical terms is always liable to lead" (*Outlines of the History of Ethics*, p. 64). But Aristotle must be doing more than analyzing common usage; otherwise he could not recognize the existence of virtues for which there are no names (see, for example, IV.4 1125b17, IV.6 1127a7, IV.7 1127a14). He is trying to show why temperance, courage, and so on deserve a prominent place in *any* human life. Excellent theoretical and practical thinking are the proper ultimate ends of human life, just as reproduction is the proper end of plants. See, for example, *Pol.* VII.15 1334b15: "For us, reason and understanding are the end of nature." This commits him to the view that any society that impedes the full development of this end is defective, even if "the Common Sense Morality" of that society makes rational excellence subordinate to certain other "virtues." For example, if a political community makes fierceness in battle the ultimate "virtue," Aristotle will criticize it, because excellent reasoning, not martial valor, should play that role. See *Pol.* VII.2 1324b41–1325a7. If such a society has no notion of practical or theoretical wisdom, and no terms for these virtues of thought, that will not excuse it: Aristotle takes his theory of the human good to be valid for all human beings, and not just those who have words or practices close to those of fourth-century

According to the interpretation I have been presenting, the various virtues of the soul are hierarchically organized, whichever of the two lives
one leads. In the philosophical life, one's ultimate aim is the exercise of
theoretical wisdom, and one is best off if one exercises other virtues to
the extent that they contribute to this highest goal. Similarly, the political
life is devoted to the fullest possible expression of practical wisdom, and
the ethical virtues are desirable because they facilitate this intellectual activity. Performing well on the battlefield—steadily facing the enemy, as
reason dictates—is a means to a higher goal, since we go to war in order
to lead our lives in peace. And this suggests that Aristotle should draw
the following conclusion: secondary happiness does not consist in courageous activity, or in any other exercise of virtue (such as the moderate
enjoyment of sexual activity) in which one is not actually engaged in
practical reasoning. After all, happiness is not a composite of all the goods
contained in a flourishing life, but consists only in the highest end for
which it is lived. And so Aristotle should apparently conclude that, just
as perfect happiness consists in contemplation, secondary happiness consists solely in the exercise of practical wisdom. Of course, this virtue of
thought can sometimes be exercised simultaneously with other practical
excellences: if one's anger really is moderate and responsive to reason,
then one should be able to think just as well when one is angry as when
one is not experiencing this emotion. But there are times when exercising
an ethical virtue—such as courage—is incompatible with carrying on a
deliberative inquiry. And so Aristotle should say that these activities in
accordance with virtue are not among the activities in which happiness
consists.

I do not think he ever draws this conclusion. On the contrary, he says
that happiness consists in activity in accordance with *perfect* virtue, and I
take the ethical virtues to be among the excellences he has in mind (4.17).
But I think we can understand why he includes ethical virtues, as well as
the virtues of thought, in his account of what happiness is. Even though
the press of action may prevent one from deliberating while exercising
the ethical virtues, one is still acting out of a conception of the good that
one has arrived at through excellent reasoning. Practical reasoning is part

Greece. Contrast Nussbaum, *The Fragility of Goodness*, pp. 245–250. She takes Aristotle to
be confining himself to the question of what *we* should think, where "we" is restricted to
those whose linguistic practices and way of life resemble those of fourth-century Greeks. I
am in agreement with Irwin, who holds that although in some passages "Aristotle simply
reports and organizes the common beliefs and prejudices of his contemporaries," this characterization "does not express a just view of his account as a whole" ("Aristotle's Methods
of Ethics," p. 219). In defending the political and the philosophical lives, Aristotle is not
simply recording "Common Sense Morality," for both lives were objects of criticism (VI.8
1142a1–9, X.7 1177b31–3), and Aristotle's response to these criticisms is not merely an
appeal to what most people think.

of a process that is designed to eventuate in action, and so when one finally acts, in light of that reasoning, one's ethically virtuous behavior can be understood only if it is seen as the issue of prior deliberation. Furthermore, if the arational part of the soul is not properly trained to follow one's reasoning, then the action at which one is aiming may easily misfire. So the actions that reflect our nature as creatures who have reason are guided not solely by the part of the soul that takes thought, but also by the part that listens to reason. When we trace ethical actions from their origin in excellent reasoning about the human good to their conclusion in successful action, we recognize that we are studying a single organized process. Different parts of the soul, rational and arational, contribute to that process, but they work together as a single unit, and this is why Aristotle equates secondary happiness not just with the exercise of practical wisdom but with the whole activity that runs from excellent reasoning through moderate feeling to successful action. But the fact that practical wisdom and ethical virtue form a single unit should not prevent us from seeing that there is a hierarchical structure within this unit: the ethical virtues are obedient to reason, and the latter provides the standard by which the ethical mean is found.

We should also recall that Aristotle's argument in defense of the ethical virtues does not rest on a commitment to any maximizing form of egoism. He wants to show why a good life for any human being must be one in which we possess and exercise the ethical virtues, but this does not mean that we should always seek to maximize our own good. There are many reasons for acting courageously, temperately, and so on, and some of them concern one's own well-being. But obviously ethical activity benefits others as well, and Aristotle is not saying that the self-regarding reasons for engaging in these activities have greater weight than the other-regarding reasons.[28] In fact, he must say that altruistic considerations sometimes take priority, for when the pursuit of one's highest end—

[28] See *NE* V.1 1129b25–1130a13: every ethical virtue is capable of being exercised in ways that benefit others as well as oneself. In the *Politics*, Aristotle emphasizes the need to inculcate habits that will be of value to the other citizens living in a particular kind of political system. See *Pol.* I.13 1260b13–18, V.9 1310a12–36, VIII.1 1337a11–30. He is of course not denying that the ethical virtues will benefit the person who possesses them. His claim, rather, is that it would be pointless to train people in habits that would make them good citizens of a democratic regime if in fact they are growing up in an oligarchy. (I take him to be assuming that these constitutions are equally reasonable approximations of the ideal, when they are not extreme democracies or extreme oligarchies.) Skill in the use of an expensive weapon may be required for the exercise of courage in an oligarchy, but in democracies courage may be shown through the use of other, less expensive weapons. In general, the training a person receives should look not only to his good but to that of others as well. And this point holds for ideal political communities as well as those that approximate the ideal: Aristotle emphasizes it in VIII.1 no less than in V.9.

whether it consists in theoretical or practical reasoning—would interfere with the like pursuit of others, the appropriate course of action may be to choose less happiness for oneself so that others may have their fair share.

6.8. THE POLITICAL LIFE

Even if we see why Aristotle thinks that the best ultimate end (aside from philosophy) is activity in accordance with such practical virtues as justice, courage, and temperance, we may still ask how this leads to the conclusion that those who adopt this end should choose a *political* life. To lead such a life is to take an active part in the governance of one's community, but surely it is possible to possess and exercise the virtues of courage, temperance, generosity, justice, mildness, and so on even if one stays away from politics. Why does Aristotle think that the political life is better than a private life in which one exercises the virtues by devoting oneself to the well-being of a small circle of friends and family? Of course, he thinks that withdrawal from politics is the best course of action: the philosophical life is better than the political life, because the former has a better ultimate end. But why should those who adopt practical activity as an ultimate end be involved in politics?

We know from *NE* VI.8 that a life of withdrawal appealed to some of Aristotle's contemporaries. To them, concern with matters beyond one's own immediate circle is a form of hyperactivity, and political leaders are mere busybodies (1142a1–9). But Aristotle is disappointingly brief in his criticism of this attitude. He simply says: "And yet presumably one's own well-being does not exist without household management and a political system" (a9–10). The idea seems to be that the private person is dependent on the political leader, and so those who advocate widespread withdrawal from politics are subverting their own lives. But this argument will not take Aristotle very far, for he himself believes that the philosophical life is superior to the political life, and he cannot concede that this thesis is undermined by the observation that one cannot lead a philosophical life "without household management and a political system." The fact that we all need politicians is compatible with the possibility that their work is very disagreeable, and that we should avoid it if we can.

I suggest that Aristotle's high regard for the political life rests on the assumption that ruling the state takes more practical wisdom than does exercising the practical virtues in the private sphere. Providing for the well-being of a whole community is a more difficult task than any other worthwhile practical undertaking, and to do it well requires a great deal of thought and experience. When sciences and crafts can be arranged hierarchically, so that superior disciplines have governance over those that are inferior, the higher-order disciplines require a greater degree of wisdom than the lower-order disciplines (*Met.* I.2 982a10–19). And the greater degree of wisdom one exercises, the more desirable one's activity. Accordingly, since politics is the practical discipline that has jurisdiction over all others, it most fully exercises our skills as practical reasoners. Once we accept Aristotle's claim that our highest end (philosophy aside) is the excellent exercise of practical reason, and his further claim that political problems provide the greatest opportunity for the use of these skills, we should see why a private life devoted to ethical virtue is inferior to an outstanding public life. Though it is possible to be just, generous, temperate, and so on without taking an active part in political matters, one's efforts will not call forth a high degree of practical wisdom, which, as we have seen, is the principal virtue of the nonphilosophical life. Those who cannot lead a life devoted to theoretical wisdom therefore do best by devoting themselves to the well-being of others—not merely for the sake of others, but because this will allow for the fullest possible development and use of the second-best virtue.

This attitude is evident in *NE* I.2, where Aristotle takes politics to be the discipline that understands the human good, and rules all others in light of that understanding. Even at this early point in his discussion, he asserts the superiority of public over private life: "For even if [the good] is the same for one [person] and for the city, it seems greater and more perfect to attain and preserve that of the city. For although one must be content [to do this] even for one [person] alone, it is finer and more divine to do so for a people and for cities" (1094b7–10). I take him to be saying that it is finer to lead a political life because political success is a more difficult and therefore greater achievement. Those who promote well-being "for a people and for cities" exercise a greater degree of skill than those who are concerned with just one person. And it is more godlike to do this: just as gods are at the pinnacle of the cosmic order, so political leaders occupy the topmost position in the hierarchy of causal forces that affect the well-being of all other citizens. The point is not simply that statesmen have great power, but that the exercise of that power for the well-being of large numbers requires considerable wisdom.

Superficially, there seems to be a conflict between what Aristotle says in this passage and what he later says in defense of the philosophical life. For philosophers do not promote the good of a whole city; at most, through their teaching, they benefit a small circle of intellectuals. And yet we are told in X.8 that they are more godlike than any other human beings. I suggest that we resolve this apparent contradiction in the following way: Aristotle is not claiming, at this early point in Book I, that the political life is superior to the philosophical life. He does not even raise that issue until I.5, and there he postpones it to X.7–8. Accordingly, we should also take I.2 to be setting aside the philosophical life for later treatment, and assuming, for the sake of simplicity, that the good "is the same for one [person] and for the city" (1094b7–8). Proceeding on that assumption, Aristotle asserts that it is better to promote that good among a large group than to promote it for just one person. This is not the controversial claim that attaining good A for few is worse than attaining an inferior good B for many. Were Aristotle making that claim, he could be asked why differences in quality are never enough to outweigh differences in quantity. Instead, he is simply saying that whatever the good turns out to be, it will be a greater accomplishment if we can secure it not only for ourselves, but for a whole city as well. As it turns out, however, the highest human good is not one that whole cities will ever pursue; Aristotle's claim requires refinement, and turns into the point that it is better to exercise practical wisdom and the ethical virtues in ways that benefit the whole community than to exercise these same skills on a far smaller scale. The political life is more divine than a private life when the latter is devoted to the exercise of the same excellences on a smaller scale. This point is entirely compatible with the thesis that a different kind of virtuous activity—one that is theoretical rather than practical—is even more godlike.

6.9. The Philosophical Life

I have tried to show (6.1–2) how the function argument of I.7 defends excellent reasoning as an ultimate end, and (6.3–8) how moral virtue and political activity are connected with that argument. It should be clear that Aristotle does not use the function argument by itself as a way of establishing the superiority of the philosophical over the political life. In I.7, he merely wants to support the more general point that our ultimate end should be to use reason well. He alludes to theoretical wisdom when he speaks of the "best and most perfect" virtue (1098a17–18), but that is because he is anticipating the arguments he will give later, in X.7–8, not because he thinks the function argument itself establishes the supremacy of theoretical reasoning. For all I.7 shows, it could turn out that the best life is devoted to excellent *practical* reasoning, or that our ultimate end should be a composite of political and philosophical activity. It is not until X.7–8 that we are given any reasons for taking contemplation by itself to be our ultimate end.

But just as it would be a mistake to take I.7 as a complete argument on behalf of the theoretical life, so too it would be wrong to read the arguments of X.7 as though they constituted a self-sufficient argument for the supremacy of contemplation.[29] Instead, I.7 and X.7 must be read together

[29] Although the arguments of X.7 are not independent of the function argument, I think that the argument from divinity in X.8 does stand on its own.

if we are to understand Aristotle's case for philosophy. For example, one of the points he makes in favor of contemplation is that it requires fewer external goods than political activity (1177a27–b1). It would be wrong-headed to isolate this argument from all the others, and take him to be saying that the best choice for an ultimate end is the activity that requires the fewest external goods. On such a reading, he would be vulnerable to the criticism that perception is a higher activity than philosophical thought: to be perceivers, we need no help at all from others, whereas co-workers do facilitate our intellectual activities, as Aristotle himself recognizes (1177a34). He is not open to this objection, because in I.7 perception is eliminated as a candidate for the ultimate end, and so it does not matter whether it requires less external equipment than philosophy. Book I taken as a whole has established that reasoning well should be our ultimate end, and the only question that remains, in X.7–8, is this: on the assumption that the two best types of reasoning activity are those that express theoretical and practical wisdom, are there any grounds for thinking that one of these activities is a better ultimate end than the other? And Aristotle clearly indicates that X.7–8 is to be connected in this way with I.7. For in X.6, he summarizes some of the main results of Book I, and insists that happiness consists not in amusement but in activity in accordance with virtue (1177a1–2, 9–11)—a conclusion reached in the function argument, and confirmed by further material in I.8–11. And the opening lines of X.7 ("if happiness is activity in accordance with virtue, it is reasonable that it is in accordance with the best," 1177a12–13) indicate that the points to be made on behalf of contemplation are dependent on the function argument.

A number of those points have already been discussed. In 3.6 and 5.11, we considered Aristotle's claim that theoretical activity has more self-sufficiency than practical activity (1177a27–8), and in 3.11–12 we examined his statement that philosophy "alone seems to be loved for itself" (1177b1–2). And of course, the argument from divinity (1178b7–32) received a good deal of attention in 1.13–16. But several of the arguments of X.7 have not been mentioned, and I would now like to say something about them.

First, Aristotle says that *nous* (understanding) is the best thing in us, and that the objects of knowledge with which it is concerned are the best objects of knowledge (1177a19–21). I take him to mean that the knowledge to be had by the philosopher is of a higher order than that to be had by the excellent practical reasoner. Theoretical wisdom gives us an understanding of necessary truths about eternal objects (VI.3 1139b19–24), and the sciences that study these objects admit of a precision that cannot be matched by practical studies.[30]

---

[30] For Aristotle, the better objects of knowledge are those about which a higher degree of

Second, he says that theoretical activity is more continuous than any other (1177a21–2). I take this to mean that it is possible to think uninterruptedly about theoretical matters for longer periods than one can do anything else uninterruptedly. Presumably Aristotle says this because he and his colleagues could go on thinking about a problem for a large part of the day without needing a break, whereas he observed that those involved in the discussion of political issues, athletes, craftsmen, and so on would need a change after just a few hours of work. No doubt his powers of concentration were formidable, but his point is vulnerable to empirical disconfirmation. Aside from this problem, we may wonder how greater continuity can provide a reason for preferring an activity. Continuity may affect how much we can engage in an activity, but what does this point about quantity have to do with quality? Aristotle needs to show that theorizing is better than practical activity, not that more of it is available to us.

But the question of duration is not irrelevant to the choice between lives. For suppose that good A is better than good B, but that one can engage in A for only short periods of time, which must be followed by long periods of rest and inactivity, whereas one can engage in B far more continuously. In such a case, the intrinsic superiority of A to B might be outweighed by the fact that one can have much more of B. It would be reasonable to avoid A entirely because so little of one's time can actually be devoted to it, and so much of one's time must be spent recovering from it. What Aristotle is saying is that no such criticism can be made of contemplation; on the contrary, we can spend more time on this activity than on any other. So even if greater continuity is not in itself evidence of superiority, it is a consideration that cannot be neglected.

Furthermore, greater continuity can be construed as a sign that we are better adapted to pursue one activity than another. If someone can think about theoretical problems all day long, but physical labor exhausts him after a few minutes, then the former activities are more suited to his nature; they are the activities he should choose, because he can excel at them

---

precision is possible. See *Met.* I.2 982a19–28. Given the imprecision of practical reasoning (see the texts cited in Chapter 1, note 16), it is understandable that he takes it to be a less satisfactory expression of reason than theoretical activity. Our own views have this degree of similarity to Aristotle's: since deliberation, unlike nonpractical theorizing (in mathematics, history, or physical science, for example), is necessarily directed at the future, and knowledge of the future is often scarce and imprecise, reason normally has less material to work with when it deliberates than it does when it studies theoretical matters. According to Wilkes, "The Good Man," p. 348, Aristotle is saying that since philosophy studies divine objects, and practical reasoning concerns human affairs, the former has a higher object than the latter. But if that were his argument, he would be committed to the view that politics is a better pursuit than the study of animals. And that is not what he thinks. As we saw in 1.19, his defense of philosophy also constitutes a defense of the study of animals, mathematics, and any other source of necessary truths.

more than he can excel as a physical worker. Similarly, Aristotle may be saying that since the best theoreticians can keep at their activity longer than the best politicians, craftsmen, or athletes can continue with theirs, contemplation is the activity at which human nature can most excel. The best activity is the one that comes to us most naturally, once we have trained for it, and what human beings can do most continuously, without being interrupted by physical or mental fatigue, is that for which they have the most talent.[31]

Third, Aristotle says, "it is agreed that the most pleasant of activities in accordance with virtue is that in accordance with wisdom" (1177a23–5). The superiority of contemplation to practical activity is established not simply by means of argument, but by experience as well. I take him to be saying that those who have enjoyed the pleasures of the philosophical life have also experienced the pleasure of exercising the practical virtues, and are generally agreed that the former are greater as pleasures. For a comparison can be made only by those who have felt both. We should be careful not to dismiss Aristotle's observation too quickly: he is not saying that all those who have tried intellectual work have immediately reported that they find it more pleasant than exercising practical excellence. It must have been as obvious to him as it is to us that some people do not enjoy intellectual activity. Rather, his claim is that those few who have acquired theoretical wisdom have found its associated activity more pleasurable than any other virtuous activity. If Aristotle has included in his sample a large enough number of those who have acquired both kinds of virtues (theoretical and practical), then he is right to be impressed by this unanimity of experience. And we should remember that the greater pleasure provided by contemplation is not by itself put forward as a reason to pursue it as an ultimate end. The mere fact that one activity is more pleasurable than another would at most show that, other things being equal, we should spend more time on it. It would not by itself show that all other ends should be pursued for the sake of the greater pleasure. And there is no reason for thinking that Aristotle is making this mistake.

After X.7 considers the pleasantness of contemplation, it moves on to two points we have already considered, namely, that this activity is most self-sufficient, and is alone loved for itself. And it then comes to a fourth point that has not been mentioned so far: happiness depends on *scholē* ("leisure," 1177b4), but practical activities are deficient in this respect, whereas contemplation is not (b4–15). The term "leisure" has the unfortunate suggestion of relaxation, but Aristotle is not saying that intellec-

---

[31] This does not commit Aristotle to the view that one should strive to lead a philosophical life whether or not one has a talent for theoretical pursuits. He can say that if someone finds such subjects laborious, and cannot think about them for long periods of time without needing to relax, then the philosophical life is not for him.

tual activity is what we should do in order to relax: that role is played by amusement rather than by virtuous activity (X.6 1176b33–5). His point emerges more clearly when he goes on (1177b4–5) to use the verb (*scholazein*) corresponding to *scholē*, and contrasts it with *ascholazein*: the latter is a matter of engaging in an activity that is to some degree troubled, wearying, or painful. The sentence in question might best be translated: "we take on trouble (*ascholoumetha*) in order to do something untroubled (*scholazōmen*)."[32] So when he says that happiness depends on *scholē*, his point is that it consists in some untroubled activity, and the lines that follow point out that practical activities are troublesome in varying degrees:

> We take on trouble in order to do something untroubled, and we make war in order to bring about peace. Now, in the case of the practical virtues, there is activity in political and military matters, but the actions that concern these matters seem to be troublesome (*ascholoi*), and are completely so in military matters. For no one chooses to make war, or prepares for war, for the sake of making war. For someone would seem completely defiled by blood if he made war upon friends so that there would be battles and gore. But the activity of the politician is also troublesome, and obtains, beyond political action, positions of power and honors, or at any rate happiness for himself and for the citizens, which is different from the activity of politics, and which we obviously seek as something different. (1177b4–15)

Though courageous acts on the battlefield are outstanding in virtue, and mastery of fear guided by practical wisdom is good in itself, whether or not it eventuates in victory, everyone but a bloodthirsty person hopes that something better than war will emerge from it. So the soldier cannot be unconcerned with the way his present action is connected with the future, and since the future is uncertain, this concern must take its toll. War is wearying, and not just because of the physical efforts it requires. But Aristotle says here that some of these same features appear even in the peacetime activities of the politician. For he says that military actions are *completely* troublesome; that is, political and military activities are both troublesome, but the latter are more so than the former.

Why the difference? Aristotle does not explain, but merely asserts that political action aims at something beyond itself. I take his point to be as follows: The soldier undertakes military activity for the sake of a different type of activity: he makes war not for the sake of war, but for the sake of something better than war. And so he has to be concerned about whether his actions will have the effect he wants them to have. Now, the politician's attitude toward his activity shares one of these features but not the

---

[32] Irwin translates: "we accept trouble so that we can be at leisure."

other. His activity is wearying and troubled to some extent because he too has to be concerned about the future: though he enjoys the activity of making decisions (it is, after all, something at which he excels), he is not making this particular decision just for its own sake, but is aiming at something in the future—"positions of power and honors, or at any rate happiness for himself and for the citizens." True, he is not necessarily aiming at an end other than political activity: if his aim is to make the citizens (himself and others) active in accordance with practical virtue, then he is trying to promote the conditions in which future political activity will flourish. His present deliberations are for the sake of future excellence in deliberation.[33] But even though his present activity is directed at activity of the same type (and so he is not like the soldier, who makes war for the sake of something else), it is still future-directed, and is for this reason troubled and wearying to some degree.

When we look at our passage in this way, we can see why Aristotle thinks that contemplation is "as untroublesome (*scholastikon*) and unwearying" as human activity can get (1177b22). For one's present contemplation is something that can be enjoyed entirely for itself; one is simply bringing to mind certain truths, and one enjoys reflecting on these matters, giving no thought to the future. By contrast, however much the political thinker enjoys deliberating, his present pleasure is accompanied by the somewhat troubling thought that the success of what he is now doing depends partly on what the future will bring. This wearisome aspect of practical thought perhaps accounts for the fact that it is less continuous and pleasant than contemplation.

This completes my account of Aristotle's argument on behalf of the contemplative life.[34] That argument begins in I.7 but remains incomplete

---

[33] See note 19 above, and contrast the way our passage is interpreted by Korsgaard, "Aristotle and Kant on the Source of Value," pp. 493–4. She says, p. 494: "The statesperson makes laws and establishes conditions in which the citizens can have a good life: a life that will not consist of making laws and establishing conditions but, rather, of something else." She takes that "something else" to be contemplation. In effect, on her interpretation Aristotle is saying that political activity has value only on condition that it promotes contemplation. Such a reading would be credible only if I.7 had placed ethically virtuous activity in the same category as craft activity: in that case, both would be ends worth pursuing only on condition that they lead to some other type of good. But I take Aristotle to be saying in I.7 that the ethical virtues are unlike the craft virtues in precisely this respect. See the discussion of the distinction between perfect and imperfect virtues in 4.17.

[34] Aristotle says at 1178a2–7 that *nous* is most of all what a human being is, but I take this to be a consequence of the six points he has been making in favor of contemplation, rather than a seventh advantage of the philosophical life. He says, "each [person] would seem to be this [*nous*], if [this] is what is controlling and better" (a2–3). The antecedent of this conditional is supported by the previous arguments, and the identity of a person with theoretical reason is the consequent. (For the sense in which this is our controlling part, see 4.23.) We should not be surprised to find Aristotle saying this: when he equates the function of a

until these four additional points (and the two discussed earlier) are made. And it is then supplemented, in X.8, by the argument from divinity, which stands on its own. It should also be remembered that, according to Aristotle, any argument on behalf of an ultimate end must be confirmed: if it really is the good for the sake of which all others are pursued, then the many goods we took for granted at the beginning of our inquiry must be included in a life devoted to that ultimate end. Aristotle is attentive to this point in I.8–11, where he shows that a life devoted to the exercise of practical virtues will require the support of external goods. And although he does not remind us in X.7–8 that such confirmation is also needed for his defense of contemplation, we have seen (3.12) that he gives some attention to the subordinate goods that promote a philosophical life. A life devoted to theorizing will not abandon these other goods, but will include them all. It is "choiceworthy and in need of nothing" (1097b15), and contemplation is what makes it so, by being the ultimate end around which all other goods are organized.

6.10. Final Thoughts

I have now done all I can to support my reading of the *NE*. My main aim has been to show how Aristotle's discussions of happiness in Books I and X fit together as a unity. Proceeding on the assumption that Aristotle intends these portions of his theory to complement each other, I have argued that the apparent contradictions between them are merely apparent. But even if my interpretation is not in the end accepted by the reader,

---

human being with activity of the rational soul in accordance with the most perfect virtue, he is telling us what a human being is. Human beings are, by definition, philosophical animals, because their function consists in contemplating, and living things are defined in terms of their function. (See *Meteor.* IV.12 390a10–13, *De An.* II.1 412b9–22, *De Gen. An.* I.2 716a23, *Met.* VII.10 1035b16–18, *Pol.* I.2 1253a23.) Of course, this definition is not something we are in a position to know at the beginning of our inquiry; rather, it is a result we achieve once we have discovered what the ultimate end of a human being is. Though few human beings satisfy the definition of the species, the lives of those who do not are defective approximations of the ideal. So any human being can be understood by means of the definition. My interpretation is the reverse of one that is sometimes proposed: according to this view, Aristotle thinks that we should *first* define what a human being is, and *then*, on the basis of that definition, we will know what the human good is. My thesis is that we discover what we are only after we have run through all of the arguments concerning what our ultimate end should be. For the contrary view, see Irwin, "The Metaphysical and Psychological Basis of Aristotle's Ethics"; Wilkes, "The Good Man," p. 343; Nussbaum, *De Motu Animalium*, p. 105; Clark, *Aristotle's Man*, p. 17; Cooper, *RHGA*, p. 157. (Unlike Cooper, I do not take Aristotle to be saying at 1177b26–7 that the contemplative life is "too exalted to suit a human being." Instead, I would translate: "Such a life would be better (*kreittōn*) than one that is human." Cf. Irwin's translation: "Such a life would be superior to the human level.")

I hope I have at least shown that many of the topics treated in the *NE* must be considered together if we are to make progress in our understanding of the whole work. For example, the question of how to read Book VI, with its complaint about the mean, cannot be separated from the question of how to interpret Aristotle's conception of happiness. This in turn cannot be understood unless we decide whether his thought can be fit into an egoistic mold, and to resolve this question we must of course turn to Books VIII and IX. And since his views about the individual's relationship to the larger community are more fully revealed in the *Politics*, that work must also be included in any thorough investigation. Furthermore, as we have seen, the question of how to understand the function argument, and its connection with the ethical virtues, cannot be isolated from a study of X.6–8 and its relationship to preceding material. The value of pressing questions about contemplation should be apparent once we see how much depends on the relation between that peculiar good and the other topics treated by the *NE*.

Though I have been reluctant to believe that Aristotle commits obvious errors, I have said nothing in defense of his conception of the human good. My task has simply been the historical one of interpretation. But it is obvious that at least some of what he says about human well-being cannot be true. The chief example of this is his argument from divinity, for although it deserves study because of the light it sheds on X.7–8, no one can now believe that there is an eternal unmoved mover who does nothing but think. So one of the arguments he uses to support his conception of happiness must be abandoned. Similarly, we cannot accept his belief that many men (natural slaves) and women have reasoning abilities so restricted that they cannot share in political activity or an intellectual life. But fortunately for Aristotle, his conception of the human good, and his defense of that conception, do not fall apart once these erroneous beliefs are abandoned.

In this final section, I would like to discuss a further problem in his theory. As we have seen, he thinks that there should be one good—reasoning in accordance with perfect virtue—for the sake of which all others are pursued. And his argument for that thesis depends in part on the assumption that human beings can lead lives that are superior to those of other animals and plants. Is this merely an expression of human arrogance and parochialism?[35] Can anything be said in its defense?

---

[35] See Gould, *Ever since Darwin*, p. 25, quoting one of Darwin's notebooks: "Why is thought, being a secretion of brain, more wonderful than gravity, a property of matter? It is our arrogance, our admiration of ourselves" (commas added). On p. 36, Gould says, "Darwin reminded himself never to say 'higher' or 'lower' in describing the structure of organisms—for if an amoeba is as well adapted to its environment as we are to ours, who is to say that we are higher creatures?" See too p. 50 on "our cosmic arrogance."

I don't think Aristotle's assumption is easy to dismiss, for it seems to be embedded in common practices that we take to be justified. Living things—plants, viruses, and so on—are intentionally killed every day for the sake of human survival, health, and well-being. If we did not eat, or combat diseases, we would die; if we did not cut down trees, we would have no books. What, if anything, justifies us in taking the lives of other creatures on such a massive scale? We do not think it right for one person to take many human lives merely because he needs to in order to survive; but it would be crazy to challenge the morality of someone who pulled mushrooms from the ground in order to stay alive. And of course there is a great deal of destruction of nonhuman life that is not needed for mere survival: even if there are some books so worthless that we regret the loss of the trees from which they were produced, it would again be crazy to say that since we can live without printed matter, we have no justification for cutting down trees. And our belief that we can justifiably take the lives of trees, mushrooms, and so on is not adequately explained by the point that, after all, they feel no pain when we kill them. We can kill other human beings painlessly, and would still be wrong in doing so. Therefore, the painlessness of taking plant life cannot by itself make this practice unobjectionable. When we take the lives of plants, we are doing something that we ourselves believe is bad for them; we think that a disease harms a tree, and that its death is even worse. And when we injure other living beings, we should have some justification. If we have none, we should stop interfering with their lives.

Once we are puzzled by this question, as I think we should be, it is natural to consider the possibility that human beings have some property that other creatures lack, and that this is what justifies our destructive practices. The idea is that human life is more valuable than the lives of certain other living beings, and so we can kill them when this is necessary for human survival or flourishing. And we might also say that other living beings can be placed somewhere in a hierarchy: some are so close to us that we can justifiably take their lives only in the most extreme circumstances (if ever); others are so distant that we can kill them so long as we do so for nonfrivolous purposes. But if we think along these lines, then we must also ask what it is about human beings that makes our lives superior. It must be some morally relevant property that all or nearly all members of the human community have, and that other living beings either lack or possess to a lesser degree. Surely one plausible candidate for such a property is our ability to reason and to be guided by standards of reasoning. This is something we value; it is widely shared among humans; and other creatures either lack it entirely or possess it at only an elementary level.

It may not be easy, then, to justify our practices unless we accept Aristotle's assumption that our lives are more valuable than those of other living beings. We might also be willing to accept a further step, and say that it is reason that makes the moral difference between us and other creatures. But even if we grant these points, we are still a long way from the conclusion he draws. He does not merely want to say that reasoning, or excellent reasoning, should be one of the goods included in our lives. That is a weak point we might be prepared to concede; for if a life leaves no room for reasoning well, then how can it be a better life than that of nonhuman creatures? But Aristotle is trying to convince us to make good reasoning the *ultimate* end of our lives. His claim is that if we make excellent thinking merely one of our activities, and subordinate it to the achievement of some further goal, then we are not living as well as we could be. And he would support this claim by asking us to consider the lives of those whose reasoning skills are directed at the achievement of some other type of good. Consider craftsmen, for example. He concedes that good craftsmen use reason well, since they employ thinking skills in producing the ends of their crafts. But, according to Aristotle, craft-reasoning cannot be the best type of thinking that humans are capable of, since it is undertaken for the sake of some other type of end—a bridle, or health, or victory. And when B is pursued for the sake of A, B is less choiceworthy than A. So craft-reasoning must be inferior to such ends as bridles, health, and victory. And these ends are in turn desired for the sake of further goals. Only ends that are not pursued for the sake of some other type of end deserve a place in the top row of the hierarchy, and only lives organized around such ends deserve to be models of human flourishing. Excellent reasoning pursued for the sake of excellent reasoning is the only goal that passes this test.

It should be clear, from what I have just said and from the interpretation I proposed in Chapter 4, that a great deal of work in Aristotle's theory is done by his conception of a hierarchy of ends linked together by the for-the-sake-of relation. He thinks we can see from many examples that when B is for the sake of A, B is less choiceworthy than A; and so our ultimate end must consist solely in ends that are not pursued for the sake of anything further. That—rather than the assumption of human superiority—is the central building block of his theory that we must resist. For it is plausible to say in many cases that when B-ing is directed at a certain goal, A or A-ing, the former is more worthwhile than the latter. For example, many people find intellectual inquiry more enjoyable than contemplating the truths reached through such inquiry; their search is undertaken for the sake of knowing the truth, but the process of inquiry is more attractive to them than the activity of bringing to mind the truths they uncover. In the same way, engineers may find the process of designing equipment far more desirable than possessing the product at which they are aiming. And Aristotle gives no reason for thinking that these evaluations are misguided. Now, once we reject his conception of the for-the-sake-of relation, we are free to challenge his assumption that philosophical and political lives are the two paradigms of human well-being. We can grant that excellence in reasoning must play some role in any good human life, but deny that lives in which this activity is undertaken for its own sake are better than those in which reasoning skills are put to use for some purpose other than reasoning.

Aristotle must settle for the thesis that lives devoted to philosophy and to the expression of ethical virtue are among the good lives human beings can have. He cannot reach the stronger conclusion that they are best. But the claim that a life devoted to ethical activity is a good life, when it is properly sustained by other goods, should itself be of great interest to us. And Aristotle has provided some of the materials needed for the defense of this thesis. Ethical virtue of the highest order cannot be divorced from such skills as judgment, insight, rational planning, and the other qualities of mind that comprise practical wisdom. We think that ideally one should have the ability to reflect on one's goals, to adjust or abandon them in light of experience and reasoned criticism, and to apply them in particular circumstances. To develop these qualities, and to integrate them properly with one's feelings, is a difficult achievement, and it is in part an intellectual achievement. So Aristotle is not too distant from the truth when he sees a kinship between the philosophical and the moral lives, and gives a common defense of both.

Bibliography

Ackrill, J. L. *Aristotle's Ethics*. London: Faber & Faber, 1973.

———. "Aristotle on *Eudaimonia*." In *Essays on Aristotle's Ethics*, edited by A. Rorty, pp. 15–33. Berkeley and Los Angeles: University of California Press, 1980.

Adkins, A.W.H. "*Theoria* versus *Praxis* in the *Nicomachean Ethics* and the *Republic*." *Classical Philology* 73 (1978): 297–313.

———. "The Connection between Aristotle's *Ethics* and *Politics*." *Political Theory* 12 (1984): 29–49.

Allan, D. J. *The Philosophy of Aristotle*, 2d ed. London: Oxford University Press, 1970.

Annas, Julia. "Plato and Aristotle on Friendship and Altruism." *Mind* 86 (1977): 532–554.

Anscombe, G.E.M. *Intention*, 2d ed. Ithaca, N.Y.: Cornell University Press, 1963.

Barnes, Jonathan. "Aristotle and the Methods of Ethics." *Revue Internationale de Philosophie* 34 (1980): 490–511.

Brandt, Richard B. *Ethical Theory: The Problems of Normative and Critical Ethics*. Englewood Cliffs, N.J.: Prentice-Hall, 1959.

———. *A Theory of the Good and the Right*. Oxford: Clarendon Press, 1979.

Broad, C. D. "Egoism as a Theory of Human Motives." In *Broad's Critical Essays in Moral Philosophy*, edited by C. D. Broad, pp. 247–261. London: George Allen & Unwin, 1971.

———. "Self and Others." In *Broad's Critical Essays in Moral Philosophy*, edited by C. D. Broad, pp. 262–282. London: George Allen & Unwin, 1971.

Burnet, John. *The Ethics of Aristotle*, edited with introduction and notes. New York: Arno Press, 1973.

Bywater, I. *Aristotelis Ethica Nicomachea*. Oxford: Clarendon Press, 1894.

Clark, Stephen R.L. *Aristotle's Man: Speculations upon Aristotelian Anthropology*. Oxford: Clarendon Press, 1975.

Cooper, John M. "The *Magna Moralia* and Aristotle's Moral Philosophy." *American Journal of Philology* 94 (1973): 327–349.

———. *RHGA = Reason and Human Good in Aristotle*. Cambridge: Harvard University Press, 1975.

———. "Aristotle on Friendship." In *Essays on Aristotle's Ethics*, edited by A. Rorty, pp. 301–340. Berkeley and Los Angeles: University of California Press, 1980.

———. "Aristotle on the Goods of Fortune." *The Philosophical Review* 94 (1985): 173–196.

———. "Contemplation and Happiness: A Reconsideration." *Synthese* 72 (1987): 187–216.

Devereux, Daniel T. "Aristotle on the Essence of Happiness." In *Studies in Aris-*

totle, edited by Dominic J. O'Meara, pp. 247–260. Washington, D.C.: Catholic University of America Press, 1981.

Dirlmeier, Franz. *Aristoteles, Magna Moralia, übersetzt und erläutert*. Darmstadt: Wissenschaftliche Buchgesellschaft, 1958.

Düring, Ingemar. *Aristotle's Protrepticus: An Attempt at Reconstruction*. Göteborg: Elanders Boktryckeri Antiebolag, 1961.

Eriksen, Trond Berg. *Bios Theoretikos: Notes on Aristotle's Ethica Nicomachea, X,6– 8*. Oslo: Universitetsforlaget, 1976.

Field, G. C. *Moral Theory: An Introduction to Ethics*, 2d ed. London: Methuen, 1932.

Fortenbaugh, W. W. *Aristotle on Emotion: A Contribution to Philosophical Psychology, Rhetoric, Poetics, Politics and Ethics*. London: Gerald Duckworth, 1975.

Frankena, William K. *Ethics*, 2d ed. Englewood Cliffs, N.J.: Prentice-Hall, 1973.

Gauthier, René Antoine, and Jolif, Jean Yves. *L'Éthique à Nicomaque*, 2d ed., Tome 2: Commentaire, vols. 1 and 2. Louvain: Publications Universitaires, 1970.

Glassen, P. "A Fallacy in Aristotle's Argument about the Good." *Philosophical Quarterly* 7 (1957): 319–322.

Gould, Stephen Jay. *Ever since Darwin: Reflections in Natural History*. New York: W. W. Norton, 1977.

Greenwood, L.H.G. *Aristotle Nicomachean Ethics Book Six*, with essays, notes, and translation. Cambridge: Cambridge University Press, 1909.

Hammond, N.G.L., and Scullard, H. H. *The Oxford Classical Dictionary*, 2d ed. Oxford: Clarendon Press, 1970.

Hardie, W.F.R. "The Final Good in Aristotle's *Ethics*." In *Aristotle: A Collection of Critical Essays*, edited by J.M.E. Moravcsik, pp. 297–322. Garden City, N.Y.: Doubleday, 1967.

———. "Aristotle on the Best Life for a Man." *Philosophy* 54 (1979): 35–50.

———. *Aristotle's Ethical Theory*, 2d ed. Oxford: Clarendon Press, 1980.

Hutchinson, D. S. *The Virtues of Aristotle*. London and New York: Routledge & Kegan Paul, 1986.

Irwin, Terence. *Plato's Moral Theory: The Early and Middle Dialogues*. Oxford: Clarendon Press, 1977.

———. "The Metaphysical and Psychological Basis of Aristotle's Ethics." In *Essays on Aristotle's Ethics*, edited by A. Rorty, pp. 35–54. Berkeley and Los Angeles: University of California Press, 1980.

———. "Aristotle's Methods of Ethics." In *Studies in Aristotle*, edited by Dominic J. O'Meara, pp. 193–224. Washington, D.C.: Catholic University of America Press, 1981.

———. "Permanent Happiness: Aristotle and Solon." *Oxford Studies in Ancient Philosophy* 3 (1985): 89–124.

———. Translation of Aristotle, *Nicomachean Ethics*. Indianapolis: Hackett, 1985.

———. "Ways to First Principles: Aristotle's Methods of Discovery." *Philosophical Topics* 15 (1987): 109–134.

———. "Disunity in the Aristotelian Virtues." *Oxford Studies in Ancient Philosophy*, Supplementary Volume 1988, pp. 61–78. Oxford: Clarendon Press.

Jaeger, Werner. *Aristotle: Fundamentals of the History of His Development*, 2d ed., translated by Richard Robinson. London: Oxford University Press, 1948.

Joachim, H. H. *Aristotle, The Nicomachean Ethics*. Oxford: Clarendon Press, 1951.

Kahn, Charles H. "Aristotle and Altruism." *Mind* 90 (1981): 20–40.

Kavka, Gregory S. *Hobbesian Moral and Political Theory*. Princeton: Princeton University Press, 1986.

Kenny, Anthony. "Happiness." In *Moral Concepts*, edited by Joel Feinberg, pp. 43–52. London: Oxford University Press, 1969.

————. *The Aristotelian Ethics: A Study of the Relationship between the Eudemian and the Nicomachean Ethics of Aristotle*. Oxford: Clarendon Press, 1978.

Keyt, David, "Intellectualism in Aristotle." In *Essays in Ancient Greek Philosophy*, vol. 2, edited by John P. Anton and Anthony Preus, pp. 364–387. Albany: State University of New York Press, 1983.

Korsgaard, Christine M. "Aristotle and Kant on the Source of Value." *Ethics* 96 (1986): 486–505.

————. "Aristotle on Function and Virtue." *History of Philosophy Quarterly* 3 (1986): 259–279.

Kraut, Richard. "The Peculiar Function of Human Beings." *Canadian Journal of Philosophy* 9 (1979): 467–478.

————. "Two Conceptions of Happiness." *The Philosophical Review* 88 (1979): 167–197.

————. "Comments on 'Disunity in the Aristotelian Virtues' by T. H. Irwin." *Oxford Studies in Ancient Philosophy*, Supplementary Volume 1988, pp. 79–86. Oxford: Clarendon Press.

MacDowell, Douglas M. *The Law in Classical Athens*. London: Thames and Hudson, 1978.

McDowell, John, "The Role of *Eudaimonia* in Aristotle's Ethics." In *Essays on Aristotle's Ethics*, edited by A. Rorty, pp. 359–376. Berkeley and Los Angeles: University of California Press, 1980.

Moline, Jon. "Contemplation and the Human Good." *Nous* 17 (1983): 37–53.

Monan, J. Donald. *Moral Knowledge and Its Methodology in Aristotle*. Oxford: Clarendon Press, 1968.

Mulgan, R. G. *Aristotle's Political Theory: An Introduction for Students of Political Theory*. Oxford: Clarendon Press, 1977.

Nagel, Thomas. "Aristotle on *Eudaimonia*." In *Essays on Aristotle's Ethics*, edited by A. Rorty, pp. 7–14. Berkeley and Los Angeles: University of California Press, 1980.

Nussbaum, Martha Craven. *Aristotle's De Motu Animalium*. Princeton: Princeton University Press, 1978.

————. *The Fragility of Goodness: Luck and Ethics in Greek Tragedy and Philosophy*. Cambridge: Cambridge University Press, 1986.

Ostwald, Martin. Translation of Aristotle, *Nicomachean Ethics*. Indianapolis: Bobbs-Merrill, 1962.

Owen, G.E.L. "*Tithenai ta Phainomena*." In *Aristotle: A Collection of Critical Essays*, edited by J.M.E. Moravcsik, pp. 167–190. Garden City, N.Y.: Doubleday, 1967.

Parfit, Derek. *Reasons and Persons*. Oxford: Clarendon Press, 1984.

Peterson, Sandra. "*Horos* (Limit) in Aristotle's *Nicomachean Ethics*." *Phronesis* 33 (1988): 233–250.

Prichard, H. A. "The Meaning of *Agathon* in the *Ethics* of Aristotle." In H. A. Prichard, *Moral Obligation: Essays and Lectures*, pp. 40–53. Oxford: Clarendon Press, 1949.

Rawls, John. *A Theory of Justice*. Cambridge: Harvard University Press, Belknap Press, 1971.

Roche, Timothy D. "*Ergon* and *Eudaimonia* in *Nicomachean Ethics* I: Reconsidering the Intellectualist Interpretation." *Journal of the History of Philosophy* 26 (1988): 175–194.

Rorty, Amélie O. "The Place of Contemplation in Aristotle's *Nicomachean Ethics*." In *Essays on Aristotle's Ethics*, edited by A. Rorty, pp. 377–394. Berkeley and Los Angeles: University of California Press, 1980.

Ross, W. D., ed. *The Works of Aristotle Translated into English*. Vol. IX, *Ethica Nicomachea*, translated by W. D. Ross. Oxford: Oxford University Press, 1915.

———. *Aristotle*. London: Methuen, 1923.

Rowe, C. J. "The *Eudemian* and *Nicomachean Ethics*: A Study in the Development of Aristotle's Thought." *Proceedings of the Cambridge Philological Society*, Supplement No. 3 (1971).

———. "A Reply to John Cooper on the *Magna Moralia*." *American Journal of Philology* 96 (1975): 160–172.

Sidgwick, Henry. *Outlines of the History of Ethics for English Readers*, 6th ed. Boston: Beacon Press, 1960.

———. *The Methods of Ethics*, 7th ed. New York: Dover, 1966.

Siegler, Frederick. "Reason, Happiness, and Goodness." In *Aristotle's Ethics: Issues and Interpretations*, edited by James J. Walsh and Henry L. Shapiro, pp. 30–46. Belmont, Calif.: Wadsworth, 1967.

Stewart, J. A. *Notes on the Nicomachean Ethics of Aristotle*, vols. 1 and 2. Oxford: Clarendon Press, 1892.

Suits, Bernard. "Aristotle on the Function of Man: Fallacies, Heresies and Other Entertainments." *Canadian Journal of Philosophy* 4 (1974): 23–40.

Urmson, J. O. "Aristotle's Doctrine of the Mean." In *Essays on Aristotle's Ethics*, edited by A. Rorty, pp. 157–170. Berkeley and Los Angeles: University of California Press, 1980.

———. *Aristotle's Ethics*. Oxford: Basil Blackwell, 1988.

White, Nicholas P. "Goodness and Human Aims in Aristotle's Ethics." In *Studies in Aristotle*, edited by Dominic J. O'Meara, pp. 225–246. Washington, D.C.: Catholic University of America Press, 1981.

Whiting, Jennifer. "Human Nature and Intellectualism in Aristotle." *Archiv für Geschichte der Philosophie* 68 (1986): 70–95.

Wilkes, Kathleen V. "The Good Man and the Good for Man in Aristotle's Ethics." In *Essays on Aristotle's Ethics*, edited by A. Rorty, pp. 341–358. Berkeley and Los Angeles: University of California Press, 1980.

Williams, Bernard. *Morality: An Introduction to Ethics*. New York: Harper & Row, 1972.

————. "Egoism and Altruism." In Bernard Williams, *Problems of the Self: Philosophical Papers 1956–1972*, pp. 250–265. Cambridge: Cambridge University Press, 1973.

Woods, Michael. *Aristotle's Eudemian Ethics, Books I, II, and VIII*, translated with a commentary. Oxford: Clarendon Press, 1982.

General Index

Ackrill, J. L., 3 n. 1, 4 n. 6, 4 n. 7, 7 n. 12, 8 n. 13, 55 n. 31, 197 n. 1, 205 n. 4, 211–237, 242 n. 35, 245 n. 38, 251 n. 43, 267 nn. 1–2, 269 n. 4, 272 n. 7, 313–314 n. 4, 330 n. 22

Adkins, A.W.H., 4 n. 7, 312 n. 1, 323 n. 16

Albertus Magnus, 271 n. 5

Allan, D. J., 4 n. 7, 9 n. 17, 84 n. 9, 330 n. 22

amusement, 164–6, 236

anger, 338–340. *See also* emotion

animals, lower: can live well, 3 n. 1; lack happiness, 39–40, 54–8. *See also* hierarchy, of living beings

Annas, Julia, 9 n. 17

Anscombe, G.E.M., 217–218 n. 14

Aquinas, 271 n. 5

Asmis, Elizabeth, 190 n. 15

Barnes, Jonathan, 59 n. 41, 310 n. 37

Brandt, Richard B., 78 n. 1, 83 n. 8, 84 n. 10

Broad, C. D., 78 n. 1, 82 n. 6, 83 n. 8

Burnet, John, 7 n. 12, 259 n. 51, 267 n. 1, 280 n. 9, 313 n. 3

Bywater, I., 7 n. 11, 222 n. 19

children: owe debt to parents, 10–11, 29, 37, 80, 87, 111; sustain happiness of parents, 180, 254–7; virtues of, 247–9

Clark, Stephen R.L., 8 n. 14, 271 n. 5, 312 n. 2, 353 n. 34

conflict among persons, 80, 83, 90–97, 115–128, 153–4, 157–8

consistency of *NE*: internal, 4–5, 19–20, 22–3, 29–30, 76–7, 79, 128–131, 155, 177, 184–192, 274, 314, 346–7, 353–4; with *EE*, 3–4 n. 2, 169–170, 289; with *Pol.*, 103–104, 274

contemplation: arguments for supremacy of, 15, 17, 26, 28, 64–7, 74–5, 174, 188, 192–6, 299–300, 347–353; broader sense of, 15–16 n. 2, 22 n. 9, 142–4, 184; desirable only for itself, 189–192; highest objects of, 14 nn. 1–2, 73–6; identified with

perfect happiness, 4, 6, 25, 54–67, 86–90; limitless value of, 9, 11, 27, 30 n. 15, 31–5, 39–41, 45–7, 62, 76, 99–100, 102, 155, 185; nature of, 4 n. 4, 15–16 n. 2, 68 n. 48, 73, 172; not to be maximized, 11, 12, 29, 30 n. 15, 32, 76, 80, 82; sole activity of the gods, 39–41, 46, 54, 56, 64; sustained by friends, 170–175

Cooper, John M., 3 n. 1, 5 n. 1, 4–5 n. 7, 6 n. 10, 17 n. 5, 22 n. 8, 24 n. 11, 44 n. 26, 79 nn. 3–4, 131 n. 51, 141 n. 56, 144 n. 58, 162–3 n. 3, 170 n. 5, 175 n. 8, 190 n. 16, 191 n. 18, 197 n. 1, 205 n. 3, 242 n. 34, 243 n. 36, 245 nn. 38–9, 255 n. 48, 265 n. 53, 267 n. 1, 287 n. 16, 289 n. 18, 290 n. 20, 292 n. 22, 323 n. 16, 326 n. 18, 330 n. 22, 353 n. 34

courage, 180, 336–7, 340

crafts, 91 n. 17, 160, 200–202, 209, 214–215, 224, 249, 302–304, 318 n. 10, 321, 356

Darwin, Charles, 354 n. 35

Devereux, Daniel T., 5 n. 7

Dirlmeier, Franz, 144 n. 58

Düring, Ingemar, 290 n. 21

egoism: not attributable to Aristotle, 9–11, 12, 29, 77, 97, 101, 109, 112, 114, 118, 134, 139, 144–8, 153–4, 263–4; benign, 80–82; combative, 80–82; conflicts with hierarchy, 105, 108–109; nonmaximizing, 84–5; psychological, 83–4, 104–105, 109; pure, 78–9, 81–2, 98; second-order, 86 n. 14. *See also* conflict among persons; polis, prior to individual

emotion, 147, 320–321, 328, 329, 333, 334, 339–344. *See also* anger

ends. *See* for the sake of, as causal-normative relation; intrinsic goodness; perfect ends; ultimate end

equality: and egoism, 105, 108–109, 120; political, 12, 83, 98–102. *See also* inequality; slavery

Eriksen, Trond Berg, 5 n. 7

Index of Passages